XML

Language Mechanics & Applications

XML
Language Mechanics & Applications

Dwight Peltzer
C.W. POST CAMPUS
LONG ISLAND UNIVERSITY

PEARSON
Addison
Wesley

Boston San Francisco New York
London Toronto Sydney Tokyo Singapore Madrid
Mexico City Munich Paris Cape Town Hong Kong Montreal

Senior Acquisitions Editor	Maite Suarez-Rivas
Editorial Assistant	Maria Campo
Marketing Manager	Nathan Schultz
Marketing Coordinator	Lesly Hershman
Production Supervisor	Marilyn Lloyd
Project Management	Argosy Publishing
Composition and Art	Argosy Publishing
Copyeditor	Amy Lepore
Technical Editor	Karl Hilsmann
Proofreader	Heather Moehn
Indexer	Ed Rush
Text Design	Joyce Cosentino Wells and Argosy Publishing
Cover Design	Joyce Cosentino Wells
Cover Image	© 2003 EyeWire, Getty Images
Senior Manufacturing Buyer	Hugh Crawford

Access the latest information about Addison-Wesley titles from our World Wide Web site: http://www.aw.com/cs

Library of Congress Cataloging-in-Publication Data

Peltzer, Dwight.
  XML language mechanics and applications / by Dwight Peltzer.
      p. cm.
Includes bibliographical references and index.
  ISBN 0-201-77168-3
  1. XML (Document markup language) I. Title.

  QA76.76.H94P45 2003
  005.7'2--dc21

                        2003049599

                                                              CIP

ISBN 0-201-77168-3
1 2 3 4 5 6 7 8 9 10-HAM-06050403

Preface

Why XML?

Recently, an article appeared in one of the Internet online weeklies discussing the recent trend by many Fortune 500 companies to convert their legacy applications from COBOL and C among other programming languages to XML and make their corporate data XML compliant. Companies such as Fidelity Investments and Time Warner have spent millions of dollars standardizing their methods of accessing data, regardless of where data resides. One senior analyst estimates Fidelity Investments will spend approximately $2.7 billion on technology, offering new services ranging from support for wireless client devices to new trading systems that function over interactive television sets.

Converting from traditional legacy systems to XML enables this widely accepted meta-language to serve as a data-centric common language to which all corporate data, ranging from database repositories to Web-based and transactional legacy systems, is translated. This single data format eliminates the expensive necessity of writing custom applications where participating business partners must agree on a data format and protocol for exchange of documents.

Many prominent companies have created schemas shared among business partners, facilitating a seamless integration and exchange of information. The governing documents impose common methods of representing different types of data. Doing so eliminates a major portion of Web application servers that executed translations between Web and legacy systems. In many cases, single queries passed through several application servers before a response could be rendered through a browser.

The Vision

XML Language Mechanics and Applications providse you with technical expertise and guidance on how to employ XML for your own business needs. We guide you from the beginning stages of domain analysis, conceptualization, documentation, and design to application specification and implementation. We focus on the XML family of related technologies including XML, DTDs, XSD Schemas, XSLT, XPath, XHTML, and SQL Server 2000 for XML. The latter two chapters of the text focus on building applications using Visual Studio.NET. We do this to introduce the recent .NET release. We examine each XML technology in depth, demonstrating how to build scalable, enterprise XML applications.

We then go over how these are used with XML and the .NET products. After reading this book, you will be able to apply techniques directly to your own applications. Each chapter contains examples derived from real-world applications you can plug in to your own designs. XML is only as good as its application.

Target Audience

XML Language Mechanics and Applications addresses the needs of both students and IT professionals. This includes courses on XML e-commerce programming, undergraduate high-level computer science curricula, or graduate courses in Information Technology and MIS, as well as seminars on XML and family-related technologies. Readers should have a fundamental background in database technology and minimal programming experience with scripting languages such as VB Script, JavaScript, or ASP. We assume the reader has no prior experience with XML.

Contents

This book organizes its presentation into four design and implementation phases: conceptualization, algorithmic design, transformation of raw data, and rendering that information into many different formats including browser rendered data in HTML, plain text, and even XML. As such, the four parts of the Table of Contents are:

Structure

Transformation

Presentation

Implementation

Part One: Structure

In Part One we explore basic concepts and fundamentals of XML structure. The first part is appropriately labeled *Structure*. Instructors can present this material based on the students' experience and background. We begin by constructing well-formed documents. Once you have mastered the fundamentals of creating XML source documents, Chapter 2 focuses on Document Type Definitions and how they impose structure on source documents and enforce business model rules. We examine entities, entity references, and internal and external reference subsets. A review of rules and constraints DTDs impose are accompanied with numerous examples and discussion. This chapter lays the groundwork for learning about schemas in Chapter 4. However, before we examine XSD schemas, we discuss parsing in Chapter 3. Chapter 4 focuses on XSD schemas. You will benefit from the comparison between DTDs and schemas and learn why schemas extend the capabilities of DTDs.

New concepts include:

Namespaces

Open and Closed Content Models

User-defined data structures

Data Type *Complex* and *Simple*

Derivation by Extension

Derivation by Restriction

Examining these new concepts will enrich your XML vocabulary and skills with which powerful schemas enhance and extend the range of possibilities in application design. Complete examples are applicable to your own schemas.

Part Two: Transformation

Part two focuses on document transformation. XSLT technology works in tandem with a parser and the Document Object Model to construct a tree containing nodes bearing instructions on how to build a result tree. The transformation of this information is translated into several meaningful formats, i.e., HTML or text rendered documents. We learn how to create a tree manually and then explore the various forms of templates and demonstrate how they are applied to XSLT stylesheets.

Chapter 6 contains a detailed examination of XPath *expressions* and *location paths.* You will become skilled in how to use numerous *axes* (i.e., **s**iblings, ancestors, descendants and self) to retrieve specified data.

Part Three: Presentation

In part three we focus on the basics of XHTML. Chapter 7 examines the basics, whereas Chapter 8 places emphasis on modularization. Browser behavior is an integral aspect of the discussion on XHTML. Unfortunately, the major browsers are still not *XHTML strict* compliant. We will show you why XHTML is a reformulated version of HTML version 4.01 and why it is becoming the meta language for the Web. The creators of XHTML designed the DTD to separate document structure from stylistic formatting instructions and encourage the use of Cascading Stylesheets for presentation. Chapter 8 focuses exclusively on modularization and how to create a new markup language. This chapter is advanced XHTML. Modularization is applicable when you are designing modules for digital devices such as PDAs. If you are not interested in learning how to design modules for such devices, you can skip this chapter and go to Chapter 9.

Part Four: Implementation

Chapter 9 concentrates on mapping data to and from XML whereas Chapter 10 is devoted to SQL Server 2000 and its full compliance with XML. We present detailed information on new XML-based query commands contained within SQL Server 2000, i.e., the *OpenXML* function and *FOR XML* 3 individual clauses. Each returns a rowset formatted as XML data in a manner specified by the author. FOR XML AUTO returns a rowset formatted as elements, and FOR XML RAW returns a rowset with a generic *row* tag. FOR XML EXPLICIT provides you with complete control over the shape of the returned rowset. This method uses metadata to assist in shaping the rowset. We will also learn about *edge* tables and *Universal tables* and the role they play in addressing SQL *update, insert*, and *delete* queries. Additionally, we will examine XML Views. They allow us to approach relational databases as though the data were formatted in XML.

We also provide an introduction to the .NET Framework, Visual Studio.NET, and Visual Basic.NET in Chapters 11 and 12.

Chapter 11 offers a brief introduction to the new, innovative .NET Framework. We begin by examining the **Common Language Runtime**, the **Common Type Specification**, and the **Common Language Specification** to which Microsoft's programming languages **Visual C++**, **C#**, and **Visual Basic .NET** adhere. We provide examples of the **Manifest** and **Assembly** with detailed analyses.

Chapter 12 focuses on building Web Services and testing them by creating **client applications**. A series of **use cases** serve as a basis for creating an **International Foreign Currency Exchange** Web Service.

Appendix A contains the full XHTML Strict DTD for reference in conjunction with our study on XHTML and Modularization. Appendix B contains the bibliography.

This book is designed so you can begin immediately with any of the individual phases or read the text from start to finish.

Part One (Structure) serves as a review and primer on XML basics. Are you primarily interested in document transformation? Begin with Part Two where we examine document transformation with XSLT. If you are interested in creating new markup languages, Part Three provides a detailed discussion on XHTML modularization and how it facilitates XML's extensibility. Part Four begins in Chapter 9 and demonstrates how to map your data toa relationl database. Chapter 10 focuses on SQL Server 2000 and its new features. We will demonstrate how this new technology revolutionizes the manner in which you work with SQL Server. We teach you how the Document Object Model, FOR XML (three individual clauses), OPEN XML, and XML Views allow you to shape the rowsets you wish returned in a specified XML format. Views allow you to use annotations and metadata to control how you map data to relational databases from XML and vice versa. XSLT, XPath, the DOM, and the new .NET Web services

permit you to manipulate data and present this information on the
Internet. Chapter 11 serves as an introduction to the suite of .NET
products and Visual Studio. Chapter 12 focuses on Web Services.

Supplements

XML Language Mechanics and Applications includes an evaluation
copy of Altova's XML Spy and accompanying CD which contains all
source code for this book. Simply create a folder called XML
Language Mechanics and then create subfolders for each chapter.
Finally, copy the source code for each chapter to the appropriate
folder. Solutions may be downloaded from a password-protected
folder on Addison Wesley's web site.

Acknowledgements

This book is dedicated to my lifetime companion and wife, Marla,
and my two sons, Jonathan and Christopher, who provided an
encouraging, happy home environment in which I have spent countless hours writing this book. Marla has devoted an endless amount of
time checking my manuscript for grammar, syntax and style.

I would also like to dedicate this book to Dr. Susan Dorchak for
her warm friendship and support, and Professor Michael Pressman,
who started me on this long and fascinating journey.

A special word of thanks goes to Dr. Steven Heim for authoring
Chapter 7 as well as being a friend and soul mate, encouraging me
when I thought I couldn't write another word. He was always there
lending both a sympathetic and objective ear. He has also contributed
his considerable skill in visualizing information. His illustrations
clarify many of the complex issues in the book. They capture the
essence and allow the reader to gain a more global perspective. He
has reviewed each chapter many times and made numerous, helpful
comments, keeping me in line when I neglected to state in a concise
manner what I really meant to say.

Many editors, reviewers, and colleagues have contributed much
toward making this book a reality. I would especially like to thank
my acquisitions editor at Addison Wesley, Maite Suarez-Rivas, for

her warm encouragement and guidance. Thanks goes to numerous other editors at Addison Wesley. They include Maria Campo, Marilyn Lloyd, Nathan Schultz, Joyce Wells, Designer, and Katherine Hartunian. I would also like to express my gratitude to Daniel Rausch, Karen Cheng, Sally Boylan, and copy editor Amy Lepore at Argosy Publishing for their super job in editing and preparing this book for publication. We all would like to wish Karen good luck and best wishes as she pursues her Masters degree.

Karl Hilsman, a member of the SQL Server development team at Microsoft, has spent a huge amount of time scrutinizing my manuscript, making insightful suggestions, corrections, and offering his expertise on .NET. I would also like to express my thanks to Phillip Garding at Microsoft, also a member of the SQL Server development team, for introducing me to Karl.

I want to thank Alan Swan, Senior Analyst, IBM, for his valuable contribution to the case study from Fidelity Investmnts. Numerous others who have contributed their constructive comments and suggestions include Alfred C. Weaver, Department of Computer Science, University of Virginia; Ellis Horowitz, University of Southern California; Sam S. Gill, San Francisco State University; Lutfus Sayeed, San Francisco State University; Vicki L. Sauter, Professor of Information Systems, University of Missouri; St. Louis, Bruce Worthen, Salt Lake Community College; Bruce Char, Drexel University; Daniel Rosenkrantz, University at Albany-SUNY; Tom Luce, Ohio University; Brian Koontz, North Lake College Irving, Texas; and Sigmund Handelman.

I have written this book to encourage others to pursue this exciting path and explore the countless benefits XML provides. Enjoy the text. Let's hear from you regarding your comments and suggestions. You may reach me at Dwight.Peltzer@liu.edu.

About the Author

Dwight Peltzer currently teaches in the Department of Computer Science at C.W. Post College as an Assistant Professor of Computer Science in Brookville, New York. He lectures on XML, XSLT, XPath, XHTML, programming in Visual C++, SQL Server 2000, and Java 2 Enterprise Edition (J2EE). A member of the University Web

Curriculum Committee, he is active in developing new curriculums for e-Commerce.

In addition to designing new courses in XML-based technologies. Dwight teaches seminars on Site Server's Commerce Edition 3.0, COM + Objects, ASP.NET, XHTML, and XML. He is currently researching, lecturing, and writing on Microsoft's recently released suite of.NET products, including the .NET Framework, Visual Studio.NET, VB.NET, and SQL Server 2000. He is also is teaching courses in SQL Server 2000 and applying Design Patterns.

During his career, he has lectured at universities and colleges throughout the United States, Canada, and Europe. His visiting professorships include New York Institute of Technology, University of Massachusetts, Southern Illinois University, University of Victoria in British Columbia, Canada, and Keele University, Staffordshire, England, where he held the Fulbright Hays Visiting Professor chair. He has presented lectures for the Canadian Broadcasting Corporation in Montreal, Canada, and the British Broadcasting Corporation in London and Birmingham, England.

Among other credits, Dwight has served as a consultant to Sheridan Software, A.C. Nielsen, Inc., and Interboro Corporation (Columbia Broadcasting System), and local affiliates of TRW Credit Corporation (now called Esperian).

Dwight is the recipient of two consecutive Fulbright fellowships for graduate study in Germany. He also received a Martha Baird Rockefeller Foundation, Fellowship for research in the Humanities and an award from the Council for International Educational Scholars. He has served as a consultant for the Alabama State Council for the Arts and the Rhode Island State Council for the Arts. He currently lives on the North Shore, Long Island with his wife and two sons.

Understanding XML is only one aspect of program design; knowing *how* to employ XML technologies is the key factor in applying this knowledge and creating successful applications.

Guided Tour for Readers

Part One: Structure

Chapter 1 Introduction to XML

XML uses elements and attributes, providing both a logical and physical structure to your source documents.

Chapter 2 Document Type Definition

A Document Type Definition (DTD) represents a set of guidelines and rules. The DTD views a document as either parsed character data or nonparsed character data. Additionally, it further enforces business model rules and imposes document structure.

Chapter 3 Parsing Your XML Documents

The parser decomposes an XML document by converting text into a set of objects, and it further ensures that the document conforms to rules defined by the XML 1.0 specification.

Chapter 4 Introducing Schemas

An XSD schema supports a rich collection of built-in and user-defined data types as well as XML namespaces. Schemas are data intensive, whereas DTDs are text intensive.

Part Two: Transformation

Chapter 5 XSLT

This transformation technology provides the mechanism for transforming XML documents into formats including HTML, plain text, PDF, and others. XSLT uses a stylesheet for modular components called templates.

Chapter 6 Applying XPath

XPath addresses parts of an XML document by using a path notation for navigating through the hierarchical structure of the document.

Part Three: Presentation

Chapter 7 XHTML

XHTML is the new version of HTML with no future releases planned.

Chapter 8 Modularizing XHTML

Modularization provides the structure for creating new markup languages within the XHTML framework module and the XHTML core modules.

Part Four: Implementation

Chapter 9 Mapping Your Data to a Database

Mapping data to and from XML is critical in an era of web services and integration on the Internet.

Chapter 10 New SQL Server 2000 Features

SQL Server 2000 provides many new features for storage and retrieval of XML data, and it views XML as a native data type.

Chapter 11 A Brief Introduction to .NET

The Common Language Runtime (CLR) supports integration and sharing common data types between languages targeting the .NET Framework. This concept paves the way to integration, interoperability, and remote procedure calls between various technologies and web services on the Internet using XML as the metadata language.

Chapter 12 Creating Distributed Applications and Web Services

Web services stand to gain mainstream acceptance as a standard within the enterprise domain. Both J2EE and Microsoft .NET support SOAP, WSDL, and UDDI as technologies for achieving integration and interoperability.

Appendix A   XHTML Strict DTD Version 1.0

Appendix B   Bibliography

CONTENTS

Chapter Three   Parsing Your XML Documents   77

Contents

Contents

PART 1

STRUCTURE

CHAPTER

1 Introduction to XML

1.1 XML: Metadata About Data

What can the Extensible Markup Language (XML) do for your business? It can help you organize your entire base of operations by making it effortless to do the following:

- Increase your business with a user-friendly, XML-driven web site
- Organize communications with your business partners
- Optimize supply-chain operations
- Improve storage and retrieval of your data
- Provide easy online access to important information for your customers
- Validate your business documents and data

XML is plain text with self-describing, original markup tags surrounding sentences, statements, paragraphs, and even complete documents. The tags provide additional information about the data they envelop. In essence, XML is metadata about data. It uses elements and attributes to provide both a logical structure and a physical structure to your document.

The *logical* category defines which elements are to be included in a specific document order. The *physical* category identifies an element's data types surrounded by markup tags. For example, `<Price>` is the markup tag, `41.95` is a decimal data type, `<Name>` (`<Name>Dwight Peltzer</Name>`) is the markup tag, and `Dwight Peltzer` consists of a sequence of ASCII characters known as a string. (We will discuss markup tags in a moment.) The building blocks for constructing an XML document include marked-up tags, elements, attributes, text, processing instructions, and comments. When assembled as a complete unit, they represent an XML document.

After studying this chapter and doing the exercises, you will be able to utilize these building blocks to create your own well-formed XML documents. At the end of this chapter are self-review questions, exercises, and projects to serve as a review of everything we have covered.

First let's define what an XML document is. An XML document can represent any number of things, including an Excel spreadsheet, a quarterly financial report, a business letter, or the American League baseball standings. By viewing an XML document as hierarchical information grouped in categories, we then present these hierarchies in a tree-structured format. The tree paradigm allows us to define parent-child and sibling-sibling relationships. Let's consider the diagram in Figure 1.1.

A tree consists of a single root, branches, and leaves. Any parts of a tree containing children are branches, and tree components that have no children exist as leaves.

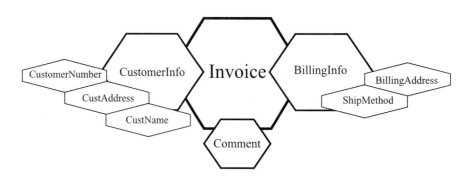

Figure 1.1   An XML hierarchical tree

In this example, `Invoice` is the tree's single root element, which must be unique. The elements `CustomerInfo` and `BillingInfo` are children of `Invoice`, so we define them as siblings to each other. The `Comment` markup tag describes any existing documentation concerning the document instance. The parser ignores it.

Additionally, both siblings have child elements. `CustomerNumber`, `CustName`, and `CustAddress` are children of the parent element `CustomerInfo`, and `BillingInfo` has two children: `BillingAddress` and `ShipMethod`. The child elements residing within the subelement categories have no children, so they exist as leaves.

We call these hierarchical components *elements*. Therefore, we deduce from this example that elements can contain other child elements and so on. The element `Invoice` resides at the top of the hierarchy, so it represents the document root.

Both HTML and XML are markup languages and use markup tags. However, let's discuss some differences between them. Let's first examine Figure 1.2, an HTML version of the Memo document. It uses markup tags just as XML does. `<title>Memo</title>` contains both an opening and closing tag. However, most of the tags are structural in nature and do not require closing tags (that is, `<br>` and `<h1>`). They also do not describe the data.

```
<html>
    <title>Memo</title>
    <body>
        <h2>From: Dr. Suzanne Smith, Department Chairperson</h2>
        <b>To: Computer Science Faculty</b>
        <br>Event
        <br>Time: 10:00 AM
        <br>Date: March 10
        <br>Place: Room 125
        <br>Subject: Curriculum Development and ECommerce
        <h1>Urgency - Middle States Evaluation Visit</h1>
        Reminder — All preliminary planning must be finished by
        March 10
    </body>
</html>
```

Figure 1.2 An HTML version of the Memo document

On the surface, an XML document resembles an HTML document. However, significant differences exist between them.

The HTML markup language depicts the structure of a web document's content plus some behavioral characteristics. The following two items accurately describe an HTML document:

- **Content:** Textual information for display on the client's screen
- **Markup:** Textual information that controls the display in the form of markup tags

The `<HTML>` tag serves as the document root, thereby signifying that this is an HTML document. The `<title>` tag has a complementary closing tag, `</title>`. A closing tag is identified by its forward slash followed by the tag name. The `<body>` element is where you place the content of your document, followed by its closing `</body>` tag. The `<br>` tag defines page layout. The `<h2>` tag is structural because it defines major sections on the page. It specifies bold, font size, and a carriage return before and after the element. The effect of the `<br>` tag also causes a carriage return. It does not require a closing tag. Finally, the `</HTML>` tag signifies the document closing. The important point to remember here is that HTML does not require that all tags be closed. None of the tags reveals anything about the data contained within them. This is not HTML's purpose. Perhaps one of the most significant issues in comparing HTML to XML is this: HTML tags define document structure but lend no semantic meaning whatsoever to content.

In contrast, XML allows you to create your own markup tags that accurately define both document structure and the meaning of data. XML separates data from formatting. The example in Figure 1.3 contains the same information as the HTML example but marked up in XML format.

```
Memo.xml
<Memo>
  <From>Dr. Suzanne Smith, Department Chairperson</From>
    <To> Computer Science Faculty</To>
      <Event>
            <Date>March 10, 2003</Date>
            <Time>10:00 A.M.</Time>
            <Place>Room 125</Place>
```

```
    </Event>
    <Subject>
    <CurriculumDevelopment>ECommerce</CurriculumDevelopment>
    <Urgency>Middle States Evaluation Visit</Urgency>
    </Subject>
    <Reminder> All preliminary planning must be finished by
    March 10 </Reminder>
</Memo>
```

Figure 1.3 An XML version of the Memo document

In many ways, this document resembles the HTML document. However, each self-describing XML tag tells a story about content residing between the tags. We know that this document is a memo. Additionally, the document contains two subelement categories, each providing specific information. For example, `<Event>` contains three child elements, `<Date>`, `<Time>`, and `<Place>`. How can you be more explicit than that? The same is true for `<Subject>`. Each individual element is explicitly descriptive.

- `<Memo>` describes the intended purpose of this document.
- `<From>` reveals the author of this memo.
- `<Event>` informs us that a meeting will take place. It also defines subcategories with additional information about the event: `<date>`, `<time>`, and `<place>`.
- `<Subject>` clearly delineates document structure by creating a new category containing information about the event.
- `<CurriculumDevelopment>` explains the purpose for the meeting.
- `<Urgency>` provides a reason for convening this meeting.
- `<Reminder>` contains any additional information concerning the event.

You can discern the differences between these two examples. HTML tags are predefined and static, and their primary function is to provide document structure and separate data from formatting. In contrast, XML tags both lend semantic meaning and provide structure to the document. Focusing on data is XML's specialty. HTML does not do that. Additionally, XML does not output formatting as HTML does.

1.2   Defining a Well-Formed Document

XML conforms to a standard set of rules called *specifications* for the XML W3C Recommendation, version 1.0. This contains all rules and defines the grammar for creating a well-formed XML document.

The W3C Working Draft Committee is a standards setting body, comprised of members from such corporations as Microsoft, Sun Microsystems, IBM, and numerous others. A specification begins as a proposal; when the Committee approves the draft, it is advanced to the Consideration stage, then finally becomes a Recommendation after all committee members agree and approve the final draft. All XML authors must adhere to the final specification.

The following criteria determine whether an XML document is well formed:

- Each XML document must contain exactly one unique element called the *root*, which serves as the top-level document element. You will also see this element referred to as the *document entity*. This term implies that the entire XML document is subsumed within this entity.
- A *source* document containing data is defined as an XML document if it is well formed and adheres to the following criteria:
  - It must conform to the XML specification.
  - A document must contain one or more elements, including the root element.
  - Elements must be properly nested within each other.
  - Each element must contain both an opening and closing tag.
  - Conceptually, the root element stores all child elements, attributes, comments, and processing instructions within it.

The self-describing root tag should accurately reflect the nature of this document. Simply labeling the element `<root>` doesn't conform to one of the main goals of XML: Apply self-describing tags that lend semantic meaning to data contained within the source document. Additionally, the author assumes full responsibility for ensuring self-descriptive tags depict the true meaning of content embedded within them. A parser processes a poorly descriptive markup tag without concern for accuracy just as it does for a well-written tag. They are not enforceable by XML rules. If we examine Figure 1.4, the element

Authors explicitly informs us that this tag does provide information concerning an author. Let's dissect this source document and see how to construct it as a well-formed document.

```
<Authors> <!-- This is the document root -->
<!-- Define the subelement category -->
    <AuthorInfo>
<!-- Define the child elements for AuthorInfo -->
        <AuthorID>101</AuthorID>
        <AuthorFName>Dwight</AuthorFName>
        <AuthorLName>Peltzer</AuthorLName>
        <AuthorAddress>PO Box 516</AuthorAddress>
        <Auth_City>Some City</Auth_City>
        <Au_State>NY</Au_State>
        <Au_Zip>11564</Au_Zip>
        <BusinessTelNo>516-111-1234</BusinessTelNo>
        <Title>Professor of Computer Science</Title>
        <Employer>Tech University</Employer>
        <!-- Close this category -->
    </AuthorInfo>
        <!-- Now define the second subelement category -->
    <AuthorPublisherInfo>
        <Publisher>Addison Wesley</Publisher>
        <Editor>MSR</Editor>
        <Address>25 Main Street Street</Address>
        <City>Major City</City>
        <State>MA</State>
        <!-- close this category -->
    </AuthorPublisherInfo>
        <!-- Define the third subelement category -->
    <BookInfo>
        <Title>XML Language Mechanics</Title>
        <Pages> 450</Pages>
        <PublishDate>Summer 2003</PublishDate>
        <ISBN>0-201-77168-3</ISBN>
        <Category>XML Markup Language</Category>
        <NumChapters>12</NumChapters>
    <AdditionalFeatures>Self-Review Exercises and
Projects</AdditionalFeatures>
        <SoftwareTools>Evaluation copy of XML Spy</SoftwareTools>
    </BookInfo>
<!-- Close the document root -->
```

```
</Authors>
```

Figure 1.4   Authors.xml as a well-formed document

The root tag contains its complementary closing tag at the document's end, immediately meeting one of the criteria for a well-formed document: an opening and closing tag.

XML is case sensitive, meaning that the opening and closing tags must be identical, either upper- or lowercase but not mixed. It must also be well formed. We have now met the second criterion. The following example is illegal: `<Authors>` . . . `</authors>`. This is not well formed. Let's digress for a moment and discuss well-formed markup tags in more detail.

A well-formed tag can begin with an ASCII character (such as A or a), an underscore, letters, digits, or with hyphens contained in the tags. The following tags are valid:

- `<Author>`
- `<_author>`
- `<author-name>`

The following are invalid:

- `<2author>` (because a tag cannot begin with a number)
- `<1 author>` (because a space cannot be embedded within a tag)
- `<%author >` (because neither a % nor a ? is allowed within a tag)

The XML specification requires matching tags. (Consider beginning all tags in lowercase because the XML community is rapidly moving toward conforming to the XHTML strict standard, version 1.0, which requires that all tags be written in lowercase.)

The XHTML (eXtensible Hypertext Markup: Language) strict version is a complete rewrite of HTML version 4.01. The strict version corrects weaknesses present in HTML by ensuring enforcement of structure and nothing else. XHTML excludes all deprecated tags and attributes in HTML version 4.01. There was no previous strict version.

Child elements must be properly nested. Consider this skeletal structure:

```
<root>
   <Book>
         <Title> some content </Title>
         <Publisher> some content </Publisher>
         <ISBN> some content </ISBN>
   </Book>

   <Book>
         <Title> some content </Title>
         <Publisher> some content </Publisher>
         <ISBN> some content </ISBN>
   </Book>
</root>
```

Notice how <Book> contains three child elements containing book information. Before we can list another book, the first <book> tag must be closed. Now let's examine <Authors>.The Authors.xml document contains exactly one root element and several properly nested child elements. Examining Authors a little closer, we divide the document into three categories.

<AuthorInfo> **Category 1**
Other child elements are leaves because they have no children.
</AuthorInfo>

<AuthorPublisherInfo>   **Category2**
Other child elements are leaves.
</AuthorPublisherInfo>

<BookInfo>   **Category3**
Additional child elements
</BookInfo>

We close the category <AuthorInfo> before defining AuthorPublisherInfo. The same holds true for <BookInfo>. Two additional elements, <AdditionalFeatures> and <SoftwareTools>, contain no children, so we properly identify them as leaves. Finally, we close the root <Authors> at the document's end. Notice that its complementary closing tag properly closes each child's opening tag.

We now have a well-formed XML source document. We have made every attempt to ensure that Authors.xml is well formed. Unfortunately, we are human and do commit occasional errors. We need a software solution to help up check our document against the specification to ensure that it does indeed conform. Good news! A processor fulfills that role and is discussed in the next section.

1.3 Why Do We Need a Processor?

XML uses a processor called a *parser* for ensuring that the XML document is well formed. Consider the following items:

- The XML document contains both a root element and other nested child elements.
- We embed elements within the < character and the > character.
- We treat these characters as markup text.
- Usually we don't include markup characters in normal text; instead, we include them in math equations and programming languages.

Here is a math example:

```
a < b; or b > c.
```

In C++, we would write the following code snippet:

```
int maxSize = 10;
for(int i = 0; i < maxSize; i++) {  }
```

Markup text requires special treatment. This is where the processor comes into play. Two separate methods exist for parsing XML. The primary method we use in this text is a tree-based parser. The other method is stream based.

The tree-based processor begins parsing at the document root and walks the hierarchical tree, parsing each element and its content. If an error exists, the parser reports the error by generating an error message stating that the document cannot be loaded. Once the parser checks the XML document and creates a hierarchical tree, a stylesheet technology such as eXstensible Style Language: Transform (XSLT uses the tree to create HTML pages). The tree might also be used for other purposes such as storing the data in a relational database. The ultimate use for an XML document is decided by the application using XML.

1.4 Defining the Role of the Browser

Internet Explorer (version 5.5 and later) comes bundled with both a built-in, tree-based parser and a stream parser, (DOM and SAX) MSXML (Microsoft XML Core Services) version 4.0, and a stylesheet. It begins parsing at the document root and subsequently visits each branch, parsing the individual elements for conformance to the specification.

Chapter 3, "Parsing Your XML Documents," is devoted almost exclusively to discussing parsers. It first examines the Document Object Model (DOM) and its tree-based method of loading the XML document into memory for parsing. It also presents another method of parsing called stream-based parsing (SAX), an acronym that stands for Simple API for XML. This type of parser reads the document and notifies the application each time a new component appears.

EXERCISE 1: Let's open the Authors.xml document in Internet Explorer 6.0 and see how it presents our well-formed document.

```
+ <Authors>
```

Figure 1.5   Authors.xml revisited

IE Explorer 6.0 places a plus sign before the root element, denoting `<Authors>` as the document root. Additionally, when we click on the plus, the document expands to expose all other child elements and their content. We can select the subelement categories' minus signs to achieve the following result:

```
- <Authors>
+ <AuthorInfo>
+ <AuthorPublisherInfo>
+ <BookInfo>
  </Authors>
```

Now we can clearly identify the individual subelement categories without viewing individual child elements residing within them. Grouping these categories clearly delineates document structure. Isn't this one of the goals we were striving for when we selected XML as our means for creating easy-to-read documents? We wanted to create documents that were both well structured and focused on data.

We can expand these categories to reveal their respective children. Explorer comes with a built-in stylesheet. This accounts for the excellent rendering in the browser. (You will learn about XSLT stylesheets in Chapter 5, "XSLT.") Returning to the subject of parsing, in the event that an error occurs, the processor generates an error similar to the example presented in Figure 1.6.

```
<Authors>
   <Author>Dwight Peltzer<Author>
</Authors>
```

Figure 1.6   InvalidAuthor.xml

Do you see the problem? Both `Author` tags represent opening tags. No closing tag exists. This is what the browser says about the error:

```
The XML page cannot be displayed.
Cannot view XML input using XSL stylesheet. Please correct the
error and then click the Refresh button, or try again later.

End tag 'Authors' does not match the start tag 'Author'. Error
processing resource 'file:///A:/InvalidAuthor.xml'. Line 5,
Position 3
</Authors>
_^
```

Now we can better understand the parser's role in checking the source documents for well-formedness. The parser is very thorough, finding every violation.

1.5   Parsed Character Data (#PCDATA)

XML makes the distinction between parsed character data (#PCDATA) and unparsed character data. Parsed character data consists of markup characters, including the lesser-than character and the greater-than character. For example, the elements in the brief example `<Description>Introduction to XML</Description>` must be parsed. Additionally, even though we consider `Introduction to XML` to be text and it does not contain any markup characters, it must be parsed as well.

Unparsed character data consists of binary data such as JPEGs and GIF files.

Frequently, text contains markup characters embedded within the body of content. If the parser encounters them, unless instructed otherwise, it will attempt to parse them as beginning markup tags. This, of course, results in an error. How do we provide instructions to the processor regarding how to handle these situations? XML provides a viable solution. We will begin by examining a concept called *entities* introduced by the XML specification.

1.6 XML Entities and Their Applications

Entities exist in many different formats and have numerous different applications. Generally speaking, entities enable you to assign a label to specific content and then refer to it by name. For example, as previously stated, the processor must be able to distinguish markup characters from content (that is, the amp, <, and > characters). Entities offer a way to represent these special characters in text. If the parser encounters one of these markup characters, without identifying it to the processor as requiring special handling, it will attempt to parse it as markup and will generate an error. Certain rules apply to these special characters.

Entity reference characters include the ampersand, apostrophe, lesser-than and greater-than characters, all of which require escaping.

Table 1.1 demonstrates how to properly embed them in text.

Table 1.1 Entity Reference Characters

Entity	Reference	Character
&	&	&#38;
<	<	&#60;
>	>	>
"	"	"
'	'	'

Character "lt" and "amp" are doubly escaped to ensure that they fulfill the requirement for entity replacements being well formed. This is why we include both &&#38, and &#60;.

The following examples demonstrate how we escape each entity reference.

```
<h2> Larry Moe & Curly</h2>
```

Web browsers correctly render this as valid HTML. In contrast, XML parsers generate an error. The ampersand requires special handling. The appropriate way to write this same example in XML is as follows:

```
<h2> Larry Moe &amp; Curly </h2>.
```

Now that we know how to handle the ampersand, let's try including both double quotes and the ampersand in the same context:

```
<Demo>
    <h2> Title=&quot; Larry Moe &amp; Curly &quot;</h2>
</Demo>
```

The output in the browser is exactly what we intended:

```
<Books>
    <h2>Title="Larry, Moe & Curly"</h2>
</Books>
```

Wow! That was easy. Nevertheless, how do we prevent the parser from improperly interpreting the lesser-than and greater-than characters? The following exercise will help you learn how to do this.

EXERCISE 2: Create a folder on your hard drive named XMLDocs. Then open an empty Notepad document. Write the following XML document exactly as presented here:

```
<EXERCISE>This demonstrates how to escape the entity refer-
ence &lt; character</EXERCISE>
```

Save it as Exercise01.xml in your newly created folder. Make sure the .xml extension is present. This identifies it as an XML document. Then open it in IE Explorer version 5.5 or 6.0. If any errors exist, the browser will notify you.

Fix the errors and attempt to open it again in your browser. Here is how the final version should look in the browser:

```
<EXERCISE>this demonstrates how to escape a <
character</EXERCISE>
```

Neat!

You can also escape the entity references using numeric character references. For example, you could use < as follows:

```
<EXERCISE>This demonstrates how to escape the entity reference
&#60; character</EXERCISE>
```

It makes no difference to the processor how you escape them. Using a name as we first wrote it is more intuitive.

Conversely, write the greater-than symbol like this:

```
<CODE> if (int a &gt; b) {do something}</CODE>
```

You manage quotes in this manner:

```
<Book title=&quot; XML Language Mechanics&quot;</Book>
```

CDATA

Why do we need character data (CDATA) when we already know how to process entity-reference characters? The XML specification provides another, better solution when there is a lot of marked-up text. In that context, it would be time consuming to escape every instance. CDATA allows us to include strings of characters containing markup characters that otherwise could cause the XML document to be ill formed. Figure 1.7 shows an example of how you can apply CDATA in this situation.

```
<Demo><![CDATA[<Watch out! y is > than x ]]></Demo>
```
Figure 1.7   CDATA markup

Ouch! This looks very complex. Let's take the example apart and see how it works. First, it contains opening and closing <Demo> tags, so let's set them aside. Then write the body content containing markup characters.

```
<![CDATA[<Watch out! y is > than x ]]>
```

Now we can begin applying the proper syntax.

1. Begin by placing an exclamation point after the < character.

2. Position two opening brackets ([) as follows: `[CDATA[`. That was easy.

3. Include any text or markup characters as you wish, following the CDATA markup.

4. Place two closing brackets (]]) and a > character after your content so that the parser knows you are finished marking up your text.

```
[<Watch out! y is > than x ]]>
```

5. Finally, put back your closing tag.

Let's consider one other easy method of applying CDATA to your document. Separate the CDATA markup characters from any markup text you wish to place in the main body of your text, as follows:

1. Separate CDATA markup in two sections: `<![CDATA[` constitutes the first part, and `]]>` (which is placed at the end of your markup) constitutes the second part.

2. Write your main text including all markup texts.

3. Place part one in front of markup text and part two behind your marked up text, as follows:

<u>element</u>   <u>part 1</u>   <u>part 2</u>   <u>closing element</u>
```
<ELEMENT><![CDATA[ markup text goes here]]> </ELEMENT>
```

Do you see how easy it is to apply CDATA to your text? All text is character data within a CDATA section.

EXERCISE 3: Prepare an HTML document containing all of its predefined tags and apply CDATA to it. It serves as an excellent example of how you can apply CDATA and cause the parser to treat the entire HTML document as normal text. Imagine escaping each HTML markup tag in such a document! That's enough to make you appreciate why CDATA was specified as a method for escaping markup characters in a large block of text.

The next step in learning XML will provide you with a greater ability to create your XML documents by focusing on data and providing more information about your content.

1.7   Including Attributes in Your Documents

An XML document contains both elements and attributes. *Attributes* contribute additional meaning by describing the meaning of the element tag and description of content.

XML makes provisions for us to create as many elements and attributes as we deem necessary in designing a well-formed XML source document. An XML application contains elements and attributes for enhancing XML documents.

Let's examine the example in Figure 1.8. It contains textual content, an element, and an attribute.

```
<Hello content="Hello XML Fans"/>
```
Figure 1.8   Chap01_1.xml

This example defines one root element and contains an attribute/value pair. Attribute content describes data embedded between the element's opening element and the closing backward slash. To understand further how to use attributes, let's rewrite Authors.xml, only this time we'll use attributes rather than elements only (refer to Figure 1.4). The results can be seen in Figure 1.9.

```
<Authors>
   <AuthorInfo>
     <AuthorID id='101' firstName='Dwight' lastName='Peltzer'
     address='PO
     Box 516' city='Some City' state='NY' zip='1154'
     telNo='516-111-1234' title='Professor of Computer
     Science' employer='Tech University
     '/>
   </AuthorInfo>
</Authors>
```

Figure 1.9   Authors.xml using attributes

The syntax for using attributes looks like this:

```
<Element_Name attribute_name='content'/>
```

This format is simple. Notice how we defined the document root, and retaining the `<AuthorInfo>` category was easy. Then we defined each child element, provided an attribute with a name, and then supplied its value. Attributes always contain an attribute/value pair. Whether you use double quotes or single quotes to delineate your content is strictly up to you. You must be consistent, however.

Attributes definitely contribute additional information. We now have a choice between using elements only or applying the element/attribute syntax to your documents.

1.8   When Should You Use Attributes

One important factor determines whether you should use attributes or not, namely that elements can contain substructures whereas attributes cannot. Elements focus on data. Attributes provide additional information about their associated element. If you need to define a subelement structure, the example in Figure 1.10 demonstrates how to achieve this.

```
<Books>
  <AuthorInfo>
    <Name>Dwight Peltzer</Name>
    <Address> Po Box 516</Address>
    <City>Some City</City>
    <State> NY</State>
    <Zip>11654</Zip>
  </AuthorInfo>
  <BookInfo>
    <Title>XML Language Mechanics</Title>
    <ISBN>0-201-77168-3</ISBN>
    <Publisher>Addison Wesley</Publisher>
    <PublicationDate>Summer 2003</PublicationDate>
  </BookInfo>
</Books>
```

Figure 1.10   NestedSubstructure.xml

The syntax for using attributes looks like this:

```
<Element_Name attribute_name='content>
```

This is simple. Notice how we defined the document root, and retaining the AuthorInfo category was easy.

NestedSubstructure.xml contains two substructure header elements: `<AuthorInfo>` and `<BookInfo>`. Extracting content from them is much easier when the document is designed using elements, whereas it is more appropriate to use an attribute for representing metadata about the current element. Consider the document in Figure 1.11.

```
<Books>
  <Book title="XML Language Mechanics">
  <Author>Dwight Peltzer</Author>
  </Book>
</Books>
```

Figure 1.11   BooksVersion2.xml

The `<title>` attribute is simply flat text, eliminating the necessity for declaring an extra title element. In this context, `<title>` is metadata explaining what the book title is.

Here's an additional reason for using attributes: IDs and IDREFs can be applied to simple data types, namely strings. ID makes an element unique, similar to a primary key in a database. An IDREF is a pointer to the ID. Essentially, they provide nice links to a specific value regardless of where they are stored. If an element containing an ID attribute is moved to another section, the IDREF always points only to that value. It doesn't break document structure. Finally, using attributes retains backward compatibility with HTML.

Comparing Attributes with Elements

Attribute names conform to the same rules as elements. They must contain one or more characters. For example, a name must begin with a letter or an underscore. However, the same element cannot have two attributes bearing the same name. For example, consider the following element declared as a triangle: `<Triangle side="8" side="8" side="8"/>`. This fragment contains duplicate attributes and is therefore illegal.

We could clear up this problem by writing the following:

```
<Triangle sideOne="8" sideTwo="8" sideThree="8">
```

1.9 Comments

Comments play an important role in providing documentation. You can place comments anywhere in your XML document. They provide invaluable information to both the user and the programmer. Comments are also valuable for debugging. Comments were included in Figure 1.4 to assist you in understanding how we created a well-formed document. The syntax for comments is as follows:

```
<!-- comments go here -->
```

Be careful when embedding comments within your documents. Examine the following document:

```
<!-- XML processing begins with the root element
<Author>
        <AuthorID>101</AuthorID>
        <AuthorFName>Joseph</AuthorFName>-->
        <AuthorLName>James</AuthorLName>
        <AuthorAddress>PO Box 555</AuthorAddress>
</Author>
```

The ending comment characters `-->` have blocked out everything but the last two lines of code. How often have we returned to modify code and wasted valuable time trying to decode what we previously did?

A software package is frequently assigned to another team of developers within a programming group for modifications. Valuable documentation is essential so that the new group can understand why a module was designed in a particular way.

> **Note:** Comments are also valuable for temporarily blocking out code when you are debugging. You may be testing a particular segment of code. Use comments in this context.

1.10 Whitespace

Whitespace plays a significant role in XML. We represent whitespace as one or more `#x20` characters, carriage returns, line feeds, and tabs. The most logical reason for using whitespace is to make text more readable. We use whitespace to separate normal text from markup. We can also place two lines between paragraphs. A processor is obligated to pass all characters to the application in order to delineate markup from normal text. Whitespace by default is always preserved outside of markup in XML.

XSLT provides the ability to strip out whitespace-only nodes based on the element they are contained within. For example, xsl:strip-space eliminates space from elements of specified types within the XML-source document. Consider the following instruction:

```
<xsl:strip-space elements ="name address"/>
```

You may also do the following depending on the specified vocabulary:

```
<xsl:strip-space elements "*"/>
```

If there are only a few non-whitespace stripping elements, it is possible to issue the following command: xsl:preserve-space which overrides the xsl:stripping command and preserves whitespace.

1.11 NMTOKEN

Frequently, you will want to provide things with a name. NMTOKENs resemble names, with the exception they can start with digits, full-stop characters such as a period (.), hyphens, and the string XML. Note: full-stop characters are periods. For example, A.full-stop.example.looks.like.this.brief.sentence. Additionally, NMTOKENs are case sensitive. They cannot contain whitespace, punctuation, or other special characters. For example, the following name is valid: `-1.first.name.last.name`. Another valid name token would be `XML-first.name-last-name-token`.

In contrast, normal names allow you to use letters or underscores anywhere within them. Characters eligible to be used anywhere in a name are called *name start characters*. These include letters, digits, hyphens, underscores, colons, or full-stop characters such as a period (.).

Characters not included in this category (that can be used within a name) are called *name characters*. Note that xml and XML are reserved keywords.

1.12 How Does XML Apply to Business Applications?

Now that you have learned how to write well-formed XML documents, how do you apply your knowledge to real-world business applications? The following list represents a few questions frequently asked by IT professionals, developers, and students. Let's address each question posed here and see if we can provide some logical answers.

- **HTML serves our purposes well. Why should we migrate to XML from HTML?**

  We now possess much knowledge about XML, and we briefly presented the case for selecting XML over HTML in Figure 1.2. Although HTML is pervasive throughout the Internet as a standard format for web development, the HTML Document Type Definition version 4.1 is a complete rewrite of HTML version 4.0, and it represents a reaction to the permissiveness of HTML. This is the reason for the reformulation of HTML, which now exists as XHTML 1.0 and comes in three versions: strict, transitional, and frameset. The strict version corrects the lack of HTML rules for requiring both opening and closing tags, among numerous other requirements. The transitional version allows for migration from permissive HTML to XHTML by overlooking certain transgressions on HTML's part. For those who use framesets in their pages, the frameset version allows for migration to the new standard. The original purpose of HTML was to provide document structure, not style. However, as the Internet evolved and the browser war between Netscape and Microsoft raged, web page developers demanded more stylistic features in their browsers. This was an unfortunate development. Stylistic considerations should be separated from both data and document structure. This is precisely the reason why XHTML was developed. XML and XHTML integrate seamlessly.

  Because XML focuses on data, using it conforms to the concept of separating data from stylistic considerations and business logic. By following this reasoning, we also preserve the integrity of our data by separating data from style and logic.

- **Is XML applicable to enterprise-size distributed applications?**

  The primary reason why XML lies at the heart of a growing number of Internet enterprise applications is its universal acceptance as a markup metalanguage. XML uses the ISO-8859-1 (Latin-1) character set. The first 128 character codes of any of the ISO 8859 character sets are identical to the ASCII character set.

  XML consists of marked-up text. Additionally, XML is readable, even by those who are not computer savvy.

  XML makes it easy for trading partners to exchange documents when presented in XML format. Because this markup language is extensible, you can use a stylesheet to transform an XML document into a variety of formats including XML.

- **We use SQL Server as our repository. Does XML map easily to a relational database?**

  The answer is yes. Let's review the Authors XML document presented in Figure 1.4., Authors.xml.

```xml
<Authors> <!-- This is the document root -->
<!-- Define the subelement category -->
   <AuthorInfo>
<!-- Define the child elements for AuthorInfo -->
      <AuthorID>101</AuthorID>
      <AuthorFName>Dwight</AuthorFName>
      <AuthorLName>Peltzer</AuthorLName>
      <AuthorAddress>PO 516</AuthorAddress>
      <Auth_City>Some City</Auth_City>
      <Au_State>NY</Au_State>
      <Au_Zip>11564</Au_Zip>
      <BusinessTelNo>516-111-1234</BusinessTelNo>
      <Title>Professor of Computer Science</Title>
      <Employer>Tech University</Employer>
      <!-- Close this category -->
   </AuthorInfo>
      <!-- Now define the second subelement category -->
   <AuthorPublisherInfo>
      <Publisher>Addison Wesley</Publisher>
      <Editor>MSR</Editor>
```

```
   <Address>25 Main Street</Address>
   <City>Major City</City>
   <State>MA</State>
   <!-- close this category -->
</AuthorPublisherInfo>
 <!-- Define the third subelement category -->
<BookInfo>
   <Title>XML Language Mechanics</Title>
   <Pages> 450</Pages>
   <PublishDate>Summer 2003</PublishDate>
   <ISBN>0-201-77168-3</ISBN>
   <Category>XML Markup Language</Category>
   <NumChapters>12</NumChapters>
   <AdditionalFeatures>Self-Review Exercises and
Projects</AdditionalFeatures>
   <SoftwareTools>Evaluation copy of XML Spy</SoftwareTools>
   </BookInfo>
<!-- Close the document root -->
</Authors>
```

This document maps easily to SQL Server 2000. `Authors` represents the database name. As a rule of thumb, elements map as table names, and attributes map directly as column headings.

Three subelement categories exist:

- `<AuthorInfo>`
- `<AuthorPublisherInfo>`
- `<BookInfo>`

The three categories represent table names, whereas their respective children map as column names. Because XML represents a hierarchy containing groups of information, we can perform query searches by category. Let's create a single table called AuthorInfo from this example. We will eliminate a few columns to display the entire table row.

```
Use Authors
GO

Create Table AuthorInfo(
AuthorID int not null,
AuthorFName varchar (25),
AuthorLName varchar(25),
Address varchar (50),
City varchar (25),
State char(2),
Zip varchar (12))
```

Here is the table as represented in row/column format:

```
Select * from AuthorInfo
_____-*/

AuthorID    AuthorFName   AuthorLName   Address   City
State    Zip
_____ _____- _____-
```

We can clearly see how easily XML maps to a relational database.

What if we wanted to write a SQL query and require that returned data be in XML format? Is this possible?

Let's execute a query against the Northwind database, which comes bundled with SQL Server:

```
Use Northwind
Go

Select * from Customers
For XML Auto
```

Here is the result of this query:

```
<Customers CustomerID="ALFKI" CompanyName="Alfreds Futterkiste"
ContactName="Maria Anders"/><Customers CustomerID="ANATR"
CompanyName="Ana Trujillo Emparedados y helados"
ContactName="Ana Trujillo"/><Customers CustomerID="ANTON"
CompanyName="Antonio Moreno Taquería" ContactName="Antonio
Moreno"/><Customers CustomerID="AROUT" CompanyName="Around the
```

PART 1 **STRUCTURE**

```
Horn" ContactName="Thomas Hardy"/><Customers CustomerID="BERGS"
CompanyName="Berglunds snabbköp" ContactName="Christina
Berglund"/><Customers CustomerID="BLAUS" CompanyName="Blauer
See Delikatessen" ContactName="Hanna Moos"/>
```

Do you see how this simple query returns the data formatted as XML? We use attributes to return the data.

This chapter has introduced many concepts. It is time to refresh our memory by reviewing them and doing the exercises and projects that follow. We will then turn our attention in Chapter 2 to the Document Type Definition, and we'll see how to govern document structure and provide business rule constraints to a source document.

Summary

- The Extensible Markup Language (XML) is a metalanguage for providing structure to many different formats and types of information.
- XML is a metalanguage about data.
- XML elements lend semantic meaning to content.
- XML imposes structure on documents (Section 1.2).
- XML is case sensitive (Section 1.2).
- XML focuses on data (Section 1.2).
- XML documents must be well formed (Section 1.2).
- Unless a good reason exists to employ attributes, it is better to store data in elements.
- Information concerning the data should be stored in attributes.
- XML uses elements and attributes to provide both a logical structure and a physical structure to your documents (Section 1.1).
- We can view an XML document as a hierarchical structure (Section 1.1).
- XML conforms to a standard set of rules called the XML specification, version 1.0.

- Each XML document must contain exactly one root plus additional child elements to qualify as a well-formed document (Section 1.2).
- Child elements must be properly nested (Section 1.2).
- XML uses a processor called a parser to validate a document against the XML specification (Section 1.3).
- XML contains both parsed and unparsed character data (Section 1.5).
- Entities exist in many different forms (Section 1.6).
- Entity reference characters include the ampersand, apostrophe, lesser-than, and greater-than characters (Section 1.6).
- Elements can contain substructures; attributes cannot (Section 1.8).
- XML documents contain comments for documentation purposes (Section 1.9).

Self-Review Exercises

1. Name three things XML does well and provide a brief explanation of how they are applicable to source documents.

2. XML is a subset of HTML. (True or False.)

3. What are the criteria for designing a well-formed document?

4. List three ways in which XML provides structure to a document.

5. An XML application consists of several elements. What are they?

6. Why is it better to store data in elements?

7. Explain what an entity reference is. Demonstrate its application in a document.

8. Explain why it is better to store information concerning data in attributes.

9. What are the building blocks for constructing an XML document?

10. Define a parent-child relationship. Define a sibling-sibling relationship.

11. A tree consists of several components, including a root, branches, and leaves. Write an XML document that demonstrates how a tree is constructed.

12. What differentiates an HTML document from an XML document?

13. XML is case sensitive. What does this mean?

14. Why do we need a processor?

15. Describe the role a browser plays in checking an XML document.

16. What is an entity character reference?

17. How do you escape the ampersand?

18. What does "parsed character" mean?

19. What constitutes unparsed character data?

20. Provide two good reasons for using attributes rather than elements.

21. Are comments necessary in an XML document?

Projects

1. Write a daily planner for the first week of September. Do not use attributes.

2. Write a daily planner for November using attributes.

3. Write an XML document that marks up the review questions in this chapter (only the first 10 questions).

4. Provide an example using CDATA.

5. Write an XML document that marks up the table of contents for this chapter.

CHAPTER

Document Type Definition

[handwritten notes: "xsd can contains multiple xsds, supports database, are extensible", "xsd", "Proc File are small", "file are large", "support for wide range of data type"]

2.1 DTD: A Description

A Document Type Definition (DTD) represents a set of guidelines and rules for your XML documents. It governs the following:

- Ensuring that the XML source document is parsed by a validating parser. Validation ensures that a source document is well formed and conforms to the XML 1.0 specification.
- Enforcing existing business model rules.
- Providing structure to your document instance.

Generating a non-validated, poorly structured business document is risky, and granting credit to a customer without performing a credit check is foolish. A poorly designed data store containing data redundancies will render the data useless. A well-designed DTD eliminates these problems.

This chapter focuses on creating well-designed XML documents. Knowing how to apply a DTD to your business can determine success or failure. Let's begin.

The DTD contains a prologue, a DOCTYPE declaration, and definitions for all element types, attributes, entities, and notations

[handwritten notes in right margin: "DTS xsd larger in size, have lots of links that have to be resolved at run time. xsd do not support conditional constraints interelement dependencies cross document validation with xml there are null values for attributes, validation of large numeric data values."]

[handwritten note at bottom: "If your send your if prefer to use DTD bec smaller in size."]

33

residing within an XML document. It determines element order and provides rules and constraints for the XML document instance.

XML focuses on data, whereas the DTD concentrates on providing organization and rules for the XML document instance. The DTD also serves as a special kind of repository or database. Let's assume we have provided a definition for an entity in a DTD, as demonstrated here:

```
<!ENTITY DPS "www.dpsoftware.com">
```

The entity contains the definition (replacement text) for DPS, so the DTD serves as a small repository containing the data, "www.dpsoftware.com". You can access this data by referencing it from the XML document as follows:

```
<EXAMPLE>
        <DEMO>For further information, log on to &dps</DEMO>
</EXAMPLE>
```

The result displayed in the browser would look like this:

```
<Demo>For further information, log on to "www.dpsoft-
ware.com"<DEMO>.
```

The ampersand is precisely the tool we need for querying the repository and accessing the replacement text.

Here are some more characteristics of the DTD:

- A DTD prologue invokes the parser to validate the XML document.
- A DTD contains both a DOCTYPE declaration and element declarations.
- The DTD can serve as a repository containing data defined internally.

A DTD can reside internally as an internal subset or externally as an external subset. As an introduction, we'll begin by examining the document prologue. Then we'll discuss internal DTDs and, finally, external DTDs. This chapter builds on what you learned in Chapter 1, "Introduction to XML." After studying the chapter and completing its exercises, you will be able to apply your newly acquired knowledge to build a successful business application.

2.2 Document Type Declarations and Definitions

As previously mentioned, a DTD contains a prologue, a DOCTYPE declaration, and definitions for elements, attributes, entities, and notations residing in the document instance. Figure 2.1 represents an internal subset by combining both a DOCTYPE declaration and a Document Type Definition, accompanied by the document instance that the DTD governs.

```
<?xml version='1.0' encoding='UTF-8', standalone='no'?>
<!DOCTYPE Author [
<!ELEMENT Author (Name, Address, City, State, Zip, Publisher,
BookTitle, ISBN)>
<!ELEMENT Name (#PCDATA)>
<!ELEMENT Address (#PCDATA)>
<!ELEMENT City (#PCDATA)>
<!ELEMENT State (#PCDATA)>
<!ELEMENT Zip (#PCDATA)>
<!ELEMENT Publisher (#PCDATA)>
<!ELEMENT BookTitle (#PCDATA)>
<!ELEMENT ISBN (#PCDATA)>
]>
<Author>
 <Name>Dwight Peltzer</Name>
 <Address>PO Box 555</Address>
 <City>Oyster Bay</City>
 <State>NY</State>
 <Zip>11771</Zip>
 <Publisher>Addison Wesley</Publisher>
 <BookTitle>XML Language Mechanics</BookTitle>
 <ISBN>0-1-23458-0</ISBN>
</Author>
```

Figure 2.1   DTD as an internal subset

This example demonstrates how we structure the DTD beginning with the XML prologue and combine both the DTD and source document into one single file called the internal subset.

```
<?xml version="1.0" encoding="UTF-8" standalone="no"?>
```

A prologue is required for only two reasons:

- Document validation
- Special handling of foreign-language characters other than English

The prologue contains three important pieces of information, beginning with `<?xml` followed by the attribute. This indicates conformance with the XML specification, version 1.0. A revised second edition has been released, but the version remains 1.0.

We mentioned character encoding, the second attribute, in Chapter 1 when we stated that XML uses the universally accepted ASCII character set. Let's delve a little further into this topic. Character encoding refers to how the processor treats special foreign characters such the German umlaut or the French accent grave. The first 128 character codes of the ISO-8859-1 (Latin-1) character set are identical to the ASCII character set. Either UTF-8 or UTF-16 can be specified in your XML documents. Unless you intend to write your application in a foreign language, simply specify the encoding as UTF-8, which is a 7-bit subset of Unicode coding.

The third attribute denotes `standalone='yes'` or `standalone='no'`. If you provide `'yes'` as the attribute's value, your document will only be checked for being well formed. If `'no'` is specified, the `<!DOCTYPE` declaration invokes a validating parser.

The document declaration begins with the keyword `<!DOCTYPE` followed immediately by an opening bracket`[`, and it ends with a bracket `]>`. The data between the brackets consists of element declarations and their data type definitions:

```
<!DOCTYPE Author [ .... Element declarations ]>
```

The root element `Author` must immediately follow the DOCTYPE declaration. The third line begins with element declarations, including a parentheses-enclosed sequence of child elements, thereby defining both document element order and the content model for this DTD. Elements containing the (#PCDATA) designation allow text within markup tags.

The preceding document declaration has introduced several important new concepts. Let's review them:

- The document root is a container holding all other document components called entities.
- Entities are storage units containing elements.
- The element's content is data.
- The DTD requires declared elements to appear in the XML source document in the exact order specified in the sequential list, as in the following:

```
<!ELEMENT Author (Name, Address, City, State, Zip, Publisher,
BookTitle, ISBN)>
```

- This DTD defines all data types as parsed character data.
- #PCDATA types allow textual content between markup tags.
- When both the source document and DTD are combined into a single unit (as we have done here), we refer to it as an internal subset.

It is also possible to refer to a DTD residing externally. We then consider it an external subset and provide a Uniform Resource Identifier (URI) that points to its location. A URI refers specifically to an XML document called a resource. Note: the web uses the Uniform Resource Identifiers to point to resources.

```
<?xml version='1.0' encoding='UTF-8' standalone='no'?>
<!DOCTYPE Author SYSTEM "Author.dtd">
```

This declaration simply states, "Look externally for the DTD." We could also specify a fully qualified URL, as in the following:

```
<?xml version='1.0' encoding='UTF-8' standalone='no'?>
<!DOCTYPE Author SYSTEM "Author.dtd"
       "http://www.dpsoftware.com/dtds/Author.dtd">
```

Many DTD authors consider a file saved with the .dtd extension, residing externally, to be a valid DTD. However, until it has been referenced and parsed, it remains just a file containing definitions.

2.3   DTD Conceptualization and Design

The DTD, a subset of Standard Generalized Markup Language (SGML), was designed expressly for validating XML documents by defining document structure and enforcing rules and constraints specified within the DTD.

The DTD's chief task is bringing organization and validation to XML documents. For example, as the parser processes each component (elements and their content), comparing the definitions with source document elements, violations are reported to the application. The DTD also performs a validity check on any given element's data type. This is in complete contrast to parsing a document for being well formed, a topic that was introduced in Chapter 1. A valid document has much more value and purpose when it adheres to a governing document.

Examine your data source first; write your DTD second. Then create the source document and test your work.

Perhaps the most important step in designing a DTD is examining your data source for content prior to beginning the application design. Careful scrutiny can help you plan both the governing document and the XML document instance. (We will refer to the XML document from this point forth as an instance rather than as a source document.) Examining its data types will help you select the proper content model (which are discussed in section 2.6). You will most likely need to reference external resources. Industrial DTDs consist of more than one DTD residing in more than one place. They can exist as separate DTDs on the Internet in many different places. You needn't necessarily re-create the wheel by always writing your own. You can import other public domain DTDs by using the DOCTYPE declaration within the document instance to reference the external entity, as follows:

```
<?xml version='1.0'?>
<!DOCTYPE LegalBrief PUBLIC "-//SOMESOURCE//DTD
LegalBrief//EN"

"http://www.somesource.com/dtds/LegalBrief.dtd">
```

Additionally, think about the DTD's ultimate purpose and usage. Consider how elements and attributes map to a relational database. Following these procedures will help guide you in structuring your document grouping elements in distinct, meaningful categories, just as we did in Chapter 1. By taking into account all these factors, you will create a well-documented strategy for designing your DTD.

A DTD allows us to focus on data while it quietly works in the background, working in tandem with the validating parser.

2.4 DTD as an External Subset

DTD authors use the SYSTEM keyword and a relative URL to provide the parser with information as to where the DTD is located.

The DOCTYPE declaration syntax is as follows:

```
<!DOCTYPE – name_ of_ root_element  SYSTEM   "DTD's name"
"DTDs_URL">
```

```
<!ENTITY Author SYSTEM "Author.xml">
```

In this example, it is assumed that the processor will accept responsibility for locating the definitions. A relative URI does not provide a qualified path and machine name to the specified resource. In contrast, the external entity subset in Figure 2.2 demonstrates a fully qualified URL.

```
<?xml version ='1.0'?>
<!DOCTYPE Author SYSTEM
"http://www.somesource.com/dtds/Author.dtd">
<Author>
<!--other code goes here-->
</Author>
```

Figure 2.2   External entity subset

By doing this, we have provided public access to the DTD, whereas an internal entity subset can only be used privately.

Storing source documents and DTDs in separate subdirectories encourages modularity and eliminates dependencies, whereas placing both source document and DTD in the same folder builds dependencies.

Frequently, attempts to validate a source document against its DTD fail because the parser fails to locate the DTD. When you are thoroughly familiar with namespaces and URLs, use the preferred method of referencing DTDs by providing a fully qualified URL, as demonstrated here:

```
<!DOCTYPE Chapters SYSTEM "http://dpsoftware.com/Example1.dtd">
```

EXERCISE 1: The example in Figure 2.3 designates the DTD as an internal subset by including both DTD and the instance document. Revise this example so that it becomes an external subset.

```
<?xml version="1.0" encoding="UTF-8"?>
<!DOCTYPE Seasons [
    <!ELEMENT Seasons (Summer, Fall, Winter, Spring)>
    <!ELEMENT Summer (#PCDATA)>
    <!ELEMENT Fall (#PCDATA)>
    <!ELEMENT Winter (#PCDATA)>
    <!ELEMENT Spring (#PCDATA)>
    ]>
    <Seasons>
     <Summer> A warm, beautiful season</Summer>
     <Fall>A colorful season</Fall>
     <Winter>Time for skiing</Winter>
     <Spring>A renewed season of eternal youth and hope
     </Spring>
    </Seasons>
```

Figure 2.3   Example 4.xml

2.5 DOCTYPE Declarations Using the PUBLIC Keyword

Authors may use the PUBLIC keyword to signify that the DTD is intended for public use.

The DTD must be given a name and provided with a URL, as follows:

```
<!DOCTYPE root_element_name  PUBLIC  "DTD_name" "DTDs_URL">
```

Such a declaration is the following:

```
<!DOCTYPE html PUBLIC "-//W3C//DTD HTML 4.0//EN">
```

You can designate a DTD as PUBLIC, define it as an external entity subset, and publish it in the public domain so that it can be shared as a common DTD for organizations, public groups, and individual XML authors. You accomplish this by creating the DTD, saving it externally, and providing a URL so that the parser can locate the DTD. It allows public organizations to agree on a common format for sharing documents and resources. It also prevents unwanted extensions from third-party vendors by not allowing an agreed-upon standard to be altered without permission.

Many HTML editors automatically place the following string at the top of an HTML file as just mentioned: <!DOCTYPE HTML PUBLIC "-//W3C//DTD HTML//EN">. It basically says, "This document conforms to a non-standards body–designed DTD for HTML created by the W3C Consortium in English." A PUBLIC identifier followed by a hyphen informs us the DTD was created by a non-standards body–approved group. The following declaration indicates that <Author> was created by Dwight Peltzer in English.

```
<?xml version='1.0'?>
<!DOCTYPE AUTHOR SYSTEM "-//Dwight Peltzer//DTD Author//EN//">
```

A plus sign would indicate that an official standards body–approved group has created the DTD. Now that we have discussed internal and external subsets, let's focus on content models.

2.6 Content Models

Content models affect the behavior of document structure dramatically.

When describing a content model, the content attribute determines whether an element can contain only elements ("ELEMENTS Only"), only text ("textOnly"), a mixture of text and elements ("mixed"), or nothing at all ("empty").

Let's discuss the ANY content model first. Consider the following example. It can contain a mixture of elements in any order and can include both parsed character data and unparsed character data.

```
<!DOCTYPE Week SYSTEM "ANYContentModel.dtd">
<Week>
    <minute>32</minute>
    <hour>11:00 am</hour>
     This is a permissive example
    <second>45</second>
    x = &#39;10&#39;, y = &#39;20&#39;. Therefore, y is &gt; x,
    &#38; this model should rarely be used!
  <Day>Monday</Day>
</Week>
```

If we examine the following example's DTD, we can understand why this content model is so permissive.

```
<!ELEMENT Week  ANY>
<!ELEMENT Day (#PCDATA)>
<!ELEMENT hour (#PCDATA)>
<!ELEMENT minute (#PCDATA)>
<!ELEMENT second (#PCDATA)>
```

The elements are out of order; additionally, text is inserted into this model with no complaint from the parser. You can use this content model when you are beta testing and become more restrictive as you develop your application and eventually phase ANY out.

There is one other aspect of the ANY model to discuss. Consider the following DTD:

```
<!ELEMENT Months ANY)>
<!ELEMENT Month (#PCDATA)>
<!ELEMENT Day (#PCDATA)>
```

The content model is ANY, the data type for Month is (#PCDATA). Therefore, the following example allows Months to contain child elements:

```
<!DOCTYPE Months SYSTEM "Months ANY.dtd">
<Months>
     <Month>January</Month>
     <Month>February</Month>
```

Now let's discuss the mixed content model.

Mixed Content Model

Element types containing mixed content are allowed to intersperse child elements with character data. An example of mixed content is a magazine article. It might contain the following:

```
<Article>This article intends to <b>emphasize</b> the
importance of writing XML documents that are both well-
formed and valid.</Article>.
```

We can provide element declarations that offer a choice:

```
<!ELEMENT Author(#PCDATA AuthorID | AuthorFName | AuthorLName |
Address)*>
```

Note the asterisk, which follows the pipe-separated list and parentheses delimited. (*Note:* A pipe symbol is almost like comma-separated ASCII. The difference is that a pipe symbol is used instead of a comma to separate the fields.) It is required where mixed content is allowed to contain a mixture of elements and character data. Whitespace is allowed before the pipe symbol and after it, just as in the example. The following example represents a data-only mixed content model:

```
<!ELEMENT Title (    #PCDATA    )>
```

Note that `#PCDATA` does contain mixed content. If you stop to consider what parsed character data means, text is interspersed with markup characters.

Whitespace may be placed before and after `#PCDATA`. You could also do the following:

```
<!ELEMENT Title (#PCDATA | subtitle | para | emph)*>
```

Empty Content Model

The Empty Content Model allows you to use attributes. Refer to Section 2.7.

An empty model cannot contain any content. The following declaration demonstrates the syntax for this model: `<!ELEMENT DEMO EMPTY>`. Although it may seem that this content model is not useful, we could look at an HTML markup tag, such as `<p>`, and see where it appears in a meaningful context. It is an empty HTML tag containing structural instructions for where to begin a new paragraph.

Valid EMPTY ELEMENT declarations include the following:

```
<!ELEMENT/>
<!ELEMENT Title name='XML Language Mechanics' ISBN='0-1-2435-0'/>
```

Although this format may surprise you, empty elements are primarily used in XML document instances to contain attributes, which provide additional meaning about their associated element.

Child Content Model (Element Only)

This model restricts the inclusion of data types to elements only. It looks like this:

```
<!ELEMENT Author (Name, Address)>
   <!ELEMENT Name (#PCDATA)>
<!ELEMENT Address (#PCDATA)>
```

This restricts `Author` to two child elements, `Name` and `Address`. Elements specified as (`#PCDATA`) cannot have other child elements. (See ELEMENT Name above.) A source document for this content model looks like this:

```
<?xml version="1.0" encoding="UTF-8" standalone="no"?>
<!DOCTYPE Author SYSTEM "AuthorContentModel.dtd">
<Author >
    <Name>Dwight Peltzer</Name>
    <Address>Oyster Bay</Address>
</Author>
```

Elements allow parsed character data within the tags. Let's alter the content model slightly to consider this content model from another point of view:

```
<!ELEMENT Author (#PCDATA)>
<!ELEMENT Name (#PCDATA)>
<!ELEMENT Address (#PCDATA)>
```

Consider the following instance document that adheres to the DTD:

```
<Author >
    <Name>Dwight Peltzer</Name>
    <Address>Oyster Bay</Address>
</Author>
```

This document would be rejected. Can you see the error? An element defined as #PCDATA cannot have other child elements. Let us fix this content model so that it's defined as Element Only.

```
<!ELEMENT Author (Name, Address)>
<!ELEMENT Name (#PCDATA)>
<!ELEMENT Address (#PCDATA)>
```

The content model as it now stands is correct. Only elements may exist. `Name` and `Address` are allowed to contain parsed character data.

2.7 Attributes

Attributes offer a way to provide additional meaning about their related elements. What distinguishes attributes from elements? Attributes cannot contain elements, whereas elements can contain other elements. Additionally, element attributes can be specified only once and can be specified in any order. Consider the following incorrect XML fragment:

```
<Triangle side='8' side='8' side='8'/>
```

A correct DTD solution would be the following:

```
<!ELEMENT Triangle EMPTY>
<!ATTLIST Triangle
          sideA CDATA #REQUIRED
          sideB CDATA #REQUIRED
          sideC CDATA #REQUIRED
>
```

Here is the XML source document with unique attributes:

```
<Triangle sideA='8'  sideB='8' sideC='8'/>
```

Everything is now correct. The XML fragment `<Triangle side='8' side='8' side='8'/>` contained attributes which were not unique.

Note: Attributes are easy to map to databases as column names. The following example demonstrates that:

```
<Book title='XML Language Mechanics' author='Dwight Peltzer'
Publisher='Addison Wesley'/>
```

Book maps as the table name; the other attributes map as column names.

Attributes and their types are enumerated in the following table:

Table 2.1   Attribute Types

`ENTITY ATTS`	Attribute values must refer to an external binary entity declared in a DTD. These should not be parsed.
`CDATA`	Attributes can only use character data.
`ENTITIES`	These are the same as ENTITY, with the exception that they allow multiple values.
`ID`	The attribute must appear as a unique identifier. This is the same as the primary key in a relational table.
`IDREF`	IDREF is a reference to an ID specified elsewhere in a document.
`IDREFS`	Multiple IDREFS can reference an ID.
`NMTOKEN`	NMTOKEN describes a mixture of characters, including letters, numbers, underscores, periods, colons, and dashes.
`NMTOKENS`	NMTOKENS allows multiple values, separated by spaces.
`NOTATION`	The DTD may include one or more notation. Each notation must have its own declaration. They usually are used to name binary entities such as an image, JPEG, or GIF.
`ENUMERATED`	The attribute value must match one of some included values, as in `<!ATTLIST attributeName (content 1| content2 |content3)>`.

Attribute List Declarations

Attributes are useful when describing the contents of an XML page, as opposed to being an integral part of content. Four attribute defaults are available for our use, as shown in Table 2.2.

Table 2.2 Attribute Defaults

Default	Usage
#REQUIRED	An element containing this attribute must specify a value.
#IMPLIED	This element is not required. The processor will ignore this attribute if none is specified.
#FIXED	This attribute must specify the value as fixed.
Default	Attribute Default identifies a default value for an attribute. If this attribute is not defined, the processor assumes that the value is the default.

The format for defining an attribute list declaration is described in the following example:

```
<!ATTLIST elementName attrName attrType attrDefault
defaultValue>
```

For example, an attribute might be used to delineate the difference between one type of textbook and another, such as a computer science text versus a medical text.

```
<!ELEMENT BOOK (#PCDATA)>
<!ATTLIST BOOK bookName CDATA #REQUIRED>.
```

BOOK is declared as the element name, bookName as the attribute name, CDATA as the attribute type, and #REQUIRED as the constraint. #IMPLIED is used only when you do not require a bookName.

```
<!ATTLIST BOOK bookName CDATA #IMPLIED>
```

The following example allows a default definition:

```
<!ATTLIST BOOK bookName CDATA "Computer Science">.
```

In some cases, the default is a number rather than text. If a default value is not specified, the processor automatically sets this attribute to the value of the default listed elsewhere, as in the following:

```
<!ATTLIST Programming Language  Type CDATA "C#">
```

Enumerated Data types

The following is an example of attribute enumerations:

```
<!ATTLIST book bookType
       (ScienceFiction |Historical | ComputerScience |
       Physics) #IMPLIED>
```

You're allowed to select one from this list of choices. `#IMPLIED`
makes the appearance of one of these enumerated attributes optional.
The DTD in Figure 2.4 demonstrates how to use attributes rather than
elements.

```
<?xml version='1.0' ?>
<!ELEMENT Book EMPTY >
<!ATTLIST    Book        name        CDATA        #REQUIRED
                         isbn        CDATA        #REQUIRED
                         title       CDATA        #REQUIRED
                         author      CDATA        #REQUIRED
                         publisher   CDATA        #IMPLIED
                         price       CDATA        #IMPLIED>
```

Figure 2.4   Attributes.dtd

`ELEMENT <Book>` is an empty content model because data resides
in the attributes.

If a default attribute is listed, its attribute/value pair is selected. It
can be overridden by providing options such as those displayed
below:

```
<?xml version='1.0' ?>
<!DOCTYPE INVOICE SYSTEM 'Invoice.dtd'>
<!ELEMENT SHIPMETHOD (UPS | USPS | FEDEX) "FEDEX">.
```

In this example, `FEDEX` is supplied by the parser if another selection is not chosen.

2.8 Entities

XML documents draw on many different sources for their data. They are not necessarily complete documents but rather exist as fragments in the form of text or images. We consider these external resources as *general entities*. They can reside in many different locations.

You will recall that in section 2.1, we defined a DTD as consisting of the following:

- An XML prologue
- A document type declaration
- Elements, attributes, comments, and processing instructions
- General entity references importing data into the root element, thereby serving as a container

How is all of this seemingly disparate data pulled together to make up a single document entity? The validating parser uses the DTD as a blueprint for collating the data into a single document entity. The DTD consists of a DOCTYPE declaration, element declarations, and a URL containing the address of the specified DTD.

Entities are containers for storing elements, and element content within those entities consists of data. We classify entities according to whether they can be used in the document instance or in the DTD, as follows:

- Entities that can be used only in a DTD are called parameter entities.
- Entities permitted in the document instance are classified as general entities.
- Entities are polymorphic because they represent containers holding different types of information. They are identifiable by name, and they can represent a single character or a large block of text. They can exist internally or externally.

Processors need a method of distinguishing between markup and content. We learned in Chapter 1 how XML predefines certain characters to identify them as the beginning of markup. Just to refresh your memory, two special characters notify the parser of the following:

- < signifies the beginning of the tag.
- > denotes the tag's ending.

Entities provide a method for inserting them into your XML document as special characters representing markup. Table 2.3 contains a list of predefined entities.

Table 2.3   Predefined Entities

Entity	Name	Symbol
<!Entity	lt	"& #60;">
<!Entity	gt	">">
<!Entity	amp	"&#38;">
<!Entity	apos	"'">
<!Entity	quot	""">

You can escape predefined characters by referring to them either by their name or by their symbols. For example, if you want to mark up <Distribution> with the more intuitive method of using the character's name, you can achieve it by doing the following:

```
<Demo>
   <PredefinedEntity> &lt;Distribution&gt;</PredefinedEntity>
</Demo>
```

The entity, when displayed in the browser, achieves the desired result:

```
- <Demo>
   <PredefinedEntity><Distribution></PredefinedEntity>
   </Demo>
```

This is easier than the following:

```
<Demo>
  <PredefinedEntity>
  &#60;Distribution&#62;</PredefinedEntity>
</Demo>
```

The result is the same:

```
<Demo>
    <PredefinedEntity><Distribution></PredefinedEntity>
</Demo>
```

Use double quotes as listed here:

```
<Demo>
  &#34;This is a quote &#34;
</Demo>
```

Viewed in the browser, the result is as follows:

```
<Demo>"This is a double quote"</Demo>
```

A single quote is escaped like the following:

```
<Demo>
  &#39;This is a single quote&#39;
</Demo>
```

Here is the result:

```
<Demo>'This is a single quote'</Demo>
```

The following example presents a mixture of escaped predefined entity characters:

```
<Demo>
  x = &#39;10&#39;, y = &#39;20&#39;. Therefore, y is
  &gt; x, &#38; this is a complicated example!
</Demo>
```

Here is the result as displayed in the browser:

```
<Demo>x = '10', y = '20'. Therefore, y is > x, & this is a com-
plicated example!</Demo>
```

It's amazing what you have to endure when escaping predefined entity characters. Nevertheless, it is fun and it works!

Entity Declarations

Entity declarations occur only in the DTD. Syntax for an entity declaration looks like this:

```
<!ENTITY    entityname "replacement text">.
```

Note that an entity reference may not contain the name of an unparsed entity. Also, one other factor must be considered. If an internal entity will be utilized in more than one document, it is better to declare it in an external DTD rather than placing it in an internal entity subset. The following example identifies dps as the entity, and the URL is its replacement text.

```
<!ENTITY dps  "www.dpsoftware.com/entities/dps">
```

Although dps is declared in the DTD, we classify this as an external entity because the replacement text is fetched from an external source. Additionally, it is referenced from the document instance using the ampersand.

Let's place this example in context (see Figure 2.5).

```
<?xml version="1.0" encoding="UTF-8"?>
<!DOCTYPE Memo [
<!ELEMENT Memo (description)>
<!ENTITY dps "www.dpsoftware.com">
<!ELEMENT description (#PCDATA)>
]>
<Memo>
  <description>You can get further information at &dps; they
will send a product description of the software package you
are interested in, and a 30 day evaluation copy.</description>
</Memo>
```

Figure 2.5 Memo.xml

Figure 2.6 demonstrates the result when the replacement text is displayed in the browser.

```
<?xml version="1.0" encoding="UTF-8" ?>
  <!DOCTYPE Memo (View Source for full doctype...)>
- <Memo>
  <description>You can get further information at www.dpsoft-
ware.com and they will send a product description of the soft-
ware package you are interested in, and a 30 day evaluation
copy.</description>
  </Memo>
```

Figure 2.6   Memo_version2.xml

Do you see how nicely the browser pulls the replacement text from the external source into the document? The example in Figure 2.7 demonstrates how we can store a large block of text as a single entity and reference it.

```
<?xml version="1.0" encoding="UTF-8"?>
<!DOCTYPE LargeEntity [
<!ELEMENT LargeEntity (Demo)>
<!ELEMENT Demo (#PCDATA)>
<!ENTITY Macro  "Entities have several uses. They allow you to
create macros for content. You simply refer to them by name.
Subsequently, they will expand in the browser when referenced.
This provides authors with a convenient means of referring to
large blocks of text stored as a single unit, without having
to retype them every time they wish to refer to it.">
]>
<LargeEntity>
    <Demo>&Macro;</Demo>
</LargeEntity>
```

Figure 2.7   LargeEntity.xml

We have defined Macro as an entity and have provided its replacement text. Let's view the results in the browser (see Figure 2.8).

```
<?xml version="1.0" encoding="UTF-8" ?>
  <!DOCTYPE LargeEntity (View Source for full doctype...)>
- <LargeEntity>
  <Demo>Entities have several uses. They allow you to create
macros for content. You simply refer to them by name.
Subsequently, they will expand in the browser when referenced.
This provides authors with a convenient means of referring to
large blocks of text stored as a single unit, without having to
retype them every time they wish to refer to it.</Demo>
  </LargeEntity>
```

Figure 2.8   LargeEntity displayed in Internet Explorer

Parameter Entities

Parameter entities are declared only in the DTD, just as general entities are, with one exception: A percentage sign (%) is placed before the entity name.

Percentage signs are not recognized in the document instance.The following individual entities are legal. However, an attempt to display the example as a complete example will not display in Internet Explorer.

```
<!ENTITY %publisher  "Pearson Publishing">
<!ENTITY legal "All Rights Reserv ed">
<!ENTITY sig  "&#xA9; 2002  %publisher;.  &legal;">
```

Parameter entities are expanded within the DTD and cannot be referenced from the instance document. Parameter entity %publisher expands to Pearson Publishing, whereas legal can be referenced from outside the DTD in the source document. The third line expands to the following:

```
© 2002 Pearson Publishers  All Rights Reserved.
```

Note that when you want to access a parameter entity, you must reference it as we do on line three:

```
<!ENTITY sig  "&#xA9; 2002 %publisher;.  &legal;">
```

Precede `sig` with an ampersand, and you will be successful in viewing the parameter entity.

Let's explore parameter entity references in a little more depth. Consider the example in Figure 2.9. Once more, each individual entity's syntax is correct.

```
<!ENTITY % name "Dwight Peltzer  Author">
<!ENTITY % publisher "Addison Wesley  Publisher">
<!ENTITY % title " Title XML Language Mechanics">
<!ENTITY  signature "%name; %title; %publisher;">
<!ELEMENT Authors ( Au_Name)>
<!ELEMENT Au_Name (#PCDATA)>
```

Figure 2.9   Parameter entities

The parameter entity declarations for `name`, `publisher`, and `title` are self-explanatory. We know they cannot be referenced directly. Let's try referencing one directly as an exercise and experience the consequences (see Figure 2.10).

```
<?xml version="1.0" encoding="UTF-8"?>
<!ELEMENT Author (Display)>
<!ELEMENT Display (#PCDATA)>
<!ENTITY % name  "Dwight Peltzer">
```

Figure 2.10   DirectReference.dtd

The parameter entity declaration for `name` is correct. Next we present the source document and try to reference the parameter entity directly (see Figure 2.11).

```
<?xml version="1.0" encoding="UTF-8"?>
<!DOCTYPE Author SYSTEM "C:\Documents and Settings\Dwight
Peltzer\My Documents\chapterRevision\DirectReference.dtd">
<Author>
        <Display>&name;</Display>
</Author>
```

Figure 2.11   DirectReference.xml

We are trying to reference the parameter entity directly with the following results:

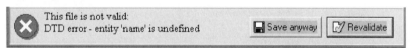

Always use Internet Explorer browser 5.5 and above when testing your examples. Netscape is not appropriate for this purpose.

The parser generates the error but incorrectly informs us that the entity name is undefined. If we examine the definition, we find that we have properly defined it. So, what is the solution? The parameter entity is not parsed until the replacement text is retrieved. Additionally, the entity must be defined first and referenced only as follows: Declare an external general entity reference by using the ampersand to reference the parameter entity and include the parameter entity within the external referencing entity (see Figure 2.12).

```
<?xml version="1.0" encoding="UTF-8"?>
<!ELEMENT Author (Display)>
<!ELEMENT Display (#PCDATA)>
<!ENTITY % name "Dwight Peltzer">
<!ENTITY ref "%name";>
```

Figure 2.12   DirectReference.dtd revised

Notice how we have declared a general entity reference called ref. Its replacement text includes the reference to the parameter entity, as demonstrated in Figure 2.13.

```
<!DOCTYPE Author SYSTEM "C:\Documents and Settings\Dwight
Peltzer\My Documents\chapterRevision\ DirectReference.dtd">
<Author>
   <Display>&ref;</Display>
</Author>
```

Figure 2.13   Revised parameter entity reference

Here is the correct result:

```
<!DOCTYPE Author (View Source for full doctype...)>
- <Author>
   <Display>Dwight Peltzer</Display>
   </Author>
```

Wow! Now you know how to declare and reference parameter entities.

EXERCISE 2: Open Notepad, try your hand at declaring a parameter entity, and reference it. The following are the specifications for this experiment.

```
Invoice.dtd
```

`Invoice` represents the root element. We need an invoice number, customerID, name, address, city, state, zip, product ID, and product name. Finally, include sales tax (8.5%) and total price. Save it to your subdirectory (XMLDocs), reference the parameter entities, and display the results in the browser.

The benefits of parameter entities become evident when referencing an external DTD. For example, if you want to modularize your DTDs and include another DTD as part of the primary DTD, reference it like this:

```
<!ENTITY % authors.dtd   SYSTEM  "authors.dtd">
```

By doing this, you inherit the external entities' data model.

Let's try our approach at declaring parameter entities. Let's assume we are preparing a catalog for a consortium of universities. Each campus shares the same content model. Here is an example of how this might be handled:

```
<!ENTITY % inlines
"(NAME | Rank | Dept | CoursesTaught)*">
<!ELEMENT Campus % inlines;>
<!ELEMENT University % inlines;>
```

If an additional element were to be added, you would simply add it to the sequential parameter entities.

As previously mentioned, you needn't necessarily reinvent the wheel. You can import other external DTDs into yours and create one large, comprehensive DTD spanning several campuses.

External Parameter Entities

Earlier in our discussion, we provided examples of DTDs that defined elements utilized in internal documents. We'll now shift our focus to assembling data from many different external sources. If you break a DTD into several components, the documents are easier to manage.

Let's assume we want to write a DTD for a book. We can begin by creating an XML instance document for an individual book and then create a corresponding DTD for it. Once we have accomplished that task, we can create a DTD for an electronic bookseller and link the book DTD with the bookseller DTD (see Figure 2.14).

```
<?xml version="1.0" encoding="UTF-8"?>
<!ELEMENT Book (Genre+, Title, ISBN, Publisher+)>
<!ELEMENT Genre              (#PCDATA)>
<!ELEMENT Title              (#PCDATA)>
<!ELEMENT ISBN               (#PCDATA)>
<!ELEMENT Publisher          (#PCDATA)>
```

Figure 2.14   Book.dtd

Notice that `Genre` has a plus sign (+) after the element, indicating that it contains more than one category. Figure 2.15 is the individual

Book document instance. Here is a valid document instance for
Book.dtd.

```
<!DOCTYPE Book SYSTEM "Book.dtd">
<Book>
  <Genre>Computer Science</Genre>
<Title>XML Language Mechanics</Title>
  <ISBN>0-15364-0</ISBN>
  <Publisher>Addison Wesley</Publisher>
</Book>
```

Figure 2.15   Book.dtd

The next task is creating a DTD for a bookseller (see Figure 2.16).
Then we will link the two DTDs.

```
<!ELEMENT Bookseller (Name, Category+, Book+)>
<!ELEMENT Name (#PCDATA)>
<!ELEMENT Category (#PCDATA)>
```

Figure 2.16   BookSeller.dtd

We need to mention a couple of items. Notice how element Book
is missing from this DTD. As a result, when you want to validate the
DTD, you will get the following error message:

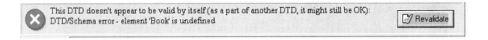

To validate this DTD, you need to add two lines to the DTD:

```
<!ENTITY % book SYSTEM "Book.dtd">
%book;
```

The following DTD is the completed DTD.

```
<?xml version="1.0" encoding="UTF-8"?>
<!ELEMENT Bookseller (Category+, Publisher+)>
<!ELEMENT Category (#PCDATA)>
<!ENTITY % book SYSTEM "Book.dtd">
%book;
```

Here is the XML document instance displayed in the browser:

```
<! DOCTYPE Book (View Source for full doctype...)>
- <Book>
  <Genre>Computer Science</Genre>
  <Title>XML Language Mechanics</Title>
  <ISBN>0-15364-0</ISBN>
  <Publisher>Addison Wesley</Publisher>
  </Book>
```

The parameter entity now links the `Bookseller` DTD to the
Book DTD. Neat! This example uses a relative URL. `Book` is defined
in the `Book` DTD.

If the processor fails to find this DTD, you can provide an absolute
URL as follows:

```
<!ENTITY % book
"http://www. dpsoftware,inc/dtds/Book.dtd">
%<!ENTITY % book SYSTEM "Book.dtd">
%book;
```

Resolving External Entities

We can also use parameter entities to assemble a portal for selling
electronic books by creating document instance files for individual
books. For example, here are individual XML files for two books:

```
A.xml
<Book>
    <Genre>Computer Science</Genre>
    <Title>VBScript</Title>
    <ISBN>0-35467-1</ISBN>
    <Publisher>XPress</Publisher>
</Book>

B.xml
<Book>
    <Genre>Computer Science</Genre>
    <Title>JScript</Title>
    <ISBN>0-46467-1</ISBN>
    <Publisher>BPress</Publisher>
</Book>
```

Here is the DTD that contains entity references for the books:

```
Portal.dtd
<!ENTITY a    SYSTEM "A.xml">
<!ENTITY b    SYSTEM "B.xml">
<!ENTITY c    SYSTEM "C.xml">
<!ENTITY d    SYSTEM "D.xml">
```

Finally, we can reference the external entities from this file:

```
Portal.xml

<?xml version="1.0" standalone="no"?>
<!DOCTYPE Bookseller SYSTEM "C:\Documents and
Settings\Dwight Peltzer\My
Documents\chapterRevision\Bookseller.dtd" [
      <!ENTITY % books SYSTEM "Portal.dtd">
      %books;
]>
<Bookseller>
<Name>DPS </Name>
<Category>Computer Science</Category>
<Book>
      <Genre>Computer Science</Genre>
      <Title>C# Made Easy</Title>
      <ISBN>0-50897-1</ISBN>
      <Publisher>ZPress</Publisher>
</Book>
 &A;
 &B;
 &C;
 &D;
 </Bookseller>
```

Let's view the results in Internet Explorer:

```
<?xml version="1.0" standalone="no" ?>
<!DOCTYPE Bookseller (View Source for full doctype...)>
- <Bookseller>
   <Name>DPS</Name>
   <Category>Computer Science</Category>
 - <Book>
```

PART 1 STRUCTURE

```
      <Genre>Computer Science</Genre>
      <Title>C# Made Easy</Title>
      <ISBN>0-50897-1</ISBN>
      <Publisher>ZPress</Publisher>
   </Book>
-  <Book>
      <Genre>Computer Science</Genre>
      <Title>VBScript</Title>
      <ISBN>0-35467-1</ISBN>
      <Publisher>XPress</Publisher>
   </Book>
-  <Book>
      <Genre>Computer Science</Genre>
      <Title>JScript</Title>
      <ISBN>0-46467-1</ISBN>
      <Publisher>BPress</Publisher>
   </Book>
-  <Book>
      <Genre>Computer Science</Genre>
      <Title>C++ in 1 Week</Title>
      <ISBN>1-35469-1</ISBN>
      <Publisher>CPress</Publisher>
   </Book>
-  <Book>
      <Genre>Computer Science</Genre>
      <Title>C#</Title>
      <ISBN>1-56467-1</ISBN>
      <Publisher>DPress</Publisher>
   </Book>
</Bookseller>
```

The possibilities are limitless using parameter entities!

2.9 Defining Element Recurrences

When we discussed content models earlier in this chapter (in section 2.6), we examined the child content model. This model contains a root element and parentheses that contain a list of child elements allowed in the element-only model. We also examined a choice list in which a selection of elements was offered, delimited by the pipe symbol (|). You can create complicated models using parentheses and the pipe symbol. Nevertheless, we need a method of specifying repeated occurrences of elements within the content model. Occurrence indicators provide this capability (see Table 2.4).

Table 2.4   Occurrence Indicators

Symbol	Usage
,	Strict ordering. This represents one element followed by the next element.
|	Selection. This is analogous to the OR symbol (either this element or that element).
+	Repetition. This element requires that an element occur once. It is allowed to repeat.
*	Minimum. This element requires that an element occur once, repeat, or not at all.
?	Optional. This element is not mandatory and is optional.
( )	Grouping. The parentheses include one or more elements.

These indicators follow an element's sequence or choice. The comma delimiter separates the sequence of elements, whereas the pipe symbol delimits the list of choices. An element that will repeat an unspecified number of times within the document instance requires an asterisk (*) indicator. An element that must appear at least once or not at all uses the plus (+) sign. A question mark means it is optional whether an element will appear. Finally, the parentheses enclose the sequential list of elements. An example of these is shown in Figure 2.17.

```
<!ELEMENT Invoice (InvoiceNo, CustNum, ClientName, Address+,
ContactName?)>
<!ELEMENT Products(SKU, ItemsOrdered+, Comments?, shipMethod)>
```

Figure 2.17   Multiple addresses

The root `Invoice` has parentheses that contain a list of child elements. A customer may have more than one address, such as a home address, a business address, and a billing address. Therefore, to accommodate multiple addresses, we use the plus (+) sign placed directly behind the `Address` element. A `ContactName` is considered optional, so we use the ? indicator to allow for this. The element needn't appear in the document instance. We previously observed how an asterisk is required when a mixed content model is specified. It can also be used to require an element to appear a minimum of one time or not at all. An element bearing no occurrence indicator must appear once in the document instance.

NMTOKEN/NMTOKENS

A name token is similar to names in XML. We define a name token as a mixture of name characters consisting of digits, hyphens, full-stop characters, and the string XML. Name tokens are case sensitive. However, they cannot contain whitespace, punctuation, or other characters not listed here. The following are valid name tokens:

- `XML-name.token-valid-name`
- `1-a-valid.name`
- `token.list.of-valid-names`

Name tokens are similar to CDATA attributes. They can be used for naming things. For example, if you were to describe a programming language, you could use name tokens to define the various constructs. Consider the example in Figure 2.18.

```
<!DOCTYPE SQLSERVER2000_DB [

<!ELEMENT Table EMPTY>
<!ATTLIST Table Name      NMTOKEN    #REQUIRED
                Columns   NMTOKENS   #REQUIRED>
. . . . .
]>
<SQLSERVER2000_ DB>
<Table Name='Invoice' Columns ="InvoiceNum CustNum CustID Name
Address">
. . . . .
</SQLSERVER2000_ DB>
```

Figure 2.18 A NMTOKEN example

Notice how the tokens are whitespace delimited.

2.10 Notation

Notations are used throughout XML documents to describe data
content for entities such as binary objects. This includes JPEGs,
GIFs, and images. The notation provides instructions for how to
interpret these non-XML objects. The link to these objects begins as
an entity declaration:

```
<!NOTATION JPEG SYSTEM "gifentity.exe">
```

The following example demonstrates how we can use notations for
a logo:

```
<?xml version="1.0" encoding="UTF-8" standalone="no"?>
<!DOCTYPE DEMO [
   <!ELEMENT DEMO ANY>
   <!ENTITY dpsLogo SYSTEM "dpsLogo.gif" NDATA GIF>
   <!NOTATION GIF SYSTEM "image/gif">
   <!ELEMENT IMAGE EMPTY>
   <!ATTLIST IMAGE SOURCE ENTITY #REQUIRED>
   ]>
<DEMO>
   <IMAGE SOURCE="dpsLogo" />
</DEMO>
```

2.11 Names

XML names allow you to include letters or underscores in a name.
Characters that are allowed to begin a name are commonly referred
to as *start characters*. Characters not allowed to start names are
called *name characters*. Symbols and whitespace cannot be used in a
name. Acceptable characters include digits, hyphens, and full-stop
characters.

2.12 Conditional Sections

In Chapter 1, we discussed the use of CDATA. Just to refresh your
memory, the CDATA syntax begins with the following:

```
<!ELEMENT><![CDATA[ markup text goes here]]></ELEMENT>
```

We can use CDATA for testing purposes, as follows:

```
<![INCLUDE[
<!ELEMENT USCatalogSection( USPrice, SKU, Discount, Comments?
)>
]]>

<!IGNORE[
<!ELEMENT EnglishCatalogSection(  UKPrice, SKU, Discount,
Comments?)>
]]>
```

This example demonstrates how we could use the conditional attributes to exclude British clients from viewing U.S. prices and vice versa. The conditionals act as a binary switch. The combinations are dependent on context.

2.13 ID, IDREF, IDREFS

These data types allow us to define the attributes ID and IDREF as references. An XML ID is similar to a database ID or primary key because both must be unique. They eliminate data redundancy within a table. The example in Figure 2.19 demonstrates how employees can have their own employee ID (empid):

```
<?xml version='1.0' ?>
<!DOCTYPE Professor [
     <!ELEMENT Professor (employee*)>
     <!ELEMENT employee (#PCDATA)>
     <!ATTLIST   employee empid ID  #REQUIRED>
]>
<Professor>
      <employee empid='103'>James Smith</employee>
      <employee empid='104'>Steven Heim</employee>
      <employee empid='105'> Michael
Pressman</employee>
</Professor>
```

Figure 2.19   DTDEx08.xml

Each professor has his own ID with attribute `empid` and its associated value. The example is well formed. Attributes referencing other
elements use the `IDREF` attribute (see Figure 2.20). An `IDREF`
attribute contains a whitespace, comma-delimited list of values
declared in the document's `ID` attributes. Several `IDREF` type attributes can refer to the same `ID` attribute. This is permissible because
the original `ID` attribute must be unique.

```
<?xml version="1.0" encoding="UTF-8" standalone="no" ?>
<!DOCTYPE Professor [
     <!ELEMENT Professor (employee*)>
     <!ELEMENT employee (#PCDATA)>
     <!ATTLIST employee empid ID  #REQUIRED>
     <!ATTLIST employee Employer IDREF #IMPLIED>
]>

<Professor>
     <employee empid='e123'>Susan Dorchak</employee>
     <employee empid='e456'> Employer='e123'>Steven
     Heim</employee>
     <employee empid='e789'  Employer='456'>Maria
     Wasser</employee>
</Professor>
```

Figure 2.20   DTDex09.xml

DTDEX09.xml includes an additional attribute list that defines an
`Employer` with data type IDREF. This example indicates that Susan
Dorchak is Steven Heim's employer and so on.

Several IDREFS can reference the same ID, as demonstrated in
Figure 2.21.

```
<!DOCTYPE Professor [
     <!ELEMENT Professor (employee*)>
     <!ELEMENT employee (#PCDATA)>
     <!ATTLIST employee empid ID  #REQUIRED>
     <!ATTLIST employee Employer IDREF #IMPLIED>
]>
<Professor>
     <employee empid='d1012'> Dean Wells</employee>
     <employee empid='e123'>Susan Dorchak</employee>
```

```
<employee empid='e456'    Employer='e123'>Steven Heim</employee>
<employee empid='e789'    Employer='456'> Julie Rooney
</employee>
<employee empid='e1010' Employer='123' > Richard
Noble</employee>
</Professor>
```

Figure 2.21   DTDEx10.xml

Similarly, we can construct a family tree in the same manner displayed previously. The example will look like Figure 2.22.

```
<?xml version="1.0" encoding="UTF-8" standalone="yes" ?>
<!DOCTYPE FamilyTree [
      <!ELEMENT FamilyTree (Member*)>
      <!ELEMENT Member (#PCDATA)>
      <!ATTLIST  Member MNumber ID #REQUIRED>
      <!ATTLIST  Member Mother  IDREFS #IMPLIED>
      <!ATTLIST  Member Father  IDREFS #IMPLIED>
      <!ATTLIST  Member Parent  IDREFS #IMPLIED>
]>
<FamilyTree>
      <Member MNumber='p1'>   Christine</Member>
      <Member MNumber='p2'>   Stanley</Member>
      <Member MNumber='c1'   Parent='p1 p2'>Maria</Member>
      <Member MNumber='c2'   Parent='p1 p2'>Richard</Member>
      <Member MNumber='c3'   Parent='p1'>James</Member>
</FamilyTree>
```

Figure 2.22   FamilyTree.dtd

p1 and p2 represent parents; c1, c2, and c3 represent children. Notice how Parent values are grouped together rather than being listing individually. IDREFS are a powerful mechanism for cross-referencing. A better design for a family tree could create family1 and family2 categories and group the references for readability. It wouldn't affect processing. Also, if you define parents as values p1 and p2 and children as c1 and c2, consider what would happen when c1 and c2 marry and have their own children. It is better to be consistent and name all member attribute values as a1, a2, and so on.

An ID attribute not only is case sensitive, it must be a valid name unique within an XML document. Now an established, valid link to an employee from another element is made possible.

Let's create a scenario in which a many-to-many relationship exists because many books share more than one author (as is the case with WROX Publication). Fortunately, XML provides a workaround for this situation by providing an IDREFS #REQUIRED attribute. The solution looks like this: <!ATTLIST book author IDREFS #REQUIRED>. Now declare a whitespace-delimited list of IDREFS within a single author attribute value:

```
<Book author="JD RUMBOUGH   RDWATERMAN   MARTHAWATERMAN">
```

The XML parser will provide this list to the XML application and identify each individual IDREF value from the list. These attributes allow us to handle one-to-many and many-to-many relationships between elements.

2.14 Practical Business Applications

When you assemble individual DTDs into a cohesive unit, it represents an organized data structure called the *document entity*. It conceptually stores both root element and all other components. If we think of the document entity as a container for storing individual chunks of data, we can understand what an entity is.

- Entities are storage units containing elements.
- The element's content is the data itself.
- The document entity stores all entities.

If we use the rosebud as a metaphor, we can better understand what the document entity represents. When the bud opens, the petals expand to reveal both their beauty and shape. The same is true with the document entity. We can conceptually expand it to reveal its polymorphic complexities and architectural structure. Although we cannot reference it, we can reference its child entities.

- The DTD mirrors and describes the actual structure of the XML document instance, beginning with the root.
- Rules and constraints express element behavior and usage, both internally and externally.

When the application invokes the parser, the document entity is the entity being parsed. Our study of DTDs has helped us appreciate the wide-ranging capabilities they offer for designing enterprise-size, distributed applications.

DTDs assembled from numerous external resources constitute a powerful business model. We benefit from modular design in numerous ways:

- Parameter entities encapsulate the inner details of a working business model, allowing us to focus on data rather than worry about designing complex functions to get an application to work as a cohesive unit.
- Parameter entities conserve on memory resources.
- Modular design eliminates dependencies, offering us the capability to use both internal and external entities to design our business model.
- Content models offer strong typing by determining both program structure and data types.
- Proper content model selection can control our entire business application.
- We can design a class of objects and then declare a module as an abstract base class and subclass to extend the range of definitions for entities.
- Entities are polymorphic because they can represent a wide range of data types.
- Entities can represent a special Unicode character.
- Entities can pull a large block of information into a document instance at runtime.
- Entities can serve as links to a wide-ranging series of DTDs owned by trading partners.
- Entities can be namespace aware, thereby preserving the uniqueness of objects bearing an ID.

What lies at the core of this powerful technology? The XML document, which can be shared by all. It is humanly readable, is accurate in describing its content, and maps easily to all types of repositories. XML is extensible, and DTDs allow us to both control and utilize this extensibility in application design.

> **Note:** Microsoft's Biztalk.Org, XML.org (sponsored by OASIS), and DTD.org (created and operated by Lumeria Inc.) are public repositories designed expressly for sharing DTDs among businesses.

Summary

- A document type declaration is positioned immediately after the XML prologue (Section 2.1).
- The document entity contains the root and all other components (Section 2.1).
- A DTD can be made up of two components: an external DTD subset and an internal DTD subset (Section 2.2).
- The SYSTEM keyword uses a relative URL for locating an external subset (Section 2.4).
- A relative URL does not provide a qualified path and machine name to the specified resource (Section 2.4).
- The PUBLIC identifier is used to identify DTDs created by a standards-setting official body such as the IEEE or W3C Consortium (Section 2.5).
- XML documents are constructed with storage units called entities, containing either parsed data or unparsed data (Section 2.1).
- Parsed data is made up of characters representing either character data or markup (Section 2.1).

- Four content models exist (Section 2.6), as follows:
  - Any content model
  - Mixed content model (Section 2.6.1)
  - Empty content model (Section 2.6.2)
  - Child content model (element) (Section 2.6.3)
- When describing a content model, the content attribute determines whether an element can contain only elements (`content="eltOnly"`), only text (`content="textOnly"`), a mixture of text and elements (`content="mixed"`), or nothing at all (`content="empty"`).
- Attributes offer a way to provide additional meaning about their related elements (Section 2.7).
- XML documents draw on many different sources for their data (Section 2.8).
- External resources are called general entities (Section 2.8).
- Parameter entity references contained within an internal subset must expand to zero or more declarations (Section 2.9).
- Three categories of entities exist (Section 2.9):
  - Internal entities
  - External entities
  - Parameter entities
- Parameter entity references begin with the percentage (%) character rather than the ampersand (&) and are expanded within a DTD (Section 2.8).
- Entities are classified as either internal or external (Section 2.8).
- NMTOKEN attributes specify valid names (Section 2.10).
- A vocabulary exists for grouping and recurrence of elements. These symbols permit XML authors to define cardinality in a document (Section 2.9).
- The ID, IDREF, and IDREFS data types allow us to define attributes ID and IDREF as references (Section 2.14).

Self-Review Exercises

1. Explain the difference between a well-formed document and a valid document.

2. Two keywords can be used in a DTD declaration: SYSTEM and PUBLIC. Describe the circumstance in which each attribute is used and provide an example of each.

3. What is an external entity subset?

4. What is an internal entity subset?

5. Explain the meaning of parsed character data.

6. Describe the difference between #PCDATA and CDATA. Provide an example of each and demonstrate how each should be used.

7. How do you reference a parameter entity? Provide an example.

8. What are the four content models? Provide examples of each type and how they can be used.

9. Three categories of entities exist. What are they?

10. A vocabulary exists for specifying how many times an element can appear in an instance document. Provide an example of each symbol and its use in a DTD.

11. An <Author> element will appear five times in a source document. How can this recurrence be specified?

12. Describe the difference between an ID and IDREF. Provide an example to show how they are used in a source document.

13. Explain why it is better to separate the source document from its DTD.

16. What are NMTOKENs? In what context are they used?

17. Describe how an ATTLIST is declared. What is its purpose? Provide an example.

18. Explain the difference between an XML name and a name token. In what context is a NMTOKEN used?

19. What is the document entity?

20. What is a general entity?

Projects

1. Write a DTD for the following memo as an external entity subset:

```
<?xml version="1.0" encoding="UTF-8"?>
<Memo>
<To>Dr. Schultheiss</To>
<CC>Dr. Stone</CC>
<Body>
Discuss the strategy for the software release.
Contact Bob W. and schedule a meeting for Sept. 10
at 10:00 am to discuss his company's involvement in
this release.
</Body>

<Addendum>Copy this memo to all staff.</Addendum>
</Memo>
```

2. Write the preceding memo as an internal entity subset.

3. Write a table of contents DTD for this chapter.

4. Write a DTD for the following example:

```
<?xml version="1.0" encoding="UTF-8"?>
<Schedule>
<Sunday>Day Off</Sunday>
<Monday>
      <am>9:00 - Faculty Meeting
          10:00 - CSC 6 Class
          11:30 - CSC121 C++
      </am>
      <pm>12:30 - Lunch with Steve
          2:00 - Dental Appointment
      </pm>
</Monday>
<Tuesday> Free for writing</Tuesday>
<Wednesday>
      <am>9:30 Appt. with Bill G.</am>
      <pm>1:30 CSC 121 Lab</pm>
</Wednesday>
```

```
    <Thursday>8:30 am Microsoft Conference</Thursday>
    <Friday></Friday>
    <Saturday>1:00 Yankees game</Saturday>
</Schedule>
```

5. Mark up the following dialogue taken from Shakespeare's
   Othello in XML format:

Duke of Venice	Nay, in all confidence, he's not for Rhodes.
1st Officer	Here is more news.
	[Enter a messenger]
Messenger	The Ottomites, reverend and gracious,
	Steering with due course toward the isle of Rhodes,
	Have there injointed with an after fleet.
1st Senator	Ay, so I thought. How many, as you guess?
Messenger	Of thirty sail, and now they do re-stem
	Their backward course, bearing with frank appearance
	Their purposes towards Cyprus. Signoir Montano,
	Your trusty and most valiant servitor,
	With his free duty recommends you thus,
	And prays you to believe him.
Duke of Venice	'Tis certain then for Cyprus

6. Write a DTD for the preceding dialog as an external entity
   subset. Write the Shakespease dialog source document and the
   DTD it adheres to as an internal entity subset.

CHAPTER

3 | Parsing Your XML Documents

3.1 Parsing: A Description

A *parser* tears apart an XML document and turns text into a set of objects. In essence, if it encounters a question, it locates a corresponding answer. It notifies the participating application of each tag encountered. Various kinds of parsers exist. One type of parser checks a source document for well-formedness (properly opening and closing tags), correct element nesting, and so forth. Another kind ensures proper document structure and enforcement of business rules. An *event-based parser* views a document as a series of events, whereas a *tree-based parser* sees an entire document as a hierarchical, tree-like structure.

This chapter examines this topic in depth. You will learn how and when to use a parser and even how to write your own. Let's begin this important journey now.

Documents come in many different formats. The following list of document types demonstrates this wide range:

- An Excel spreadsheet
- A relational database table
- A memo
- An invoice

- A quarterly report
- An HTML document

Each document type may be valid in its own environment but not when imported into the XML environment. They require some kind of parsing and transformation before we can use them. For a business application to utilize these documents, they need conversion to XML.

One of XML's primary tasks is representing these documents in a well-formed digital format, relying heavily on a software package called a parser, to make sure the document being processed conforms to rules defined by a specified language. XML uses markup to structure a document so that a computer can assist in storing and retrieving data, processing, searching, transforming, and displaying data for different purposes. The parser breaks up a document into small components, examining each unit and passing the data to other software applications for further processing or display. XML processors will load a document and provide access to its contents in the form of objects.

This chapter provides you with a comparison of parsers, both non-validating and validating, and explains how they work. Additionally, it discusses why and when to select one parser over another. Once you have completed this chapter, you will be able to select the appropriate parser for your document processing or, if necessary, write your own parser.

Figure 3.1 is the source document we will use as the base document for our discussion on parsers.

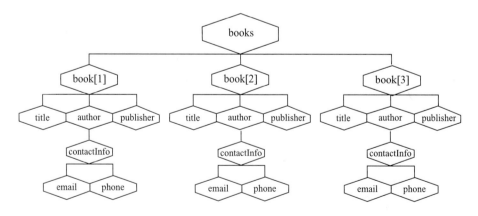

Figure 3.1   Books.xml

3.2   What Does a Parser Do?

Parsing a language means taking a source document, breaking it into small components, and checking it for conformance to the specified language's rules. The following are the four methods of categorizing a parser:

- Validating parser
- Nonvalidating parser
- Stream-based parser
- Tree-based parser

We begin by discussing the role of the validating parser.

Defining the Role of Validating Parsers

A DTD or schema invokes a validating parser to process each document component (elements and their content), comparing the definitions contained within the DTD or schema with source document elements to guarantee conformance to rules defined by the governing document. For example, the document instance in Figure 3.2 adheres to a governing document called the DTD.

This example contains three *book* elements. We refer to them as sibling elements. Refer ahead to Chapter 6, Section 6.2 for a discussion on siblings and the *context node*.

```
<?xml version='1.0' encoding='UTF-8' standalone='no'?>
<!DOCTYPE books SYSTEM "books.dtd">
<books>
    <book>
            <title>XML Language Mechanics</title>
            <author name="Dwight Peltzer">
            <contactInfo person="MWP">
            <email>dpeltzer@hotmail.com></email>
            <phone>516-922-3460</phone>
            </contactInfo>
            </author>
    <publisher>Addison Wesley</publisher>
    </book>
    <book>
      <title>The Human Interface</title>
      <author name="Steven Heim">
        <contactInfo person="MH">
```

```
            <email>sheim@hotmail.com</email>
            <phone>516-843-4567</phone>
        </contactInfo>
      </author>
      <publisher>Addison Wesley</publisher>
    </book>
    <book>
      <title>CyberCrime</title>
      <author name="Chris Malinowski">
        <contactInfo person="LIU">
            <email>cmalinow@</email>
            <phone>718-345-8765</phone>
        </contactInfo>
      </author>
      <publisher>Prentice Hall</publisher>
    </book>
</books>
```

Figure 3.2   A DOCTYPE Declaration for books.xml

Both the `standalone='no'` attribute and the `DOCTYPE` declaration in the header of the document instance indicate that a validating processor is required to parse this document. The governing document is books.dtd (see Figure 3.3).

```
<?xml version="1.0" encoding="UTF-8"?>
<!ELEMENT author (contactInfo)>
<!ATTLIST author
  name CDATA #REQUIRED
>
<!ELEMENT book (title, author, publisher)>
<!ELEMENT books (book+)>
<!ELEMENT contactInfo (email, phone)>
<!ATTLIST contactInfo
  person (LIU | MH | MWP) #REQUIRED
>
<!ELEMENT email (#PCDATA)>
<!ELEMENT phone (#PCDATA)>
<!ELEMENT publisher (#PCDATA)>
<!ELEMENT title (#PCDATA)>
```

Figure 3.3   books.dtd

The application will do one of two things with the document. It will either load the entire document in memory, view it as a hierarchical tree, and parse it. This is called the Document Object Model (DOM). Another parser will parse each part as it encounters it in document order, reporting each component to the participating application. This is called the Simple API for XML or SAX.

A parser plays many different roles:

- It validates a document for being well formed.
- It checks data types against the governing document (schemas only).
- It ensures that source document elements appear in the same order as specified in a DTD or schema.
- It enforces business rules and constraints.

It can also supply default values for attributes of related elements defined in a DTD. If an attribute is missing, the parser will supply the value. This is especially useful when you receive external documents that you haven't designed. The pattern looks like this:

```
<!ATTLIST elementName attrName attrdatatype "DefaultValue">
```

Here is an example using attributes:

```
<?xml version="1.0" standalone="yes"?>
<!DOCTYPE document [
  <!ELEMENT document (description,code)>
  <!ELEMENT description (#PCDATA)>
  <!ATTLIST description xml:lang NMTOKEN #FIXED "en">
  <!ELEMENT code (#PCDATA)>
  <!ATTLIST code xml:space (default|preserve) "preserve">
]>
<document>
  <description xml:lang="en">
    The following section of code displays the menu of user
    choices and gets the user's request.
  </description>
  <code>
  do
```

```
    {
    do
      { disp_menu();
          scanf(" %d", &amp;ans);
      } while ((ans&lt;1) || (ans&gt;3));
  </code>
</document>
```

Nonvalidating Parsers

A nonvalidating parser only requires the document being parsed to be well formed. In Chapter 1, "Introduction to XML," we defined a well-formed document. A review of those rules will serve our purposes well now.

XML conforms to a standard set of rules called the XML Recommendation, version 1.0. This contains all rules and defines the grammar for creating a well-formed XML document.

The following criteria determine conformance to the XML recommendation:

- Each XML document must contain exactly one unique element called the root, which serves as the top-level document element.
- A source document containing data is defined as an XML document if it is well formed and adheres to the following criteria:
  - It must conform to the XML specification.
  - It must contain one or more elements, including the root element.
  - Elements must be properly nested within each other.
  - Each element must contain both an opening and closing tag.

Stream-Based Parsers

Two distinct methods exist for making components known to an application:

- Stream-based parsing
- Tree-based parsing

Stream-based parsing means that the parser moves element by element, processing the document, and notifies its participating application when it encounters a new element. Two well-known terms describe the kind of parsing used to process a source document: Simple API for XML (SAX) and the Document Object Model (DOM). The latter is tree based. See section 3.6 for tree-based parsing. The DOM views an XML document as a hierarchical tree.

SAX is a processing standard developed by members of the *xml-dev* mailing list. They developed a method for describing how a parser should process a source document. A SAX parser reads the source document and fires events based on the following criteria:

- Starting element
- Closing element
- #PCDATA and CDATA
- Comments and processing instructions
- Entity declarations

3.3   Creating a SAX Parser

SAX does not come bundled with a default object model that emulates your XML document instance. Therefore, you need to create three essential components before using SAX.

1. Create your object model consisting of a single class named books. This class is based on <books> (see Figure 3.1).

2. Because the SAX parser is event based, you need to create an event handler. It initializes instances of your object model based on the source document. The handler acts as a listener for events we previously listed, such as the starting tags character. The SAX parser fires the events and sends the relevant information to the document handler.

3. Create a document handler to accept the information provided by the event handler and to utilize the information.

The example in Table 3.1 demonstrates how SAX processes a series of events.

Table 3.1   A SAX Event

`<?xml version='1.0'?>`	`startDocument()`
`<books>`	`startElement("books", attribs)`
`<book>`	`startElement("book",attribs)`
`<authorName>`	`startElement("author", attribs)`
`Dwight Peltzer`	`characters(char[],start, length)`
	`Evaluates to Dwight Peltzer.`
`</authorName>`	`endElement("author",attribs)`
`</book>`	`endElement("book", attribs)`
`</books>`	`endElement("books",attribs)`
	`endDocument()`

By examining Table 3.1, you can observe how the SAX parser encounters an event and calls a particular callback method. SAX parsing involves the registration of a content handler, with an object implementing the XMLReader interface. This interface contains a callback routine for each event type encountered by the parser. They include `startDocument()`, `startElement()`, `characters()`, `endElement()`, and `endDocument()`. Parsing is always initiated by a call to the `parser()` method of the XMLReader. The call to the `parser()` and calls to individual callback methods are synchronous. The `parser()` will only return when the last callback method returns; each callback must complete its task before the following callback method returns.

3.4   Pros and Cons of Using SAX

Selecting a parser depends on several factors. SAX is particularly useful for parsing documents in a memory-constrained environment. If your document is large, SAX is your first choice because it can parse any size document. If you need speed, SAX is fast. Another reason for selecting SAX is its flexibility. You can design your parser so that it selects only those nodes you want to process. A stream-based parser allows you to move forward to a specific element, skipping over those elements you don't need.

SAX provides you with flexible control over error handling and faults. You can generate application-specific error reports. SAX has become language independent. Additionally, it provides you with several APIs to populate your custom-designed data structures and process them.

The negative side of parsing documents with SAX is that it doesn't allow you to process elements based on their position in relation to other elements. There is a workaround, however: If you save your events, you can have random access. The context node (look ahead to Chapter 6, "Applying XPATH," where we use XPath expressions to select nodes based on their relative position to other elements) is not a factor in a SAX-oriented environment.

3.5 Creating a SAX2 Application with Visual Basic

SAX2 provides a JumpStart application for creating a SAX2 application. SAX2 is a push-model parser; therefore, when it parses a document, the SAXXMLReader (reader) reads a document and passes events to the event handlers. The SAXXMLReader generates several categories of events:

- Events occurring in the content of an XML document
- Events in a DTD
- Events as errors

To handle these events, you need to implement a handler class including callback methods for processing any type event. Notice that you only need to implement handlers for events you want to process. Table 3.2 shows the three essential components you need to implement SAX2 applications in Visual Basic.

we sax to read part of Dom tree

Table 3.2   SAX2 Components

Component	Description
ContentHandler	This handler implements the IVBSAXContentHandler interface. It is a class providing methods for processing the main content of an XML source document. The SAX2 parser passes all events to the ContentHandler. For each element in the document instance, the reader passes the startElement, Characters, and endElement events. Add code to the ContentHandler to process information passed by the reader.
ErrorHandler	ErrorHandler implements the IVBSAXErrorHandler interface. It is a class providing callback methods for handling events passed by the reader.
main form	The main form provides the user interface for the application. The main form contains code for creating instances of the SAXXMLReader, ContentHandler, and ErrorHandler.

Figure 3.4 shows the complete code provided by the SAX2 JumpStart Tutorial. Navigate to the following address to download this package: http://www.saxproject.org/.

The user interface has two text boxes and two command buttons. The first text box receives the URL and name of the XML document you want to process. Command_button1 contains code for declaring an XMLReader, a ContentHandler, and an error handler. Then create an instance of the ContentHandler to do most of the work.

```
Option Explicit
Private Sub Command1_Click()
    Dim reader As New SAXXMLReader
    Dim contentHandler As New ContentHandlerImpl
    Dim errorHandler As New ErrorHandlerImpl
        Text2.text = ""
    Set reader.contentHandler = contentHandler
    Set reader.errorHandler = errorHandler
    On Error GoTo 10
```

```
    reader.parseURL (Text1.text)
Exit Sub
10  Text2.text = Text2.text & "*** Error *** " & Err.Number &
" : " & Err.Description
End Sub


Private Sub Command2.Click()
    End
End Sub
```

Figure 3.4   Jumpstart Form.vb

The example in Figure 3.5 displays the results.

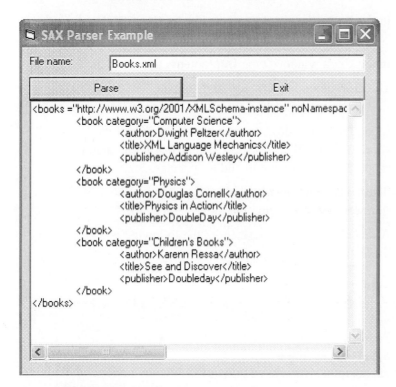

Figure 3.5   The form user interface

The next task is to provide code for the event handlers you want to implement. Notice that code is provided for only those event handlers. Do the following steps before you compile this code:

1. In Visual Studio VB6.0, create a new project and select standard.exe.

2. Create a reference to MSXML 3.0 by selecting the Project menu and clicking References.

3. Select Microsoft XML 3.0 from the drop-down menu.

4. Create a new class by selecting Add Class Module.

5. From the View menu, select the Properties menu.

6. In the Properties window, enter **ContentHandlerImpl** for the Name property.

7. In the Class window, type **Implements** and press the space bar.

8. The drop-down list will appear. Click on IVBSAXContentHandler to add code to the Class window.

9. In the Procedure drop-down list on right side of the Class window, select the IVBSAXContentHandler method and/or property that you want to add to this class.

10. Select `startElement` to add this method to the `ContentHandlerImpl` class.

11. After selecting `startElement`, the following code appears in the Class window:

```
Private Sub
IVBSAXContentHandler_startElement(strNamespaceURI
As_
String, strLocalName As String, strqName as String,
ByVal oAttributes_
as MSXML2.IVBSAXAttributes)

End Sub
```

The next step is to add the necessary code listed below to enable this method.

```
Option Explicit
Implements IVBSAXContentHandler
Private Sub
IVBSAXContententHandler_startElement(StringNamespace uri,
String name, String qname, Attributes atts)
Dim i As Integer
Form1.Text2.text = Form1.Text2.text & "<" & strLocalName
For i = 0 To (attributes.length - 1)
Form1.Text2.text = Form1.Text2.text & " " &
attributes.getLocalName(i) & "=""" & attributes.getValue(i) &
""""
Next
Form1.Text2.text = Form1.Text2.text & ">"
If strLocalName = "qu" Then
Err.Raise vbObjectError + 1, "ContentHandler.startElement",
"Found element<qu>"
End If
End Sub
Private Sub IVBSAXContentHandler_endElement(strNamespaceURI As
String, strLocalName As String, strQName As String)
 Form1.Text2.text = Form1.Text2.text & "</" & strLocalName &
">"
End Sub

Private Sub IVBSAXContentHandler_characters(text As String)
text = Replace(text, vbLf, vbCrLf)
Form1.Text2.text = Form1.Text2.text & text
End Sub
Private Property Set IVBSAXContentHandler_documentLocator(ByVal
RHS As MSXML2.IVBSAXLocator)
End Property
Private Sub IVBSAXContentHandler_endDocument()
End Sub
```

```
Private Sub IVBSAXContentHandler_endPrefixMapping(strPrefix As
String)
End Sub
Private Sub IVBSAXContentHandler_ignorableWhitespace(strChars
As String)
End Sub
Private Sub IVBSAXContentHandler_processingInstruction (target
As String, data As String)
Form1.Text2.text = Form1.Text2.text & "<?" & target & " " &
data & ">"
End Sub
Private Sub IVBSAXContentHandler_skippedEntity(strName As
String)
End Sub
Private Sub IVBSAXContentHandler_startDocument()
End Sub

Private Sub IVBSAXContentHandler_startPrefixMapping (strPrefix
As String, strURI As String)
End Sub
```

Here is the XML source code to be processed:

```
books.xml
<books>
  <book>
      <title>XML Language Mechanics</title>
      <author name="Dwight Peltzer">
      <contactInfo person="MWP">
      <email>dpeltzer@hotmail.com></email>
      <phone>516-111-1234</phone>
      </contactInfo>
      </author>
    <publisher>Addison Wesley
  </book>
  <book>
      <title>The Human Interface</title>
```

```
        <author name="Steven Heim">
        <contactInfo person="MH">
        <email>sheim@hotmail.com></email>
        <phone>718-111-1346</phone>
      </contactInfo>
    </author>
    <publisher>Addison Wesley</publisher>
  </book>
  <book>
        <title>CyberCrime</title>
        <author name="Chris Malinowski">
        <contactInfo person="LIU">
        <email>cmalinow@hotmail.com></email>
        <phone>718-111-1346</phone>
      </contactInfo>
    </author>
    <publisher>Addison Wesley</publisher>
  </book>
</books>
```

Interface ContentHandler

This interface receives notification of the logical content for an XML document. Note that this module containing both source code and documentation is in the public domain. You can get further information at http://www.saxproject.org about all SAX2 interfaces.

ContentHandler is the main interface for SAX2 events. If your application needs information concerning parsing events, it implements this interface and registers an instance with the SAX parser, utilizing the `setContentHandler` callback method. For example, the parser uses the instance to report basic events such as the start and ending elements that include character data. The order of events is important because it emulates the order of information in the document instance. All components of an element's content, including character data, processing instructions, and subelements, will appear in order between the `startElement` and `endElement` event. Table 3.3 contains a list of methods for review.

Table 3.3   SAX2 Methods

void	`characters(char[] ch, int start, int length)` Receives notification of character data.
void	`endDocument()` Receives notification of the document's end.
void	`endElement(java.lang.String uri, java.lang.String localName, java.lang.string qName)` Receives notification of the element's end.
void	`endPrefixMapping(java.lang.String prefix)` Defines end of scope of prefix-URI mapping.
void	`ignorableWhitespace(char[] ch, int start, int length)` Receives notification of ignorable whitespace in element content.
void	`processingInstruction(java.lang.String target, java.lang.String data)` Receives notification for a processing instruction.
void	`setDocumentLocator(Locator locator)` Receives an object for locating the origin of SAX document events.
void	`skippedEntity(java.lang.String name)` Receives notification of a skipped entity.
void	`startDocument()` Receives notification of the document's beginning.
void	`startElement(java.lang.String uri, java.lang.String localName, java.lang.String qName, Attributes atts)` Receives notification of the element's beginning.
void	`startPrefixMapping(java.lang.String prefix, java.lang.String uri)` Begins scope of a prefix-URI namespace mapping.

The example in Figure 3.6 demonstrates a complete SAX2 application provided by the SAX project.

```java
import java.io.FileReader;
import org.xml.sax.XMLReader;
import org.xml.sax.Attributes;
import org.xml.sax.InputSource;
import org.xml.sax.helpers.XMLReaderFactory;
import org.xml.sax.helpers.DefaultHandler;

public class MySAXApp extends DefaultHandler
{

    public static void main (String args[])
      throws Exception
    {
      XMLReader xr = XMLReaderFactory.createXMLReader();
      MySAXApp handler = new MySAXApp();
      xr.setContentHandler(handler);
      xr.setErrorHandler(handler);

      // Parse each file provided on the
      // command line.
      for (int i = 0; i < args.length; i++) {
          FileReader r = new FileReader(args[i]);
          xr.parse(new InputSource(r));
      }
    }

    public MySAXApp ()
    {
      super();
    }


////////////////////////////////////////////////////////////
/////
    // Event handlers.

////////////////////////////////////////////////////////////
/////

    public void startDocument ()
    {
```

```
      System.out.println("Start document");
    }

  public void endDocument ()
  {
    System.out.println("End document");
  }


  public void startElement (String uri, String name,
                        String qName, Attributes atts)
  {
    if ("".equals (uri))
        System.out.println("Start element: " + qName);
    else
        System.out.println("Start element: {" + uri + "}" +
name);
    }


  public void endElement (String uri, String name, String
qName)
    {
    if ("".equals (uri))
        System.out.println("End element: " + qName);
    else
        System.out.println("End element:   {" + uri + "}" +
name);
    }
  public void characters (char ch[], int start, int length)
    {
    System.out.print("Characters:    \"");
    for (int i = start; i < start + length; i++) {
        switch (ch[i]) {
        case '\\':
          System.out.print("\\\\");
          break;
        case '"':
          System.out.print("\\\"");
          break;
        case '\n':
```

```
        System.out.print("\\n");
        break;
    case '\r':
      System.out.print("\\r");
        break;
     case '\t':
        System.out.print("\\t");
        break;
    default:
        System.out.print(ch[i]);
        break;
    }
  }
  System.out.print("\"\n");
 }

}
```

Figure 3.6   A complete SAX2 application demo

Compile this document and invoke the parser as follows:

```
$ java -Dorg.xml.sax.driver=gnu.xml.aelfred2.XMLReader
MySAXApp books.xml
```

The results should be the same as presented in Figure 3.5. Since we have given you the basics for stream-based parsing, our next task is examining the DOM tree method of parsing documents.

3.6. Parsing with the Document Object Model (DOM)

The DOM views the XML source document (see Figure 3.2) as a hierarchical tree. The DOM is particularly useful when you want direct access to the source tree. It offers the following benefits:

- It provides random access to the document.
- A DTD or schema is readily available.
- The DOM is both readable and writable.

update or insert, delete

You can search elements and create complex data retrievals based on an element's attributes. Additionally, the DOM integrates with Extensible Stylesheet Language Transformation (XSLT) and XPath, giving you extreme flexibility by using the XPath axes. They provide you with forward or reverse mobility to move up the tree as well as down. The DOM views elements as nodes, beginning with the root node. (Again, see Chapter 6 for a discussion on XPath).

One of the few negative consequences of utilizing the tree-based DOM method is its memory-intensive processing. The DOM loads the entire source document into memory. If your document instance is extremely large, processing the document is slow. In fact, if your document is large enough, you can exhaust your memory resources. Then your only alternative is selecting a stream-based parser.

To provide you with a glimpse of how the DOM parser works, consider the brief example in Figure 3.7. We use the Invoice.xml source document for demonstration purposes.

```
<?xml version="1.0" encoding="UTF-8"?>
<Invoice>
  <InvoiceID>DS561</InvoiceID>
</Invoice>
```

Figure 3.7   Parsing with the DOM

To begin, instantiate the DOM document object (see Figure 3.8).

```
<html>
  <head>
    <title>DOM Invoice</title>
  </head>
  <body>
  <script type="text/vbscript">
   set xmlDoc = CreateObject("Msxml2.DOMDocument.4.0")
   xmlDoc.async="false"
   xmlDoc.load("C:\XML\Invoice.xml")
   document.write("<h1>This is the root element</h1>")
   alert(xmlDoc.documentElement.nodeName)
   alert(xmlDoc.documentElement.childNodes(0).nodeName)
   alert(xmlDoc.documentElement.childNodes.item(0).text)
   </script>
  </body>
</html>
```

Figure 3.8   Parsing Invoice.xml

The script begins by creating a DOM object (`set xmlDoc=`
`CreateObject("Msxml2.DOMDocument.4.0")`. Then it loads the
specified XML document into memory using the `xmlDoc.load`
method. `document.write` is a property of the document object, and
it allows us to write text just as is done here:
`document.write("<b>This is the root element:`
`</b>")`. Then we retrieve the object requesting the root element's
name. `xmlDoc` functions as a handle to the DOM object. See
Figure 3.9.

Figure 3.9   Document element

Next we get the child node's name.

Figure 3.10   Using the `xmlDoc.LoadXML()` Method

Finally, the content is retrieved.

Figure 3.11   View Properties

The DOM creates an internal document representation and stores it
temporarily in memory for processing by the parser. After the

document is parsed, flushing the document from memory restores memory resources with the pointer no longer valid.

You could also load the next document into memory by using the method in Figure 3.12.

```
<books>
  <book>
    <title>XML Language Mechanics</title>
    <author name="Dwight Peltzer">
      <contactInfo person="MWP">
         <email>dpeltzer@hotmail.com></email>
         <phone>516-922-3468</phone>
      </contactInfo>
    </author>
    <publisher>Addison Wesley</publisher>
  </book>
</books>
```

Figure 3.12   Using the `xmlDoc.Load XML()`

In this scenario, it is better to access the document via URL rather than using this method.

```
xmldoc.loadXML("<books><book><title>XML Language
Mechanics</title><author name="Dwight Peltzer"><contactInfo
person="MWP">
<email>dpeltzer@hotmail.com></email><phone>516-922-
3468</phone></contactInfo></author><publisher>AddisonWesley</pu
blisher>
</book></books>")
```

The DOM is Language Independent

The DOM is language independent and functions as an abstract layer between the parser and the application. A parser such as XT by James Clark, Michael Kay's Instant Saxon, or Microsoft's MSXML version 4.0 (which comes bundled with Internet Explorer 6.0) traverses the tree, instantiating objects for each node, extrapolating data from them, and subsequently handing the information to the DOM for data access. An application then takes retrieved information and exposes the information on the web or store the data somewhere in storage.

Defining a DOM Core

The DOM provides a DOM core that is implemented as a set of interfaces for working with XML documents. It also provides optional modules allowing the DOM to work with cascading style sheets, HTML, and so on. For example, in an HTML environment, when we call an interface, we are in essence asking the interface, "Which methods do you support?" Of course, given an environment like HTML or XHTML, each particular markup language supports its own list of interfaces and methods that addresses the particular language in question.

The list of optional modules includes:

> **DOM views.** Quoting the W3C specification, "A view is the root of a presentation, owned and maintained by a document. A view formats the contents of a document into a particular type presentation. It may contain general properties of the view, resource segments, and segments representing the content of a document, prepared for presentation." You can find the specification at http://www.w3.org/TR/DOM-Level-3-Views/.

Figure 3.13 shows some view properties.

```
View v = (View)((DocumentView)document).getDefaultView();
Segment q = v.createSegment();
q.setOrder("Content");
MatchSet m = q.createMatchSet(m.SET_ALL);
int hu = v.getIntegerProperty("HorizontalDPI");
int vu = v.getIntegerProperty("VerticalDPI");
n.addMatch(q.createMatchString(m.IS_EQUAL, "Type",
"VisualCharacterRun");
m.addMatch(q.createMatchInteger(m.INT_FOLLOWS_OR_EQUALS,
"LeftOffset", hu/2));
m.addMatch(q.createMatchInteger(m.INT_FOLLOWS_OR_EQUALS,
"RightOffset", hu/2));
m.addMatch(q.createMatchInteger(m.INT_FOLLOWS_OR_EQUALS,
"TopOffset", vu/2));
m.addMatch(q.createMatchInteger(m.INT_FOLLOWS_OR_EQUALS,
"RightOffset", vu/2));
m.addMatch(q.createMatchBoolean(m.IS_EQUAL, "Selected", true);
```

```
q.setCriteria(m);
ContentItem start = q.createContentItem("StartContent");
ContentItem end = q.createContentItem("EndContent");
q.addItem(start);
q.addItem(end);
v.matchFirstSegment(q, 0);
while (q.getExists())
{
  // ... do Something with range from start to end...
  q.getNext();
}
```

Figure 3.13   View properties

View Segment Properties

The following are some types and names of properties of segments of visual media types:

```
Integer TopOffset
Integer BottomOffset
Integer LeftOffset
Integer RightOffset
Integer Width
Integer Height
Boolean Visible
Boolean Selected
Integer ForegroundColor
Integer BackgroundColor
String FontName
String FontHeight
String FontBaseline
String FontSpace Width
String FontMaximum Width
```

These properties provide an overview of what views are intended to do.

- **DOM HTML.** Again quoting the standard, "An HTML document interface, derived from the core `Document` interface, specifies the operations and queries that can be made on an HTML document. An HTML interface, derived from the core

`Element` interface, specifies the operations and queries that can be made on any HTML element. Methods on HTML `Document` include those allowing for the retrieval and modification of attributes that apply to all HTML elements.

"Specializations for all HTML elements that have attributes extend beyond those specified in the HTML `Document` interface. For all such attributes, the derived interface for the element contains explicit methods for setting and getting the values."

The DOM Level 2 includes mechanisms to access and modify style specified through CSS and defines an event model that can be used with HTML documents. The address for this DOM specification is http://www.w3.org/TR/DOM-Level-2-HTML.

The goals of the HTML-specific DOM API are as follows, quoted from the specification:

- To specialize and add functionality relating specifically to HTML documents and elements
- To address issues of backward compatibility with the DOM Level 0
- To provide convenience mechanisms, where appropriate, for common and frequent operations on HTML documents

The key difference between the core DOM and the HTML application of DOM is that the HTML Document Object Model exposes a number of convenient methods and properties consistent with existing models and more appropriate to script writers. In many cases, these enhancements are not applicable to a general DOM because they rely on the presence of a predefined DTD. The transitional or frameset DTD for HTML 4.0 or the XHTML 1.0 DTD is assumed. Interoperability between implementations is only guaranteed for elements and attributes specified in the HTML 4.0 and XHTML 1.0 DTDs.

DOM stylesheets and CSS allow programs and scripts to traverse a tree and identify a range of contents in a source document. The address for this is http://www.w3.org/TR/DOM-Level-2-Traversal-Range.

- DOM Events provides applications and scripts with a generic event system. The address for this is http://www.w3.org/TR/DOM-Level-2-Events.
- Defining a DOMString data type as UTF 16-bit

The DOM guarantees uniformity between parsers by defining a DOMString data type implemented as a UTF 16-bit unit, and assures programming languages such as Visual Basic, JavaScript, and Java will interact seamlessly with the DOM. The DOMString IDL definition follows:

```
valuetype DOMString sequence<unsigned short>
```

C++ programmers beware. Because you can work in either 8-bit or 16-bit units, make sure you specify the 16-bit environment to conform to the DOM standard.

3.7 Understanding DOM Interfaces

The parser interprets a hierarchical tree by viewing each object as a node. As the parser encounters a tree node, it instantiates an object for each node. Each node exposes a set of interfaces, listed here:

- a Document node
- Node
- a NodeList
- NamedNodeMap
- an Element node
- an Attr node
- a Text node
- a Character data node
- a Document fragment

3.8 Understanding Interfaces

Let's examine the AuthorsAttributes.xml source document in Figure 3.14.

```
<?xml version="1.0" encoding="UTF-8"?>
<root>
   <AuthorElement alias="DPS">
     <AuthorFName>Dwight</AuthorFName>
     <AuthorLName>Peltzer</AuthorLName>
     <AuthorAddress>PO Box 212</AuthorAddress>
     <AuthorCity>East Norwich</AuthorCity>
   </AuthorElement>
</root>
```

Figure 3.14   AuthorsAttributes.xml

By examining the first few nodes, we can learn how the DOM implements this structure (see Figure 3.15).

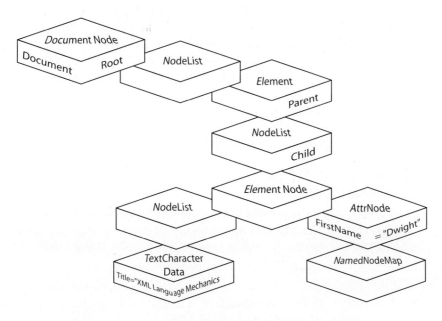

Figure 3.15   AuthorsAttributes.xml DOM representation

The internal representation of this document stored in memory accurately depicts the structure of the XML document as a hierarchical tree in which each node represents an object. The node names—DocumentNode, NodeList, NamedNodeMap, and TextCharacterData—expose interfaces implemented by each individual object, thereby allowing us to work with them.

The top node represents the Document root. This node stores conceptually all elements, attributes, text, characters, comments, and processing instructions within it. The Document node implements methods that create the objects. Therefore, it supports the Document interface.

The in-memory representation contains two other interfaces, NodeList and NamedNodeMap. The first interface manages node lists, whereas NamedNodeMap handles unordered sets of nodes. Remember, attributes are unordered among themselves.

Referring back to the in-memory internal representation of the <Authors> XML document, the NodeList node does not support the node interface itself; rather, it functions as a handler or supervisor of lists. Nodes we insert are automatically reflected in the list.

The diagram in Figure 3.15 demonstrates a parent/child relationship in which <Parent> supports the <Element> interface. This allows us to insert other elements at the same node level. The <child> element implements both Node and Element interfaces. The Name attribute represents a child of the NamedNodeMap and implements the Node and Attribute interfaces. In the diagram, NamedNodeMap handles the attribute/value ="Dwight" and is a child of the NamedNodeMap. NodeList manages element content.

3.9 DOM Core APIs

"The DOM core APIs present two separate sets of interfaces to an XML/HTML document: The first is an *object-oriented* approach with a hierarchy of inheritance, and the second set is a *simplified* view allowing all processing directly through the Node interface." The simplified approach represents a flattened view in which one can work directly with the Node interface. The following list represents the most commonly used set of DOM APIs.

- **The document object.** The document object is the root element in the node tree. All nodes in the node tree are `childNodes` of the document element. It must be present in all XML documents. Listed in Table 3.4 are the properties and methods of the document object.

Table 3.4 Document Properties

Name	Description
`documentElement`	Returns the root element of the document.
`Doctype`	Returns the DTD or schema for the document
`implementation`	Returns the implementation object for this particular document

Document Methods

Name	Description
`createAttribute (attributeName)`	Creates an attribute node with the specific attribute name
`createCDATASection (text)`	Creates a CDATASection containing the specified text
`createComment(text)`	Creates a comment node containing the specified text
`createDocument Fragment()`	Creates an empty documentFragment object
`createElement (tagName)`	Creates an element with the specified tag name
`createEntityReference (referenceName)`	Creates an entityReference with the specified text referenceName
`createProcessing Instruction (target,text)`	Creates a processingInstruction node, containing the specified target and text
`createTextNode(text)`	Creates a text node containing the specified text

- **Document methods.** Notice that `documentElement` returns the root element where document methods allow you to create new child elements and attributes. Let's learn how to utilize these interfaces and manipulate XML source documents. The template in Figure 3.16 demonstrates the basic structure for writing DOM queries.

```
<html>

   <head>
      <title>DOM Example</title>
   </head>
   <body>
   <script language="vbscript">
<!--Declarations go here -->
set xmlDoc = CreateObject("Msxml2.DOMDocument.4.0")
xmlDoc.async= False
xmlDoc.Load("c:\XML\Authors.xml")
   </script>
   </body>
</html>
```

Figure 3.16 A DOM template

Let's test various DOM interfaces. A few items require some explanation. An example written in JavaScript should contain the syntax `objDOM = new ActiveXObject("Msxml2.DOMDocument.4.0")`, whereas VBScript uses this syntax to create the object: `xmlDoc = CreateObject("Msxml2.DOMDocument.4.0")`.

We set the `async` property to false, meaning that our program can perform other tasks while the document is loading. Otherwise, any ancillary task would have to wait until the document is loaded. Let's load a simple DOM document (see Figure 3.17) and see how it works. The document loads the file and displays the elements in the browser (see Figure 3.18).

```
<html>
<body>
<script type="text/vbscript">
Text="<h1>Some DOM examples</h1>"
```

```
document.write(Text)
set xmlDoc=CreateObject("Msxml2.DOMDocument.4.0")
xmlDoc.async="false"
xmlDoc.load("C:\XMLBusinessSolutions\Chapter3\chap3No7.xml")
for each n in xmlDoc.documentElement.childNodes
   document.write(n.nodename)
   document.write(": ")
   document.write("<br>")
next
</script>
</body>
</html>
```

Figure 3.17   A simple DOM document

```
InvoiceNumber:
CustomerName:
CustomerAddress:
CustomerState:
CustomerZip:
ItemPurchased:
Manufacturer:
Price:
```

Figure 3.18   DOM Node Names

It is also possible to cycle through the elements and grab the data within them, as follows:

```
for each x in xmlDoc.documentElement.childNodes
      document.write(x.text)
      document.write("<br/>")
   next
```

We can also retrieve information using the getElementsByTagName, which grabs information by specifying the zeroeth element for each node, as demonstrated in Figure 3.19. We use JavaScript in this document.

```
<html>
<head>
<script type="text/javascript" for="window" event="onload">
var xmlDoc = new ActiveXObject("Msxml2.DOMDocument.4.0")
xmlDoc.async="false"
xmlDoc.load("note.xml")
to.innerText =
xmlDoc.getElementsByTagName("to").item(0).text
from.innerText=
xmlDoc.getElementsByTagName("from").item(0).text
header.innerText=
xmlDoc.getElementsByTagName("heading").item(0).text
body.innerText=
xmlDoc.getElementsByTagName("body").item(0).text
</script>
</head>
<body bgcolor="white">
<h1>DP Software</h1>
<b>To: </b>
<span id="to"></span>
<br>
<b>From: </b>
<span id="from"></span>
<hr>
<b><span id="header"></span></b>
<hr>
<span id="body"></span>
</body>
</html>
```

Figure 3.19   GetElementsByTagName

The results are shown in Figure 3.20.

```
DP Software
To: Dwight
From: Susan
Reminder
Don't overlook the publishing deadline!!
```

Figure 3.20   A memo

Notice how "to", "from", "heading", and "body" prefix item(0).text from innerText refers to the corresponding memo document *to, from, heading,* and *body* in the source document.

3.10 Creating Document Fragments

In many cases, it is convenient to assemble a number of fragments and place them in an XML document. However, these components will not necessarily contain a root element. Fortunately, this is easy to do. Consider the following code. Declare objFragment and then create the object.

```
var objFragment;
objFragment = objDOM.createDocumentFragment();
```

Next declare an objNode variable and use it to create a child element:

```
objNode = objDOM.createElement("Joe");
```

Append the child by doing the following:

```
objFragment.appendChild(objNode);
```

AppendChildNode takes objNode as a parameter. Next create another child element:

```
objNode = objDOM.createElement("Bob");
```

Append child2 and add both elements to the root element:

```
objDOM.documentElement.appendChild(objFragment);
```

Display the results with an alert, as shown in Figure 3.21.

Figure 3.21   A fragment demo

We assume that document fragments are not necessarily fully XML compliant documents; therefore, we can dynamically program the entire document using the API interfaces, just as we demonstrated.

We can also create and retrieve attributes. The following code retrieves DEP, an attribute of the `<AuthorElement>`.

```
<html>
<body>
<script type="text/vbscript">

set xmlDoc=CreateObject("Msxml2.DOMDocument.4.0")
xmlDoc.async="false"
xmlDoc.load("C:\XML\AuthorElement.xml")

set x=xmlDoc.getElementsByTagName("AuthorElement")
document.write(x.item(0).getattribute("name"))
</script>
</body>
</html>
```

Figure 3.22   Retrieving an attribute

Here is the result: DEP.

The script in Figure 3.23 first creates a root element, followed by a text node where both root and text nodes are appended to the document element. DOM interfaces such as the one we use in the next example (Figure 3.23) use `createNodeType` to produce the type of node we want to construct. In this example, we generate both a root element and a text node. `CreateElement` takes `root` as the `Element` parameter; `createTextNode` takes the text we want to insert as parameter (`AuthorElement`). Following this step, we can add them to our document root element, which conceptually holds all elements, attributes, processing instructions, comments, and so on.

```
<script language="JavaScript">
     objDOM = new ActiveXObject("Msxml2.DOMDocument.4.0");
     objDOM.async = false;
     var objNode;
     var objText;
     objNode = objDOM.createElement("root");
     objText = objDOM.createTextNode(" root AuthorElement");
     objDOM.appendChild(objNode);
     objNode.appendChild(objText);
     alert(objDOM.xml);
 </script>
```

Figure 3.23   Create a root element

The result is shown in Figure 3.24.

Figure 3.24   AuthorElement

3.11 Retrieving NextNode Siblings

In many cases, we would like to retrieve information about nodes following the root node. We accomplish this by using the `document.write` interface in VBScript to return node names and their siblings. Before we execute the following, let's take another glance at the source document (see Figure 3.25).

```
<root>
    <AuthorElement>DPS</AuthorElement>
        <AuthorFName>Dwight</AuthorFName>
        <AuthorLName>Peltzer</AuthorLName>
        <AuthorAddress>PO Box 212</AuthorAddress>
        <AuthorCity>East Norwich</AuthorCity>
</root>
```

Figure 3.25   DomAuthor2.xml

The content model is elements only.

Figure 3.26 contains the script.for NextSibling.nodeName.

```
<html>
<body>
<script type="text/vbscript">
set xmlDoc=CreateObject("Msxml2.DOMDocument.4.0")
xmlDoc.async="false"
xmlDoc.load("DomAuthor2.xml")
document.write(xmlDoc.documentElement.childNodes(0).nodeName)
document.write("<br />")
document.write(xmlDoc.documentElement.childNodes(0).nextSibling
.nodeName)
</script>
</body>
</html>
```

Figure 3.26   NextSibling.nodeName

In this example, we began by using VBScript and created the DOM object. We set the `async` property to `false`. Then we loaded the document and retrieved the `documentElement`'s first child node name (`AuthorElement`). The `<br />` element caused a line break. Then we retrieved the `AuthorFName` element. Notice how `documentElement.childNodes` retrieves the `NodeName` by specifying the zeroeth array element. The result is shown in Figure 3.27.

```
AuthorElement
AuthorFName
```

Figure 3.27   Sibling results

3.12 Creating a Source Document from Scratch

Now that we understand some of the DOM basics, let's create an XML document from scratch. Comments describe the action as we proceed. We use the DOM DocumentFragment attribute for this XML instance. Figure 3.28 displays the output that the script (see Figure 3.29) creates.

Figure 3.28   Creating a DOM document

And now here's the script:

```
<HTML>
<HEAD><TITLE>DOM Demo</TITLE>
<SCRIPT language="JavaScript">
  var objDOM;
  objDOM = new ActiveXObject("Msxml2.DOMDocument.4.0");
  objDOM.async = false;
  var objNode;
  var objFragment;
  <!-- create root element-->
  objNode = objDOM.createElement("root");
  objDOM.appendChild(objNode);
  <!-- create the Document Interface Object to which other
objects can be added -->
  objFragment = objDOM.createDocumentFragment();
  <!-- Now create all child elements -->
  objNode = objDOM.createElement("FName");
  <!-- append the child node -->
  objFragment.appendChild(objNode);
  <!-- create the text node for the child elements; Note the
firstChild specifier -->
```

```
objFragment.firstChild.appendChild(objDOM.createTextNode
("Dwight"));
objNode = objDOM.createElement("LName");
objFragment.appendChild(objNode);
objFragment.lastChild.appendChild(objDOM.createTextNode
("Peltzer"));
objNode = objDOM.createElement("Publisher");
objFragment.appendChild(objNode);
objFragment.lastChild.appendChild(objDOM.createTextNode
("AddisonWesley"));

objNode = objDOM.createElement("Address");
objFragment.appendChild(objNode);
objFragment.lastChild.appendChild(objDOM.createTextNode
("PO Box 355"));

objNode = objDOM.createElement("City");
objFragment.appendChild(objNode);
objFragment.lastChild.appendChild(objDOM.createTextNode
("Oyster Bay"));

objNode = objDOM.createElement("State");
objFragment.appendChild(objNode);
objFragment.lastChild.appendChild(objDOM.createTextNode
("NY"));

objNode = objDOM.createElement("ZipCode");
objFragment.appendChild(objNode);
objFragment.lastChild.appendChild(objDOM.createTextNode
("11731"));
<!-- Finally add the elements to our document root element -->
objDOM.documentElement.appendChild(objFragment);
alert(objDOM.xml);
</SCRIPT>
</HEAD>
<BODY>
<P>Building an XML Document.</P>
</BODY>
</HTML>
```

Figure 3.29   `DocumentFragmentFromScratch.htm`

Examining the code step by step (see Figure 3.30) reveals insights as to how to build an XML document dynamically.

```
<script language="JavaScript">
   var objDOM;
   var objNode;
   var objFragment;
   objDOM = new ActiveXObject("Msxml2.DOMDocument.4.0");
   objDOM.async = false;
   objNode = objDOM.createElement("root");
   objDOM.appendChild(objNode);


   alert(objDOM.xml);


   </script>
```

Figure 3.30   Creating the root element

The next step requires that we declare and build the `DocumentFragment` interface so that we can add other elements to our Document root.

```
objFragment = objDOM.createDocumentFragment();
```

Next we can create the `Fname` element and append it as follows:

```
objNode = objDOM.createElement("Fname");
objFragment.appendChild(objNode);
```

Element nodes don't contain text; therefore, let's form a text node so that we can insert some text into it. The DOM provides a good method for accomplishing this task:

```
ObjFragment.firstChild.appendChild(objDOM.createTextNode
("Dwight"));
```

One final step must be taken before we obtain the proper results. Namely, we need to add the following line of code to complete our task:

```
ObjDom.documentElement.appendChild(objFragment);
```

This adds the elements in `DocumentFragment` to the document root. You can view the results in Figure 3.31.

Finally, the XML source in Figure 3.32 was generated dynamically using the DOM interfaces.

Figure 3.31   TextNode()

```
<?xml version="1.0" encoding="UTF-8"?>
<root>
    <FName>Dwight</FName>
    <LName>Peltzer</LName>
    <Publisher>Addison Wesley</Publisher>
    <Address>PO Box 355</Address>
    <City>Oyster Bay</City>
    <State>NY</State>
    <ZipCode>11771</ZipCode>
</root>
```

Figure 3.32   DOM-generated source document

3.13 Working with Attributes

We have already seen how to retrieve attributes using the `getAttribute("parameter")` method. It is also possible to create attributes using `setAttribute("parameter")`. The code in Figure 3.33 retrieves the document root `Invoice` and then displays it in an alert. It then displays the attribute value to be replaced and finally uses the `setAttribute` method to insert a new value, `James`, subsequently displaying it.

```
<SCRIPT language="JavaScript">
  var objDOM;
  var objAttribute;
  objDOM = new ActiveXObject("MSXML2.DOMDocument.4.0");
  objDOM.async = false;
  objDOM.load("ch7_ex1.xml");
  //our code will go here...
document.write("<b>This is the root element: </b>");
  varInvoice = objDOM.documentElement;
  alert(varInvoice.tagName);
  document.write(varInvoice.tagName);
    alert(varInvoice.getAttribute("ID"));
    objAttribute = objDOM.documentElement;
  objAttribute.setAttribute("ID", "James");
  alert(objAttribute.getAttribute("ID"));
</SCRIPT>
```

Figure 3.33   SetAttribute("newAttributeName")

Figure 3.34 displays the old attribute and Figure 3.35 displays the new attribute.

Figure 3.34   Old attribute

Figure 3.35   New attribute

We can also create a purchase order number to append to this small document. Use the methodology in Figure 3.36 to accomplish this.

This is the way the XML document looks before it is modified to reflect the new purchase order number:

```
<?xml version="1.0"?>
<Invoice ID="PD11" Date="12/21/2001">
</Invoice>
```

Figure 3.36   Creating a purchase order date

Here is the way it looks after modification:

```
<?xml version="1.0"?>
<Invoice ID="PD11" Date="12/21/2001">
            <PurchaseOrder>PO5651</PurchaseOrder></Invoice>
```

Figure 3.37   Creating a purchase order date

3.14 Inserting and Updating

We can retrieve existing values, update data, insert before data, and remove values from a source document. The script in Figure 3.38 does precisely these things.

```
  varSalesInfo= objDOM.documentElement;
//show the original XML document
  alert(varSalesInfo.xml);
//Find the Customer elements and select the first one
  varElemCust1 =
varSalesInfo.getElementsByTagName("Customer").item(0);
//create a new element
  varNewElem = objDOM.createElement("MonthlySalesData");
//append the element
  varNewElem = varSalesInfo.insertBefore(varNewElem,
varElemCust1);
//create a new text-type node and append it
  newText = objDOM.createTextNode ("a new element");
  varNewElem.appendChild(newText);
  alert(objDOM.xml);
```

```
<!-- adding an attribute -->
//create a new attribute and give it a value
  varElemCust1.setAttribute("telephoneNo", "3591765524");
  alert(objDOM.xml);
```

Figure 3.38 Inserting and positioning elements

Figure 3.39 shows the results, demonstrating the versatility that the DOM interfaces offer us.

Here is the second updated screen shot:

```
<?xml version="1.0"?>
<SalesData Status="Updated">
          <Invoice InvoiceNumber="102"
TrackingNumber="57823" OrderDate="10/25/2001"
ShipDate="10/27/2001" Shipmethod="FedEx"
CustomerIDREF="Customer202">
          <LineItem Quantity="5" Price="10.95"
          PartIDREF="Part2"/>
          <Invoice>
          <MonthlySalesData>Can you see that we have cre-
ated a new element?</MonthlySalesData><Customer
ID="Customer202" firstName="James" lastName="Watts" Address="PO
Box 355" City=="Hempstead" State="NY" PostalCode="11634"/>
<Part PartID="Part2" PartNumber="13" Name="FeltHammer"
Color="White" Size="2 3/4"/>
</SalesData>
```

Finally, here's the last update:

```
<?xml version="1.0"?>
<SalesData Status="Updated">
          <Invoice InvoiceNumber="102"
TrackingNumber="57823" OrderDate="10/25/2001"
ShipDate="10/27/2001" ShipMethod="FedEx"
CustomerIDREF="Customer202">
          <LineItem Quantity="5" Price="10.95"
          PartIDREF="Part2"/>
          </Invoice>
          <MonthlySalesData>Can you see that we have cre-
ated a new element?</MonthlySalesData>
<CustomerID="Customer202" firstName="James" lastName="Watts"
```

```
Address="PO Box 355" City="Hempstead" State="NY"
PostalCode="11634" telephoneNo="3591765524"/>
<Part PartID="Part2" PartNumber="13" Name="FeltHammer"
Color="White" Size="2 3/4"/>
</SalesData>
```

Figure 3.39   Demonstrating inserts, updates, and positioning

3.15 DOM Remove/Replace Methods

The DOM offers a `removeChild` method, using a reference to the child node we want to remove. Let's view the appropriate code:

```
ObjOldChild = objParent.removeChild(objParent.lastChild);
```

We can also replace a child node by removing a node and then replacing it with another node. This is achieved by writing the following code:

```
ObjOldChild = objParent.replaceChild(objnewChild,
objParent.firstChild);
```

3.16 Cloning Nodes

We can create a copy of a node by cloning a node as a separate new node. Two separate methods of copying exist:

- Shallow cloning
- Deep cloning

These require some explanation: The *shallow cloning* method copies only the node itself, whereas the *deep cloning* method recursively clones the subtree under the node. (All child nodes are copied in deep cloning.) Additionally, a clone node takes a Boolean parameter indicating whether the copy is shallow (false) or deep (true). Here is code for this:

```
objNewNode = objNode.cloneNode(false), meaning the cloning will
be shallow.
var objNode;
objNode= objDOM.documentElement.firstChild;
var objNewNode;
objNewNode = objNode.cloneNode(false);
objNode.appendChild(objNewNode);
alert(objDOM.xml);
```

This example demonstrates how we copy the node and then append it back to the tree. Because this is a shallow copy, no child nodes of the node being cloned are copied.

3.17 NodeList

The `NodeList` interface provides two properties:

- The length property
- The item property

The length property returns the number of items in a `NodeList`, whereas the item property returns a specified item. Items in a `NodeList` function just as a normal array does, where numbering begins at 0. The code for this is as follows:

```
document.write(xmlDoc.documentElement.childNodes(0).nodeName)
```

Let's assume a list has four items. The length property would return 4 because the first item begins at zero, not 1.

3.18 String Handling

Let's assume we have a node object named `objText` containing the string `"Dwight"`. We would write the following code:

```
alert(objText.length)
```

This would present a message box saying 6, whereas if we write the following:

```
alert(objText.data)
```

It would return the string "Dwight".

The DOM also provides a method for handling substrings, as follows:

- The offset specifies where to begin counting characters.
- Examine the code below to see how this is done. The offset begins with the 12th character. "str" is the substring (3 characters) we are looking for.

```
"Here is the string we wish to process"
Alert(objText.substring(12, 3);
```

A message box pops up and displays the following: `str`. One can also modify strings by appending content such as `ObjText.appendData(" ? ")`.

The DOM supports the CDATA section just as it does with comments. When we create a CDATA section, the DOM adds `<![CDATA[    ]]>`" to it.

3.19 Notation and Entity References

The Notation interface represents a notation declared in the DTD. Chapter 2, "Document Type Definition," covered this topic. A notation can represent an unparsed entity such as a GIF or JPEG file. The Node interface supports the `NodeName` property and is set to the name of the notation. `EntityReference` objects can be inserted into the DOM if an entity reference is present in the source document. They are read-only.

We have basically covered the essentials of how the DOM functions. Only when we understand DTDs, schemas, and XPath expressions can we fully appreciate and understand the powerful interfaces that the DOM provides us. It is just one more tool in our arsenal of XML-related tools. The next topic, the Microsoft MSXML 4.0 parser, is fully documented with tutorials via the downloadable documentation and parser online at MSDN Microsoft.com.

3.20 Microsoft's MSXML 4.0 Parser Brief Overview

The recent release of Microsoft's MSXML 4.0 parser provides information concerning new features that this parser supports in Internet Explorer 5.5 and above. Basically, these interfaces introduce features presented in this chapter and others. For developers using C, C++, or Microsoft Visual Basic, these objects are exposed as follows:

- IXMLDOMDocument/DOMDocument
- IXMLDOMNODE
- IXMLDOMNODELIST
- IXMLDOMNamedNodeMap
- IXMLDOMParseError

3.21 What's New in MSXML Version 4.0? Plenty!

The following new features are supported in version MSXML 4.0 and are Microsoft extensions:

- Support for XSD, thereby conforming to the W3C proposed recommendation. Note that it doesn't support regular expressions and identity constraints.
- Support for XML Path Language (XPath) extension functions. XPath 1.0 doesn't recognize expressions that evaluate nodes based on data type. Therefore, this new version offers a number of XPath extension functions to do this:
  - String-compare for lexicographical string comparison
  - Format-date and format-time, which convert standard XSD date/time formats to characters appropriate for output

- `IXMNamespaceManager` and `IXMNamespacePrefixes` inter-faces. These provide an easy way to manage namespace pre-fixes and namespace URIs.

- SAX to DOM support. These allow us to integrate DOM objects into Simple API for SAX. With the SAX IMXWriter interface, we can now create a DOM document object from SAX events by setting the output property as an input parameter of the parse method of the ISAXXMLReader interface.

- DOM to SAX support.

- MSXHTMLWriter CoClass. This is an implementation of the IXMWriter interface, allowing us to generate HTML output from SAX applications.

- A wizard for creating C++ SAX applications. This is available from Microsoft Product Support Services.

- Enhanced XSLT development guide.

- New GUIDs and PROGIDs. MSXML 4.0 provides three DLL files installable in your system folder when downloading the parser: msxml4.dll, msxml4a.dll, and msxml4r.dll.

- Schema Object Model (SOM). This provides a set of interfaces to explore information in a schema document and to create schema nodes through the use of the DOM document.

For more information concerning these interfaces, navigate to www.msdn.microsoft.com and download the SDK for MSXML Parser 4.0. Complete documentation is available through the SDK.

Summary

A comparison of parsers—validating vs. nonvalidating, stream-based vs. tree-based—has provided us with an overview of the role parsers play in processing source documents.

When parsing a document, the application will do one of two things:

- Load the entire document in memory, view it as a tree, and parse it.

- Parse each component in document order, reporting each element to the application.

We also learned the parser's many different roles:

- It validates a document for being well formed.
- It checks data types against a governing document.
- It ensures that source document elements will appear in the same order specified in a DTD or schema.
- It enforces business rules and constraints.
- It can supply default values for attributes of related elements.

Event-based parsing means that the parser reads a document and notifies the participating application when it encounters a new component.

We learned about two separate kinds of parsing: Simple API for XML and the Document Object Model.

The SAX parser reads a source document and fires events based on the following criteria:

- Starting elements
- Closing elements
- PCDATA and CDATA sections of a document
- Comments and processing instructions
- Entity declarations

SAX does not come with a default object model. Therefore, you need to create a class, an event handler, and a document handler before you can use a SAX parser.

Criteria for selecting a SAX parser depends on several different factors:

- Memory constraints
- Size of the document
- Flexibility in processing only those elements you need to process
- Error-handling capabilities
- Speed

SAX is inappropriate if you need to determine the position of a node in relation to other elements. SAX offers only forward-motion parsing and lacks support for random access.

We also learned how the Document Object Model provides a set of interfaces allowing us to dynamically access data, create elements and attributes, update data, clone nodes, and replace, position, and delete nodes. One of the most important concepts provided by the DOM explains how the document root conceptually stores all elements, child elements, text nodes, attributes, comments, and processing instructions within it.

The DOM provides a powerful tool to dynamically process data using XPath expressions. By creating an internal representation of a source document, we can easily ascertain the current context node, thereby enabling quick access to important data.

The DOM is language independent and serves as an abstract layer between parser and application. It provides a DOM core, implemented as a set of interfaces for processing XML source documents.

Optional modules included with the DOM include the following:

- DOM views, which provide a view existing as the root of a presentation owned and maintained by the document. It formats document contents into a particular type presentation.

- An HTML DOM, which specifies how operations and queries can be made on an HTML document.

- A DOM for stylesheets and cascading style sheets, which allows programs and scripts to traverse a tree and identify a range of contents in a source document.

- A DOM defining a DOMStringDataType as UTF 16-bit, thereby guaranteeing uniformity between parsers.

We learned that the internal representation of an XML document stored in memory accurately depicts the structure of the source document as a hierarchical tree in which each node represents an object. The node names `DocumentNode`, `NodeList`, `NamedNodeMap`, and `TextCharacterData` expose interfaces implemented by each individual object.

The DOM core APIs present two separate sets of interfaces to an XML/HTML document:

- An object-oriented approach
- A simplified approach

The first is an OOP approach with a hierarchy of inheritance. The second is a simplified view that allows all processing to be accomplished through the Node interface. It represents a flattened view in which we can work directly with the Node interface.

Other features provided by the DOM allow us to do the following:

- Create document fragments in which we can assemble a number of separate documents and provide a root to make the composite document XML conforming.
- Create and retrieve elements and attributes.
- Use XPath expressions to retrieve data from a specified node.
- Create a source document from scratch using the DOM interfaces.
- Work with CDATA sections.
- Work with all forms of string handling.
- Clone, replace, and update nodes.
- Use notation and entity references.

We also provided a brief overview of Microsoft's recent release of its MSXML 4.0 SDK and parser.

Self-Review Exercises

1. Explain what the parser does.

2. Several kinds of parsers exist. What are they and what role do they play?

3. XML Documents exist in many different formats. Name three formats and provide an example of each.

4. Explain the meaning of attribute Standalone="no".

5. A source document containing marked up data is defined as an XML document if it meets several criterion. What are they?

6. Describe how a Stream-based parser works. Provide an example.

7. What is an event handler?

8. What role does an event handler play?

9. What is a document handler?

10. Discuss the pros and cons for using SAX.

11. What does a SAXXMLREADER do?

12. How does the Document Object Model (DOM) view an XML document?

13. List three benefits the DOM offers developers.

14. What is the DOM Core?

15. What is a DOM view?

16. Provide a list of DOM interfaces.

17. What are the COMCore APIs?

18. What is a document fragment. How do you use it?

19. Demonstrate how to use a document fragment.

20. Create a source XML document from scratch.

21. Demonstrate how you can update data in a document.

22. Demonstrate how to insert a value before another node.

Projects

1. Describe the role of the EventHandler.

2. Explain the role of the SAXXMLReader.

3. What does the document handler do?

4. Use the DOM Document 4.a below to generate the following output:

```
Some DOM Examples
DesignPattern: The intent is to add additional responsibilities
to an object dynamically.
```

Document 4.a

```
<DOMDocument>
<DesignPattern>
<Decorator>The intent is to add additional responsibilities to
an object dynamically</Decorator>
</DesignPattern>
</DOMDocument>
```

5. Write a program to create a root element followed by a single child element and a text node. Insert some text into this node.

6. Write a program demonstrating how we can retrieve information about nodes following the root node. Use the following XML document:

```
<?xml version="1.0" encoding="UTF-8"?>
<Invoice>
        <InvoiceNumber>L1035</InvoiceNumber>
        <CustomerName>Joe Schmidt</CustomerName>
        <CustomerAddress>PO Box 367</CustomerAddress>
        <CustomerState>NY</CustomerState>
        <CustomerZip>11983</CustomerZip>
        <ItemPurchased>XMLSpy v.4.4</ItemPurchased>
        <Manufacturer>Altova</Manufacturer>
        <Price>Inexpensive for the value</Price>
</Invoice>
```

7. Write a program to output just the content. Use the preceding Invoice program to do so.

8. Write a program and substitute a new attribute for the old one. Output first the old attribute and then display the replaced attribute. Use the following example for the source document:

```
<?xml version="1.0" encoding="UTF-8"?>
<Invoice number="DSH134"/>
```

9. Write a program to create a comment containing the specified text.

10. Write a program that splits a text at a specified character and finally returns the remaining text.

CHAPTER

4 Introducing Schemas

4.1 Schemas, a Better DTD

Schemas allow you to emulate accurately your entire base of business operations. They enforce your business rules and provide document structure. Schemas view XML document instances as a collection of data types. The advantages that schemas bring to us represent a significant increase in software technology. For example, in contrast, DTDs view a source document as an entire entity, typing content as either parsed character data or unparsed non-XML data.

This chapter places emphasis on schema data types, derivation, and extension of those types, both predefined data and primitive. After studying this chapter, you will have increased exponentially your knowledge of XML, DTDs, and schemas, and you will be able to build successful distributed applications using the wide-ranging set of tools that schemas offer. They allow you to express the business model in XML without the constraints that DTDs impose on document authors.

4.2 Schema Data Types

Part 2 of the XML Schema Specification provides facilities for defining datatypes.

The XML schema W3C 2001 specification lists 44 built-in data types. Of the 44 built-ins, 19 are primitive data types, and 25 are built-in, derived data types. The primitive data types are the base types from which all other data types are constructed. The built-in, derived types can be either derived from or built upon. No fundamental difference exists between the built-in data types and the user-derived data types. User-derived data types and built-in data types are constructed using the `simpleType definitions`. A simple type definition restricts text that is allowed to appear as content for an attribute value or text-only elements without elements. A complex type definition constrains the permissible element contents. Consider the following examples, first the simple type:

```
<xsd:simpleType name="isbnType">
    <xsd:restriction base="xsd:string">
    <xsd:pattern value="[0-9] {10}"/>
    </xsd:restriction>
</xsd:simpleType>
```

Now the complexType:

```
<xsd:complexType name="bookType">
    <xsd:sequence>
        <xsd:element name="Fname" type="xsd:string"/>
        <xsd:element name="Address" type="xsd"string"/>
    </xsd:sequence>
</xsd:complexType>
```

A schema data type contains three components:

- A value space
- A lexical space
- A set of facets

Value Space

The *value space* consists of a set of values for a specified data type. For example, book is a string data type. The title, XMLPrimer, is a sequence of literals, known as a *lexical representation* for this specified data type. Consider for example the first sentence which is XML code.

1. `<book>XML Primer</book>`. The value space and lexical space are the same in this example. `<book>` is a string data type representing a string of characters, and the title `XML Primer` contains a set of literals of type string (`XML Primer` is one string) for this value space. Therefore, they are of the same type, string.

2. `<number>125</number>`. The value space for `number` consists of a set of literals for this value space. The lexical representation for this value space contains a specified number of characters (3) of type digit.

3. Schemas view the document instance as a collection of data types. The schema in Figure 4.1 is the governing document for Author.xml.

```
<?xml version="1.0" encoding="UTF-8"?>
<xs:schema xmlns:xs="http://www.w3.org/2001/XMLSchema">
<xs:element name="Author">
<xs:annotation>
    <xs:documentation>
```

This example represents a simple schema for Author.xml:

```
    </xs:documentation>
  </xs:annotation>
  <xs:complexType>
    <xs:sequence>
        <xs:element name="Name" type="xs:string"/>
        <xs:element name="Address" type="xs:string"/>
        <xs:element name="City" type="xs:string"/>
        <xs:element name="State" type="xs:string"/>
        <xs:element name="Zip" type="xs:string"/>
    </xs:sequence>
  </xs:complexType>
 </xs:element>
</xs:schema>
```

Figure 4.1   AuthorSchema.xsd

Literals

The Author schema in Figure 4.1 contains five elements representing value spaces for a string data type. The value space for element `Name` is a single string, whereas the string is a sequence of characters. The lexical representation consists of a string. Although it seems confusing, when examining a value space for a given type, first begin by determining the data type for the value space. Second, ascertain whether the literals are equal to the data type for the value space. Finally, the lexical representation is the sequence of literals for the specified data type, as follows:

```
<simpleType name='sizes'>
  <list itemType='decimal'/>
</simpleType>
<shoeSizes xsi:type='sizes'> 8 10.5 12 </shoeSizes>
```

Figure 4.2 is the source document for our schema.

```
<?xml version="1.0" encoding="UTF-8"?>
<Author>
    <Name>Dwight Peltzer</Name>
    <Address>Po Box 555</Address>
    <City>Oyster Bay</City>
    <State>NY</State>
    <Zip>11771</Zip>
</Author>
```

Figure 4.2 An Author document instance

`Author.xsd` demonstrates a significant contrast between DTDs and schemas by focusing on data types: built-in types, derived data types, and user-defined types.

The most important advance is the focus on data types. Schemas provide definitions for both simple and complex types. *Simple types* define attributes and elements containing only text and do not contain other attributes. They are derived from `AnyType`, the apex of the data type hierarchy. The diagram in Figure 4.3 demonstrates this.

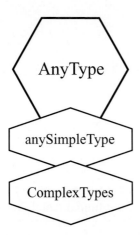

Figure 4.3   SimpleType hierarchy

The following example uses the `simpleType model` to enumerate a list of string type values.

```
<xs:simpleType name="Title">
    <xs:restriction base="xs:string">
        <xs:enumeration value="Sir Edward"/>
        <xs:enumeration value="Professor Peltzer"/>
        <xs:enumeration value="XSLT and
        Transformation"/>
    </xs:restriction>
</xs:simpleType>
```

A `Type` declaration describes the relationship between the element name and its behavior in the document instance. An element we define as a simple type string must appear in the XML document in that context. The same is true for an element defined as type short, type integer, or any other simple type. An element cannot violate that rule.

4.3 Facets

Facets define the value space and properties for a specified data type. Facets consist of two types:

Refer to the XML Schema
Specification, Part 2,
Facets.

- Fundamental facets
- Nonfundamental facets

Fundamental facets *define* a data type, whereas nonfundamental facets *impose* restrictions on the data type by limiting the range of a data type. The following is a list of the fundamental facets:

- Equal
- Ordered
- Bounded
- Cardinality
- Numeric

The `equal` facet allows you to compare two values. For example, for values a and b in a value space, only one of the following is true: a — b or a != b.

The `ordered` facet allows us to place a group of words in a predefined order relative to each other. `Ordered` can be applied to the partial list of data types presented here:

- Double decimal
- Float
- Duration
- Date
- Time

The `bounded` facet allows us to provide a lower limit and an upper limit on values within a value space. Attributes `minExclusive` and `maxExclusive` allow us to restrict a range of values. The following example demonstrates this concept:

```
<xs:simpleType name="less-than-ten">
    <restriction base="integer">
        <maxExclusive value="10"/>
    </xs:restriction>
</xs:simpleType>
```

The *cardinality* facet defines numeric relationships between occurrences of entities. An example would be something like the following:

```
<xs:ComplexType name = "CarDealership">
   <xs:sequence>
       <xs:element name="InventoryItem" type="carPart"
           minOccurs="0" maxOccurs="unbounded" />
   </sequence>
</xs:ComplexType>
```

We can define `Dealership` as a class and show a `"0"` to many relationships between `Dealership` (`0..*`) and `carPart` (many).

Dealership ——> carPart
PartID
Name
Price

We used cardinality and the plus (+) sign in the DTD to allow an element to appear repeatedly in a document instance. Schemas offer a better method whereby we can precisely specify cardinality. Consider the following example:

```
<xs:complexType>
  <xs:sequence>
       <xs:element name="optionalAddress" type="xs:string"
minOccurs="0" maxOccurs="unbounded"/>
   </xs:sequence>
   </xs:complexType>
```

The attribute `minOccurs="0"` makes the address optional. Conversely, `maxOccurs` allows the address to appear in the document instance as needed. If we set `maxOccurs="10"`, we restrict

element recurrences to the specified amount, a significant improvement over the DTD method.

Every value space contains an association with cardinality.
Lengths of a string and defining the number of digits in an ISBN are
two examples of cardinality.

The `numeric` facet allows you to classify a value as either
numeric (`value="true"`) or nonnumeric (`value="false"`). In the
following example, we restrict the `ISBN` to 10 digits. We apply the
numeric facet as follows in this example:

```
<xs:simpleType name="isbnType">
   <xs:restriction base="xs:string">
      xs:pattern value= "[0-9] {10}"/>
   </xs:restriction>
</xs:simpleType>
```

> **Note:** the expression `[0-9]` in this example refers to digits between 0
> and 9. `{10}` restricts the number of digits to 10. The data type digit is
> of type `string`.

Nonfundamental facets allow you to restrain the values within a
value space. The following example demonstrates how we define a
euro and limit the decimal base to 10 digits, two `fractionDigits`
to the right of the decimal:

```
<xs:element name="EuroDollar">
   <xs:simpleType name="EuroDollarType">
    <xs:restriction base="decimal">
        <xs:totalDigits value="10"/>
           <xs:fractionDigits value="2"/>
      </xs:restriction>
   <xs:simpleType>
</xs:element>
```

The document instance would look like this:

```
<EuroDollar>55.95</EuroDollar>
```

Derived User Types: Restriction

We construct user-derived data types by utilizing the simple type definitions and applying one of the following three methods:

- Restriction
- List
- Union

The restriction method uses one or more constraining facets to restrict the value space or lexical space for the base data type. For example, in the following example, the `pattern` facet restricts the permissible pattern for a U.S. postal code:

```
<xsd:simpleType name="addressType">
    <xsd:restriction base = "xsd:string">
        <xsd:pattern value="[0-9] {9}"/>
    </xsd:restriction>
</xsd:simpleType>
```

Derived User Types: List

The list method uses a predetermined `itemType` sequence of attributes to derive a new type. In this example, we use the list type to define a whitespace-separated list of values of type `decimal`. A list must be based on an existing built-in or custom `simpleType`.

```
<?xml version='1.0'?>
<xs:schema xmlns:xs=http://www.w3.org/2001/XMLSchema
<xs:simpleType name="myLottoNumbers">
    <xs:list itemType name="decimal"/>
 </xs:simpleType>
</xs:schema>
```

The instance document would look like this:

```
<numbers xsi:type="myLottoNumbers"> 10 18 35 47 34</numbers>
```

Another example of list types would be as follows:

```
<?xml version='1.0'?>
<xs:schema xmlns:xs=http://www.w3.org/2001/XMLSchema>
<xs:element name="intvalues" type="intvalueList">
    <xs:simpleType name"intvalueList">
         <xs:list itemType="integer"/>
    </xs:simpleType>
</xs:schema>
```

The source document would look like this:

```
<intvalueList>10 20 30 —40 1028</intvalueList>
```

Derived User Types: Union

The union element creates a data type that is derived from more than one data type. The union element utilizes an attribute that defines all base types participating in the union. Note that any of the defined base data types can be used. The following example allows any declared data type:

```
<xsd:simpleType name="demoTypeUnion">
  <xsd:union memberTypes="AType BType"/>
</xsd:simpleType>
```

In the following example, AType and BType are the defined member types:

```
<Month> Jan Feb Mar</Month>
<Month> 1 2 3 </Month>
```

Notice how the Month element contains two different data types: The first is a decimal type, and the second is a string type. The element consists of a list of whitespace-delimited data types. Remember, union types are always derived from atomic or list data types that include the value space and lexical spaces on all data types utilized to create the union type.

Practical Application for Simple Types

Schemas are designed to accommodate business needs of every type. Data types are an integral component of every business, ranging from email and e-commerce business transactions to messaging between trading partners and database queries. Table 4.1 lists a sample hierarchy of built-in data types. After reviewing them, we will discuss both how and why to apply these data types to your applications.

Table 4.1   Data Type Definitions

TypeName	Type	Derivation
anyType	Urtype	Base type for all schemas
anySimpleType	UrType	anyType
All complex types	Complex types	anyType
duration	Built-in primitive	anySimpleType
dateTime	Built-in primitive	anySimpleType
time	Built-in primitive	anySimpleType
date	Built-in primitive	anySimpleType
gYear	Built-in primitive	anySimpleType
gYearMonth	Built-in primitive	anySimpleType
gMonthDay	Built-in primitive	anySimpleType
float	Built-in primitive	anySimpleType
double	Built-in primitive	anySimpleType
anyURI	Built-in primitive	anySimpleType
string	Built-in primitive	anySimpleType
decimal	Built-in primitive	anySimpleType
integer	Built-in Derived	decimal
long	Built-in Derived	integer
Name	Built-in Derived	token
int	Built-in Derived	non-Negative Integer
NMTOKENS	Built-in Derived	NMTOKEN
ID	Built-in Derived	NCName
IDREF	Built-in Derived	NCName
IDREFS	Built-in Derived	NCName

If we want to use one of these data types, a facet, or a facet contained within a data type, we do the following:

- Begin with the base URI, which is the XML schema namespace.
- Include a fragment identifier, as follows:
  - Data type: `XMLSchema #float`
  - Facet: `XMLSchema #pattern`
  - Fragment identifier within a data type: `XMLSchema #string.pattern`

Usually, a data type contains the following items:

- Facets
- Name
- Value

Let's present a few examples to demonstrate the concepts we have discussed.

```
<!--schema-->
<xs:element name="myString" type="xs:string"/>
<!--instance document-->
<myString> This example represents a simple string</myString>
```

If we examine this schema fragment, the following constraining facets would apply:

- `length`
- `maxLength`
- `minLength`
- `pattern`

Another example would limit the `IsbnType` to 10 digits:

```
<Schema>
 <xs:simpleType name="myIsbnType">
   <xs:restriction base="xs:decimal">
```

```
            <xs:pattern value="[0-9]{10}"/>
          </xs:restriction>
     </xs:simpleType>
</Schema>
```

This example demonstrates how we define the value space as type myIsbnType. The base type is decimal, and the pattern facet constrains the value to 10 digits.

Another example demonstrates how a money element is restricted by the totalDigits and fractionDigits facets:

```
<Schema >
<xsd:element name="money">
  <xsd:simpleType>
  <xsd:restriction base="xsd:decimal">
          <xsd:totalDigits value="4"/>
               <xsd:fractionDigits value="2"/>
  </xsd:restriction>
 </xsd:simpleType>
</xsd:element>
</xsd:Schema>
```

The instance document would look like this:

```
<money>20.95</money>
```

One other example is in order:

```
<Schema>
<xsd:element name="houseCharge">
  <xsd:simpleType>
  <xsd:restriction base="xsd:float">
          <xsd:minExclusive value="30.00"/>
          <xsd:maxExclusive value=="300.00"/>
  </xsd:restriction>
 </xsd:simpleType>
</xsd:element>
<!-- Instance document -->
<houseCharge>99.95</houseCharge>
```

4.4 Complex Types

A `complex type` element contains other elements and attributes. We use complex types to build other content models. Consider the following example. Before we examine Figure 4.4, a review of the meaning of global and local scope is in order. Elements declared within the context of schema declarations are global in scope and are visible to the entire application. In contrast, when we see the declaration pair `<xs:complexType>` followed by `<xs:sequence>`, element declarations following this are local in scope and are not visible to the application, rendering them as not reusable within application context. Local scope ends with `</xs:sequence>` and `</xs:complexType>`.

```
<xs:complexType>
    <xs:sequence>
      <xs:element name="Author" type="xs:string"/>
       <xs:element name="Name" type="xs:string"/>
       <xs:element name="Address" type="xs:string"/>
       <xs:element name="City" type="xs:string"/>
       <xs:element name="State" type="xs:string"/>
       <xs:element name="Zip" type="xs:string"/>
    </xs:sequence>
  </xs:complexType>
```

Figure 4.4 `ComplexType` declarations

This declaration has several important implications. It signifies the end of global scope and marks the beginning of local element declarations. All elements and attributes declared within this model are local in scope. We defined Author (refer to Figure 4.1) as an immediate child of the schema, whereas the five elements declared within `complexType` are child elements of `Author` and are constrained to functioning as local elements.

Notice how each element declaration specifies a data type. In this model, all elements are simple data types. Because we declare the elements within the `complexType` model, they are hidden and are not reusable. Additionally, the five elements contain no dependencies on root `Author`.

The impact of the restriction on local elements depends on how you want to structure your document model. Remember, one of the main benefits that schemas offer document authors is the ability to define elements as reusable. Alternatives to this model exist, but we will defer that discussion until Section 4.7, "Exposing/Hiding Namespaces," where we examine three different models: the Russian Doll model, the Salami Slice model, and the Venetian Blind model.

We can declare an element as type complex and create a new data type based on the original type, as demonstrated here:

```
<xs:Schema
        xmlns:xs="http://www.w3.org/2001/XMLSchema">
<xs:element name="consumer" type="consumerType">
    <xs:complexType>
        <xs:choice>
                <xs:element name="creditCard" type="xs:string"/>
                <xs:element name="cash" type="xs:decimal"/>"
                <xs:element name="PaymentMethod"
type="xs:string"/>
        </xs:choice>
    </xs:complexType>
    <xs:element>
</xs:Schema>
```

We use the `choice` attribute to provide the document author with flexibility for this document model by enumerating the options. The new data type is `consumerType`. The following document instance demonstrates this concept:

```
<consumer>
        <PaymentMethod>credit Card</PaymentMethod>
</consumer>
<consumer>
        <PaymentMethod>cash</PaymentMethod>
</consumer>
```

Declaring an element as a type component makes it reusable, thereby conforming to the object-oriented principle of modularization and component reuse. Keep in mind that elements declared within `complexType` are local, rendering them not reusable. They do not interact with other elements within the schema, nor are they visible to other components within the schema. The following example demonstrates this concept.

```
<xs:schema xmlns:xs="http://www.w3.org/2001/XMLSchema"
elementFormDefault="qualified">
    <xs:element name="ComputerScienceCurriculum">
      <xs:complexType>
        <xs:sequence>
          <xs:element ref="CourseLevel"/>
          <xs:element name="CourseList" type="CourseListType"/>
        </xs:sequence>
      </xs:complexType>
    </xs:element>
    <xs:element name="CourseLevel" type="xs:string"/>
    <xs:complexType name="CourseListType">
      <xs:attribute name="courses" type="xs:string"
use="required"/>
    </xs:complexType>
</xs:schema>
```

The elements `CourseLevel` and `CourseList` exist as reusable components. They are visible and useful to other parts of the schema or other schemas.

The source document for this schema is as follows:

```
<ComputerScienceCurriculum>
    <CourseLevel>Graduate</CourseLevel>
    <CourseList courses="CSC690 CSC540 CSC600 CSC602 CSC670"/>
</ComputerScienceCurriculum>
```

4.5 Compositors

Compositors provide us with three convenient methods:

- Sequential order of elements in the document instance
- Choice of elements used in the source document

- The ALL compositor, which provides an unrestricted freedom in defining order and selection of elements allowed to appear in the document instance

Sequence

`Sequence` determines element order in the document instance. For example, the following eight elements must appear in the document instance in the order listed within the `complexType` component:

```
<xs:complexType>
  <xs:sequence>
    <xs:element name="Name" type="xs:string"/>
    <xs:element name="Address" type="xs:string"/>
    <xs:element name="City" type="xs:string"/>
    <xs:element name="State" type="xs:string"/>
    <xs:element name="Zip" type="xs:short"/>
    <xs:element name="Publisher" type="xs:string"/>
    <xs:element name="BookTitle" type="xs:string"/>
    <xs:element name="ISBN" type="xs:string"/>
  </xs:sequence>
</xs:complexType>
```

Choice

`Choice` allows the author to choose between two or more defined options. Frequently, it is useful to declare an element containing a group with choices, similar to a DTD in which we offer a selection of elements. You can select only one from the list in the document instance. For example, consider the following DTD element definition:

```
<!ELEMENT Book (Romance | History | Computer Science)>
```

The schema fragment in Figure 4.5 represents a `NamedType` declaration offering a list of choices.

```
<xsd:complexType name="employee" type= "EmployeeType">
     <xsd:choice>
    <xsd:element name="employeeCategory"/>
```

```
      <xsd:sequence>
            <xsd:element name="salaried" type="xsd:string"/>
            <xsd:element name="hourly" type="xsd:decimal"/>
      </xsd:sequence>
   </xsd:choice>
```

Figure 4.5   EmployeeType.xsd

A source document for this schema would look like this:

```
<?xml version='1.0' encoding="UTF-8'?>
<Employee>
      <salaried>Jonathan</salaried>
      <hourly>7.50</hourly>
</Employee>
```

ALL

ALL is similar to ANY, the compositor that allows element declarations to appear in any order but must occur. (Refer to Chapter 2, "Document Type Definition," for a discussion of the ANY content model.)

```
<xs:element name="FamilyName">
   <xs:complexType>
       <xs:all>
     xs:element name="firstName" type="xs:string"/>
     xs:element name="middleName" type="xs:string"/>
     xs:element name="lastName" type="xs:string"
minOccurs="0"/>
       </xs:all>
      </xs:complexType>
</xs:element>
```

Figure 4.6   The ALL compositor

Although the schema may define the sequential order of elements, ALL allows the document author to list the elements in any order. Note that, by including the minOccurs attribute, we define an open-ended model allowing any element to appear in any order.

4.6 Defining Namespaces

Schemas introduce the concept of using namespaces to delineate the difference between elements sharing the same name but containing different meanings.

Each country, for example, has its own format for user-defined `postal codes`, `telecom`, `money`, and `date`. The American format for zip codes consists of five digits, a hyphen, and then four more digits, as in `11732-1225`. The Swedish postal code is formed as in `432-00`, whereas the United Kingdom postal code is expressed as `Lancashire WN8-7PD`. How can the processor handle this unique situation? The answer is simple: Provide a unique namespace for each country, containing the definitions for each unique postal code, and attach a unique prefix to it. The consequence of providing a distinctive prefix and namespace is that all declared elements and attributes belong to the namespace containing the prefix.

Schema declarations occur within the schema. Syntax for this can be somewhat confusing. Let's demystify it for you. The prefix `xs` serves as the default prefix for all `XSD` schemas.

```
<xs:schema:xmlns:xs="default URL namespace"
```

Both the prefix `xs` and `xsd` are used interchangeably. Just make sure the schema extension is `.xsd`, as in `MySchema.xsd`.

Three separate schema namespaces exist:

- The XML schema namespace
- The XML schema data type namespace
- The XML schema instance namespace

We use the first namespace for W3C schema elements. The prefix `xs` or `xsd` precedes the default URI, which is `<xs:schema:xs="http://www.w3.org/2001/XMLSchema">`.

The schema for schema definitions is dependent on four separate documents:

- Schema for data type definitions
- The XML InfoSet

- Namespaces
- XPath language

These contain definitions for the schema framework and components of an XML schema. You can locate the schema for schemas at `www.w3.org/TR/2001/REC-xmlschema-1-20010502/#normative-schemaSchema`. Schema is defined as an abstract data model consisting of 13 schema components divided into three groups:

- Simple type definitions
- Complex type definitions
- Element declarations

We suggest you consult the official schema definitions for each group.

The second namespace specifies the use of built-in data types. The URL where data type definitions reside is `http://www.w3.org/2001/XMLSchema-datatypes`.

The default namespace we provided first also contains the built-in data type definitions. Therefore, it is unnecessary to use the data type URI provided here because the first namespace we mentioned contains the same data type definitions.

The third namespace specified for XMLSchema attributes utilized in document instances includes definitions for `xsi:type`, `xsi:nil`, and `xsi:noNamespaceSchemaLocation`. Always use prefix `xsi` when you use this namespace. The URL for this namespace is `http://www.w3.org/2001/XMLSchema-instance`.

We use `xsi:type` when we map our schema to the schema-instance namespace and employ the XML schema extensions in the instance document. For example, the `xsi:noNamespaceSchemaLocation` and `xsi:schemaLocation` allow you to bind a document to the W3C schema. The following example demonstrates this:

```
<book isbn="0-201-24356-1"
        xmlns:xsi="http://www.w3.orf/2001/XMLSchema-
        instance"
         xsi:noNamespaceSchemaLocation="mydocument.xsd">
```

One other use of `xsi` attributes provides information concerning how an element is related to the schema. They include `xsi:type`, which allows you to define an element as simple or complex, and `xsi:nil`, which enables you to specify a null value for an element. You use nillable in the schema utilizing a `nillable="true"` attribute. This is comparable to the relational database model in which we restrict a field to either null or not null.

Global vs. Local Scoping

The declaration for element Author (refer to Figure 4.1) occurs in the context of the schema declaration, which means that Author is a child of Schema. All elements declared before `xs:complexType` are global elements. For example, if we declared elements `Name` and `Address` within the schema context, they would become global elements, thereby preventing their redefinition as local elements. The example in Figure 4.7 is a schema with `Name` and `Address` declared as global elements:

```
<?xml version="1.0" encoding="UTF-8"?>
<xs:schema xmlns:xs="http://www.w3.org/2001/XMLSchema">
    <xs:element name="Name" type="xs:string"/>
    <xs:element name="Address" type="xs:string"/>
    <xs:element name="Author">
<!--this is where global declarations stop -->
    <xs:complexType>
       <xs:sequence>
          <xs:element name="City" type="xs:string"/>
          <xs:element name="State" type="xs:string"/>
       </xs:sequence>
    </xs:complexType>
    </xs:element>
</xs:schema>
```

Figure 4.7   Global elements

Figure 4.8 shows the document instance for global elements. It does not contain a target namespace but specifies `noNamespaceSchemaLocation` to indicate where the schema resides. Do not use a prefix in this context.

```
<Author
     xmlns:xsi="http://www.w3.org/2001/XMLSchema-instance"
     xsi:noNamespaceSchemaLocation="global.xsd">
   <City>String</City>
   <State>String</State>
</Author>
```

Figure 4.8   Global.xml

If you decide to use a namespace with your document instances, you must define a target namespace within your source document: `targetNamespace="http://www.your namespace.com"`. The target namespace binds your XML document to the schema to which it adheres.

```
<?xml version="1.0" encoding="UTF-8"?>
<Author
xmlns:xs="http://www.myNamespace.com/schemas/Authors">
   <Name>Dwight Peltzer</Name>
   <Address>PO Box 555</Address>
   <City>Oyster Bay</City>
   <State>NY</State>
   <Zip>11771</Zip>
   <Publisher>
       <Name>Addison Wesley</Name>
       <City>Boston</City>
       <State>Massachusetts</State>
     </Publisher>
   <BookTitle>XML Language Mechanics</BookTitle>
   <ISBN>0-1-23458-0</ISBN>
</Author>
```

Figure 4.9   A target namespace within the source document

XML schemas allow you to define a target namespace for any document(s) you want to adhere to a schema:

```
<schema
      targetNamespace
='http://www.dpsoftware.com/schemas/Author'>
 . . . . .
  </schema>
```

Frequently, you may decide not to use a namespace for your document instance. In that case, simply omit the target namespace attribute as in Figure 4.10.

```
<?xml version="1.0" encoding="UTF-8"?>
<xs:schema xmlns:xs="http://www.w3.org/2001/XMLSchema">
<xs:element name="Author">
     <xs:complexType>
       <xs:sequence>
          <xs:element name="Name" type="xs:string"/>
          <xs:element name="Address" type="xs:string"/>
          <xs:element name="City" type="xs:string"/>
          <xs:element name="State" type="xs:string"/>
          <xs:element name="Zip" type="xs:short"/>
          <xs:element name="Publisher" type="xs:string"/>
          <xs:element name="BookTitle" type="xs:string"/>
          <xs:element name="ISBN" type="xs:string"/>
       </xs:sequence>
     </xs:complexType>
   </xs:element>
</xs:schema>
```

Figure 4.10   Target Namespace Not Defined

By not declaring a target namespace, you are using the built-in data types provided by the schema and mapping all declared elements/attributes to the default namespace. This prevents you from reusing the locally declared elements, deriving from them, or extending the base type.

```
<xs:Schema
          xmlns:xs="http://www.w3.org/2001/XMLSchema">
```

It follows that the document instance would not have a namespace, as demonstrated in Figure 4.11.

```
<?xml version="1.0" encoding="UTF-8"?>
<Author
        xmlns:xsi=http://www.w3.org.2001.XMLSchema-instance"
        xsi:noNamespaceSchemaLocation="Author.xsd">
    <Name>Dwight Peltzer</Name>
    <Address>PO Box 555</Address>
    <City>Oyster Bay</City>
    <State>NY</State>
    <Zip>11771</Zip>
    <Publisher>
        <Name>Addison Wesley</Name>
        <City>Boston</City>
        <State>Massachusetts</State>
    </Publisher>
    <BookTitle>XML Language Mechanics</BookTitle>
    <ISBN>0-1-23458-0</ISBN>
</Author>
```

Figure 4.11   `NoNamespaceSchemaLocation`

By now you know that a target namespace defines a namespace for your own user-defined declarations and definitions. You accomplish this by adding the target namespace to the schema root. Figure 4.12 shows how to achieve this.

```
<?xml version="1.0" encoding="UTF-8"?>
<xs:schema xmlns:xs="http://www.w3.org/2001/XMLSchema"

targetNamespace="http://www.dpsoftware.com/namespaces/Author"
    xmlns="http://www.dpsoftware.com/namespaces/Author">
    <xs:element name="Author">
      <xs:complexType>
        <xs:sequence>
            <xs:element name="Name" type="xs:string"/>
            <xs:element name="Address" type="xs:string"/>
            <xs:element name="City" type="xs:string"/>
            <xs:element name="State" type="xs:string"/>
            <xs:element name="Zip" type="xs:string"/>
```

```
            <xs:element name="Publisher" type="xs:string"/>
            <xs:element name="BookTitle" type="xs:string"/>
            <xs:element name="ISBN" type="xs:string"/>
        </xs:sequence>
    </xs:complexType>
  </xs:element>
</xs:schema>
```

Figure 4.12   Document with target namespace

Notice the changes we have made to this schema. First, we added the `targetNamespace` attribute. The second addition is the default namespace for the schema document itself. The target namespace must be included in the document instance.

```
targetNamespace="http://www.dpsoftware.com/namespaces/Author"
xmlns="http://www.dpsoftware.com/namespaces/Author">
```

The consequence for these additions is that all elements declared belong to the www.dpsoftware.com namespace.

All global elements must be qualified in the document instance when you declare a target namespace, whereas you need not qualify local elements. This rule is specified in the XML schema recommendation. Let's view such a document. In the example in Figure 4.13, Author must be qualified using the prefix dp and the target namespace. Local elements are not qualified.

```
<?xml version="1.0" encoding="UTF-8"?>
<dp:Author
    xmlns:dp="http://www.dpsoftware.com/namespaces/Author"
    xmlns:xsi="http://www.w3.org/20011/XMLSchema-instance"
xsi:schemaLocation="http://www.dpsoftware.com/namespaces/author
/AuthorV1.xsd">
    <Name>Dwight Peltzer</Name>
    <Address>Po Box 555</Address>
    <City>Oyster Bay</City>
    <State>NY</State>
    <Zip>11771</Zip>
    <Publisher>Addison Wesley</Publisher>
```

```
    <BookTitle>XML Language Mechanics</BookTitle>
    <ISBN>0-1-23458-0</ISBN>
</dp:Author>
```

Figure 4.13   Global element qualification

Namespace Qualification

Namespace qualification means we hide or expose the namespace for
each element in the document instance. Two global attributes exist:

- `elementFormDefault ="qualified | unqualified"`
- `attributeFormDefault =""`

As previously mentioned, you must qualify global elements in the
instance document. However, by using `elementFormDefault` and
setting it to `unqualified`, which is the default, the document
instance hides the namespace qualifications. Conversely, we can set
`elementFormDefault="qualified"`. Then all document elements must be exposed using a prefix, such as `dp`, which binds that
particular element to a specified namespace. Let's view a document
instance containing all qualified elements (see Figure 4.14).

```
<?xml version="1.0" encoding="UTF-8"?>
<dp:Author
    xmlns:dp="http://www.dpsoftware.com/namespaces/author"
    xmlns:xsi="http://www.w3.org/2001/XMLSchema-instance"
xsi:SchemaLocation="http://www.dpsoftware.com/namespaces/author
/Author.xsd">
    <dp:Name>Dwight Peltzer</dp:Name>
    <dp:Address>PO Box 555</dp:Address>
    <dp:City>Oyster Bay</dp:City>
    <dp:State>NY</dp:State>
    <dp:Zip>11771</dp:Zip>
    <dp:BookTitle>XML Language Mechanics</dp:BookTitle>
    <dp:ISBN>0-1-23458-0</dp:ISBN>
</dp:Author>
```

Figure 4.14   Qualified elements

Notice how we qualify every element with prefix dp in the document instance. The same rules apply to attributes.

4.7   Exposing/Hiding Namespaces

An important decision you must make when designing your schema depends on whether you need to expose or hide your namespaces in the document instance. Three schema design models are available to help you make this decision:

- The Russian Doll design
- The Salami Slice design
- The Venetian Blind design

Russian Doll Design

The first design model emulates a Russian doll, containing a single box with nested boxes inside it. You can think of elements as separate components (boxes) with nested elements contained within. This model mirrors the document instance. Figure 4.15 shows the source document it emulates.

```
<Book>
  <Title>XML</Title>
  <Author>Dwight Peltzer</Author>
</Book>
```

Figure 4.15   RussianDoll.xml

Figure 4.16 shows the schema for the Russian Doll model.

```
<xs:schema xmlns:xs=http://www.w3.org/2001/XMLSchema>
 <xs:element name="Book">
    <xs:complexType>
      <xs:sequence>
        <xs:element name="Title" type="xs:string"/>
        <xs:element name="Author" type="xs:string"/>
      </xs:sequence>
    </xs:complexType>
```

```
        </xs:element>
    </xs:schema>
```

Figure 4.16   RussianDoll.xsd

<Book> is global, whereas <Title> and <Author> are local elements. They are not visible to other components in the schema. They remain localized within the schema.

Salami Slice Design

The Salami Slice model represents the other end of the design spectrum. Figure 4.17 displays Name and Title as global components. Additionally, they are separated and presented as individual components.

```
<xs:element name="Title" type="xs:string"/>
<xs:element name="Author" type="xs:string"/>
<xs:element name="Book">
    <xs:complexType>
        <xs:sequence><xs:schema
xmlns:xs="http://www.w3.org/2001/XMLSchema"
elementFormDefault="qualified">
    <xs:element name="Title" type="xs:string"/>
    <xs:element name="Author" type="xs:string"/>
    <xs:element name="Book">
      <xs:complexType>
        <xs:sequence>
            <xs:element ref="Title"/>
            <xs:element ref="Author"/>
        </xs:sequence>
      </xs:complexType>
    </xs:element>
</xs:schema>
<!--reassemble Title and Author -->
            <xs:element ref="Title"/>
            <xs:element ref="Author"/>
        </xs:sequence>
      </xs:complexType>
    </xs:element>
```

Figure 4.17   Salami.xsd

You can clearly see how `Title` and `Author` represent independent global elements.

It also is visually clear how we take elements `Title` and `Author` and group them by referencing them. Anytime you see elements pointed to using the `ref` attribute, you know those elements are global.

We have effectively coupled the disparate components and built dependencies between them. Therefore, they are both coupled and cohesive. Contrast this with the Russian Doll design in which we grouped all components together. However, they are not coupled with elements residing outside the root element. Here's a final comment concerning the Salami Slice model: `Title` and `Author` must be exposed in the document instance using a unique prefix.

Venetian Blind Design

The third document model, Venetian Blind, offers a flexible design model. This is where we can easily employ the attributes `elementFormDefault` and `attributeFormDefault` as a binary switch to facilitate hiding or exposing namespaces in the source document. If we want to expose the namespace in the document instance, set `elementFormDefault` to `qualified`. Conversely, set the switch to `unqualified`, thereby effectively confining the namespace declarations within the schema. The key to understanding this design model lies with type definitions. By creating a global type definition and enclosing `Title` and `Author` declarations within it, we provide the flexibility needed to use the `elementFormDefault` switch without redesigning the Salami content model. See Figure 4.18.

```
<?xml version="1.0" encoding="UTF-8"?>
<xs:schema xmlns:xs="http://www.w3.org/2001/XMLSchema"
elementFormDefault="qualified" attributeFormDefault=
"unqualified">
   <xs:element name="Employer">
   <xs:annotation>
   <xs:documentation>Comment describing your root element
   </xs:documentation>
   </xs:annotation>
   </xs:element>
```

```
    <xs:complexType name="employeeType">
    <xs:sequence>
        <xs:element name="name" type="xs:string"/>
        <xs:element name="contact" type="xs:string"/>
    </xs:sequence>
</xs:complexType>
 <xs:complexType name="employeeTypeExt">
  <xs:complexContent>
   <xs:extension base="employeeType">
      <xs:sequence>
      <xs:element name="empName" type="employeeType"/>
      </xs:sequence>
   </xs:extension>
  </xs:complexContent>
 </xs:complexType>
 <xs:element name="employee" type="employeeTypeExt"/>
</xs:schema>
```

Figure 4.18   The Venetian Blind model

All `NamedType` components are reusable (see Figure 4.19).

```
<xs:simpleType name="Title">
  <xs:restriction base="xs:string">
    <xs:enumeration value="Sci_Fi"/>
    <xs:enumeration value="Information Systems"/>
  </xs:restriction>
</xs:simpleType>
<xs:simpleType name="Name">
  <xs:restriction base="xs:string">
  <xs:minLength value="1"/>
  </xs:restriction>
</xs:simpleType>
<xs:complexType name="Editor">
  <xs:sequence>
    <xs:element name="Title" type="Title"/>
    <xs:element name="Author" type="Editor"/>
  </xs:sequence>
</xs:complexType>
<xs:element name="Book" type="Editor"/>
```

Figure 4.19   Reusable components

The components `Title`, `Name`, `Editor`, and `Book` represent reusable components. Defining type definitions is the key to this model. You can easily use `elementFormDefault` to turn on or off the ability to expose or hide namespaces. You needn't redesign your schema each time you want to expose or hide your namespaces.

4.8   Content Models

Content models allow you to reuse, extend, or restrict content models. You accomplish this via the complexType definition. Consider the prototype in Figure 4.20.

```
<xs:complexType name="nameType">
   <xs:sequence>
      <xs:element ref="firstName"/>
      <xs:element ref="middleName"/>
      <xs:element ref="lastName"/>
   </xs:sequence>
</xs:complexType>
```

Figure 4.20   Content model template

Once you have named the complex type, you can reference the named complex type definitions using the type attribute.

ANY Content Model

The ANY content model is the data type from which all other types are derived. It allows both text and any subelements that the author desires. This content model is located at the top of the data type hierarchy and serves as the base model for all other types.

```
<xs:element name="book">
    <xs:complexType>
      <xs:sequence>
        <xs:ANY minOccurs="1" maxOccurs="unbounded"
        processContents="skip"/>
      </xs:sequence>
    </xs:complexType>
  </xs:element>
```

The attribute `processContents="skip"` is a directive to the processor to bypass validation.

The ANY element serves as a placeholder for other elements residing in a content model. You can validate this model against any namespace by providing a target namespace. Consider the following example:

```
<xs:element name="books">
  <xs:complexType>
    <xs:sequence>
        xs:any namespace="http://www.yournamespace.com"
        minOccurs="0" maxOccurs="unbounded"
        processContents="lax"/>
        <xs:sequence>
    </xs:complexType>
</xs:element>
```

Note: `processContents` contains three definitions:

- `strict`
- `lax`
- `skip`

We are referring to validation when we use these attributes:

- `strict` requires validation, and a namespace must be located.
- `skip` requires no validation.
- `lax` means validate if possible.

The Empty Content Model

The *Empty Content Model* allows you to use attributes when you wish to provide additional information about data.

This model is similar to the DTD `Empty` content model. It doesn't allow child elements or text to appear. Frequently, you will use attributes with this model. The example in Figure 4.21 demonstrates this concept. You simply remove any text or element declarations from the tag.

```
<?xml version="1.0" encoding="UTF-8"?>
<Book>
   <Author/>
   <Title/>
</Book>
```

Figure 4.21   Empty content model

A schema for this document instance is as follows:

```
<xs:schema xmlns:xs="http://www.w3.org/2001/XMLSchema"
 elementFormDefault="qualified">
   <xs:element name="Book">
     <xs:complexType>
       <xs:sequence>
         <xs:element name="Author">
            <xs:complexType/>
         </xs:element>
         <xs:element name="Title">
            <xs:complexType/>
         </xs:element>
       </xs:sequence>
     </xs:complexType>
   </xs:element>
</xs:schema>
```

Take note of how we declare the empty elements for `Author` and `Title`. Especially observe where we place the closing forward slash for complexType:

```
<xs:complexType/>
```

The Mixed Content Model

The mixed content model allows a combination of text and child elements to appear within this model, as demonstrated in Figure 4.22.

```
<xs:schema xmlns:xs="http://www.w3.org/2001/XMLSchema"
elementFormDefault="qualified">
   <xs:element name="Author" type="xs:string"/>
   <xs:element name="Book">
```

```
    <xs:complexType mixed="true">
      <xs:choice minOccurs="0" maxOccurs="unbounded">
        <xs:element ref="Author"/>
      </xs:choice>
    </xs:complexType>
  </xs:element>
</xs:schema>
```

Figure 4.22 Mixed Content Model.xsd

The document instance for this schema is shown in Figure 4.23.

```
<Book
xmlns:xsi="http://www.w3.org/2001/XMLSchema-instance"
xsi:noNamespaceSchemaLocation="C:\Documents and Settings\Dwight
Peltzer\My Documents\Spy04\Mixed.xsd">
    <Author> Dwight Peltzer</Author>
    Maite is an excellent editor.
</Book>
```

Figure 4.23 Mixed content model

The Element Content Model

This content model allows only other elements to appear. Child elements may not contain other nested elements (see Figure 4.24).

```
<Author xmlns:xsi="http://www.w3.org/2001/XMLSchema-instance"
xsi:noNamespaceSchemaLocation="Catalog.xsd">
    <Name>Dwight Peltzer</Name>
    <Address>PO Box 555</Address>
    <City>Oyster Bay</City>
    <State>NY</State>
    <Zip>11771</Zip>
</Author>
```

Figure 4.24 Element-only model

4.9 Deriving Complex Types from Existing Complex Types

Subclassing based on existing complex types conforms to object-oriented principles, which allows us to derive objects from existing complex types. All base class properties are made available to the new type. Subclassing begins with the definition of a base type.

This technique is applicable to many different contexts. We can extend a base USAddress type to accommodate a UK address or some other country's address type. This applies as well to different currencies, different university courses, and so on. The example in Figure 4.25 demonstrates how we extend the USCurrency type to accommodate the euro. Invoice is the root element, whereas USCurrency represents the base class.

```
<?xml version="1.0" encoding="UTF-8"?>
<xs:schema xmlns:xs="http://www.w3.org/2001/XMLSchema"
elementFormDefault="qualified" attributeFormDefault=
"unqualified">
<xs:element name="Invoice">
<xs:annotation>
<xs:documentation>derivation by extension</xs:documentation>
</xs:annotation>
</xs:element>
<xs:complexType name="EuroCurrency">
<xs:complexContent>
<xs:extension base="USCurrency">
<xs:sequence>
<xs:element name="EuroDollar" type="xs:decimal"/>
</xs:sequence>
</xs:extension>
</xs:complexContent>
</xs:complexType>
</xs:schema>
```

Figure 4.25   Deriving by extension for foreign currencies

`<xs:complexType>` and `<xs:complexContent>` signify the intent to extend the base `USCurrency` type. Through derivation, we can easily create new instances of currency. An instance document conforming to the euro currency type will be validated if the specified content appears within the document where a type of currency is anticipated. The derived type must be specified in the instance document using the `xsi:type` attribute defined within the XML instance namespace.

Deriving Simple Types from Existing Built-In Types

Defining a simple type is similar to defining a complex type. An `integer` data type is defined as a simple type because simple types include built-in primitive types like `integers`, `floats`, `doubles`, `date`, `CDATA`, `tokens`, `bytes`, `binary`, `long`, `unsignedInts`, and so on. The `attribute` type declares its data type rather than declaring the element content model, as demonstrated in the following schema fragment:

```
<AttributeType name="invoiceNum" dt:type="int"
required="yes"/>.
```

New simple types can be derived from existing built-in types. Restrict an existing simple type using the keyword `restriction` to describe the base type and then apply facets. (A *facet* is a delimiting property of a data type uniquely identifying it from other properties.) String length is used to constrain the range of values:

```
<xsd:simpleType name="MyRestrictedInteger">
    <xsd:restriction base="xsd:integer">
        <xsd:minInclusive value ="100"/>
        <xsd:maxInclusive value ="250"/>
    </xsd:restriction>
</xsd:simpleType>
```

We combine two facets with the base type to define `MyRestrictedInteger`. By doing so, the integer must fall within the 100 to 250 range to qualify for validation.

The next example uses the `enumeration` facet to provide a list of states based on the simple type `USState`.

```
<xsd:simpleType name="USState">
        <xsd:restriction base ="xsd:string">
            <xsd:enumeration value="AR"/>
            <xsd:enumeration value="NY"/>
        </xsd:restriction>
</xsd:simpleType>
```

The restriction limits an acceptable range to two specified white-space-delimited states: `<USState> AR NY</USState>`.

Creating Anonymous Type Definitions

You can define anonymous type definitions by creating named type sets such as `ContestantParticipantType`. The element `ContestantParticipant` references types using the `"type="` construct. Although anonymous types are confusing, one easy method of identifying them is look for a missing `"type="` in an element or attribute declaration. Also, look for an unnamed simple or complex type definition. The schema in Figure 4.26 demonstrates this. The element `bookName` contains `bookItem` and `quantity`, representing the anonymous elements in this schema.

```
<xsd:complexType name="BookInventory">
<xsd:sequence>
<xsd:element name="bookName" minOccurs="0"
maxOccurs="unbounded">
<xsd:complexType>
<xsd:sequence>
<xsd:element name="bookItem" type="xsd:string"/>
<xsd:element name="quantity">
<xsd:SimpleType>
<xsd:restriction base="positiveInteger">
<xsd:maxExclusive value="10"/>
</xsd:restriction>
</xsd:simpleType>
```

```
      </xsd:element>
      <xsd:element name="bookPrice" type="xsd:decimal"/>
      <xsd:element name="shipDate" type="xsd:date" minOccurs="0"/>
      </xsd:sequence>
      <xsd:sequence>
      <xsd:attribute name="ISBN" type="SKU" use="required"/>
      </xsd:complexType>
      </xsd:element>
      </xsd:element>
      </xsd:sequence>
      </xsd:complexType>

      <?xml version="1.0" encoding="UTF-8"?>
      <xsd:schema xmlns:xs="http://www.w3.org/2001/XMLSchema"
      elementFormDefault="qualified" attributeFormDefault=
      "unqualified">
      <xsd:complexType name="BookInventory">
      <xsd:element name="bookName" minOccurs="0"
      maxOccurs="unbounded">
      <xsd:complexType>
      <xsd:sequence>
      <xsd:element name="bookItem" type="xsd:string"/>
      <xsd:element name="quantity" type="xsd:integer"/>
      </xsd:sequence>
      </xsd:complexType>
      </xsd:element>
      </xsd:complexType>
      <xsd:simpleType>
      <xsd:restriction base="positiveInteger">
      <xsd:maxExclusive value="10"/>
      </xsd:restriction>
      </xsd:simpleType>
      </xsd:schema>
```

Figure 4.26   BookInventory.xsd

The quantity element has an anonymous simple type derived from integer, whose value is limited to top range '9' and bottom range '1'. bookName has an anonymous complex type containing the elements `bookItem` and `quantity`.

Deriving Complex Types from Simple Types

The Items example previously discussed contained an attribute and a simple value. In an instance document containing a bookPrice, this element might appear as follows:

```
<bookPrice USCurrency="US">55.95</bookPrice>
```

Notice the absence of a "`type=`". This identifies the element as an anonymous type. A new schema for a new instance document could declare a "`bookPrice`" `type="decimal"` in the following manner:

```
<xsd:element name="bookPrice" type="xsd:decimal"/>.
```

We could add an attribute to this element by defining a `complexType` to hold an attribute declaration. The content required is a simple type decimal:

```
<!--Note: the following code is a document fragment.-->
<xsd:element name="USCurrency">
   <xsd:complexType>
   <!--We create an anonymous data type here-->

   <xsd:simpleContent>
      <xsd:extension base="xsd:decimal">
      <xsd:attribute name="USCurrency" type="xsd:string"/>
      </xsd:extension>
   </xsd:simpleContent>
   </xsd:complexType>
<xsd:element>
```

Use the `complexType` to create an anonymous data type. The content model of the new type contains only character data and no elements. We extend the simple type by deriving the new type. Then we use a standard attribute declaration to extend a `USCurrency` attribute.

4.10 Attribute Definitions

Defining attributes is similar to defining element types. You can create attributes in the following manner:

```
<AttributeType
        default="defaultValue"
        dt:type="built-in type"
        dt:values="enumerated-values"
        name="idref"
        required="{yes | no}" />
```

Attributes are more limited than elements in several ways. For example, attributes cannot contain child elements nor are they required to appear in a specific order. In addition, they can appear only once per element. Specify them as optional or required.

Attributes offer certain capabilities that elements do not. For example, attributes can restrict their values to a limited set of strings:

```
<AttributeType name="priority" dt:type="enumeration" dt:values=
"small medium large"/>
```

Specifying a Default Value

Attributes allow you to specify a default value by using it as demonstrated in Figure 4.27.

```
<?xml version='1.0' ?>
<Schema xmlns="<xsd:schema
xmlns:xsd="http://www.w3.org/2000/10/XMLSchema" >
   <xsd:element name="Customer" type="xsd:string"/>
     <ElementType name="customer">
     <AttributeType name="custID" />
     <AttributeType name="custName" />
     <AttributeType name="city" />
     <AttributeType name="state" default="CA"/>
            <attribute type ="custID" />
            <attribute name="custName" />
            <attribute name= "city" />
            <attribute name="state" />
```

```
    </Element>
</Schema>
```

Figure 4.27   DefaultValue.xsd

Let's consider a document instance containing a `<customer>`
element and an absent `state` attribute. Automatically, the validating
parser applies the default value, which in this case is `CA`. To clarify
this even further, examine the following document fragment:

```
<Customer custID="PO132"custName="SHHeim"  city="GlenEllyn"
state="IL"/>
<Customer custID="PD11"  custName="PDJames" city="Redwood City"
state="" />
```

Customer "`PO132`" specifies state `Illinois`; therefore, the
default value is ignored. However, customer "`PD11`" does not list a
state, so the parser will fill in the default, which is declared as `CA`. If
we use the `required="yes"` attribute, it ensures that the default
value will be provided. The `<customer>` element is required to
contain a `<state>` attribute, which declares `CA` as the default.

The next example demonstrates syntax for defining and referencing attributes:

```
<AttributeType name="invoiceNum" dt:type="int"
required="yes" />
<AttributeType name="invoiceDate" dt:type="date"
required="yes" />
```

Reference them as follows:

```
<elementType name="invoice" content="eltOnly"
order="many" model="closed" />
    <attribute Type ="invoiceNum" />
    <attribute Type ="invoiceDate" />
    ...
    </elementType>
```

This example specifies elements only, and the content model is
`closed`. Once an attribute is defined, we are free to reference it at
will.

Attribute Groups

We define an attribute group as an association between an attribute group name and a set of attributes. The example in Figure 4.28 demonstrates this concept.

```
<xs:attributeGroup name="myAttributeGroup">
      <xs:attribute name="Author" type="xs:string"/>
      <xs:attribute name="Publisher" type="xs:string"/>
      <xs:attribute name="Title" type="xs:string"/>
      <xs:attribute name="Price" type="xs:decimal"/>
</xs:attributeGroup>
```

Figure 4.28   Attribute group

Now you can simply reference the attribute group within the schema, as follows:

```
  <xs::attributeGroup ref="myAttributeGroup"
  </xs:complexType>
</xs:element>
```

You can also add other elements to the group without breaking the content model.

Substitution Groups

Substitution groups allow you to substitute one group of elements for another. This is especially useful if you are working with a prede-fined schema. Using this method, you could redefine a content model or substitute a content model that's satisfactory for development pur-poses. We include a substitution group that we can use as a replace-ment for the final version. The genericType represents the substitution group. See the following example in Figure 4.29.

```
<xs:element name="book" type="bookType"
    SubstitutionGroup="genericType"/>
    <xs:element name="periodical" type="periodicalType"
    substitutionGroup="genericType"/>
    <xs:complexType name="genericType">
    <xs:sequence>
    <xs:element ref="title"/>
```

```
        <xs:element ref="author"/>
        <xs:element ref="description"/>
        </xs:sequence>
        </xs:complexType>
```

Figure 4.29   A GenericType Model

Model Group Definitions

This group model allows the document author to define and reuse
components. Let's examine the example in Figure 4.30.

```
<?xml version="1.0" encoding="UTF-8"?>
<xs:schema xmlns:xs="http://www.w3.org/2001/XMLSchema"
elementFormDefault="qualified" attributeFormDefault=
"unqualified">
    <xs:annotation>
        <xs:documentation>.This schema demonstrates how we cre-
ate an attribute group</xs:documentation>
    </xs:annotation>
   xs:element name="OrderData" minOccurs="0"
maxOccurs="unbounded">
   <xs:complexType>
     <xs:sequence>
       <xs:element name="ProductName" type="xs:string"/>
       <xs:element name="quantity">
       <xs:simpleType>
          <xs:restriction base="xs:positiveInteger"
          xsi:type="decimal">
             <xs:maxExclusive value="250"/>
          </xs:restriction>
       </xs:simpleType>
       </xs:element>
       <xs:element name="price" type="xs:decimal"/>
       <xs:element name="shippingDate" type="xs:date"/>
     </xs:sequence>
    <!-- Here is where the attribute group would be substituted
         for individual element declarations -->
    <xs:attributeGroup ref="ProductShippingInfo"/>
   </xs:complexType>
```

```
      </xs:element>
      <xs:attributeGroup name="ProductShippingInfo">
        <xs:attribute name="productNum" type="SKU"
        use="required"/>
        <xs:attribute name="ShippingMethod">
          <xs:simpleType>
             <xs:restriction base="xs:string">
                <xs:enumeration value="USPS"/>
                <xs:enumeration value="UPS"/>
                <xs:enumeration value="FedEx"/>
                <xs:enumeration value="AirborneExpress"/>
             </xs:restriction>
          </xs:simpleType>
        </xs:attribute>
      </xs:attributeGroup>
</xs:schema>
```

Reference `ProductShippingInfo` in the following manner:

```
  <xsd:element name="Invoice">
     <xsd:complexType>
     <xsd:complexContent>
     <xsd:extension base="xsd:type">
<!-- now you reference the attribute group with your schema-->
     <xsd:attributeGroup ref="ProductShippingInfo">
     </xsd:extension>
     </xsd:complexContent>
     <xsd:complexType>
</xsd:element>
</:xsd schema>
```

Figure 4.30   AttributeGroup.xsd

Because we are extending the base type indicated above, as in `<xsd:extension base="xsd:type">`, we are defining the attribute group as a user-defined type. Note that attribute groups may be compared to DTD parameter entities because the group is expanded when referenced by providing access to individual attributes residing within the group. Additionally, you must declare attributes and attribute groups after declaring elements.

4.11 Identity Constraints

Schemas offer you a flexible mechanism for defining identity constraints. Three methods exist:

- `Key` and `KeyRef`
- `Unique` element
- `ID` data type

The `Key` and `Keyref` elements allow you to define relationships between elements. They are similar to `ID` and `IDREF`; however, whereas an `ID` must be unique for the entire document, a `Key` can be applied to a specified element set. You must use XPath expressions to identify an element set. (This is the main topic for Chapter 6, "Applying Xpath.")

You can use the unique element to specify any attribute or element value within scope. This attribute uses a selector or field element. The selector element defines the element for the unique constraint. The field element identifies the attribute or element field.

The third method uses the `ID/IDREF` data type. The `ID` must be unique to the entire document.

XML schemas allow us to generate business reports for many different purposes, including quarterly reports, annual reports, and so on. For example, let's examine a quarterly sales report and use the identity constraints (see Figures 4.31 and 4.32).

```xml
<?xml version="1.0" encoding="UTF-8"?>
<QuarterlySalesReport Quarter="P3M" PeriodEnding="2002-12-31"
xmlns:xsi="http://www.w3.org/2001/XMLSchema-instance"
xsi:noNamespaceSchemaLocation="C:\XML\QuarterlySalesReport.xsd"
>
    <CountryArea>
      <zip Code="11731">
        <ISBN num="0-123-1235" sold="200"/>
        <ISBN num="0-453-6804" sold="1001"/>
        <ISBN num="0-684-4568" sold="1456"/>
        <ISBN num="0-459-1234" sold="1795"/>
      </zip>
      <zip Code="11932">
```

```
        <ISBN num="0-123-1234" sold="1795"/>
      </zip>
  </CountryArea>
  <ISBNnum>
    <ISBN num="0-123-1235">XML Primer</ISBN>
    <ISBN num="0-453-6804">DTDs</ISBN>
    <ISBN num="0-684-4568">XSLT</ISBN>
    <ISBN num="0-459-1234">XPath</ISBN>
  </ISBNnum>
</QuarterlySalesReport>
```

Figure 4.31   Quarterly sales report v1

```
<?xml version="1.0" encoding="UTF-8"?>
<xs:schema xmlns:xs="http://www.w3.org/2001/XMLSchema"
           xmlns:r="http://www.dpsoftware.com/Report"
           xmlns:xipo="http:www.dpsoftware.com/FIPO"
elementFormDefault="qualified">
<!-- import namespace for SKU -->
<import namespace="http://www.dpsoftware.com/Schemas/FIPO"/>
   <xs:element name="QuarterlySalesReport">
   <xs:complexType>
   <xs:sequence>
   <xs:element name="CountryArea" type="a:CountryAreaType">
   <xs:keyref name="NorthEast" refer="a:ISBNnumKey">
   <xs:selector XPath="a:zip/a:num"/>
   <xs:field XPath="@num"/>
   </xs:keyref>
   </xs:element>
   <xs:element name="ISBNnum" type="a:ISBNnumType"/>
   </xs:sequence>
   <xs:attribute name="Period" type="duration"/>
   <xs:attribute name="PeriodEnding" type="date"/>
   </xs:complexType>

   <xs:unique name="MidAtlantic">
   <xs:selector XPath="a:ISBNnum/a:ISBN"/>
   <xs:field XPath="@num"/> //Note: @num is an attribute
   </xs:unique>
```

```
      <xs:key name="ISBNnumKey">
      <xs:selector XPath="a:ISBNnum/a:ISBN"/>
      <xs:field XPath="@num"/>
      </xs:key>
</xs:element>

<xs:complexType name="CountryAreaType">
   <xs:sequence>
   <xs:element name="zip" maxOccurs="unbounded">
   <xs:complexType>
   <xs:sequence>
   <xs:element name="ISBN" maxOccurs="unbounded">
   <xs:complexType>
   <xs:complexContent>
   <xs:restriction base="anyType">
   <xs:attribute name="num" type="xipo:SKU"/>
   <xs:attribute name="sold" type="positiveInteger"/>
   </xs:restriction>
   </xs:complexContent>
   </xs:complexType>
   </xs:element>
   </xs:sequence>
   <xs:attribute name="Code" type="positiveInteger"/>
   </xs:complexType>
   </xs:element>
   </xs:sequence>
   </xs:complexType>

<xs:complexType name="ISBNnumType">
   <xs:sequence>
   <xs:element name="ISBN" maxOccurs="unbounded">
   <xs:complexType>
   <xs:simpleContent>
   <xs:extension base="string">
   <xs:attribute name="number" type="fipo:SKU"/>
   </xs:extension>
   </xs:simpleContent>
```

```
  </xs:complexType>
  </xs:element>
  </xs:sequence>
  </xs:complexType>
</xs:schema>
```

Figure 4.32   QuarterlySalesReport.xsd v2

The root element `QuarterlySalesReport` indicates the nature of the report, followed by the attributes `Period` and `PeriodEnding`. In the Schema specification, "Schemas, Part Two, DataTypes," note the definitions for `period` and `duration`, section 2.4.2.15. `Quarter` denotes a period of recurring time. The official definition states that "`period` is the frequency of recurrence for values for the data type recurring duration." Additionally, the value of `period` must be `time duration`. The instance document reflects this concept and declares the period ending as `2002-12-31`.

Notice how `CountryArea` includes more than one zip code. For example, `11731` denotes a Long Island zip code, whereas `11932`, a fictitious zip code, would indicate another area, perhaps the Philadelphia area. Therefore, using an XPath expression, we can search by zip code. Additionally, searching by element `ISBN`, we could locate a specific book number to procure the number of books sold. We import the namespace where `SKU` is defined: "`http://www.dpsoftware.com/Schemas/FIPO`". This pertains to the `partnum` for a book's CD containing solutions for projects and exercises.

We define the root element `QuarterlySalesReport` as both a global element and `complexType`. Next we import the namespace where `SKU` is defined in another schema. We use the `import` mechanism in our schema because it allows us to bring components from other targeted namespaces into our central schema. This schema does not share or define a targeted space, so it is not possible to use the `include` mechanism we previously used in earlier examples. You will recall that the `include` mechanism can only bring in definitions and declarations from a schema whose target namespace is identical to the including namespace. That is not the case here. To identify the `SKU` part number defined in the `ForeignSpecifications.xsd` schema, we establish a unique prefix, `fipo`, and associate it with the imported namespace, thereby identifying its unique namespace.

Uniqueness

Another important concept we must discuss is specifying uniqueness. We use the `unique` element to select a set of elements/attributes. We identify the element or attribute field relative to each chosen element unique within scope of the selected elements. Here we use a `selector` element's XPath expression, selecting all zip elements in the source document such as `CountryArea/zip`. Here is the snippet of code that does that:

```
<xs:element name="CountryArea" type="a:CountryAreaType">
     <xs:keyref name="NorthEast" refer="a:ISBNnumKey">
     <xs:selector XPath="a:zip/a:num"/>
     <xs:field XPath="@num"/>
     </xs:keyref>
</xs:element>
```

Notice how we define the `prefix a:CountryAreaType`. This allows us to reference a country region (`NorthEast`) by providing a key to establish its uniqueness, much the same as when we define a primary key or ID in XML parlance.

We can also define an XPath expression to access the ISBN num's value by writing the following code:

```
<xs:field XPath="@num"/>
```

XML schemas provide new mechanisms for ensuring uniqueness through the `Key` and `Keyref` mechanisms. Whereas the validity constraint for attribute `ID` applies to a single ID per element type, element `Key` can be applied to indicate foreign key relationships in a schema. You begin this process by first defining key fields using the `<key>`element. Then use the `selector` element to specify nodes for which this definition applies, just as we did in our example. Finally, utilize the key name to define references to it by applying the `Keyref` element. You can apply them to any element or attribute content, regardless of their data type.

We can also select unique combinations of fields. For example, if we want the combined values of `zip code` and `ISBN num` to be unique, we could do the following: {211950-123-1235}, {117310-123-1235}, and so on. For a detailed discussion on

XPath expressions, see Chapter 6, where we examine all aspects of XPath's powerful querying technology.

4.12 Practical Business Application Suggestions

We have focused on several important concepts that schemas offer us:

- Data types represent the core technology for schemas.

  We recommend commencing your study of schemas by learning to apply the 44 built-in data types to your business model. They are comprehensive in scope, offering you the ability to meet all challenges that your business model requires.

- SimpleType content models provide complete control of your model through derivation.

- Facets allow you to restrict the range of your data types.

- ComplexType content models allow you to build on existing data types through extension.

- Namespaces allow you to import and include other schemas containing industry-specific schemas as well as define your own namespaces.

Begin your application design with an analysis of data types needed to implement your application. Schemas provide a comprehensive solution to all of your business requirements. Then consider which content model fits your needs. The Russian Doll design may satisfy your requirements by allowing your schema to mirror the document instance. Just keep in mind that local elements are not reusable. The Salami Slice model definitely enhances your ability to design reusable components. This is true when you want your global elements visible to external schemas. An alternative to this model is the Venetian Blind model. It is flexible and requires no modification if you decide to either expose or hide your namespaces.

Identity constraints are useful. Whereas ID/IDREFS are applicable to an element throughout the entire document, utilizing the `Key`/`Keyref` attributes allows you to apply uniqueness to your elements on an individual basis. This provides much more flexibility. You are not constrained to applying these attributes to simple types only. `Keys`/`Keyrefs` apply to any data type.

Summary

- An XML schema is a language for describing a class of objects.
- Schemas are created with XML metalanguage, making them much easier to understand.
- Elements, attributes, tags, entities, and content models are objects, the building blocks for constructing an XML schema.
- Schema construction is based on object-oriented programming concepts.
- Schema modular design allows for easy application maintenance.
- Schemas encourage reuse of code.
- Schemas view XML document instances as a collection of individual data types.
- Schema data types consist of three components: value space, lexical space, and facets.
- Schemas focus on data types.
- Schemas provide definitions for both simple and complex data types.
- Simple types define attributes and elements containing only text and do not contain other attributes.
- complexTypes signify the end of global scope and the beginning of local scope.
- Declaring an element as a named type makes it reusable.
- A `type` declaration describes the relationship between the element name and its behavior in the document instance.
- Facets define the value space and properties for a specified data type.
- Fundamental facets define a data type.
- Nonfundamental facets impose restrictions on a data type.
- Restriction applies restraining facets to restrict the value space or lexical space for a base data type.
- The list method uses a predetermined `itemType` sequence of attributes to derive a new type.
- Compositors consist of three types: sequential, choice, and ALL.

- Schemas introduce the concept of namespaces to delineate the differences between elements sharing the same name but contain different meanings.
- Schemas provide support for uniquely identifying specific data via namespace targeting.
- Schemas contain open and closed content models.
- Schemas offer three design models: Russian Doll, Salami Slice, and Venetian Blind.
- Schemas allow global and local scoping.
- Open content models have several constraints:
  - Do not add or remove content or you will destroy the content model after it has been defined.
  - Undeclared elements are permissible, provided they are defined in different namespaces.
- Two categories exist for schema data types:
  - Complex types
  - Simple types
- Elements can have child elements embedded within them.
- Complex type elements bearing similar properties can share the same content model.
- Schemas support four kinds of typeComplex elements:
  - Element-only elements, containing other elements and attributes but allowing no text
  - Mixed content elements, containing a combination of elements, attributes, and possibly text
  - Empty elements, containing attributes only but never elements or text
  - Text-only elements, containing only text
- Three options for a schema exist: choice, unordered group, or reference another group declared elsewhere.
- Defining a simple type is similar to defining a complex type.
- Union types allow an element or attribute to exist as one or more instances of a specified type derived from the union of a multiple value list and atomic types.

- An attribute group is an association between an attribute group name and a set of attributes.
- Model group definitions allow you to define and reuse components.
- Schemas offer a flexible mechanism for defining identity constraints.

Self-Review Exercises

State whether the following statements are true or false. If false, provide an explanation.

1. An application can use a schema to validate document structure but not its content.

2. Schemas allow XML authors to create user-defined types.

3. Schema construction is built on object-oriented programming principles.

4. Schemas encourage reuse of code. (Provide an explanation whether this is true or false.)

5. Schemas support encapsulation.

6. Schemas do not allow global and local scoping.

7. Elements can have nested child elements but not attributes.

8. Elements containing subelements or attributes are simple types.

Answer the following statements:

1. Explain: You are allowed to redefine a group of elements.

2. You can define an element as abstract. What procedure must you follow to accomplish this?

3. Two categories exist for schema data types. What are they?

4. Open content models impose several constraints. Explain what they are.

5. Provide explanations and examples for each of the following content models:

   a. Element only

   b. Mixed content

   c. Empty elements

   d. Text only

6. Three options exist for a schema. Describe what they are and their use in a schema.

7. An integer is a simple type. Describe the differences between simple and complex data types.

8. Namespace declarations include two default types. Provide examples of each.

9. Demonstrate how a variable is declared globally.

10. Provide a description for a list type and show how it applies to a document.

11. How do you declare an anonymous type? Provide an example of one and discuss its characteristics.

12. How do you build an attribute group?

13. How do you reference an attribute group?

14. What is the difference between the import mechanism and the include mechanism?

15. How do you use the attribute `form`?

16. Provide an example demonstrating the difference between attribute ID and key.

Projects

1. Write a schema for the following daily planner :

```
<?xml version="1.0" encoding="UTF-8"?>
  <DailyPlanner>
    <Sunday>
```

```
        <am>Leisure Day</am>
        <pm>1:00 Jets Game</pm>
    </Sunday>
    <Monday>
        <am>10:00 meeting with Steve
            11:00 Faculty Meeting
            12:00 Lunch
        </am>
        <pm>
            1:00 CSC 504
            3:00 Meeting with Susan
            6:30 CSC 602
            8:40 CSC 600
        </pm>
    </Monday>
    <Tuesday>
        <am>9:00 Meeting with Editor 805 8th Avenue</am>
        <pm>2:00 Meeting with Microsoft</pm>
    </Tuesday>
    <Wednesday>
        <am>9:30 Conference at Microsoft</am>
            12:00 Luncheon Meeting with Bill
    </Wednesday>
    <Thursday>
        <am>9:00 11:30 Conference call with editors</am>
        <pm>1:30 Meeting with Time Warner</pm>
    </Thursday>
    <Friday>
        <am>Keep free for writing</am>
        <pm>1:00 Luncheon meeting at ICM</pm>
    </Friday>
    <Saturday>
        <am>Free</am>
        <pm>Free</pm>
    </Saturday>
</DailyPlanner>
```

2. Write a schema for the Booking Manager XML source document:

```
<?xml version="1.0" encoding="UTF-8"?>
  <bookingmanager>
     <event>Business Meeting</event>
       <date>
          <year>2003</year>
          <month>October</month>

          <day>18</day>
       </date>
    <rooms>
       <equipment>projector</equipment>
       <sound>Bose</sound>
       <musicalInstrument>piano</musicalInstrument>
       <bar>yes</bar>
    </rooms>
    <association>
       <name>XML University</name>
       <address>1201 Hempstead Turnpike</address>
       <city>Hempstead</city>
       <state>NY</state>
       <zip>11549</zip>
     </association>
     <purpose>Discuss the Economy</purpose>
     <speaker>J Politician</speaker>
    </bookingmanager>
```

3. Convert the following DTD to a schema for the source document listed here:

```
<!DOCTYPE FamilyTree [
<!ELEMENT FamilyTree (Member*)>
<!ELEMENT Member (#PCDATA)>
<!ATTLIST Member
   MNumber ID #REQUIRED
   Parents IDREFS #IMPLIED
>
]>
<FamilyTree>
<Member MNumber="p1">   Christine</Member>
<Member MNumber="p2">   Stanley</Member>
```

```
<Member MNumber="c1">    Parents='p1'
'p2'>Maria</Member>
<Member MNumber="c2">    Parents='p1'
'p2'>Richard</Member>
<Member MNumber="c3">    Parents='p1'
'p2'>James</Member>
</FamilyTree>
```

4. Write a schema for a three-tiered document. Create your own source document.

5. Write a schema for the following table of contents:

```
<?xml version="1.0" encoding="UTF-8"?>
<TableOfContents>
    <PhaseOne>A Recursive Approach to XML Programming</PhaseOne>
    <ChapterOne>XML's Path to the Internet</ChapterOne>
    <subtitle>Two Design Strategies</subtitle>
    <subheading>
        <subelement>Top Down Strategy</subelement>
        <subelement>Recursive Programming Strategy</subelement>
    </subheading>
    <subheading>
        <subelement>Defining Parsed Character Data</subelement>
    </subheading>
    <subtitle>Three Content Models</subtitle>
    <subheading>
        <subelement>Element Content Model</subelement>
        <subelement>Mixed Content Model</subelement>
        <subelement>Empty Content Model</subelement>
    </subheading>
    <subheading>
        <subelement>XML Data Types</subelement>
        <subelement>XML Document Structure</subelement>

        <subelement>Modeling Data and Text</subelement>
        <subelement>Designing Modular Data</subelement>
```

```
        <subelement>Mapping XML to a Relational
        Database</subelement>
        <subelement>Mapping from A Repository to
        XML</subelement>
    </subheading>
    <ChapterTwo>Selecting A Parser</ChapterTwo>
    <ChapterThree>Introducing Schemas</ChapterThree>
    <subheading>
        <subelements>Schemas, a Better DTD</subelements>
        <subelements>Introducing Namespaces</subelements>
    </subheading>
    <subheading>
        <subelements>Schemas, a Better DTD</subelements>
    </subheading>
    <subtitle>Four Schema Content Models</subtitle>


    <subheading>
        <subelement>Open Content Model</subelement>
        <subelement>Closed Content Model</subelement>
        <subelement>Complex Content Model</subelement>
        <subelement>Simple Content Model</subelement>


    </subheading>
</TableOfContents>
```

6. Write a schema for the following invoice source document:

```
INVOICE
SUNNYVALE INC.
380 WEST OLD COUNTRY RD.
HICKSVILLE, NY.11801
Invoice No.: L0105318
Invoice Date: 05/30/02        SALES: 1-516-555-8900
Order No.: 16698              SERVICE: 1-516-555-8900
Cust  P/O # PD11:             FAX:   1-516-555-8966


SOLD TO: (PD 11)              SHIPTO:
Joseph Fingers                Joseph Fingers
PO Box 355                    172 Lawn Lane
East Meadow NY. 11542         Old Brookville, NY. 11542


TEL: 516-555-5600              TERMS: CASH ONLY
SALES PERSON    DATE SHIPPED   *SHIP VIA*   USPS UPS
FEDEX GROUND    PAYMENT        UPS GROUND        CHECK
Q'ty   1
Item No.   Description                 Unit Price   Total
1          DL-DSH5 D-LINK 5-PORT 10/100 HUB/SWITCH  61.00 61.00
                              SUB-TOTAL:US$        61.00
                              TAX:US$               5.95
                              UPS: US$
                              *TOTAL US$           65.95
```

7. Demonstrate how you declare elements as local, using the Russian Doll format.

8. Write a schema example demonstrating how you derive by restriction. Use an `xsd:integer` type as the base type.

9. Write a schema example demonstrating how you derive by extension.

10. Write a schema example demonstrating how to use derivation and how to apply facets for an ISBN type.

PART 2

TRANSFORMATION

5 XSLT

5.1 Transform Your Documents with XSLT

XSLT is an essential member of the XML family, providing the mechanism for transforming and manipulating XML data. XSLT uses a stylesheet to serve as a container for modular components called templates. A *template* is similar to a block of code in Java or C++ where it contains processing instructions and defines local scope. Consider the following C++ example:

```
int maximum( int, int, int);
int main()
{
    int a, b, c;
    cout << "Enter three integers ";
    cin >> a >> b >> c;
    cout << "Maximum is: " <<maximum( a, b, c ) << endl;
    return 0;
}
int maximum( int x, int y, int z )
{
   int max = 0;
       . .  . . .
}
```

This C++ fragment represents two code modules. Now let's view an XSLT template:

```
<xsl:stylesheet version='1.0'
xmlns:xsl="http://www.w3.org/1999/XSL/Transform">
<xsl:template match="book">
    <tr>
    <td><xsl:number/></td>
    <xsl:apply-templates/>
    </tr>
</xsl:template>
```

This stylesheet consists of both a declaration that maps prefix xsl to the default namespace for stylesheets, and a template that includes instructions for processing book and its child elements. The following example is the source document:

```
<books>
    <book>
        <author></author>
        <title></title>
        <publisher></publisher>
    </book>
</books>
```

An XSLT stylesheet usually contains several templates, each carrying instructions for how to process each specific node or node set.

XSLT views the document instance as a hierarchical tree containing a root, branches, and leaves. Similar to the DOM, XSLT views elements and attributes as nodes or node sets. They contain the content we want to access and copy to a result tree.

Here is how an XSLT processor examines and manipulates a source document:

- **Examination.** The processor examines two documents:
  - The input XML source document:
    ```
    <?xml-stylesheet
    xmlns:xsl="http://www.w3.org/1999.XSL/Transform">
        <Document>
            <subject>
                <element>content1</element>
    ```

```
        <element>content2</element>
        </subject>
    </Document>
```

- XSLT stylesheet for the source document:

```
?xml version="1.0" encoding="UTF-8"?>
<xsl:stylesheet version="1.0"
xmlns:xsl="http://www.w3.org/1999/XSL/Transform">
  <xsl:output method="html"/>
    <xsl:template match="element">
        <p>
            <xsl:apply-templates/>
        </p>
    </xsl:template>
</xsl:stylesheet>
```

The output is as follows:

```
<p>content1</p>
<p>content2</p>
```

- **Parse and instantiate nodes.** Instructions contained within a stylesheet template process a specified node based on several factors: the current context node, context size, namespaces currently in scope, core library functions, and variable bindings for other languages such as Java and C++. (We will explain these in detail later in this chapter.)
- **Create the result tree.** The processor creates a structured XML output tree containing literal element results, HTML tags, and content.
- **Render the document.** This is done in a browser or other format.

Three separate components exist as part of the transformation process:

1. The document instance represents a hierarchical tree serving as the source document (see Figure 5.1).

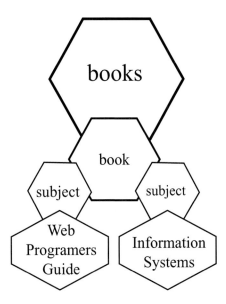

Figure 5.1   Example1.xml

Figure 5.2 is the XML markup version for the hierarchical tree just displayed.

```
<?xml version="1.0" encoding="UTF-8"?>
<books>
        <book>
          <subject topic="the Web Programmers
          Guide">XML</subject>
          <subject>Information Systems</subject>
        </book>
  </books>
```

Figure 5.2   Example1.xml

2. The stylesheet (see Figure 5.3) contains instructions for how to apply the appropriate template to the document instance, instantiate an instance of the node being processed, and copy the information to a result tree.

```
<?xml version="1.0" encoding="UTF-8"?>
<xsl:stylesheet version="1.0"
xmlns:xsl="http://www.w3.org/1999/XSL/Transform">
   <xsl:output method="html"/>
        <xsl:template match="subject">
      <p>
         <xsl:apply-templates/>
      </p>
        </xsl:template>
   </xsl:stylesheet>
```

Figure 5.3   Example1.xsl

3. The result tree is the third component. The XML output is as follows:

```
<p>XML</p>
<p>Information Systems</p>
```

The result tree demonstrates how the processor encloses XML content within HTML tags called literal result elements. This constitutes the result tree from which the processor generates output to the browser. Observe the following results:

```
XML
Information Systems
```

Notice the structure of the stylesheet in Figure 5.2. The `<xsl:template match='subject'>` contains instructions to search the document instance for node `<subject>`. Once it locates this node, the template contains instructions to insert HTML literal tag p into the result tree. Next, XSLT outputs the content within `<subject>` enclosed by opening and closing tags. Instruction template `<xsl:apply-templates/>` causes the processor to output all children of this node: XML and Information Systems. One final note concerning the XML output: It is not well formed because XSLT processors do not parse output.

Now that you have a 20,000-foot overview of XSLT, we recommend that you study this chapter and the next in sequence. In this chapter, we concentrate on XSLT templates; in Chapter 6, "Applying XPath," we examine XPath. Templates contain XPath expressions and functions used to process the nodes. It is impossible to discuss XSLT without applying XPath functionality to the process of parsing and instantiating nodes. We will first examine XSLT in depth with limited reference to XPath until Chapter 6, where we expand our exploration of XSLT templates as we study XPath. You will learn how the two technologies are inseparable.

We begin our study of XSLT with a discussion on stylesheet structure. XSLT provides numerous top-level elements and instruction templates. We will show you how to integrate them and will explain how they apply to any given situation. Later, we will include a discussion on *why* we select a particular instruction template and where to apply it.

5.2   Presenting Your Document in HTML

Transformation requires an XSLT processor for processing XML documents. Several choices are available:

- XML Spy Suite version 5.4 from Altova, Inc.
- Saxon, an open-source XSLT processor developed by Michael Kay and available for free downloading
- XT, a processor developed by James Clark (also free and available for downloading)
- Tibco's Extensibility Turbo 2.2
- Internet Explorer version 5.5 and above with a built-in stylesheet, available from Microsoft
- A Perl module called XML::XSLT, which provides XSLT processing
- Xalan from Apache, which is intended for a Java application

We used XML Spy to prepare all examples in this book. It offers a full range of tools for fulfilling any task you need. It supports the W3C Recommendation specifications for XML, DTDs, schemas,

XSLT, XPath, XHTML and XSL:FO transformation. The IDE is intuitive and user friendly. You can also prepare your stylesheets using Notepad in combination with Internet Explorer.

5.3 XSLT Stylesheet Structure

An XSLT stylesheet is an XML document using an XSLT engine to perform a transformation on other XML documents. The stylesheet conforms to XML well-formed rules and utilizes XSLT-specific namespace declarations. It may contain other stylesheets by importing or including them. XSLT never alters the source document but generates output according to specified template rules. It sorts, manipulates, and reorganizes nodes but never touches the original data.

A stylesheet contains two item categories:

- Top-level elements
- Instruction templates

Top-Level Elements

Top-level elements are children of the document element and perform a specific task. The first three elements we include are as follows:

- `<xsl:include>` allows a style sheet to reference templates and instructions from external sources. It must be the immediate child of the stylesheet.
- `<xsl:output>` provides three methods: `xml`, `html`, `text`.
- `<xsl:strip-space>` removes all whitespace for nodes containing only whitespace before further processing.

Let's assume we want to write a module that includes a sylesheet defined elsewhere. Figure 5.4 is the input XML document for this example.

```
<?xml version="1.0" encoding="UTF-8"?>
<Meeting>
   <Agenda>Book Publishing</Agenda>
   <Authors>Dwight Peltzer</Authors>
   <Place>Pell Hall</Place>
   <Room>125</Room>
   <publisher/>
   <abstract>XML Primer</abstract>
</Meeting>
```

Figure 5.4   XSLT's include Element

Notice the `publisher` tag. We define it as a placeholder by declaring an empty element. Figure 5.5 shows the main stylesheet.

```
<xsl:stylesheet version="1.0"
xmlns:xsl="http://www.w3.org/1999/XSL/Transform">
<xsl:include href="publisher.xsl"/>
<xsl:output method="xml" version="1.0" encoding="UTF-8"
indent="yes"/>
<xsl:strip-space elements="*"/>
```

Figure 5.5   Main Stylesheet.xsl

We use `<xsl:include>` and the attribute `href` to reference the external stylesheet module. The `<xsl:strip-space>` element removes whitespace from nodes containing only whitespace.

```
<xsl:template match="publisher">
   <publisher><xsl:call-template name="publisher"/></publisher>
</xsl:template>
```

The preceding block of code demonstrates how we set the `<publisher>` element to a string identifying the publishing company that owns the book. Note how we place an opening tag for publisher before calling the publisher template. This allows us to avoid outputting a new line before publisher's text. Let's continue to the next block:

```
<xsl:template match="*">
<xsl:copy>
<xsl:copy-of select="@*"/>
<xsl:apply-templates/>
</xsl:copy>
</xsl:template>
</xsl:stylesheet>
```

`template match="*"` causes the processor to match any element. The next two instructions, `<xsl:copy>` and `<xsl:copy-of>`, need clarification. `<xsl:copy>` performs a shallow copy, meaning only `publisher` is copied to the result tree, whereas `<copy-of>` executes a deep copy by copying `publisher`'s child elements to the result tree. We have used attribute symbol (@) to provide the ability to select attributes as they appear in the source document. The asterisk following the attribute sign causes the processor to output all child attributes. The following generated XML output matches the input source document:

```
<Meeting>
    <Agenda>Book Publishing</Agenda>
    <Authors>Dwight Peltzer</Authors>
    <Place>Pell Hall</Place>
    <Room>125</Room>
    <publisher>Pearson Publishing 2002 </publisher>
    <abstract>XML Primer</abstract>
</Meeting>
```

The stylesheet is shown in Figure 5.6.

```
<xsl:stylesheet
        xmlns:xsl="http://www.w3.org/1999/XSL/Transform"
        version="1.0">
<xsl:variable name="editor">Pearson Publishing</xsl:variable>
<xsl:template name="publisher">2002 <xsl:value-of
select="$editor"/>   </xsl:template>
</xsl:stylesheet>
```

Figure 5.6 XML stylesheet

The `<value-of> select` template represents a precise method of pulling elements from the source document. In contrast, `apply-templates` offers less control. When you apply this template, you are leaving element choice in the hands of the processor to select whatever is contained within the specified block of code. You needn't do this. If you want to select a particular node, `value-of select` is an excellent choice. Another less precise method is `apply-templates select="expression"/>`.

Figure 5.7 includes the fourth top-level element, `<xsl:variable>`. We declare variable `$editor` and supply the text for it. `variable` defines a specific value that's usable in other elements in a stylesheet. We reference the variable by placing a dollar ($) sign before its name. Figure 5.7 demonstrates how to declare a variable. (Note: The `<xsl:variable>` also appears in Figure 5.6.)

```
<xsl:variable name="editor">Pearson Publishing</xsl:variable>
```

Figure 5.7   Publisher.xsl

The fifth top-level element we discuss is `<xsl:import>`. We could replace `include` with `import` to bring an external module into the main stylesheet. However, the imported stylesheet has lower precedence than definitions specified in the main stylesheet. In the event of conflicting definitions, the calling stylesheet definition always takes precedence over the imported definition(s). Suppose we want to reuse the publisher stylesheet in another context and with a different editor's name. We could keep the same stylesheet and substitute `import` for `include` as follows:

```
<xsl:stylesheet version="1.0"
xmlns:xsl="http://www.w3.org/1999/XSL/Transform">
<xsl:import href="publisher.xsl"/>
<xsl:output method="xml" version="1.0" encoding="UTF-8"
indent="yes"/>
```

The sixth top-level element we discuss is `<xsl:key>`. This associates a key with a specified node declared in an XML document instance. Each key paired with a node requires defining a value with the `key()` function. Key uses three required attributes, as shown here:

PART 2 TRANSFORMATION

```
<xsl:key>
        name=QName
        match=pattern
        use=expression
```

The key element employs the qualified `name` attribute to create the key name, `match` identifies a specific node, and the `use` attribute defines information to be utilized to apply a value to the key.

```
<xsl:key name="person-identification" match="person"
use="@req"/>
```

Another example for key would apply to a SKU code:

```
<xsl:key name="product-code" match="product" use="@code"/>
```

The key name is `product-code`; the template must match the product element with a given product code. For example, to find the product Dlink–DSH5, we could do the following:

```
<xsl:apply-templates select="key('product-code',
'Dlink-DSH5')"/>
```

`apply-templates` generates output of all children elements in the current document containing code `Dlink-DSH5`. An alternate output method would be `value-of select ="."`.

The seventh top-level element, `<xsl:decimal-format>`, allows you to control the format for decimal numbers by controlling the pattern. The stylesheet in Figure 5.8 displays several decimal formats. This element does not affect the behavior of the `xsl:number` and `xsl:value-of` elements when they are used to format a number for display in the output.

```
<?xml version="1.0" encoding="UTF-8"?>
<xsl:stylesheet version="1.0"
xmlns:xsl="http://www.w3.org/1999/XSL/Transform" version="1.0">
<xsl:decimal-format name="number" digit="D"/>
<xsl:template match="/">
<html>
<body>
```

```
<xsl:value-of select='format-number(123456789,"#.000000000")'/>
<br/>
<xsl:value-of select='format-number(123456789,"#########")'/>
<br/>
<xsl:value-of select='format-number(123456789,"#.0")'/>
<br/>
<xsl:value-of select='format-number(0.123456789,"##%")'/>
<br/>
<xsl:value-of select='format-
number(123456789,"D.0","number")'/>
<br/>
<xsl:value-of select='format-
number(123456789,"$DDD,DDD,DDD.DD","number")'/>
</body>
</html>
</xsl:template>
</xsl:stylesheet>
```

Figure 5.8   Format decimal

The output is as follows:

```
123456789.000000000
123456789
123456789.0
12%
123456789.0
$123,456,789
```

The eighth top-level element, `<xsl:namespace-alias>`, allows you to declare a specified namespace URI as a replacement for another. This facilitates using more than one namespace in a document. This can only be a child of `<xsl:stylesheet>`. The next stylesheet (see Figure 5.9) demonstrates the following concepts.

The `stylesheet-prefix` attribute represents the namespace (prefix) you want to modify. The `result` prefix is the new namespace prefix (in our case, dps). We use the top-level element `param` to declare name `var` and `blank`. Notice how the namespace alias is used in the last five lines, such as `<dps:value-of select="{$var}">` dps replaces `xsl`.

```
<xsl:stylesheet xmlns:xsl="http://www.w3.org/1999/XSL/Transform" version="1.0"
xmlns:dps="dps.xsl">
<xsl:param name="var">name</xsl:param>
<xsl:param name="blank"></xsl:param>
<xsl:namespace-alias stylesheet-prefix="dps" result-prefix="xsl" />
<xsl:template match="/">
<dps: stylesheet version="1.0">
<dps:variable name="{$var}">
<dps:value-of select="{$blank}" />
</dps:variable>
</dps:stylesheet>
</xsl:template>
</xsl:stylesheet>
```

Figure 5.9 Namespace aliases

{$var} and {$blank} are attribute value templates. They represent a string in which curly braces contain an XPath expression. The processor first evaluates the expression and then converts it to a string. Finally, the string is substituted into the attribute value as a replacement for the expression.

The ninth top-level element, <xsl:attribute-set>, defines a named set of attributes eligible for use as a group in an output element. Each xsl:attribute element is output in the order declared in the set element. You can create a reusable set of attributes by calling the attribute set by name more than once.

Figure 5.10 provides a perspective on how components are reusable. Frequently, programmers need a specific set of definitions for formatting HTML tables. A stylesheet is appropriate for this purpose. We may reference it in an instance document. In essence, we are creating a macro. Define it first and then apply it wherever needed.

```
<?xml version="1.0" encoding="UTF-8"?>
<xsl:stylesheet version="1.0"
xmlns:xsl="http://www.w3.org/1999/XSL/Transform">
    <xsl:output method="xml" version="1.0" encoding="UTF-8"
indent="yes"/>
<xsl:attribute-set name="normal_table">
    <xsl:attribute name="border">0</xsl:attribute>
    <xsl:attribute name="cellpadding">3</xsl:attribute>
    <xsl:attribute name="cellspacing">4</xsl:attribute>
</xsl:attribute-set>
```

```
<xsl:attribute-set name="border_table">
    <xsl:attribute name="border">1</xsl:attribute>
    <xsl:attribute name="cellspacing">2</xsl:attribute>
    <xsl:attribute name="cellpadding">3</xsl:attribute>
</xsl:attribute-set>

<xsl:template match="city">
  <xsl:call-template name="table_cell"/>
</xsl:template>

<xsl:template match="street">
  <xsl:call-template name="table_row"/>
</xsl:template>

<xsl:template match="state">
  <xsl:call-template name="table_row"/>
</xsl:template>
<xsl:template match="main">
<xsl:element name="table" use-attribute-sets="border_table">
</xsl:element>
</xsl:template>
<xsl:template match="/">
  <html>
  <head><title>Attribute-set example</title></head>
  <body>
     <xsl:apply-templates/>
  </body>
  </html>
 </xsl:template>
<xsl:template name="table_row">
   <tr>
     <xsl:apply-templates/>
   </tr>
</xsl:template>

<xsl:template name="table-cell"></xsl:template>
    <td>
        <xsl:apply-templates/>
    </td>
</xsl:stylesheet>
```

Figure 5.10   Attribute sets

`<xsl:template>` represents the construct for selecting specified nodes for processing, and it contains instructions for that node. We have witnessed the application of several different type templates.

A Review Exercise

We have demonstrated how to use top-level elements. The following list represents instruction templates applied in previous examples:

- `<xsl:apply-imports>`
- `<xsl:apply-templates>`
- `<xsl:attributes>`
- `<xsl:call-template>`
- `<xsl:apply-imports>`
- `<xsl:copy>`
- `<xsl:copy-of>`
- `<xsl:apply-imports>`
- `<xsl:number>`
- `<xsl:value-of>`
- `<xsl:apply-imports>`
- `<xsl:variable>`

Now it is your turn to write an XML document instance and corresponding stylesheet. Here are the specifications:

- Create a source document providing a list of graduate courses in computer science, such as Java, C++, data structures, and so on.
- Create a stylesheet including an external document that contains a definition for a special topics course.
- Use the `include` element to achieve this.
- Apply the `number` template to your list so that the courses are numbered.
- Use the HTML table format to output the course list.

Solutions are included on the accompanying CD under Chapter 5 solutions.

PART 2

TRANSFORMATION

5.4   Parsing with XSLT's Processor

Before we continue, you will benefit from learning how the XSLT processor parses the document instance. The processor (we will refer to it from now on as XSLT to avoid writing "the processor" repeatedly) consults both the source document and the stylesheet for instructions on how to process nodes.

Determining the Current Context Node

The XSLT traverses the tree, grouping elements, reordering them, sorting, and copying text to their appropriate node/node sets. It manipulates nodes by applying template rules and creating a result tree for rendering documents in the desired format.

We refer to processing the order of nodes as the *document order* and call it the *depth-first* traversal, beginning with the document root and subsequently visiting each node. We must be able to determine at any given moment where we are in the tree. The node XSLT is the current context node.

This node is composed of the following items:

- The context node
- The context position
- The context size
- All namespaces in scope for the expression
- Core library functions
- A set of variable bindings for namespaces, such as Java

The current context node refers to the node that the parser is currently processing. We determine the context position by comparing the position of the current node in relation to its immediate parent. The context size is an integer > 1 describing the number of nodes in the current node list we are examining. Figure 5.11 (<book>) contains three child nodes. (Note: This is a document fragment; see the complete instance later in this section.)

```
<books>
  <book category="Computer Science">
      <author> Dwight Peltzer></author>
      <title>AML Language Mechanics</title>
      <publisher>addison Wesley</publisher>
  </book>
</books>
```

Figure 5.11   books.xml

The three nodes follow below.

- <author>
- <title>
- <publisher>

Therefore, the context size is 3.

XSLT begins processing by applying `<xsl:template match="/">` to the root node (`<books>`). Once XSLT locates the root element, `<books>` becomes the current node. At this stage, XSLT then examines the size of the current context node.

We must also examine the namespace and scope for each node/node set. XSLT namespaces are the same as XSD:Schema namespaces. The same rules apply for both.

Let's assume the parser is processing the sibling `<book>` node. XSLT determines its position by recursively referring to its parent node, `<books>`. (Note: XML allows only one parent element in a document. Child elements can have ancestors but never more than one parent). Next, XSLT determines its context size by examining the nodes within scope. `<book>` (the document instance fragment) contains three child nodes, so scope begins with first child node `<books>` and ends with its closing tag. The processor proceeds to the next node, `<author>`, the child element. `<author>` replaces `<book>` as the current context node. XSLT then reverts to `<book>`, replacing `<author>` as the current context node. Next, XSLT traverses the tree to `<title>`, replacing `author` as the new current context node. Next, XSLT reverts to `<book>`, replacing `<title>` as the current context node. The final child node, `publisher`, becomes the current context node and so on. Note that the processor always reverts to its parent before proceeding to the next child node, as demonstrated in this figure.

The schema prefixes *xs* and *xsd* are used interchangeably in Altova Spy.

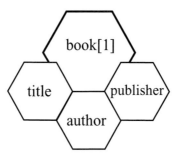

The root element for this document instance is <books> (which is not present in diagram). Nested within the root element is the child element <book>, containing three separate categories: Computer Science, Physics, and Children's Books. (This is the following three-tier example.)The content model for each group is element only and is identical in structure. The complete document is as follows:

```
<?xml version="1.0" encoding="UTF-8"?>
<books>
    <book category="Computer Science">
        <author>Dwight Peltzer</author>
        <title>XML Language Mechanics</title>
        <publisher>Addison Wesley</publisher>
    </book>
    <book category="Physics">
        <author>Douglas Cornell</author>
        <title>Physics In Action</title>
        <publisher>XPublisher</publisher>
    </book>
    <book category="Children's Books">
        <author>Karenn Ressa</author>
        <title>See and Discover</title>
        <publisher>YPublisher</publisher>
    </book>
</books>
```

Here is the skeletal version of the stylesheet for books. It contains the XML prologue, stylesheet declaration, output method, and a template for the document root.

```
<?xml version="1.0" encoding="UTF-8"?>
<xsl:stylesheet version="1.0"
xmlns:xsl="http://www.w3.org/1999/XSL/Transform">
   <xsl:output method="html" />
       <xsl:template match="/">
       </xsl:template>
</xsl:stylesheet>
```

Applying `<xsl:template match="/">` simply locates the root element for this document. Let's modify the template so that it will generate output for the book categories and their content:

```
<?xml version="1.0" encoding="UTF-8"?>
<xsl:stylesheet version="1.0"
xmlns:xsl="http://www.w3.org/1999/XSL/Transform">
   <xsl:output method="html" />
       <xsl:template match="book">
        <p>
           <xsl:apply-templates/>
        </p>
       </xsl:template>
</xsl:stylesheet>
```

`<book>` represent the target node that the parser needs to locate to process the child node and its descendants. `apply-templates` is an instruction template. It generates output for all child elements of the current node. The following example displays the XML content with surrounding HTML paragraph tags.

```
<?xml version="1.0" encoding="UTF-8"?>
<p>Dwight PeltzerXML Language MechanicsAddison Wesley</p>
<p>Douglas CornellPhysics in ActionXPublisher</p>
<p>Karenn RessaSee and DiscoverYPublisher</p>
```

The output includes both literals and content but is not yet suitable for presentation. The content looks like run-on sentences. Let's use an HTML table to achieve the results we desire. Figure 5.12 shows the modified stylesheet.

```
<?xml version="1.0" encoding="UTF-8"?>
<xsl:stylesheet version="1.0"
xmlns:xsl="http://www.w3.org/1999/XSL/Transform">
    <xsl:output method="html" version="1.0" encoding="UTF-8"
indent="yes"
    Doctype-public='-//W3C//DTD HTML 5.0 Final//EN'/>
        <xsl:template match= "/">
    <html><body>
    <h1>Book Publisher Catalog</h1>
        <table width='650'>
            <xsl:apply-templates/>
        </table>
    </body></html>
    </xsl:template>
        <xsl:template match='book'>
        <tr>
        <td><xsl:number/></td>
        <xsl:apply-templates/>
        </tr>
        </xsl:template>
        <xsl:template match='author | title | publisher'>
            <td><xsl:value-of select="."/></td>
        </xsl:template>
    </xsl:stylesheet>
```

Figure 5.12   Books.xsl

The difference between this stylesheet and the previous
example is significant. The first template contains instructions to
signify to the processor that the document is in HTML format.
`<apply-templates>` generates the literal result elements `html`,
`body`, `h1`, and the text `Book Publisher Catalog` to be inserted
into the result tree. The second template inserts `tr` and applies the
template `<xsl:number>` enclosed by `td` tags to number each node
sequentially. We position `<xsl:template match="/">` before we
insert `html` and `body` tags, as demonstrated here:

```
<?xml version="1.0" encoding="UTF-8"?>
<xsl:stylesheet version="1.0"
xmlns:xsl="http://www.w3.org/1999/XSL/Transform">
    <xsl:output method="xml" version="1.0" encoding="UTF-8"
indent="yes"/>
```

```
    <xsl:template match="/">
<html><body>
<h1>Book Publisher Catalog</h1>
    <table width="650">
```

We are getting there. The forward slash represents an XPath pattern that matches the root node. The processor applies this template pattern to the document root element. If you don't specify the template rule, the processor applies a default template rule. It is a good idea to take the matter out of the processor's control and specify your own template rule because the default will not always do what you may expect. Another method of specifying the document root is supplying the document name instead of the / template rule, as in `<xsl:template match="books">`. book is the only child of books; therefore, when we use `<apply-templates>`, its immediate children are output.

The next stage is critical. Immediately after applying `template match`, you should add any other code you want, including table width, before the `html` tag. The processor then knows to output HTML literals before it applies the next template rule:

```
<xsl:apply-templates/>
```

This template functions as a trigger by generating output of all child nodes and their content for book. We could also express the template like this to achieve the same results: `<xsl:apply-templates select="."/>`. We are not done because we must still provide the processor with further instructions on how to process all book categories. Let's apply the next template rule:

```
<xsl:template match="book">
```

The processor searches for this category and applies the most appropriate rule for `<book>`. In this context, it will generate output for each book until it has processed all three book nodes. Embedded HTML instructions instruct the processor to use the HTML table `<th>`, `<tr>`, and `<td>` attributes. Additionally, we apply the XSLT instruction number template for each book. Once the processor sees this directive, it administers the `<xsl:apply-templates/>` rule. One final step: Apply the template rule for author, title, and publisher. The `<xsl:value-of select="."` template generates output for all child node content for author, title, and publisher. Then provide closing tags for each element, template rule, and HTML tag.

Finally, Figure 5.13 shows the result as displayed in Internet Explorer version 6.0.

Figure 5.13   Books.htm

Book Publisher Catalog

1 Dwight Peltzer	XML Language Mechanics	Addison Wesley
2 Douglas Cornell	Physics in Action	XPublisher
3 Karenn Ressa	See and Discover	YPublisher

Figure 5.14 demonstrates how the processor generates XML output for this example. All HTML tags are output as literal result elements.

```
<! DOCTYPE html PUBLIC "-//W3C//DTD HTML 5.0
Final//EN"><html>
<body>
<h1>Book Publisher Catalog</h1>
<table width="650">
<tr>
<td>1</td>
<td>Dwight Peltzer</td>
<td>XML Language Mechanics</td>
<td>Addison Wesley</td>
</tr>
<tr>
<td>2</td>
<td>Douglas Cornell</td>
<td>Physics in Action</td>
<td>XPublisher</td>
</tr>
<tr>
<td>3</td>
<td>Karenn Ressa</td>
<td>See and Discover</td>
<td>YPublisher</td>
</tr>
</table>
</body>
</html>
```

Figure 5.14   Literal result elements in HTML

Just a reminder: If you intend to output the document in HTML, place your root template immediately before the HTML declaration, as demonstrated in the following example:

```
<xsl:template match= 'books'>
   <html>
       . . . . .
</xsl:template>
```

The `<xs:apply-templates/>` instruction causes the processor to apply a specified template rule to the most appropriate rule for each node. If you want, apply the `select="expression"` to elements in the source document to which `select=expression` is applicable. The latter instruction provides you with more selective control over your output. It you don't include a `select="expression"`, the processor will search for and apply a template to every one of the current node's children. Children are nodes one step or more below the current context node.

5.5 Exploring XSLT Templates and Elements

This section begins with an exploration of varying techniques in stylesheet and template design. We discuss some of the more commonly used templates, but a comprehensive examination of XSLT elements is beyond the purview of this text. In addition, in Chapter 6, we include several of the templates and elements not discussed in this chapter when we examine XPath expressions and functions.

Let's begin by embedding a stylesheet in a source document. Embedding a stylesheet is a simple task. There is a recommended procedure for enabling a document author to embed a stylesheet within an XML document. The W3C suggests using a processing instruction (PI) at the top of an XML document to allow XML to locate the top of a stylesheet. The PI uses an `href` and a URI to refer to the ID of the stylesheet. The recommendation states, "Stylesheets can be associated with an XML document by using a processing instruction whose target is `xml-stylesheet`." This processing instruction follows the behavior of the HTML 4.0 `<LINK REL="stylesheet"`. The `xml-stylesheet` processing instruction

is allowed only in the prolog for an XML document. Here are some examples:

```
<LINK href="mystyle.css" title="Compact" rel="stylesheet"
type="text/css">
```

The equivalent XML syntax would be as follows:

```
<?xml-stylesheet href="common.css" type="text/css"?>
```

Figure 5.15 demonstrates how we can achieve this. We use the same Book.xml source document and stylesheet for this discussion.

```
<?xml version="1.0" encoding="UTF-8"?>
<?xml-stylesheet type="text/xsl" href="#style1"?>
<books>
    <book category="Computer Science">
      <author>Dwight Peltzer</author>
      <title>XML Language Mechanics</title>
      <publisher>Addison Wesley</publisher>
    </book>
    <book category="Physics">
      <author>Douglas Cornell</author>
      <title>Physics in Action</title>
      <publisher>XPublisher</publisher>
    </book>
    <book category="Children's Books">
      <author>Karenn Ressa</author>
      <title>See and Discover</title>
      <publisher>YPublisher</publisher>
    </book>

    <xsl:stylesheet id="style1" version="1.0"
     xmlns:xsl="http://www.w3.org/1999/XSL/Transform">
      <xsl:template match="xsl:stylesheet"/>
      <xsl:template match="books">
        <html>
          <body>
            <h1>An embedded stylesheet</h1>
```

```
              <table>
                  <xsl:apply-templates/>
              </table>
          </body>
      </html>
  </xsl:template>
  <xsl:template match="book">
      <tr>
          <xsl:apply-templates/>
      </tr>
  </xsl:template>
  <xsl:template match="author|title|publisher">
      <td>
          <xsl:value-of select="."/>
      </td>
  </xsl:template>
  </xsl:stylesheet>
</books>
```

Figure 5.15   Embedded stylesheet

Following the XML document instance declaration, the stylesheet declaration uses #style1 to point to the included stylesheet embedded within the document. You will not find support for this feature in all XSLT processors. Note that XSLT version 1.1 is not being developed beyond the draft stage. The W3C committee decided instead to use this version as a base for version 2.0, now in the draft stage. It explores several of the new features included in the schema recommendation release. For further information on this topic, consult the W3C at www.w3.org.

Embedding a stylesheet within a source document raises some important issues. Embedding a stylesheet provides immediate access to the source document. However, reusing the stylesheet in another context is not possible. Consider these factors carefully before doing so.

A Simple Stylesheet

The syntax for a simple stylesheet is slightly different. Notice how the declaration begins with HTML (see Figure 5.16).

PART 2 TRANSFORMATION

```
<html xmlns:xsl="http://www.w3.org/1999/XSL/Transform" xsl:ver-
sion= "1.0">
<head><title>A Table Rendering</title></head>
<body>
<h2>My Simple Stylesheet</h2>
<table border="2">
   <xsl:for-each select="//book">
   <xsl:sort select="author"/>
     <tr>
       <td><xsl:value-of select="author"/></td>
       <td><xsl:value-of select="title"/></td>
       <td><xsl:value-of select="publisher"/></td>
     </tr>
   </xsl:for-each>
</table>
</body>
</html>
```

The following code is the output:

```
<html>
<head>
<META http-equiv="Content-Type" content="textÆ/html";
charset="UTF-16">
<title>My simple stylesheet</title></head>
<body>
<h2>My Simple Stylesheet</h2>
<body>
<table border="2">
<tr>
<td>Douglas Cornell</td>
<td>Physics in Action</td>
<td>XPublisher</td>
</tr>
<tr>
<td>Dwight Peltzer</td>
<td>XML Language Mechanics</td>
<td>Addison Wesley</td>
</tr>
<tr>
<td>Karenn Ressa</td>
<td>See and Discover</td>
```

```
<td>YPublisher</td>
</tr>
</table>
</body>
</body>
</html>
```

Figure 5.16 My Simple Stylesheet syntax

Figure 5.17 displays the output for this stylesheet:

Figure 5.17 A simple stylesheet

My Simple Stylesheet

Douglas Cornell	Physics in Action	XPublisher
Dwight Peltzer	XML Language Mechanics	Addison Wesley
Karenn Ressa	See and Discover	YPublisher

Many different output styles can be generated. Let's generate a modified version of `<books>`. We have restructured the template by defining the order of nodes in the body; we apply `<xsl:template match='/ '>` and include HTML formatting instructions within the body. `<xsl:value-of select="."/>` generates content for each node as specified. It may not be the most desirable representation, but it demonstrates how the original data remains intact and XSLT has restructured the output. Additionally, it represents a different approach to restructuring output. Refer to figure 5.18. It is the code for figure 5.19 which represents the generated output.

```
<xsl:template match= 'books'>
    <html>
    <head>
    <title>Reordered Books Structure</title>
    </head>
    <body>
        <xsl:apply-templates select="book/title"/>
        <xsl:apply-templates select="book/author"/>
        <xsl:apply-templates select="book/publisher"/>
    </body>
    </html>
```

```
  </xsl:template>

  <xsl:template match='title'>
    <h3><xsl:value-of select="."/></h3>
  </xsl:template>

  <xsl:template match='author'>
    <h3><xsl:value-of select="."/></h3>
  </xsl:template>

  <xsl:template match='publisher'>
    <h3><xsl:value-of select="."/></h3>
  </xsl:template>

  </xsl:stylesheet>
```

Figure 5.18   Altered books structure

The following is the generated output for the code in Figure 5.18.

```
XML Language Mechanics
Physics in Action
See and Discover
Dwight Peltzer
Douglas Cornell
Karenn Ressa
Addison Wesley
XPublisher
YPublisher
```

Figure 5.19   Books.htm restructured

Refer to the document instance to observe how the processor applies the template for each category. It generates output first for title, followed by author and publisher.

5.6 Template Rules and Expressions

This section focuses on template rules and expressions. Whereas we were previously discussing stylesheet structure, we now shift our attention to rules expressed within templates.

Document structure usually determines the order in which elements appear in the source tree. As previously mentioned, each document begins with a document root followed by child elements, attributes, text nodes, comments, and processing instructions. Keep in mind that attributes are not ordered within themselves. Consider the document order to be the order in which an XML document is read. Additionally, the ordering of elements is usually predetermined by business model requirements.

Templates consist of a sequence of elements and text nodes. Comments, processing instructions, and whitespace text nodes are ignored. The most frequently used template formats include the following, some of which we have already seen:

1. `<xsl:template match='/'>`

Note: The preceding template searches for the root node.

---

2. With `<xsl:apply-templates>`, all child elements of the current node will be processed. For example, if we are processing the root node, it will contain only one child element, the document element. `<xsl:apply-templates>` identifies a set of nodes and specifies that nodes should be processed at the point where the most appropriate template applies. A conflict-resolution policy exists to resolve any clashes if more than one template rule is present.

3. The `<xsl:apply-templates select="."/>` rule is more specific. The dot between quotes processes all elements within the current node's context. In addition, the dot denotes the root. The `select` = template calls other templates. Note: This template requires a node set to be valid.

4. The `<value-of select ='expression'>` identifies the node set from which the source document node content should be output.

5. We frequently use `<xsl:for-each select 'expression'` to create HTML tables. The format for this template is demonstrated here:

```
<xsl:for-each select="Chapter">
  <p><xsl:value-of select="."/></p>
  </xsl:for-each>
```

In this context, we are processing a table of contents. Specifically, this template instructs the processor to select all nodes bearing the value `Chapter` and its related text within the current context. The correct syntax for this code fragment is shown in Figure 5.20.

Figure 5.20   OUTPUT.html

A Recursive Approach to XML Programming
Chapter One . . . XML's Path to the Internet
Chapter Two . . . DocumentTypeDefinitions
Chapter Three . . . . . Schemas

We will see this example again when we generate a table of contents later in this chapter.

5.7 Conditional Processing

XSLT provides an `<xsl:if test='boolean condition'>`

```
<!-- do something -->
```

Note: XSLT uses a two-tiered truth table in contrast to SQL, which uses a three-tiered truth table. The boolean condition returns either true or false. If the condition is matched, the nodes are processed. Figure 5.20 demonstrates how to write syntax for this template. We list complete code for this template when we process a poem by Wordsworth.

```
<xsl:template match='line'>
   <xsl:if test="position() mod 2 = 0">  </xsl:if>
     <xsl:value-of select="."/><br/>
</xsl:template>
```

Figure 5.20   Template `Match='line'`

We are testing for the position of a specified line within the source document. For example, a poem stanza usually contains an even number of lines. The line's position is tested within the stanza. If the remainder is zero, the position is even, whereas the position is uneven if not true. If true, we apply two nonbreaking whitespaces.

Another method of conditional processing provides several choices. Write the following code within a template rule:

1. Type `<xsl:choose>`.

2. Type `<when>` to begin the initial condition.

3. Type `test='expression'` where `expression` specifies a certain node set, a string, or a number.

4. Specify the processing that will occur if the element is not empty.

5. Finally, type `</xsl:when>`. If an option is available, type `<xsl:otherwise>` to continue processing the node set and specify what should be done.

6. `</xsl:otherwise>` ends the processing. If the first condition tests true, the following conditions are ignored. We will use the `book` example we have used previously Refer to the code in Figure 5.21.

```
<?xml version="1.0" encoding="UTF-8"?>
<xsl:stylesheet version="1.0"
xmlns:xsl="http://www.w3.org/1999/XSL/Transform">
<xsl:output method="xml" version="1.0" encoding="UTF-8"
indent="yes"/>
<xsl:template  match="text()"/>
<xsl:template match="*">
<xsl:choose>
<xsl:when test="authors">
<xsl:text>Found the author name.
</xsl:text>
</xsl:when>
<xsl:otherwise>
<xsl:text></xsl:text>
<xsl:value-of select="."/>
</xsl:otherwise>
</xsl:choose>
</xsl:template>
</xsl:stylesheet>
```

Figure 5.21   Conditional processing

The output for this example is as follows:

```
Dwight Peltzer XML Language Mechanics Addison Wesley
```

When the processor fails to locate `authors`, it drops through to the `otherwise` template and generates output for the first element it finds. If we changed `<xsl:template match="*">` to `books` and corrected the `authors` name to its proper name, the output would be as follows:

```
Found the author name.
```

5.8 Sorting

A sorting template allows us to specify an order of elements using the `sort` element.

If no child `<xsl:sort>` processing instruction exists, selected nodes are processed in document order. In other words, the nodes will be processed in the order they are encountered in the source document. Elements are always sorted before their children. In the event that attributes belonging to the same element exist, they may be processed in any order by applying the `sort` rule. If nodes are imported from other source documents, as is the case when we use the `document()` function,the order is not specified. Here is the basic template format for `sort`:

```
<xsl:sort>
    select=expression
    order={'Ascending' | 'descending'}
    case-order={'upper-first' | 'lower-first'}
    lang={language-code}
    data-type={'text' | 'number' | 'Qname'}
```

The default data type for `sort` is text. Text sorting converts the value of a node to a string prior to sorting by using lexicographical algorithms. In our case, data type number is converted to a string prior to sorting.

Figure 5.22 shows the source document for numbers.xml.

```
<numbers>
    <num>07</num>
    <num>003</num>
    <num>02</num>
    <num>4</num>
    <num>006</num>
    <num>005</num>
    <num>1</num>
</numbers>
```

Figure 5.22   Numbers sorted

The simple type stylesheet is shown in Figure 5.23, beginning with the root declaration.

PART 2

TRANSFORMATION

225

```
<numbers xsl:version="1.0"
    xmlns:xsl="http://www.w3.org/1999/XSL/Transform">

    <xsl:for-each select="//num">
    <xsl:sort data-type="number" order="ascending"/>
    <xsl:value-of select="."/>
    <xsl:text>
    </xsl:text>
    </xsl:for-each>
    </numbers>
```

Figure 5.23   Sorting numbers

The output is as follows:

```
<numbers>1 02 003 4 005 006 </numbers>
```

We can also sort a list of cities to accomplish the same thing we did with numbers. Figure 5.24 shows the source document.

```
<?xml-stylesheet type="text/xsl"
href="C:\SaxonApps\citysort.xsl"?>
<cities>
    <city>New York</city>
    <city>Chicago</city>
    <city>Los Angeles</city>
    <city>San Francisco</city>
    <city>Cleveland</city>
</cities>
```

Figure 5.24   Sorting text

The stylesheet, shown in Figure 5.25, is similar to when using numbers.

```
<cities xsl:version="1.0"
    xmlns:xsl="http://www.w3.org/1999/XSL/Transform">
    <xsl:for-each select="//city">
    <xsl:sort data-type="text"
            order="ascending"/>
    <xsl:value-of select="."/>
    <xsl:text>
    </xsl:text>
    </xsl:for-each>
</cities>
```

Figure 5.25   Sorting text stylesheet

The output for cities is as follows:

```
Chicago Cleveland Los Angeles New York San Francisco
```

5.9   Including Other Source Documents

The `document()` function applies a template rule to an outside source document:

```
<xsl:apply-templates
```

```
select='document('financeMgr.xml')/total/[name=$amount]'
mode='finances'/>
</xsl:template>
```

This function specifies the name of the external source document, financeMgr.xml. The XPath expression provides the path to the total amount. Read the path from right to left: `$amount` is the value we are seeking; its attribute is `name`. `financeMgr` contains a subdirectory named `total`, where the desired total amount is accessed. We will discuss this subject in Chapter 6.

5.10 Generating Elements from Attributes

You can output elements from attributes by using literal result elements in the stylesheet or by copying nodes from the source document. Figure 5.26 shows the source document.

```
<?xml version="1.0" encoding="UTF-8"?>
<?xml-stylesheet type="text/xsl" href="C:\Documents and
Settings\Dwight Peltzer\My
Documents\Spy04\attsToElements.xsl"?>
<book title="XML Primer" author="Dwight Peltzer"
publisher="Addison Wesley" price="44.99"/>
```

Figure 5.26　Attributes to elements

The stylesheet utilizes `<xsl:for-each select="@*">` to select the attributes. The next step is defining a placeholder for the name element. Finally, use `<xsl:value-of select="."/>` to generate output for all attributes.

This approach is especially valuable when you are using different namespaces. See for example, Figure 5.27.

```
<xsl:transform
xmlns:xsl="http://www.w3.org/1999/XSL/Transform" version="1.0">
<xsl:output indent="yes"/>
<xsl:template match="book">
 <book>
    <xsl:for-each select="@*">
    <xsl:element name="{name()}">
    <xsl:value-of select="."/>
    </xsl:element>
    </xsl:for-each>
  </book>
 </xsl:template>
</xsl:transform>
```

Figure 5.27　The attributes-to-elements stylesheet

The output for this example is as follows:

```
<book>
    <title>XML Primer</title>
    <author>Dwight Peltzer</author>
    <publisher>Addison Wesley</publisher>
    <price>44.99</price>
</book>
```

5.11 Inserting Formatted Numbers

We can use the `xsl:number` element to insert a formatted number into a result tree. The expression for doing this is as follows:

```
<xsl:template match="items">
   <xsl:for-each select="item">
       <xsl:sort select="."/>
<p>
   <xsl:number value="position() " format="1. "/>
 </p>
     </for-each>
</xsl:template>
```

The `xsl:number` element insertion is based on the position of the current node. Chapter 6 will discuss a number of steps involved in using the `xsl:number` element in our study of axes.

We have examined the most frequently used templates rules. Our next task is to generate an HTML rendering of a poem written by William Wordsworth. The approach we take is traditional because the output matches the source document. The stylesheet treats the document in document order. Please see Figure 5.28 for the unformatted text. Then see the formatted text in Figure 5.29.

```
PoemVersion1.xml
<?xml version="1.0" encoding="UTF-8"?>
<Poem>
    <author>William Wordsworth</author>
    <title>Lines</title>
    <date>1798</date>
 <stanza>
    <line>I hear a thousand blended notes,</line>
    <line>While in a grove I sate reclined,</line>
    <line>In that sweet mood when pleasant thoughts</line>
    <line>Bring sad thoughts to the mind.</line>
    </stanza>
 <stanza>
    <line>To her fair works did nature link</line>
    <line>The human soul that through me ran;</line>
    <line>And much it griev'd my heart to think</line>
    <line>What man has made of man?</line>
    </stanza>
 <stanza>
    <line>Through primrose-tufts, in that sweet bower,</line>
    <line>The periwinkle trail'd its wreathes;</line>
    <line>and 'tis my faith that every flower</line>
    <line>Enjoys the air it breathes.</line>
    </stanza>
 <stanza>
    <line>The birds around me hopp'd and play'd:</line>
    <line>Their thoughts I cannot measure,</line>
    <line>But the least motion which they made,</line>
    <line>It seemed a thrill of pleasure.</line>
    </stanza>
</Poem>
```

Figure 5.28   A Wordsworth poem

Figure 5.29   Lines by Wordsworth

Lines by
William Wordsworth
I hear a thousand blended notes,
 While in a grove I sate reclined,
In that sweet mood when pleasant thoughts
 Bring sad thoughts to the mind.
To her fair works did nature link
  The human soul that through me ran;
And much it griev'd my heart to think
  What man has made of man?
Through primrose-tufts, in that sweet bower,
  The periwinkle trail'd its wreathes;
and 'tis my faith that every flower
  Enjoys the air it breathes.
The birds around me hopp'd and play'd:
  Their thoughts I cannot measure,
But the least motion which they made,
  It seemed a thrill of pleasure.
                    1798

This document begins with the required header and namespace declaration:

```
<?xml version="1.0" encoding="UTF-8"?>
<xsl:stylesheet version="1.0"
xmlns:xsl="http://www.w3.org/1999/XSL/Transform">
<xsl:output method='html'
        indent='yes'
        doctype-public='-W3C//DTD HTML 5.0 Final//EN'/>
```

Next we must write a template rule for each element in the original source document. The <Poem> element creates the basic HTML format for the entire document by defining the order of elements displayed. The only variation in document order is the placement of the date element at the end of the poem. See how this is achieved in Figure 5.30.

```
<xsl:template match='Poem'>
  <html>
    <head>
      <title><xsl:value-of select="title"/></title>
    </head>
  <body>
    <xsl:apply-templates select='title'/>
    <xsl:apply-templates select='author'/>
      <xsl:apply-templates select='stanza'/>
      <xsl:apply-templates select='line'/>
      <xsl:apply-templates select='date'/>
    </body>
  </html>
</xsl:template>
```

Figure 5.30   Poem.xsl

The document root is `<Poem>`. After defining the standard `tem-plate match="Poem"`, the following line is the proper place to embed the HTML elements within the stylesheet. The `<xsl:value-of >` template rule inserts the value of the specified element in the input order, whereas the `<xsl:apply-templates>` instruction processes all child elements residing within that node set. Each child element has its own template rule. For example, both the `<title>` and `<author>` elements specify their individual placement as center-aligned with HTML formatting instructions using the `<h1>` font heading. The `<xsl:value-of select='.'` specifies that all content contained within the selected element is to be inserted.

```
<xsl:template match='title'>
    <h1><xsl:value-of select="."/></h1>
</xsl:template>
<xsl:template match='author'>
    <h2><xsl:value-of select="."/></h2>
</xsl:template>
```

Figure 5.31   Title.xsl

The template rule for the `<stanza>` element formats each stanza into an HTML paragraph and then processes individual lines within the specified element.

```
<xsl:template match='stanza'>
   <p><xsl:apply-templates select='line'/></p>
</xsl:template>
```

Figure 5.32   Stanza.xsl

The template rule for `<line>` is more complex. The `position()` function determines if the line position is an even number. If true, the line is preceded by two nonbreaking space characters ( ). `<xsl:if` calls the `position()` function to ascertain the relative position of the present line. Subsequently, if true, the content of the line is output followed by an HTML `<br/>` element.

```
<xsl:template match='line'>
   <xsl:if test="position() mod 2 = 0">  </xsl:if>
   <xsl:value-of select="."/><br/>
</xsl:template>
```

Figure 5.33   Line2.xsl

One important item is the placement of the closing element forward slash, either before or after the element. A significant difference exists between the following two document fragments:

Example 1:
```
<stanza>
    <line></line>
</stanza>
```

Example 2:
```
<stanza/>
    <line></line>
```

The difference is subtle but significant. The first example's parent element `<stanza>` contains child `<line>` elements. When written in this format, all stanza child elements are properly rendered (see Figure 5.34).

Figure 5.34 Poem.txt

I hear a thousand blended notes,
  While in a grove I sate reclined,
In that sweet mood when pleasant thoughts
  To her fair works did nature link
  The human soul that through me ran;
And much it griev'd my heart to think
  What man has made of man?

However, Example 2's code does not output the desired effect. Why is this so? Because `<stanza/>` does not view `<line>` elements as children, whereas the following

```
<stanza>
  <line></line>
</stanza>
```

sees the subsequent four `<line>` elements as its children. The current scope begins with the `<stanza>` element and ends with the `</stanza>` closing tag. Test it yourself. Unfortunately, something seemingly insignificant can have considerable impact on your output, as we just demonstrated.

Figure 5.35 shows the complete stylesheet for PoemVersion1.

```
<?xml version="1.0" encoding="UTF-8"?>
<xsl:stylesheet version="1.0"
xmlns:xsl="http://www.w3.org/1999/XSL/Transform">
<xsl:output method='html'
       indent='no'
      doctype-public='-W3C//DTD HTML 3.2 Final//EN'/>
    <xsl:template match='Poem'>
  <html>
    <head>
       <title><xsl:value-of select="title"/></title>
    </head>
```

```
<body>
  <xsl:apply-templates select='title'/>
  <xsl:apply-templates select='author'/>
  <xsl:apply-templates select='stanza'/>
  <xsl:apply-templates select='line'/>
  <xsl:apply-templates select='date'/>
</body>
</html>
</xsl:template>
<xsl:template match='title'>
    <h1><xsl:value-of select="."/></h1>
</xsl:template>    <xsl:template match='author'>
     <h2><xsl:value-of select="."/></h2>
</xsl:template>
  <xsl:template match='date'>
<p><i><xsl:value-of select="."/></i></p>
</xsl:template>
```

Figure 5.35   PoemStyleSheet.xsl

A stylesheet can be written in several other ways. Most stylesheets will contain a variety of different template rules. Each template is defined as an `<xsl:template>` element with an accompanying `match` attribute. Its attribute value is expressed as a pattern, determining which nodes in the source tree are applicable to this rule. The pattern / matches the root node; the pattern `<title>` matches a `<title>` element, and so forth. Remember, when you "apply a template," you're actually specifying a set of nodes to be processed by whatever templates are appropriate for a given context; you're not executing a specific template. Frequently, this concept is misunderstood. The difference seems subtle but is significant.

5.12 Formatting Lists

Frequently, it is convenient to format a list of names. Figure 5.36 shows the source document for this example.

```
<composers>
   <Classical>A Discography of Composers</Classical>
      <composer>Bach</composer>
      <composer>Beethoven</composer>
      <composer>Brahms</composer>
      <composer>Chopin</composer>
      <composer>Debussy</composer>
</composers>
```

Figure 5.36 A formatted list of names

We use three templates for this example. `<xsl:template match="composers">` locates the root. Then we apply `value-of select` to element `Classical`. Finally, we use `<xsl:if test="position() != last()">` and `</xsl:if test="position() = last() -1>` to generate and format the list. The `position()` function provides punctuation based on position.

Figure 5.37 shows the stylesheet for composers.

```
<xsl:transform xmlns:xsl="http://www.w3.org/1999/XSL/Transform
" version="1.0">
   <xsl:template match="composers ">
      <xsl:value-of select=" Classical " />
      authored by  <xsl:for-each select=" composer ">
      <xsl:value-of select= "." />
         <xsl:if test="position() != last() ">,  </xsl:if>
         <xsl:if test="position() =last() -1">and  </xsl:if>
      </xsl:for-each>
   </xsl:template>
</xsl:transform>
```

Figure 5.37 List punctuation

PART 2 TRANSFORMATION

The output for this stylesheet is as follows:

```
<?xml version="1.0" encoding="UTF-16"?>
A Discography of Composers
authored by Bach,  Beethoven,  Brahms,  Chopin,  and  Debussy
```

A Table of Contents

Let's write a stylesheet to generate a table of contents. Figure 5.38 shows the input document.

```
<?xml version="1.0" encoding="UTF-8"?>
<TableOfContents>
   <PhaseOne>A Recursive Approach to XML Programming</PhaseOne>
   <ChapterOne>XML's Path to the Internet</ChapterOne>
   <subtitle>Two Design Strategies</subtitle>
   <subheading>
     <subelement>Top Down Strategy</subelement>
     <subelement>Recursive Programming Strategy</subelement>
   </subheading>
   <subheading>
     <subelement>Defining Parsed Character Data</subelement>
   </subheading>
   <subtitle>Three Content Models</subtitle>
   <subheading>
     <subelement>Element Content Model</subelement>
     <subelement>Mixed Content Model</subelement>
     <subelement>Empty Content Model</subelement>
   </subheading>
   <subheading>
     <subelement>XML Data Types</subelement>
     <subelement>XML Document Structure</subelement>
     <subelement>Modeling Data and Text</subelement>
     <subelement>Designing Modular Data</subelement>
```

```
  <subelement>Mapping XML To A Relational Database</subelement>
  <subelement>Mapping from A Repository to XML</subelement>
 </subheading>
<ChapterTwo>Selecting A Parser</ChapterTwo>
<ChapterThree>Introducing Schemas</ChapterThree>
 <subheading>
  <subelements>Schemas, a Better DTD</subelements>
  <subelements>Introducing Namespaces</subelements>
 </subheading>
 <subheading>
  <subelements>Schemas, a Better DTD</subelements>
 </subheading>
<subtitle>Four Schema Content Models</subtitle>
 <subheading>
  <subelement>Open Content Model</subelement>
  <subelement>Closed Content Model</subelement>
  <subelement>Complex Content Model</subelement>
  <subelement>Simple Content Model</subelement>
 </subheading>
</TableOfContents>
```

Figure 5.38   TableOfContents.xml

We expect to output the title: "A Recursive Approach to XML Programming." Figure 5.39 shows the stylesheet.

```
<?xml version="1.0" encoding="UTF-8"?>
<xsl:stylesheet version="1.0"
xmlns:xsl="http://www.w3.org/1999/XSL/Transform">
   <xsl:output method="html" version="1.0" encoding="UTF-8"
indent="yes"
   Doctype-public="-//W3C//DTD HTML Final 5.0//EN"/>
   <xsl:template match="/">
   <html>
   <head>
     <title>Table of Contents</title>
   </head>
   <body>
```

```
        <xsl:apply-templates select="TableOfContents/PhaseOne"/>
    </body>
    </html>
    </xsl:template>
</xsl:stylesheet>
```

Figure 5.39   Stylesheet.xsl

The output is correct. The next step is modifying the stylesheet so that all chapter titles and subheadings will be displayed (see Figure 5.40).

```
<?xml version="1.0" encoding="UTF-8"?>
<xsl:stylesheet version="1.0"
xmlns:xsl="http://www.w3.org/1999/XSL/Transform">
    <xsl:output method="html" version="1.0" encoding="UTF-8"
indent="yes"
    Doctype-public="-//W3C//DTD HTML Final 5.0//EN"/>

    <xsl:template match="/">
    <html>
    <head>
    <title><xsl:value-of select="TableOfContents"/></title>
    </head>
    <body>
        <xsl:apply-templates select="TableOfContents"/>
        <xsl:apply-templates select="PhaseOne"/>
        <xsl:apply-templates select="ChapterOne"/>
        <xsl:apply-templates select="ChapterTwo"/>
        <xsl:apply-templates select="ChapterThree"/>
        <xsl:apply-templates select="subheading"/>
        <xsl:apply-templates select="subtitle"/>
    </body>
    </html>
    </xsl:template>
    <xsl:template match="PhaseOne">
```

```
<h2><xsl:value-of select="."/></h2>    </xsl:template>
<xsl:template match="ChapterOne">
 <h2>Chapter One. . .<xsl:value-of select="."/></h2>
</xsl:template>
<xsl:template match="ChapterTwo">
  <h2>ChapterTwo<xsl:value-of select="."/></h2>
  </xsl:template>
<xsl:template match="ChapterThree">
   <h2>ChapterThree<xsl:value-of select="."/></h2>
   </xsl:template>
<xsl:template match="subtitle">
  <h2><i><xsl:value-of select="."/></i></h2>
  </xsl:template>
<xsl:template match="subheading">
  <p><xsl:apply-templates select="subelement"/></p>
  </xsl:template>
  <xsl:template match='subelement'>
  <xsl:value-of select="."/><br/>
  </xsl:template>
</xsl:stylesheet>
```

Figure 5.40   TableOfContentsV2.xsl

Once more, the output is as anticipated (see Figure 5.41).

Figure 5.41   StylesheetOutput.htm

A Recursive Approach to XML Programming

Chapter One. . .XML's Path to the Internet

Two Design Strategies
Top Down Strategy
Recursive Programming Strategy
Defining Parsed Character Data

Three Content Models
Element Content Model
Mixed Content Model
Empty Content Model
XML Data Types
XML Document Structure
Modeling Data and Text
Designing Modular Data
Mapping XML to a Relational Database
Mapping from a Repository to XML

ChapterTwo   Selecting A Parser

ChapterThree   Introducing Schemas

Four Schema Content Models
Open Content Model

Closed Content Model

Complex Content Model

Simple Content Model

The secret to achieving the correct results lies in two separate areas:

1. You set up the format you desire in the body, as is done here:

```
<xsl:apply-templates select="TableOfContents"/>
<xsl:apply-templates select="PhaseOne"/>
<xsl:apply-templates select="ChapterOne"/>
<xsl:apply-templates select="ChapterTwo"/>
<xsl:apply-templates select="ChapterThree"/>
<xsl:apply-templates select="subheading"/>
<xsl:apply-templates select="subtitle"/>
```

PART 2

TRANSFORMATION

2. Then you apply the `value-of select` template to each individual node:

```
<xsl:template match="PhaseOne">
   <h2><xsl:value-of select="."/></h2>
</xsl:template>
```

```
<xsl:template match="ChapterOne">
   <h2>Chapter One. . .<xsl:value-of select="."/></h2>
</xsl:template>
```

Note the paragraph formatting for subheading and subelement nodes. Also note how `<xsl:apply-templates>` is applied to `subelement` to achieve the desired rendering.

```
<xsl:template match="subheading">
   <p><xsl:apply-templates select="subelement"/></p>
</xsl:template>
```

```
<xsl:template match='subelement'>
<xsl:value-of select="."/><br/>
</xsl:template>
```

What if we decided to display only chapter titles? We could use the `for-each` template rule to accomplish this. The syntax for this rule is as follows:

```
<xsl:for-each="Chapter">
<p><xsl:value-of select="."/></p>
</xsl:for-each>
```

Here is the output for this template rule:

A Recursive Approach to XML Programming

Chapter One . . . XML's Path to the Internet

Chapter Two . . . Selecting A Parser

Chapter Three . . . Schemas, A Better DTD

5.13 A Table of Template Rules

Table 5.1   Template Rules

Node Type	Built-In Template Rule
Root node	Call `<xsl:apply-templates>` to process child nodes of the root.
Element	Call `<xsl:apply-templates>` to process all children of the current node, in the same node as the calling node.
Attribute	Copy the attribute to the result tree, not as the attribute node.
Text	Copy all text to the result tree.
Comment	Don't process anything.
Processing-instruction	Don't process anything.
Namespace	Don't process anything.

Call these templates when there is no template rule matching a node anywhere within the stylesheet. Remember that we cannot override a built-in template for namespaces. For example, if we call `<xsl:apply-templates`, nothing will occur. We can use `<xsl:for-each select= "namespace::*>` for processing all namespace nodes for an element. This syntax is a simple XPath expression. The next chapter provides in-depth information concerning XPath.

5.14 Resolution Conflict Policy

XSLT provides a resolution conflict policy for resolving situations in which more than one template rule resides within a stylesheet matching a particular situation. Here is how it works:

1. Consider the import precedence of each rule. Within a stylesheet, invoke the `<xsl:import>` element to use another stylesheet within the same document. For instance, if stylesheet

A imports stylesheet B, the rules for stylesheet A always take precedence over B.

2. Examine the priority of each rule. Priorities have a numeric value. For example, the higher the number, the higher the priority. Either the priority element can be specified within the `<xsl:template>` element, or the system can allocate a default priority. The system range will always be within –0.5 to +0.5.

3. If there is more than one rule within the same import precedence and priority, the system can report an error, or the XSLT engine can choose whichever rule appears last within the stylesheet using the `import` element.

5.15 Expressions, Variables, and Data Types

In section 5.15, we will examine expressions, variables, and data types.

```xml
<?xml version="1.0" encoding="UTF-8"?>
<bookingMgr>
   <typeEvent>BusinessMeeting</typeEvent>
   <typeRoom>GrandBallroom</typeRoom>
   <dateBooked>2001/07/13</dateBooked>
        <eventDate>
           <year>2001</year>
           <month>August</month>
           <day>15</day>
        </eventDate>
        <meeting>
           <timeDuration>
               <from>1300</from>
               <to>1600</to>
           </timeDuration>
        <clientName>MorganStanley</clientName>
           <address>
```

```
<billingAddress>1225 Ave.of the Americas</billingAddress>
   <city>New York</city>
   <state>NY</state>
   <zip>10025</zip>
</address>
<NumberGuests>20</NumberGuests>
<MeetingTitle>Planning the Future Economy</MeetingTitle>
<GuestSpeaker>Irwin J. K</GuestSpeaker>
</meeting>
</bookingMgr>
```

Figure 5.42   bookingMgr.xml

The stylesheet begins with the usual XML declaration followed by the stylesheet declaration. The only option we currently have is conformance to version 1.0, which refers to the stylesheet namespace at http://www.w3org/1999/TR/Transform. The output method is declared as HTML, with a doctype declaration conforming to the HTML DTD. Our next task is generating the HTML document in Figure 5.43.

Figure 5.43 is the HTML output. Figure 5.44 is the stylesheet.

```
<!DOCTYPE HTML PUBLIC "-//W3C//DTD HTML 5.0 Final//EN">
<html>
   <head>
      <title>The Booking System</title>
   </head>
   <body>
      <p><h1>The Booking Manager System</h1> </p>
   </body>
</html>
```

Figure 5.43   HTML document output

```
<?xml version="1.0" encoding="UTF-8"?>
<xsl:stylesheet version="1.0"
xmlns:xsl="http://www.w3.org/1999/XSL/Transform">
<xsl:output method="html" version="1.0"  indent="yes"
doctype-public='-W3C//DTD HTML 5.0 Final//EN'/>
<xsl:template match='/'>
<html>
<head>
<title>The Booking System</title>
<body>
    <p><h1>The Booking Manager System</h1></p>
</body>
</head>
</html>
</xsl:template>
</xsl:stylesheet>
```

Figure 5.44   BookingMgr.xsl

The output element specifies the following items:

1. The document is an XML file.

2. The output document must be rendered as an HTML file.

3. Indentation is specified.

4. The document contains an `<xsl:template>` element.

5. The HTML output file conforms to version 5.0 of the HTML DTD.

Moving to the next line, the processor locates a template matching the document root. Note that the document root is specified, not the root element. The `match` attribute is identified as `/`.

The processor provides a default template when none is specified. However, it does not always do what you desire, so it is wise to declare one. Now that we know how to specify a template for matching the root, let's modify the XSL stylesheet to output the type event specified in the source document by adding the following code to the existing template:

```
<h2><xsl:value-of select="BookingTypeEvent"/></xsl:value-
of></h2>
```

The output is what we expected: `BusinessMeeting`. Let's define a template to output not only the type of meeting but also the date specified in the source document (see Figure 5.45).

Figure 5.45   Business meeting

The event is a Business Meeting
The meeting date is: 2002 July 15

Let's output the desired date required for the catering business: See Figure 5.46.

```
<?xml version="1.0" encoding="UTF-8"?>
<xsl:stylesheet version="1.0"
xmlns:xsl="http://www.w3.org/1999/XSL/Transform">
<xsl:output method="html" version="1.0"  indent="yes"
doctype-public='-//W3C//DTD HTML 3.2 Final//EN'/>
<xsl:template match='/'>
<html>
<head>
<title>The Booking System</title>
<body>
   <p><h2>The event is a <xsl:value-of
select="bookingMgr/typeEvent"></xsl:value-of></h2></p>
   <h2>The meeting date is: <xsl:value-of
select="bookingMgr/eventDate/year"/> 
<xsl:value-of select="bookingMgr/eventDate/month"/> 
<xsl:value-of select="bookingMgr/eventDate/day"/>
   </h2>
<xsl:apply-templates select='meeting'/>
   <h1><xsl:value-of select="bookingMgr/dateBooked"/></h1>

</body>
</head>
</html>
</xsl:template>
</xsl:stylesheet>
```

Figure 5.46   The BookingSystem.xsl

We have output the type of meeting and the booking date. Also note the path defined to access the date node: `bookingMgr/bookingDate`. We have made a lot of progress. Now we need to output the event date by defining the template. It contains three separate elements: `year`, `month`, and `day`. Render the desired output in this format: `August 15, 2002`. This is a bit tricky. We need to modify our stylesheet so that it will match the event date and subsequently grab the `year`, `month`, and `day` elements. Let's match the event date: `<xsl:template match='eventDate'>`. Then define a template that properly renders the date in its desired format.

```
<h2><xsl:value-of select='month'/>  <xsl:value-of
select='day'/>  <xsl:value-of select=year/> </h2>.
```

We are getting there, but the syntax, if left in its current form, would process the date elements again. We need to ensure that this will not happen. The proper solution is to provide a `select` element so that it will not occur. Here is the solution: `<xsl:apply-templates select='meeting'/>`. Figure 5.47 shows the template written in its proper format.

```
<xsl:template match='eventDate'>
<h2><xsl:value-of select='month'/> 
<xsl:value-of select='day'/> 
<xsl:value-of select=year/> </h2>
<xsl:apply-templates select='meeting'/>
</xsl:template>
```

Figure 5.47   Event date

5.16 Stylesheet Design Considerations

Processing nodes requires control. Simply applying a template does not necessarily produce the results you desire. `<apply-templates>` means one thing in a given context but something different in another. Let's consider the following three template rules:

- `<xsl:apply-templates>`
- `<xsl:apply-templates select =" ">`
- `<xsl:value-of select ="."/>`

The first template simply generates output for whatever LREs and nodes the processor is examining. Be sure of your content before you apply this template. In a context in which the template rule finds a match, such as `<xsl:template match="author|title|pub-lisher">`, you are simply asking the processor to cycle through each node and output its child nodes and content. We assume in this context that a value exists for each element. Say, for example, author contains a name, title has a value, and the publisher name is specified. `<xsl:apply-templates>` is adequate for the job.

The second template provides more control. We request that the processor explicitly select first author, then title, and finally publisher. However, this template will produce uneven results if any element lacks a value. If this scenario exists, the third template rule, `<xsl:value-of select ="."/>`, gives the control we need.

We use `<xsl:for-each>` where we want to do batch processing or build an HTML table.

Modes

Modes allow us to treat elements in a different manner within a stylesheet. The table of contents is a perfect example. A TOC contains three categories: front matter, book, and back matter. We could specify a mode for each category. The XML document in Figure 5.48 serves as the model for this discussion. Here is the document instance.

```
<conference>
<TITLE>Microsoft Boot Camp</TITLE>
<agenda>Presenting the .NET Framework</agenda>
<date>October 31 through November 4</date>
<Speech>
<ProjectManager> Mike Pizzo </ProjectManager>
<Topic>SQL Server 2000 for XML works in a disconnected
mode!</Topic>
<Topic>SQL Server appends For XML Auto to a query</Topic>
```

```
</Speech>
<Speech>
<ProjectManager> Phillip Garding</ProjectManager>
<Topic>VB.NET supports inheritance and multi-threading.</Topic>
<Topic>VB.NET is a significant improvement over VB 6.0.</Topic>
</Speech>
</conference>
```

Figure 5.48   Microsoft conference

The stylesheet demonstrates how we apply modes to our document instance:

```
<xsl:transform
xmlns:xsl="http://www.w3.org/1999/XSL/Transform" version="1.0">
<xsl:template match="conference">
<html><body>
<h1><xsl:apply-templates select="TITLE"/></h1>
<xsl:variable name="productManagers"
select="//ProjectManager[not(.=preceding::ProjectManager)]"/>
<h2>Presenters:  <xsl:apply-templates select="$productManagers"
mode="presenters-list"/> </h2>
<xsl:apply-templates select="*[not(self::TITLE)]"/>
</body></html>
</xsl:template>

<xsl:template match="date">
<p><b><xsl:apply-templates/></b></p>
</xsl:template>

<xsl:template match="agenda">
<b><xsl:apply-templates/></b>
</xsl:template>
```

```
<xsl:template match="ProjectManager" mode="presenters-list">
<xsl:value-of select="."/>
<xsl:if test="not(position()= last() )">, </xsl:if>
</xsl:template>

<xsl:template match="TITLE">
<h1><xsl:apply-templates/></h1>
</xsl:template>

<xsl:template match="Speech">
<p><xsl:apply-templates/></p>
</xsl:template>

<xsl:template match="ProjectManager">
<b><xsl:apply-templates/></b>
</xsl:template>

<xsl:template match="Topic">
<xsl:apply-templates/><br/>
</xsl:template>
</xsl:transform>
```

Within the first template, a lot is happening. We declare a variable named `productManagers` to serve as a node set containing all project manager elements appearing in the document. The second complex XPath expression, `//ProjectManager`, selects all product manager elements representing descendants of the root. The predicate in square brackets eliminates all product managers previously selected: `select="//ProjectManager[not(.=preceding:: ProjectManager)]"/>`. The result of this expression presents speakers only once with their comments (see Figure 5.49).

Figure 5.49   Mode example output

Microsoft Boot Camp

Presenters: Mike Pizzo, Phillip Garding
Presenting the .NET Framework
October 31 through November 4
Mike Pizzo SQL Server 2000 for XML works in a disconnected mode!
SQL Server appends For XML Auto to a query
 Phillip Garding VB.NET supports inheritance and multithreading.
VB.NET is a significant improvement over VB 6.0.

The following demonstrates how to use a mode:

```
<h2>Presenters:  <xsl:apply-templates select="$productManagers"
mode="presenters-list"/> </h2>.
```

Then we create the following template:

```
<xsl:template match="ProjectManager" mode="presenters-list">
<xsl:value-of select="."/>
<xsl:if test="not(position()= last() )">, </xsl:if>
</xsl:template>
```

Notice how we use the `xsl:if test` template to provide punctuation: `<xsl:if test="not(position()= last() )">, </xsl:if>`.

The following block of code selects the `TITLE` node once again, only this time the processor treats the nodes in normal mode rather than as previously done with the `presenters-list` mode.

```
<xsl:template match="TITLE">
<h1><xsl:apply-templates/></h1>
</xsl:template>
```

Why do we use modes? They provide design flexibility. Not all documents exist in the same format. Therefore, keep your audience interested. Apply imagination to your documents and web sites. XSLT can help you accomplish this.

XSLT version 1.1 offers several extension functions. Unfortunately, XSLT version1.1 is not supported beyond the draft stage and will not be supported in the future. Therefore, we will not present them in Chapter 6 where we discuss extension functions. We will only discuss those that XSLT and XPath support.

Before we proceed to Chapter 6, XSLT allows you to control output escaping. Usually, when you try to output a special character such as < or > in text mode, the processor escapes the character in the normal manner: x > y. You can avoid this by using the following:

```
<xsl:text disable-output-escaping="yes">&lt;</xsl:text>
```

The engine will output special characters as they appear: > or x > y and so on.

One final comment: We have presented the most frequently used templates and discussed both the how and why of applying them to our business applications.

Additionally, debugging is problematic when applying XPATH. We recommend using comments to block out specified sections of code to trace the problem. You can also use `<xsl:text>` to assist in following the stylesheet logic. One of the perceptive reviewers of this text suggests that `<xsl:text>` is useful when tracing `<xsl:apply-templates>` calls.

The next chapter represents a continuation of this discussion. XPath expressions enhance our ability to write powerful business documents. Let's proceed immediately to XPath and increase exponentially our knowledge of XSLT before we move on to XHTML and modularization.

Summary

- XSLT uses a stylesheet serving as a container for modular components called templates (Section 5.1).
- XSLT views the document as a hierarchical tree (Section 5.1).

- Three components exist as part of the transformation process (Section 5.1):
  - Document instance
  - Stylesheet
  - Result tree
- A stylesheet can include or import other stylesheets (Section 5.1).
- A stylesheet contains two item categories (Section 5.1):
  - Top-level elements
  - Instruction templates
- Top-level elements are children of the document element (Section 5.1):
  - `<xsl:include>` allows a stylesheet to reference templates and instructions from external sources. `<xsl:include>` must be the immediate child of the stylesheet (refer to Figure 5.4).
  - `<xsl:output>` provides three methods: `xml`, `html`, `text` (refer to Figure 5.4).
  - `<xsl:strip-space>` removes all whitespace for nodes containing only whitespace before further processing continues (refer to Figure 5.4).
  - `<xsl:call-template>` allows you to call a named template anywhere within a document (refer to Figure 5.4).
  - `<xsl:copy:of>` performs a deep copy (refer to Figure 5.4).
  - `<xsl:copy>` performs a shallow copy. (Figure 5.4).
  - `<xsl:call-template>` references an external stylesheet. (Figure 5.4).
  - `<xsl:variable>` defines a specific value applicable in other stylesheet elements (Figure 5.5).
  - `<xsl:import>` allows you to import an external stylesheet into the main stylesheet (Figure 5.6).
  - `<xsl:key>` associates a key with a specified node declared in an XML document instance (Refer to the key section following Section 5.6).

- `<xml:decimal-format>` allows you to control the format for decimal numbers by controlling the pattern (refer to Figure 5.7).
- `<xsl:namespace-alias>` allows you to declare a specified namespace URI as a replacement for another namespace (refer to Figure 5.8).
- `<xsl:attribute-set>` defines a named set of attributes eligible for use as a group in an output element (refer to Figure 5.9).

- The current context node consists of six items (Section 5.4):
  - Context node
  - Context position
  - Context size
  - Namespaces in scope
  - Core library functions
  - A set of variable bindings
- XSLT allows you to:
  - embed a stylesheet within a source document (Section 5.5).
  - perform condition processing (Section 5.7).
  - sort elements in ascending or descending order (Section 5.8).
  - sort lists (Section 5.12).
- Section 5.13 provides a list of template rules.
- Section 5.16 includes a discussion on using modes.

Self-Review Exercises

1. Answer true or false to the following statements. If false, include an explanation.
2. The primary role for an XSLT processor is constructing a result tree.
3. A parser constructs a result tree.
4. XSLT uses cascading style sheets for transforming the result tree into an HTML-rendered format.

5. Three separate components exist in the transformation process:

    Source document

    Schema

    HTML page

6. Identifying the context node requires four separate steps.

7. Tree nodes include only elements and attributes.

8. The document order is the order in which the tree is traversed.

9. A root element cannot contain a child element.

10. A root element contains siblings and ancestors of the context node.

11. XSL is a language for transforming the structure of XML documents into other formats.

12. You can include or import other stylesheets into your main stylesheet.

13. The document() function is supported in XSLT.

14. You cannot embed stylesheets in a source document.

15. You can sort nodes in ascending order.

16. Modes allow you to process elements twice with different formatting.

Projects

1. Write a template to render the following source document in XML:

```
<?xml version="1.0" encoding="UTF-8"?>
<?xml-stylesheet type="text/xsl"
href="C:\XMLBusinessSolutions\Chapter5\SolutionNo5_1.xsl"?>
<Books>
   <book category="reference">
     <author>James Smith</author>
     <title>XML Language Mechanics</title>
     <publisher>X Press</publisher>
   </book>
   <book category="Web Publishing">
```

```
      <author>Steve Heim</author>
      <title>The Human Interface</title>
      <publisher>Y Press</publisher>
   </book>
   <book category="music">
      <author>Joe Schmidt</author>
      <title>Beethoven's Life</title>
      <publisher>Z Press</publisher>
   </book>
</Books>
```

2. Write a template to render the preceding example in HTML.

3. Write a simple stylesheet to render the preceding document in the following format:

My Simple Stylesheet

Dwight Peltzer	J2EE and NET, A Comparison	ZPress
James Smith	XML Language Mechanics	X Press
Steve Heim	The Human Interface	Y Press

4. Write a stylesheet using the same document to generate the following output:

> James Smith
> XML Language Mechanics
> X Press
> Steve Heim
> The Human Interface
> Y Press
> Dwight Peltzer
> J2EE and NET, A Comparison
> ZPress

5. Write a stylesheet to sort a column of numbers.

6 Applying XPath

6.1 Applying XPath Expressions, Patterns, and Functions

XSLT and XPath view the source document as a hierarchical tree, representing an abstract data type. The top of the tree has a document node but does not correspond to any other part of the source document. It consists of one single element, zero or more processing instructions, comments, and zero or more DOCTYPE declarations. Do not make the frequent mistake of confusing the document node with the root element containing all other elements. Note that each document can have only one root element. All other elements are nested within it. The XPath expression / identifies the document node, as demonstrated here:

There are 13 axes altogether. We present only the most frequently used axes in this chapter.

XPath: /		Evaluate

XPath syntax	XPath origin	Real-time evaluation
⊙ Allow Complete XPath	⊙ From Document Root	⊙ Evaluate when typing
○ XML Schema Selector	○ From Selected Element	○ Evalute on button click
○ XML Schema Field		

name	value / attributes
<Document Root>	

The root element begins with `<books>`, as demonstrated in the following example:

```
XPath: /                                                    Evaluate

┌─XPath syntax──────┐ ┌─XPath origin──────┐ ┌─Real-time evaluation──┐   Close
│ ⊙ Allow Complete XPath │ ⊙ From Document Root │ ⊙ Evaluate when typing │
│ ○ XML Schema Selector  │ ○ From Selected Element │ ○ Evalute on button click │
│ ○ XML Schema Field     │                        │                        │

  name                     value / attributes
  <Document Root>
```

Use two dots to locate this node. This is similar to DOS, in which we type two dots to move up one level in a subdirectory until we finally reach C:\, the root of the directory tree.

Applying XPath technology requires addressing the document tree as a series of nodes. The processor walks the tree in depth-first traversal, evaluating each respective node in succession. If you want to identify the current node, simply type a single dot (.) denoting the self-node, `<book>`. You will learn in a moment that "self" represents an axis, instructing the processor to take a forward or reverse direction in traversing the tree. You can type this expression anywhere in the tree to ascertain the current node. For example, let's assume we are currently processing `book[2]`'s `title` element (see Figure 6.1), and we want to locate `title`'s parent node. Just type `'..'` and `<book>` is returned as the parent of `title`. Note the distinction between the dot (.) and `/`. The single dot references `<book>`, the outermost top-level element, whereas `/` selects the `<document root>`, an important distinction.

```
<?xml version="1.0" encoding="UTF-8"?>
<books>
        <book>
            <title>XML Language Mechanics</title>
            <author name="Dwight Peltzer">
                <contactInfo person="MWP">
                    <email>dpeltzer@hotmail.com></email>
                    <phone>516-922-3460</phone>
                </contactInfo>
            </author>
```

```
            <publisher>Addison Wesley</publisher>
        </book>
        <book>
            <title>The Human Interface</title>
            <author name="Steven Heim">
                <contactInfo person="MH">
                    <email>sheim@hotmail.com</email>
                    <phone>516-843-4567</phone>
                </contactInfo>
            </author>
            <publisher>Addison Wesley</publisher>
        </book>

        <book>
            <title>CyberCrime</title>
            <author name="Chris Malinowski">
                    <contactInfo person="LIU">
                        <email>cmalinow@</email>
                        <phone>718-345-8765</phone>
                    </contactInfo>
            </author>
            <publisher>Prentice Hall</publisher>
        </book>
</books>
```

Figure 6.1   The source document (Books.xml)

The XSLT processor views the tree as a group of node categories called *axes*. The *axis specifier* defines a direction (path) originating from a named node (called the context node) to other related nodes. The axes are as follows:

- parent
- child
- ancestor
- descendant
- preceding-sibling
- following-sibling
- self

PART 2 TRANSFORMATION

If we examine Figure 6.1, we can view it from either a vertical or a horizontal point of view. The vertical category includes the parent, child, ancestor, and descendant axes. The horizontal category includes the preceding-sibling and following-sibling axes. Technically, the axis direction is either a forward axis or a reverse axis.

Additionally, XPath uses a *step* (look ahead to Section 6.2 for a definition of step), which selects a set of nodes in the document related to an originating node. It can find either children of node N or ancestors of node N and so on.

We suggest you make a copy of Figure 6.1, and follow along as we explain the individual axes. The context node for this discussion varies, so we will specify the originating node (the context node) for each example as we examine the axis in order.

Delineating the differences between XPath expressions and patterns is one of our primary tasks. Determining the context node is key to understanding the differences between them.

After examining XPath expressions, location steps, patterns, and functions, you will have mastered both XSLT templates and XPath technologies. Combining XSLT and XPath represents a fully comprehensive range of technologies that you can apply to your applications. We will also include exercises throughout this chapter to reinforce what you have learned. Let's begin.

6.2 XPath Expressions and Steps

An evaluated XPath expression returns an object that can be one of four different types:

- A string consisting of a sequence of characters
- A boolean (true or false)
- A number (floating point)
- A node set containing an unordered group of nonduplicating nodes.

A node set is the result of an expression. Additionally, a node set is either empty or contains only one node. Nodes can be ordered as they are referenced.

Location Steps

A *location step* defines a path from the context node to other related nodes. Syntax for this is as follows: `Axis-specifier` — `Node Test` — `Predicate`. For example, you would interpret the expression `parent::node()` as follows: `parent` represents the axis-specifier, the two colons are separators, and the node test is `node()`. If we were attempting to specify the position of a particular node, we would use a predicate to locate that particular node. For example, `.//book[2]` would locate the second book sibling. A predicate always embeds an XPath expression inside a beginning ([) bracket and closing (]) bracket.

By using `author` (refer to Figure 6.1) as the current context node, we can define a path to `book` because the immediate parent of `author` is `book`.

A step comes in two different forms: long and short. Use the short form, called an abbreviated step, to locate the context node or the parent of the context node. You may not use it otherwise. Use the long form to follow any axis and locate any type of node.

A step always follows the initial / path operator and looks like this: `'//'`. The left side of the path operator always evaluates to a node set. For example, if we type `'/'`, we locate the document's topmost element which is the document root.

The forward slash following the initial slash represents a step. Here is how XPath evaluates the step function:

1. Select all nodes of a specified step, beginning at the context node.

2. Select those nodes that satisfy the node test.

3. Number the remaining nodes from 1 to *n* in document order for a forward axis or in reverse order for a reverse axis.

4. Apply the leftmost predicate to each node.

The following list of examples emphasizes the concepts just presented. The context node for these examples is `author[1]`:

- `parent::node()` selects the first `book[1]` node.
- `child::node()` selects child elements (`contactInfo`) of the context node (`book`).

name	value / attributes
() contactInfo	person="MWP"

- `ancestor::node()` selects all ancestor nodes of the context node. The results are returned in reverse order: book, books, and Document Root.

name	value / attributes
() book	
() books	
<Document Root>	

- `descendant::node()` selects all descendants of the context node.

name	value / attributes
= version	1.0
= encoding	UTF-8
() books	
() book	
() title	XML Language Mechanics
Abc	XML Language Mechanics
() author	name="Dwight Peltzer"
() contactInfo	person="MWP"
() email	dpeltzer@hotmail.com>
Abc	dpeltzer@hotmail.com>
() phone	516-922-3460
Abc	516-922-3460
() publisher	Addison Wesley

- `preceding-sibling::node()` selects all nodes preceding the context node (author). They are children of the same parent node in reverse document order.

name	value / attributes
() title	CyberCrime

- `following-sibling::node` selects all nodes following the context node. They are children of the same parent node.

name	value / attributes	
() publisher	Prentice Hall	

- `self::node()` selects the current context node (`author`).

name	value / attributes
() author	name="Dwight Peltzer"

The Originating Node

The originating node represents the context node. For example, `<book>` contains three siblings. If `book` is the originating node (the point at which we start evaluating the context node) and we type `parent::node()`, the result returned is `books`.

The child axis selects all children of the originating node in document order.

If we type `child::node()` using `book[1]` as the current context node, the expression returns `title`, `author`, and `publisher`.

Typing `preceding::node()` returns the following values:

name	value / attributes
= encoding	UTF-8
= version	1.0
() XML	

Assuming the context node is `title[2]`, if we type `following-sibling::node()`, the result returned is as follows:

name	value / attributes
() author	name="Steven Heim"
() publisher	Addison Wesley

The originating node in this case is `book[2]`. In Chapter 5, "XSLT," we listed detailed procedures for determining the current context node. We needn't always begin with the root node but can process a particular node based on criteria determined by a business model. This could mean restructuring the order of nodes for presentation purposes or generating a report. Let's review those procedures.

PART 2

TRANSFORMATION

We must be able to determine at any given moment our position in the tree. Let's assume we want to navigate to sibling node `book[2]` and reference it from the root `<books>`. Here is the XPath expression:

```
.//book[position()=2]/author.
```

Let's examine this XPath expression beginning with the dot. The dot (.) refers to the self axis, the originating node itself. If we type this as the sole expression, it says "select the outermost document node." The result is as follows:

name	value / attributes
<Document Root>	

The dot combined with the first forward slash does nothing. The single forward slash by itself would always select the document root. However, in this case, we are constructing an XPath expression. The second forward slash `//` represents a step, providing the path to the desired node. The following expression selects: `.//book`. Next include the predicate and type the name of the node we want to process, as in (`.//book[2]`) to select the second book. This example includes both the node name and a predicate. The predicate allows us to test the expression, returning true if it finds a match or false if no match is found. We need to retrieve the content from the second author node. Type **`.//book[position() =2]/author`** to retrieve the following output:

name	value / attributes
() author	name="Steven Heim"

The predicate incorporates the `position()` function to specify the location followed by a forward slash. Typing **`.//book[position() =last()]/author`** would return the last author:

() author	name="Chris Malinow

6.3 A Stylesheet-Embedded XPath Expression

The example in Figure 6.3 demonstrates how to embed an XPath expression within a stylesheet.

```
<xsl:stylesheet version="1.0"
xmlns:xsl="http://www.w3.org/1999/XSL/Transform">
<xsl:output method="xml" version="1.0" encoding="UTF-8"
indent="yes"/>
  <xsl:template match='/'>
  <html>
  <body>
    <xsl:value-of select="//book[position()=2]/author/@name "/>
  </body>
  </html>
  </xsl:template>
</xsl:stylesheet>
```

Figure 6.3   Selecting the name attribute

We want to select only the name of the second author in books. Therefore, following author, add an additional step and use the @name attribute to achieve the desired result, as displayed here:

If we selected only the author without applying the name attribute, we would get the following output: sheim@hotmail.com 516-843-4567. That is not what we asked for. An XPath expression combined with the appropriate steps provides us with complete control over the results we want to return. Study them carefully and experiment. The results are worth it.

PART 2 TRANSFORMATION

> **Note:** XPath is an essential component of the recently released .NET framework, so you need to master XPath concepts.

6.4 Evaluating XPath Expressions

The following sections demonstrate the usage of the various axes. We will not include the entire stylesheet for each axis; rather, we'll include only the `value-of select` instruction. Again, we identify the context node for each example.

The Document Root

We select the document root by writing the following `value-of select` statement:

```
<xsl:value-of select="/"/>
```

This expression selects the following nodes. The output is not pretty, but it represents an accurate query. Do not confuse this instruction with `template match='/'`.

```
XML Language Mechanicsdpeltzer@hotmail.com&gt;516-922-
3460Addison WesleyThe Human Interfacesheim@hotmail.com516-843-
4567Addison WesleyCyberCrimecmalinow@718-345-8765Prentice Hall
```

To unscramble the results, we would need to apply a template rule to each individual component, just as we did in Chapter 5.

Child

`child::author` selects all element children of the context node. Another way to express this is `child::*`. `book[2]` is the context mode. The output is as follows:

name	value / attributes
() title	The Human Interface
() author	name="Steven Heim"
() publisher	Addison Wesley

`child::book[position()=1]/title` selects the title element of the first book that is a child of the context node, `books`.

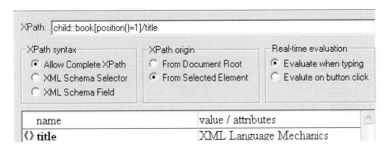

This expression selects the last title element of `book`.

```
child::book[position()=last()-1]/title
```

The output is as follows:

name	value / attributes
⟨⟩ title	CyberCrime

This expression selects the second-to-last title element of `book`.

```
child::book[position()=last()-1]/title
```

name	value / attributes
⟨⟩ title	The Human Interface

6.5 Attributes

Attributes select all attributes of the context node. The context node is `author[1]` for this example: `attribute::*`.

The output for this expression is as follows:

name	value / attributes
= name	Dwight Peltzer

If we changed the expression to begin at the root element, it would look like this: `//attribute::*`. The expression selects all elements functioning as attributes of the context node:

name	value / attributes
= name	Dwight Peltzer
= person	MWP
= name	Steven Heim
= person	MH
= name	Chris Malinowski
= person	LIU

Ancestors

We can select all ancestors of the context node. The expression `ancestor::*` returns the following result:

name	value / attributes
() book	
() books	

`ancestor-or-self::book` selects the book ancestors of the context node. If the context node is a `book` element, it will select the context node as well. The result is as follows:

name	value / attributes
() book	

Descendants

Descendants select all children of the context node, including their children. The following expression selects the `book` element descendants of the context node and, if the context node is a `book` element, selects the context node as well:

```
<xsl:value-of select="descendant-or-self::books"/>
```

The output for this example is as follows:

name	value / attributes
() book	
() book	
() book	

The following expression selects the third descendant of `author`:

```
/descendant::author[position()=3]
```

The output is as follows:

name	value / attributes
() **author**	name="Chris Malinowski"

Self

Self selects a single node, which is the original node itself.

```
<xsl:value-of select="//self::author"/>
```

() **author**	name="Dwight Peltzer"

Following-Sibling

The following-sibling selects all nodes that follow the context node `book[1]`. They are children of the same node:

```
following-sibling::book[position()=1]/*
```

The result is as follows:

name	value / attributes
() **title**	CyberCrime
() **author**	name="Chris Malinowski"
() **publisher**	Prentice Hall

Preceding-Sibling

The preceding-sibling selects all nodes preceding the original node in reverse order.

The following statement selects `book` by selecting all nodes in reverse order with `book[2]title` as the context node:

```
preceding-sibling::node()
```

The result is as follows:

() title	The Human Interface

6.6   Abbreviated Expressions

Now let's examine the list of abbreviated expressions. The same XML document applies. Use the same example we have previously used.

- `book` selects all book element children of the context node. The output is as follows:

```
book
book
book
```

- `text()` selects all text node children of the context node.

```
<xsl:value-of select="//text()"/>
```

The Output is:

name	value / attributes
Abc	XML Language Mechanics
Abc	dpeltzer@hotmail.com>
Abc	516-922-3460
Abc	Addison Wesley
Abc	The Human Interface
Abc	sheim@hotmail.com
Abc	516-843-4567
Abc	Addison Wesley
Abc	CyberCrime
Abc	cmalinow@
Abc	718-345-8765
Abc	Prentice Hall

- `@name` selects the name attribute of the context node.

```
<xsl:value-of select="//@name"/>
```

The output for the `name` attribute is as follows:

name	value / attributes
☰ **name**	Dwight Peltzer

- `book[1]` selects the first `book` child of the context node.

  ```
  <xsl:value-of select="//book[1] "/>
  ```

  The output generated is `book`.
- `book[last()]` selects the last `book` child of the context node. The output is `book`.
- `*/book` selects all `book` grandchildren of the context node.
- `//book` selects all `book` descendants of the document root and thus selects all `book` elements in the same document as the context node.
- `"."` selects the context node.
- `.//book` selects the `book` element descendants of the context node.
- `".."` selects the parent of the context node.

Note the significant difference between the unabbreviated version and the abbreviated syntax. It is much easier to trace the path using the latter format.

Here are some general principles for selecting a node:

- When referring to the current node, type a period (.). We do not always have to select the entire node set. Use a predicate to test the specified node. However, keep in mind that, when utilizing predicates, processing is expensive because each single node selected will temporarily become the context node in turn. The node test, meaning `self::node()`, is the least expensive. Generally speaking, selecting siblings and ancestors of the context node is less costly. Descendants are more expensive in computing power.
- If an `xsl: apply-templates` instruction exists, the current node becomes the node matched by the appropriate template.

- As you process more than one node in succession utilizing a `for-each` instruction, each node in turn becomes the current node. After the node has been processed, it reverts to its former state before it was selected. (See Section 5.6 of Chapter 5 for a review of `for-each` processing.)

- If the current node contains elements you want to process, you can refer to the specific node by name without having to spell out the entire path to the node, such as `author`.

- Selecting all descendants of the root node requires the following syntax: `//` (two forward slashes). To select all descendants of the current node, place a period before them, as in `.//`.

- Selecting an attribute requires typing the `@name`. Including an asterisk selects all node attributes.

- Selecting a subset requires several steps. Begin by creating the path to the node containing the node you are interested in processing. Then type the opening square bracket [. Follow with the expression identifying the subset and close with the closing square] bracket.

EXERCISE 1: Now it is your turn. Copy the following source document into your folder. Then follow the instructions listed.

```
<?xml version="1.0" encoding="UTF-8"?>
<Books>
   <book category='reference'>
     <author>Joseph Professor</author>
     <title>An XML Primer</title>
     <publisher>X Press</publisher>
   </book>
   <book category='Sci-Fi'>
     <author>Steve Heim</author>
     <title>The Human Interface</title>
     <publisher> Y Press</publisher>
   </book>
```

```
   <book category ='music'>
     <author>Frank Hauser</author>
     <title>A Composers Life</title>
     <publisher>Z Press</publisher>
   </book>
   <book category = 'Computer Science'>
     <author>DPeltzer</author>
     <title>How to Compute</title>
     <publisher>AA Press</publisher>
     </book>
</Books>
```

The following list of instructions should be applied to this source document:

1. Write an XPath expression selecting all ancestors of the current context node book[2].

2. Select all descendants of book containing categories.

3. Select the category identifying Computer Science.

4. Select all //title elements in the document.

5. Select the //title element containing How to Compute.

6. Use book[2] as the context node. Select the preceding-sibling containing title An XML Primer.

6.7 Placing XPath Expressions in Context

Table 6.1 lists the context in which you can use XPath expressions within a stylesheet.

Table 6.1 Permissible XPath Expressions Used Within a Stylesheet

Context	Data Type
`<xsl:with-param select=' '>`	Any
`<xsl:param-select=" ">`	Any
`<xsl:variable select=" ">`	Any
`<xsl:when test=" ">`	Boolean
`<xsl:if test=" ">`	Boolean
`<xsl:number value=" ">`	Number
`<xsl:value-of select = " ">`	String
`<xsl:sort select=" ">`	String
`<xsl:apply templates=" ">`	Node set
`<xsl:copy-of select = " ">`	Node set
`<xsl:key use=" ">`	Node set or string

An XSLT stylesheet places certain constraints on syntax of XPath expressions. For example, certain stylesheet contexts require a node set. Table 6.1 defines these constraints. If we use `<xsl:value-of select=". ">`, the data type required is a string, whereas `<xsl:apply-templates>` requires a node set for the expression to be valid. Using `<xsl:if test=" ">` requires a boolean as the data type and so on. Always consult the chart when you use these instruction templates.

XPath applies two rules to an expression:

- Static context
- Dynamic context

The first rule can be determined by examining the stylesheet as follows:

- Examine the variable names in scope where the XPath expression appears.
- Examine the namespaces in effect where the expression appears.
- Examine the corresponding namespace URI.

- Inspect the data type to see if it conforms to the rule listed in the table.
- Determine whether any extension functions are in use.

The dynamic context of the expression can only be determined at runtime. Examine all referenced variables in the expression. Also examine context node, context position, and context size. In any given context, the context changes. In essence, context is polymorphic. Understanding a given context will help you select the proper template and design the appropriate XPath expression. Refer to Chapter 5 for a review of these ideas.

The examples in Table 6.2 clarify the concepts presented in this section.

Table 6.2   Clarifying Some XPath Expressions

Expression	Description
`book and author`	Returns boolean true value if the context node contains both elements
`3.14159`	Returns numeric value 3.14159
`//author	//publisher`	Requires a node set containing all author and publisher elements in the same document

6.8 Applying Patterns

A pattern can be used in only four different contexts: `<xsl:template match>`, `<xsl:key>`, `<xsl:number>`, and its associated `count` and `from` attributes. A pattern allows only two axes: child and attribute. Remember, the child axis selects all child elements of the current context node. Attribute selects all attributes if the original node is an attribute. Additionally, pattern allows the operator `//`. The | operator (or) is allowed in a pattern at the top level. Note that evaluating a pattern means you are always looking to the ancestor or self to serve as the current context node.

Let's begin by examining `<xsl:template match ="author"/>`. The `match` attribute represents a pattern. Use the pattern to prescribe a condition that a node must satisfy to be chosen. The pattern determines which nodes should have the specified pattern applied to them. The context node is the determining factor. For example, `<xsl:template match="author"/>` specifies a template rule (pattern) matching every `<author>` element *if* its parent is the current context node *and* `<author>` is a member of that node set. The formal definition of a pattern can be determined by asking the following questions:

- Is pattern `author` a member of a node set where parent `<book>` is the context node?
- Additionally, does `<book>` exist as `ancestor or self` of child `<author>`?
- If both questions are true, the answer will return a node set including `child <author>`.

`Ancestor-or-self` is the key to understanding a pattern, especially when you consider that a pattern only allows two axes: child and attribute.

Identify patterns by node name, type, and string value. The position of the node relative to its parent is essential. Patterns cannot use the `position()` and `last()` functions except within a predicate, as in `<xsl:value-of select="author[position() = last()-1]"/>`. Context plays a major role in determining whether a pattern is valid. For example, if we define `author` as a pattern, it represents an abbreviated version for `./child::author`, meaning "select all `author` children of the current context node." Does the XPath expression `author` mean it represents all `author` children of the context node? Does this include the particular `author` element we are attempting to match? The answer depends on the current context node. In our example, the `author` element resides within three different `book` categories. The conclusion we must come to says, "If pattern `author` matches a particular `author` node containing a `parent` node, when used as the context node for the expression ' `./child::author`', it returns a node set including the specified author element."

Usually, it is possible to test a pattern by examining only the node itself, or you can include its ancestors, the ancestor's children, and/or attributes.

Let's examine `<xsl:template>` in more depth. It introduces a template for generating output. Invoke it either by matching specified nodes against a pattern or by calling it explicitly using the following template rule: `<xsl:apply-templates>`. Syntax for this pattern is as follows:

```
<xsl:template
name="QName"
match="pattern"
    node="QName"
    priority="Number"
    <xsl:param> *
</xsl:template>
```

`<xsl:template>` is a top-level element, meaning it appears as the child of `<xsl:stylesheet>`.

The `match` is optional. Its attribute is `pattern`, meaning "determine which nodes are eligible to be processed by this template." If the attribute is missing, a `name` attribute must be present. The `name` is optional. Its value is `QName` and represents the name of the template. `priority` is also optional; its value must be a `Number`. A `Number` denotes the priority of this template. Use this when several templates match the same node. `mode` is also optional. Its value is a `QName`. We use mode when `<xsl:apply-templates>` is used to process a set of nodes.

We used the `match` attribute in a number of different contexts in the Chapter 5. Let's review Figure 5.48.

We begin by applying `<template match="conference>"`, the root node for this example. `conference` is the outermost top-level root element. The template rule searches for the document root to find a match. Within the body, `<xsl:apply-templates select="TITLE">` can be appropriately applied because its parent is the current context node and serves as an ancestor or self to element `TITLE`. Even though `TITLE` is a single node, it is a member of a node set, where `conference` is `TITLE`'s ancestor. Also, within this complex template body, we are able to use `<xsl:apply-templates select="$productManagers">` in another context, where the mode attribute is also specified. The XPath expression says, "Select all Project Managers not previously selected who are members of the current context mode." This valid expression uses a predicate to test the node before selecting it. It also uses the `.=preceding` axis to specify the location. Two `ProductManager` elements exist within this source document. Therefore, the current context node must be ascertained before determining which node set `ProductManager` belongs to.

The `<xsl:template match="ProjectManager" mode=presenters-list">` is applied in another template body to provide appropriate punctuation where necessary. The XPath expression `<xsl:value-of select=".">` selects all children of the current context node. This context requires a string data type. The source document for this discussion is as follows:

```
<xsl:transform
xmlns:xsl="http://www.w3.org/1999/XSL/Transform" version="1.0">
<xsl:template match="conference">
<html><body>
<h1><xsl:apply-templates select="TITLE"/></h1>
<xsl:variable name="productManagers"
select="//ProjectManager[not(.=preceding::ProjectManager)]"/>
<h2>Presenters:  <xsl:apply-templates select="$productManagers"
mode="presenters-list"/> </h2>
<xsl:apply-templates select="*[not(self::TITLE)]"/>
</body></html>
</xsl:template>
<xsl:template match="date">
<p><b><xsl:apply-templates/></b></p>
</xsl:template>

<xsl:template match="agenda">
<b><xsl:apply-templates/></b>
</xsl:template>
```

```
<xsl:template match="ProjectManager" mode="presenters-list">
<xsl:value-of select="."/>
<xsl:if test="not(position()= last() )">, </xsl:if>
</xsl:template>
<xsl:template match="TITLE">
<h1><xsl:apply-templates/></h1>
</xsl:template>
<xsl:template match="Speech">
<p><xsl:apply-templates/></p>
</xsl:template>
<xsl:template match="ProjectManager">
<b><xsl:apply-templates/></b>
</xsl:template>
<xsl:template match="Topic">
<xsl:apply-templates/><br/>
</xsl:template>
</xsl:transform>
```

We used the `<xsl:key>` template in Chapter 5. For your convenience, we have brought this section into this chapter to serve as illus-
tration of the topic we are currently discussing, patterns.

`<xsl:key>` is used to associate a key with a specified node
declared in an XML document instance. Each key associated with a
node requires defining a value with the `key()` function. Key uses
three required attributes as shown here:

```
<xsl:key>
name= "QName"
match="pattern"
use="expression"
</xsl:key>
```

The key element uses the qualified `name` attribute to create the key
name. `match` identifies a specific node, whereas the `use` attribute
defines information to apply a value to the key. The first example
where `match` is applied is the following:

```
<xsl:key name="person-identification" match="person"
use="@req"/>.
```

Another example for key would apply to a "SKU" code:

```
<xsl:key name="product-code" match="product" use="@code"/>
```

The key name is `product-code`; the template must match the product element with a given product code. For example, to find product `Dlink–DSH5`, we could do the following:

```
<xsl:apply-templates select="key('product-code',
'Dlink-DSH5')"/>
```

`<xsl:number>` represents the third `pattern` we discuss. This element performs two functions:

- It provides a sequential number for the current node.
- It formats a number.

The format for `number` is as follows:

```
<xsl:number
      level="single" | "multiple| "any"
      count=pattern
      from=Pattern
      value=Expression
      format={format-string}
      lang={language-code}
      letter-value=(  "alphabetic" | "traditional" )
      grouping-separator=(character)
      grouping-size=(number)
```

`<xsl:number>` represents an instruction and is always used within a template body.

- The `level` attributes, `single`, `multiple`, and `any`, are optional. This controls the manner in which a sequential number is allocated, based on the position of the node.
- `count` is also optional, representing a pattern. This attribute determines nodes counted to determine a sequence number.
- `from` is optional, representing a pattern. This specifies a starting point for counting.

- `value` is optional and is an expression. This is a user-supplied number rather than the present node sequential number.
- `format` is optional, representing an attribute value template and returning a formatted string.
- `lang` is optional, representing an attribute value template. It returns a language code (`xml:lang`) as defined in XML specification.
- `letter-value` is optional, returning an alphabetic or traditional character.
- `grouping-separator` is optional, representing an attribute value template and returning a single character.
- `grouping-size` is optional, representing an attribute value template and returning a single number.

In summary, `<xsl:number>` executes the following tasks:

- It determines a sequential number.
- It analyzes a format string into a sequence of formatted tokens.
- It formats each component of the sequence number, applying the appropriate format token.
- It writes the string to the output as a text node.

You will recall in that, in Chapter 5, we used `<xsl:number>` in the following context:

```
<xsl:template match='book'>
   <tr>
    <td><xsl:number/></td>
    <xsl:apply-templates/>
    </tr>
    </xsl:template>
    <xsl:template match='author | title | publisher'>
    <td><xsl:value-of select="."/></td>
    </xsl:template>
   </xsl:stylesheet>
```

The generated output using the `<xsl:number>` template is as follows:

Book Publisher Catalog

1 Dwight Peltzer	XML Language Mechanics	Addison Wesley
2 Douglas Cornell	Physics in Action	DoubleDay
3 Karenn Ressa	See and Discover	DoubleDay

EXERCISE 2: Write a short paragraph explaining the difference between a pattern and an XPath expression. Create a stylesheet to query a node and determine whether it is a member of a node set.

6.9 Data Types

XPath supports four data types: numbers, strings, booleans, and node sets. Operations include the following: and, or, !=, < , <=, >, and >=. The comparison operators are = and !=. The operators <, >, <=, and >= are called relational operators. All of them are left associative.

1 < 2< 3 means (1 < 2) < 3. Additionally, arithmetic operations +, -, *, / , and unary negative – are used for numbers.

Strings

Comparison operations take strings as operands. All other operations convert string operands to whatever data type is appropriate for the operation being executed. All characters are significant, including whitespaces. Determining whether strings are equal is simple. If they contain identical character sequences, they are equal. Strings in a relational operation are converted to a number and then used for the operation being performed. For example, 10 < 5 will always return false.

Numbers

Addition and subtraction use the traditional + and − signs. One caveat: Because − is a valid XML character in names, embed the subtraction operator between whitespaces, as in `xyz  − lmn`. When converted to numbers, the result returned is a number. In another context, the same expression means evaluating the location path. The result would be a node set.

Multiplication, Division, and Remainder

We use the asterisk (*) operator for multiplication and `div` for division. Use `mod` for the remainder of division.

String Conversions

A number can have the following values:

- Positive zero
- Negative zero
- Positive infinity
- Negative infinity
- NaN, not a number
- A normal number

We represent a normal number by its decimal number. Precede negative numbers with a minus sign. For NaN, (not a number), string NaN is utilized. Use zero (0) for positive and negative numbers. For positive infinity, use string Infinity. For negative infinity, place a minus sign in front of it.

- Convert a string to a number by using the `number` function. An example of this conversion is `number(95)`. The result is 95.
- When converting a string to a boolean value, if a string contains at least a single character, the string returns true when converted. If the string is empty, it is converted to false.
- Convert a boolean value to a number by doing the following: `(boolean('ShipMethod'))` becomes number 1.

- The union operator | takes two node sets and combines all nodes together after removing any duplicate nodes.
- Converting the root node into a string requires removing all XML markup from the XML document. The string value of the root is character data.
- Converting an element node into a string requires removing all markup contained by the element.
- Convert a node set to a number by converting the node set to a string and then convert the string to a number.

```
string( X) = 10 + 2+ 3+ 5+7 + 9+22="10235922"
number('10235922') = 10235922
```

6.10 What Is a QName?

XML namespaces provide an easy method for qualifying element and attribute names. The method is associating an NCName with namespaces identified by URI references. We have previously defined an XML namespace as a collection of names identified by a URI reference. Names from XML namespaces may appear as qualified names. They contain a single colon, separating the name into a namespace prefix and a local part. The prefix maps to a URI reference and selects a namespace. URI references can contain characters not allowed in names. This means such references cannot be used as namespace prefixes.

```
<x xmlns:dps="http://www.ecommerce.org/schema">
  <dps:USAddress="PO Box ">215</dps:USAddress>
</x>
```

A node test containing a QName is true if the node type is the principal node type, containing an expanded name equal to the expanded name defined by the QName. `child::book` selects the book element children of the context node. If the context node has no `para` (paragraph) children, it will select an empty set of nodes.

`attribute::href` selects the `href` attribute of the context node. If the context node has no `href` attribute, it will select an empty set of nodes.

In the node test, a QName is extended into an expanded name using the namespace declarations from the expression context. This is the same way expansion is done for element type names in start and end tags except that the default namespace declared with `xmlns` is not used. If the QName does not have a prefix, the namespace URI is null (attribute names are similarly expanded). If the QName has a prefix for which there is no namespace declaration in the expression context, an error is generated.

A node test `*` is always true for any principal node type. `child::*` selects all element children of the context node. `attribute::*` selects all attributes of the context node.

A node test can have the form `NQName:*`. (Nonqualified name). In this particular context, the prefix expands in the same way as a Qname, using the context namespace declarations. If no namespace declaration exists for a prefix in the expression context, an error is generated. The node test for `text()` is true for any text node. For example, `//child::text()` will select all text node children of the context node.

6.11 Functions

Several different node set functions exist for testing the node set:

- The `last()` function returns a number equal to the context size from the context node.

- The number `position()` function returns a number equal to the context position from the evaluation context.

- The `id(object)` selects elements carrying a unique ID. Usually, the `id()` returns a string by calling the `string` function. If the `id()` is a node set, the result is a union of the result of applying `id` to the `string-value` of each individual node in the argument set.

- `namespace-uri(node-set)` returns the `namespace-uri` of the expanded name of the node in the argument node set that is first in document order.

- The `name()` function returns the expanded QName of the node set that is first in document order.

- `ceiling(value)` `number` returns the smallest integer that's greater than or equal to the numeric value of an argument. For example, `ceiling(1.2)` returns 2 and so on.

- `count` takes a node set as its parameter and returns the number of nodes existing within a node set. For example, `count(../book[title])` returns 3.

- `current()` returns a node set containing a single node, the current node.

- `floor(11.3)` returns 11. This means it returns the largest integer that is <= to the numeric value provided as an argument.

- `local-name()` returns the local part of the node name. For example, `<email>dpeltzer@hotmail.com></email>` returns `email`.

- `(name)` returns the name of a function. It returns `email` if applied to the expression in the preceding example.

- `round (5.6)` returns 6.

Evaluate function call expressions by using the function name to identify a function in the expression evaluation context function library. As usual, zero or more arguments are passed to the function.

Convert an argument to type string by calling the `string` function. An argument is converted to type number by calling the `number` function. The same is true for booleans.

One can perform the following expression tests:

Comparing two values. To locate the node set you want to manipulate, begin by creating the path to the desired node. Then create the comparison test using one of the following operators:

- `=` `(equals)`
- `!=` `(not equal to)`
- `&gt;` `(greater-than)`
- `&lt;` `(less-than)`

Next type the path to the node set containing the two values you want to compare. You can use "`and`" or "`or`" to test the condition.

```
<xsl:template match='condition'/>
  <xsl:choose>
  <xsl:if test="0">
  <font color='red' title='the bill has not been paid'>Not
  paid</font>
  <xsl::when>
  </xsl:choose>
</xsl:template>
```

You can also test the position of the node by using the `posi-tion()` function.

```
<xsl:value-of select="Books/book[position()= last()]"/>
```

You can also test for the last position by using the `last()` function. Including an exclamation point ! (not) operator verifies that the selected node is not the last position and so on.

```
<xsl:value-of select="Books/book[position()!= last()]"/>
```

Another node test we can use was demonstrated in Chapter 5 when we tested for line position in the Wordsworth poem.

```
<xsl:template match='line'>
    <xsl:if test="position() mod 2 = 0">  </xsl:if>
    <xsl:value-of select="."/><br/>
</xsl:template>
```

Let's examine the following string-handling functions.

- The `concat` function concatenates its arguments. For example, 'one', 'two'. four' becomes 'onetwofour'.
- The function `starts-with (string, string)` returns true.
- The function `starts-with` returns true if the first argument string begins with the second argument string.
- `string substring-before` returns the substring of the first argument string preceding the first occurrence of the second argument string in the first argument string. For example, `"substring-before('2001/05/01','/')"` returns 2001.

- string" substring-after('2001/05/01','/')"
  returns 05/01.

- The function substring(string, number, number?)
  returns the substring of the first argument beginning at the specified position in the second argument with length specified in
  the third argument. For example, "substring('12345'
  2,3)" returns "234".

- The function string "string-length('string?')" returns
  the number of characters residing in the string, which is 7.

The function string translate(string, string, string)
returns the first argument string with occurrences of characters in the
second argument string replaced by the character at the corresponding position in the third argument string. For example,
<xsl:value-of select="translate('one' ,'abc',
'ABC') "/> returns one.

6.12 Extension Functions Using the Document Object Model

You use extension functions in much the same manner as normal
functions provided by XSLT and XPath. Occasionally you might
need to retrieve data from an external source such as a database.
Alternatively, you might need to access a system function (say, a
date) or random number generator. There may be complicated situations, such as numbers crunching, where a specific function is not
available in XPath or XSLT. Then you need to call an extension function. Extension functions are always called within an XPath expression. The name of the extension function will always include a
namespace prefix and a colon, as in dps:function($arg1, 10,
string(title)). The function will take any number of arguments,
including the needed parentheses. Your selected language can include
Java, JavaScript, or VBScript. JScript is particularly appropriate for
MSXML 3.0 or above (now you should use MSXML 4.0). Java is
appropriate if you are using Saxon or Xalan.

Note that XSLT version 1.1 is not being developed beyond this
version, so check with www.w3.org for bindings for Java and ECMA

script. You must also use the Document Object Model to take advantage of Java bindings.

When using an extension element within a template, the following code demonstrates its application:

```
<xsl: template match='/'>
    <xsl:variable name='var' select = '25'/>
    <ext:while test ='var' > 0
    update $var −1'>
    <p><xsl:value-of select='var'/></p>
    </ext:while>
</xsl:template>
```

Apply either the `element-available()` or `function-available()` to ascertain whether an extension element is available. XSLT provides an `xsl:fallback` function; this represents an exception handler for `xsl:fallback`. For example, fallback elements are placed inside instruction elements. If an element containing the fallback elements is not available, these elements are processed in document order. Otherwise, the engine ignores them.

6.13 Reconsidering Patterns

After reviewing this chapter in detail, you need to remember the distinction between XPath expressions and patterns. Once you understand these differences, applying the appropriate template becomes an easy task in any given context. The following suggestions highlight some of the most important concepts we have covered:

- Always examine your context node.
- Examine the context node's size.
- Evaluate variables being currently referenced.
- Consider the namespaces in effect while evaluating the current node.
- Evaluate functions currently in effect.
- Use abbreviated axes as much as possible.
- Always look to the ancestor or self node to determine whether the node you are evaluating is a child of the context node.

Summary

- XSLT creates a data structure based on the source document.
- The XSLT processor traverses the tree, grouping elements, reordering them, sorting them, and copying text to their appropriate node/node sets.
- The processor manipulates nodes by applying template rules and creating a result tree for rendering documents in the desired format.
- XPath makes provisions for testing whether a node matches a pattern by viewing an XML document as a set of nodes representing a hierarchical tree.
- We refer to the order of nodes representing elements as the document order and call it a depth-first traversal, beginning with the document root and visiting each node.
- An XPath expression returns objects of four different types:
  - A string consisting of a sequence of characters.
  - A boolean (true or false).
  - A number (floating point).
  - A node set containing an unordered group of non-duplicating nodes. A node set is the result of an expression. It can either be empty or contain only one node. These sets can be ordered as they are referenced.
- Base an expression evaluation on the current context node.
- The following five items represent the context node:
  - The context node itself
  - The context position and context size
  - A core function being used from the core function library
  - A determination of all namespaces in scope for the expression
  - A set of variable bindings
- A location path consists of two separate types:
  - The relative location path
  - The absolute location

- A location step consists of three individual components.
  - The first component is an axis defining the tree relationship between nodes selected by both the location step and context node.
  - The second component defines the type of node being selected, including the expanded name of nodes selected by the location step.
  - The third component contains zero or more predicates that use arbitrary expressions to specify further the set of nodes being selected by the location step.
- Thirteen separate axes exist, and every axis has a principal node type. They include the following:
  - An attribute axis
  - A namespace axis

    For other axes, the principal node type is the element.
- XML namespaces provide an easy method for qualifying element and attribute names.
- Expressions are always dependent on the context node, whereas patterns are context free.
- Function call expressions are evaluated by using the function name to identify a function in the expression evaluation context function library.
- Extension functions are used in much the same manner as normal functions provided by XSLT and XPath.

Self-Review Exercises

The following statements are either true or false. If false, provide an explanation why.

1. XSLT creates a data structure based on a stylesheet.

2. An XML source document contains a set of nodes representing a hierarchical tree.

3. The order of nodes representing elements is called the in-depth traversal.

PART 2

TRANSFORMATION

4. An XPath expression is a formula for creating a tree.

5. The current context is the root element.

6. An XPath expression is evaluated to return an object of two different types.

7. The context position and context size are the same.

8. An expression is context free, whereas a pattern is not.

9. A location path consists of three separate types.

10. Thirteen separate axes exist. You can apply them to a source document.

Projects

1. Write an XPath expression to return the third author name in books.xml. Use the following example for this query.

```xml
<?xml version="1.0" encoding="UTF-8"?>
<books>
  <book>
    <title>XML Language Mechanics</title>
    <author name="Dwight Peltzer">
        <contactInfo person="MWP">
          <email>dpeltzer@hotmail.com</email>
          <phone>516-922-3555</phone>
        </contactInfo>
     </author>
     <publisher>Addison Wesley</publisher>
  </book>
  <book>
    <title>The Human Interface</title>
    <author name="Steven Heim">
        <contactInfo person="MH">
          <email>sheim@liu.edu</email>
          <phone>516-299-2046</phone>
        </contactInfo>
     </author>
     <publisher>Addison Wesley</publisher>
  </book>
```

```
<book>
    <title>CyberCrime</title>
    <author name="Chris Malinowski">
        <contactInfo person="LIU">
            <email>xmalinow@liu.edu</email>
            <phone>516-299-2047</phone>
        </contactInfo>
    </author>
    <publisher>XPress</publisher>
</book>
</books>
```

2. Write an XPath expression to return the third title element in books.xml.

3. Write an XPath expression to return the third publisher in books.xml.

4. Write an XPath expression to return the following-sibling node in books.xml, containing the `publisher` child node from context node (the second book node). It should return following:

name	value / attributes
() publisher	XPress

5. Assuming in books.xml that the context node is `title[2]`, return the following-sibling node. It should return the following:

name	value / attributes
() author	name="Steven Heim"
() publisher	Addison Wesley

6. Using books.xml, write an expression that selects all children elements of context node `book[2]`. It should return the following:

name	value / attributes
() title	CyberCrime
() author	name="Chris Malinowski"
() publisher	XPress

7. Assume the context node is `author[1]` in books.xml. Write an XPath expression using attributes to return the following result:

name	value / attributes
☰ name	Dwight Peltzer
☰ person	MWP
☰ name	Steven Heim
☰ person	MH
☰ name	Chris Malinowski
☰ person	LIU

8. Write an XPath expression that uses the following-sibling syntax to return the following results. The current context node is `book[1]`. The nodes are all children of the same node.

name	value / attributes
{} title	CyberCrime
{} author	name="Chris Malinowski"
{} publisher	XPress

9. Write an XPath expression using descendant syntax to return the third descendant of `author`. It returns the following:

name	value / attributes
{} author	name="Chris Malinowski"

10. Write an example using the `text()` function. The current context node is `<DailyPlanner>`. The source code is as follows:

```
<?xml version="1.0" encoding="UTF-8"?>
<DailyPlanner>
  <Sunday>
    <am>Leisure Day</am>
    <pm>1:00 Jets Game</pm>
  </Sunday>
  <Monday>
    <am>10:00 meeting with Steve
        11:00 Faculty Meeting
        12:00 Lunch
    </am>
    <pm>
```

```
                  1:00 CSC 504
                  3:00 Meeting with Susan
                  6:30 CSC 602
                  8:40 CSC 600
         </pm>
</Monday>
<Tuesday>
  <am>9:00 Meeting with Editor 805 8th Avenue</am>
  <pm>2:00 Meeting with Microsoft</pm>
</Tuesday>
<Wednesday>
  <am>9:30 Conference at Microsoft</am>
         12:00 Luncheon Meeting with Bill
</Wednesday>
<Thursday>
  <am>9:00 11:30 Conference call with editors</am>
  <pm>1:30 Meeting with Time Warner</pm>
</Thursday>
<Friday>
  <am>Keep free for writing</am>
  <pm>1:00 Luncheon meeting at ICM</pm>
</Friday>
<Saturday>
  <am>Free</am>
  <pm>Free</pm>
</Saturday>
```

`</DailyPlanner>` should be as follows:

name	value / attributes
Abc	Leisure Day
Abc	1:00 Jets Game
Abc	10:00 meeting with Steve
Abc	1:0
Abc	9:00 Meeting with Editor 805 8th Avenue
Abc	2:00 Meeting with Microsoft
Abc	12:00 Luncheon
Abc	9:30 Conference at Microsoft
Abc	9:00 11:30 Conference call with editors
Abc	1:30 Meeting with Time Warner
Abc	Keep free for writing
Abc	1:00 Luncheon meeting at ICM
Abc	Free

PRESENTATION

PART **3**

7 | XHTML

7.1 Why Do We Need XHTML?

The question posed in the Introduction was "Why do we need XML?" The same question can be asked of Extensible Hypertext Markup Language (XHTML), and the answer is simple. The balkanization of HTML, a subset of Standard Generalized Markup Language (SGML), led browser developers astray. They lost sight of the original intent of HTML: searchable text documents. Both Netscape and Internet Explorer developers, just to mention a few, responded to calls for more and more bells and whistles to be included in each new release. Unfortunately, these new features were presentation oriented, having little to do with HTML's main purpose: to provide document structure.

For the most part, XHTML is identical to HTML version 4.01. In reality, most of the revisions to HTML were actually done in version 4.0.

7.2 What Is XHTML?

XHTML, just like its predecessor (HTML), defines document structure. It consists of three separate versions:

- Strict DTD

PART 3

PRESENTATION

Appendix A contains the complete XHTML Strict DTD.

- Transitional DTD
- Frameset DTD

The *strict* version corrects weaknesses present in HTML by ensuring enforcement of structure and nothing else. XHTML excludes all deprecated tags and attributes in HTML 4.01. This forces web page authors to use only those features fully supported in the strict HTML DTD. The XHTML DTD doesn't include `<font>` tags. Cascading style sheets (levels 1 and later) support styling. However, many web page authors find the strict version too restrictive and use the second XHTML version, *transitional* DTD, which includes all deprecated features. HTML authors love the transitional version because it allows them to migrate their legacy HTML applications to XML and still enjoy some of the deprecated features in HTML 4.0.

The third version, called *framesets*, is identical to the transitional version with the exception that frames replace the document body with appropriate frames. The transitional DTD serves as basis for the frameset DTD.

7.3 Nonconforming User Agents

Despite well-meaning efforts by the W3C Consortium to create three separate DTDs for XHTML, both Netscape version 6.2 and Microsoft Internet Explorer version 6.0 (and other browsers not listed here) do not support the XHTML strict DTD. Microsoft's XML specialist informs us that the MSXML parser version 4.0, embedded in IE Explorer, does not support the strict DTD. One successful method for testing XHTML strict code uses XML Spy version 4.2. The embedded browser in the Spy IDE catches all nonconforming code violations. Use HTML Validator at http://validator.w3.org/ as an alternative. We hope future browser releases from all vendors will conform to XHTML's strict DTD and therefore ensure the viability and integrity of extensible languages.

7.4   Creating XHTML Documents

Specifying the XML version as 1.0 informs the browser how to interpret the document:

1. Declare the XML prologue as per usual, specifying version 1.0.

2. Declare the markup language's DTD.

The declaration looks like the following:

```
<?xml version="1.0" encoding="UTF-8"?>
<!DOCTYPE html PUBLIC "-//W3C//DTD XHTML 1.0 Strict//EN"
"http://www.w3.org/TR/xhtml1/DTD/xhtml1-strict.dtd">
<html xmlns="http://www.w3.org/1999/xhtml">
```

HTML defines the document root in the DTD. Specify the PUBLIC identifier as "-//W3C//DTD XHTML 1.0 Strict//EN". The URL following the public identifier instructs the browser where to locate the DTD file. If the file resides locally, the browser knows where to locate it. The <! DOCTYPE declaration instructs the browser to use the strict version.

The declaration for the transitional version is as follows:

```
<?xml version="1.0" encoding="UTF-8"?>
<!DOCTYPE html PUBLIC "-//W3C//DTD XHTML 1.0 TRANSITIONAL//EN"
"http://www.w3.org/TR/xhtml1/DTD/xhtml1-transitional.dtd">
<html xmlns="http://www.w3.org/1999/xhtml">
```

Finally, the frameset version replaces the transitional version in the declaration.

7.5   Writing Our First XHTML Document

We begin the examination of XHTML by presenting a properly structured XHTML document. Required elements include the DOCTYPE declaration specifying the DTD version (strict, transitional, or frameset), the xmlns namespace declaration, and the ubiquitous

<html>, <head>, <title>, <body>, and corresponding closing tags. XHTML is case sensitive; therefore, write all tags in lowercase.

```
<?xml version="1.0" encoding="UTF-8"?>
<!DOCTYPE html PUBLIC "-//W3C//DTD XHTML 1.0 Strict//EN"
"http://www.w3.org/TR/xhtml1/DTD/xhtml1-strict.dtd">
<html xmlns="http://www.w3.org/1999/xhtml">
   <head>
     <title>Chapter Eight</title>
   </head>
   <body>
     <p>This chapter focuses on XHTML</p>
   </body>
</html>
```

Figure 7.1   My first XHTML document

This structurally correct XHTML document should always be applied to every document. However, if you include the following document fragment and validate using the strict version, the parser generates an error:

```
<body>
     <b>This chapter focuses on XHTML</b>
     <i>XHTML and Namespaces</i>
</body>
```

Why? The strict DTD does not allow such tags unless they are embedded within a paragraph tag. The parser requires a <p> tag for this fragment to work:

```
<body>
     <p><b>This chapter focuses on XHTML</b></p>
     <p><i>XHTML and Namespaces</i></p>
</body>
```

If we revert to the transitional version, it is back to the good old days where you can enjoy all the permissive bells and whistles in HTML version 4.0. Although the transitional version is convenient, whenever possible, we recommend migrating your legacy applications to the strict version, referencing stylesheets for presentation, and using all of XML's benefits.

7.6   Namespaces and XHTML

A DTD defines elements, attribute names, and markup characters as part of the markup language. For example, you will recall that a DTD views a document as either parsed character data or character data. CDATA is unparsed data. The parser reacts to any markup symbol, such as the lesser-than and greater-than characters, by treating the < character as the beginning of a markup tag. An XHTML document may contain numerous markup characters that are not part of a beginning or closing markup tag. The correct way to instruct the parser to ignore them is placing those characters within a CDATA section, and the parser will not attempt to treat them in the normal manner.

Consider the following fragment of code:

```
<Demo><![CDATA{<This code contains markup characters, i.e. the
< and > characters]]></Demo>
```

The declarations and definitions for these elements reside in a namespace that's unique to the DTD. The browser consults the DTD for instructions on how to interpret these elements as they are referenced. Depending on context, you can include multiple DTDs in your document. In the event that more than one DTD uses the same name for defining elements that are different, the `xmlns` attribute resolves this namespace clash. For example, the math `div` attribute is used for division, whereas the XHTML `<div>` tag is a block-level container. We recommend using the `xmlns` attribute accompanied by its URL value and placing it in the starting tag to uniquely identify the element/attributes. Applied in this context, the URL uniquely identifies the namespace. The following example demonstrates how the URL is declared:

```
<html xmlns="http://www.w3.org/1999/xhtml>
```

If you are going to apply a specific tag to many different elements within your document, declare and label the unique namespace in the document header. Then reference the label at will by placing it in a starting tag. For example, we can do the following:

```
<html xmlns="http://www.w3.org/1999/xhtml"
 xmlns:Math ="http://www.w3.org/1998/Math/MathML">
```

Once you have made your declarations, reference the `xmlns` attribute in the following manner: `<math:div>a1/x</div>`. Observe how convenient and simple it is. This concept applies to any situation requiring a unique namespace. (Refer to Chapter 4, "Introducing Schemas," for a discussion on namespaces.)

7.7   End Tags

One unique feature in HTML allows us to leave out closing tags for elements such as `<br>` and `<li>`. Most browsers render tags officially requiring closing tags such as `<p>` even if the closing tag is omitted. However, XHTML does not allow this. You must think in pairs of elements, meaning opening and closing tags. To write a well-formed document, every opening tag requires a closing tag, as in `<p></p>`, `<li></li>`, `<th></th>`, `<tr></tr>`, and `<td></td>`. We realize how much more effort it requires to close every element tag and how illogical it is to write `<br></br>`. For singlets or empty tags like `<br>` and objects like `<img>`, concatenate into one tag both the opening and closing tags, as follows: `<br />` or `<img src="my_image.gif" />`. Include a space and closing slash before the > symbol.

A list of empty HTML tags in acceptable XHTML format includes the following:

```
<area />, <param />, <img />, <hr />, <input />, <isindex />,
<base />, <basefont />, <link />, <br />, <col />, <frame />,
<meta />
```

7.8   Nested Elements

Both XHTML and XML well-formed documents require correct nesting. Three situations exist in which this might become an issue:

- Improper nesting order:

  ```
  <body><p><b>This chapter focuses on XHTML</p></b>
  <p><i>XHTML and Namespaces</p></i></body>
  ```

- Obvious inclusion conflicts:

  The `<label>` tag cannot contain another `<label>` tag.

  The `<form>` tag cannot contain other `<form>` tags.

  The `<button>` tag may not contain the following:

  ```
  <select>, <input>, <label>, <textarea>, <button>,
  <form>, <fieldset>, <iframe>, <isindex>
  ```

  The `<pre>` tag cannot contain `<big>`, `<small>`, `<object>`, `<sub>`, or `<sup>`.

- Nonobvious inclusion conflicts:

  ```
  <cite><p>…</p> </cite>
  <a href="myFile.html"><h3>This is my file</h3></a>
  ```

It is always a good policy to close tags from the inside out. The element tag preceding the content should be closed immediately after the content. Then close the outer tag. Other nesting restrictions apply and are covered in the Appendix A, "XHTML Strict DTD Version 1.0."

7.9 Enclosing Attributes in Quotes

XHTML requires enclosing attributes with double quotes. For example, XML source documents require them as shown in Figure 7.2.

```
<books>
   <book category="CS">
   </book>
   <book category="History">
   </book>
</books>
```

Figure 7.2   Double quotes

The following example is incorrect in XHTML: `<table colspan=5>`. It generates an error, whereas syntax in this example is correct: `<table colspan="5">`. Here's yet another example: `<table border="0" cellpadding="5">`.

For those authors who want to generate server-side scripts dynamically in XHTML, wrapping attributes in double quotes presents a problem. For example, consider an ASP script that dynamically places an image in the document:

```
<%
Response.Write("img src=" & queryResults (dps.gif") &
"/>")
%>
```

Inside the `Response.Write ()` function, incorporate a dynamically built string in the document being sent to the browser, as follows:

```
<%
Response.Write ("img src=" & Chr (22) & queryResults
("dps.gif") & Chr(22) & "/>")
%>
```

Use the `Chr()` VBScript function in such a situation.

> **Note:** The `Chr` function converts an ANSI character code value to a character.

7.10 Attribute Minimization in XHTML

XHTML does not allow attribute minimization. This refers to situations in which explicit attribute values or one-word attributes should not be used. Instead, write `name="value"`. For example, the `nowrap` attribute forces the browser to write the text on a single line; therefore, write it in the following manner: `nowrap="nowrap"`. All browsers can handle these new values. A list of new attribute values includes `noresize="noresize"`, `compact="compact"`, `nowrap="nowrap"`, `selected="selected"`, `noshade="noshade"`, `ismap="ismap"`, `checked="checked"`, `disabled="disabled"`, `declare="declare"`, `readonly="readonly"`, `multiple="multiple"`, and `defer="defer"`.

7.11 Character Data in XHTML

To be properly interpreted, place markup within CDATA sections in XHTML. For example, let's assume we are going to gain control over objects embedded within JavaScript. We could write the following example:

```
<script language="JavaScript">
<![CDATA[ place your JavaScript here. . .
 ]]>
</script>
```

Client-side script code is not subject to the same rules as XHTML. The JavaScript code fragment in Figure 7.3 allows users to select the correct RPM access time for a new hard drive.

```
<?xml version="1.0" encoding="UTF-8"?>
<!DOCTYPE html PUBLIC "-//W3C//DTD XHTML 1.0 Transitional//EN"
"http://www.w3.org/TR/xhtml1/DTD/xhtml1-transitional.dtd">
<html xmlns="http://www.w3.org/1999/xhtml">

<head>
<title>MaximOnline.com Order Form</title>
<script type="text/javascript">

<![CDATA[
    function validate(myForm) {
        var rbchecked = 0;
        for(int i = 0; i < myForm.type.length; i++) {
          if (myForm.type[i],checked) {
              rbchecked=1;
      }
        }
        if(rbchecked) {
            alert("Please select the size for your hard
drive!");
            return false;
        }
        else {
```

```
                    return true;
        }
    }
]]> <!-- CDATA ends here -->
</script>
</head>
<body bgcolor="white">
<h1> MaximOnline.com</h1>
<p> Order your hard drive online in our form:</p>

<form action="orderprocess.pl" method="post" onsubmit="return
validate(this)">

<table border="0" cellpadding="6">

<tr valign="top">
            <td><b> RPM Speed:</b></td>
            <td>
            <input type="radio" name="type" value="7200"/>
            7200 RPM
            <input type="radio" name="type"  value="5200"/>
            5200 RPM
            </td>
            </tr>
<tr valign="top">
            <td><b>RPM:>3200</b></td>
        <td>
        <select name="RPM"  multiple="multiple">
        <option>7200</option>
        <option>5200</option>
        <option>3200</option>
            </select>
            </td>
</tr>
<tr><td colspan="2"><input type="submit" value="Order
Item!"/></td></tr>
</table>
</form>
</body>
</html>
```

Figure 7.3 RPM access time

Unfortunately, a caveat exists. HTML browsers like to ignore XML CDATA contents. If your browser ignores CDATA, use the `src` attribute of the `<script>` element to read in your client-side code from an external source. Then you do not need to create a CDATA section inside the script element.

XHTML does not like special characters such as the ampersand, greater-than, and lesser-than symbols when they are embedded within attributes. Use entity references to escape them, as follows:

```
<img src="LarryMoeCurly.gif alt="Larry Moe &amp; Curly" />.
```

Refer to Chapter 2, "Document Type Definition," for a review of entity references.

7.12 Binding Elements with the ID Attribute

The `name` attribute was used in early versions of HTML to create a fragment identifier. This enabled scripts to identify and manipulate a specific object on the page. It was also associated with the `input` tag and used as a group delimiter, thereby enabling radio buttons to function properly. However, the `name` attribute fragment identifier is now deprecated and replaced by the `id` attribute now fully supported by XHTML. Simply add the `id` attribute to an element and then reference it anywhere within your document. The attribute for the `input` tag is necessary for all but the `submit` and `reset` types. Include the following NMTOKEN tags as an implied attribute: `select`, `textarea`, `button`, `meta`, `param`, the `a  object` and `map`.

7.13 Converting Your Documents to XHTML

One of the predicaments HTML authors face when trying to make a shift from HTML to XHTML is converting all document element tags to lowercase to conform to the new standard. One product available for doing this is Allaire's Homesite version 4.5. You simply navigate to the Edit column drop-down menu and select Convert Tag Case. Then select one of two options: Upper Case or Lower Case. Choose the latter and eliminate this time-consuming task.

7.14 Examining a Well-Formed HTML Document

Let's convert a well-formed HTML document to XHTML. The web page in Figure 7.4 conforms to the HTML 4.0 DTD.

```
<html>
<head><title> DP Software Inc.</title></head>
<body bgcolor="white" link="#660000" vlink="blue"
alink="#cc0099">
<center>
<!--Outside table-->
<table border="0" cellpadding="0" cellspacing="2"
background="Graphics/sun.jpg">
<tr>
<td>
<!--Inside table-->
<table border="0" cellpadding="0" cellspacing="2"  width="500"
background="Graphics/trans.gif">
<tr>
<td align="right" width="90" height="250"> </td>
<td width="5" bgcolor="#6666ff"> </td>
<td width="200"><br>
<br>
<!--DP Software address-->
<h3>DP Software</h3>
<address>
PO Box 202 <br>
EAST NORWICH, N.Y. <br>
11732 </address>
</td>
<td width="5" rowspan="3" bgcolor="#6666ff"> </td>
<td rowspan="3" width="200" valign="top"><br>
<br><br><br><br><br><br><br>
<!--DP Contact--><b>Tel: </b>(516) 922-2822
<br>
<b>Fax: </b>(516) 922-2835
<br><br>
<b>Email:</b>
<br>
```

```
<a
href="mailto:dpeltzer@dpsoftware.com">dpeltzer@dpsoftware.com</
a>
<br>
</td>
</tr>
<tr>
<td colspan="3" height="10">
<hr width="100%" noshade>
</td>
</tr>
<tr>
<td align="right" height="250"></td>
<td width="5"> </td>
<td align="right" valign="top"><!--Web Alliance Members-->
<h3>Web Alliance</h3>
<a href="http://www.st-eve.com" target="_top">St. Eve</a>
</td>
</tr>
</table><!--End Inside table-->
</td>
</tr>
</table><!--End outside table-->
</center>
</body></html>
```

Figure 7.4   DP Software's incorrect version

This simple example includes a few HTML tag presentational features to achieve a conservative yet attractive "look" for the contact page of a larger site. Utilizing the `bgcolor` aspect in an empty table cell in combination with the `font color` attribute presents a pleasing appearance with minimal load time. The background image of the outside table relates to the overall graphic look of the site, one that utilizes frames to organize its navigation. Note how we use a transparent image for the inside table and insert the background image into the outside cell table. This guarantees proper Netscape rendering for the background image of the table.

As the browser parses this document, it first checks to see if the document is well formed. Several items must be altered to properly convert this frame to strict XHTML. All `<br>` elements generate errors because they are defined in the DTD as empty, thereby allowing no content within them. Closing all <br> elements by using
 </br> generates undesirable results in some HTML agents. Therefore, resolve this issue by closing all empty tags as follows: <br />.

The browser rejects the `noshade` attribute of the `hr` tag because this presentational attribute is now deprecated. Eliminating `noshade` eliminates the problem. The responsibility for `noshade` should be transferred instead to cascading style sheets. The next task is closing the `hr` tag, just as we did for the `br` tag. Doing this does not, however, eliminate the problem for boolean attributes in general. When using attributes like `ismap` and `nohref`, add a new value to this attribute, namely the attribute name itself, as in `nohref="nohref"`. Another error occurs when the browser looks for the `doc type` and `namespace` definitions. Both of these replace the HTML opening tag.

```
<?xml version="1.0" encoding="UTF-8"?>
<!DOCTYPE html PUBLIC "-//W3C//DTD XHTML 1.0 Strict//EN"
"http://www.w3.org/TR/xhtml1/DTD/xhtml1-strict.dtd">
<html xmlns="http://www.w3.org/1999/xhtml">
```

The browser attempts to validate the document and returns an error when it encounters the `bgcolor` attribute of the body tag. Link attributes (`link="#660000"` `vlink="blue"` `alink="#cc0099"`) generate an error and should be removed. Additionally, the unexpected `center` tag does not conform and must be removed. Also remove the `background="…"` attributes for tables; the `width`, `height`, and `bgcolor` attribute for table cells, and `width` for the `hr` tag. Finally, to conform to the strict DTD, remove the reference for the target frame (`_top`). We now have a well-formed valid document (see Figure 7.5) in which all presentational aspects of the page are gone, leaving a barely recognizable version of the original. If we had utilized a few more basic graphic elements, we might have faired slightly better by retaining the "look" of the page. Layout diminishment was unavoidable, and links no longer function in the frameset as required. The obvious reason for this is we are trying to convert a legacy HTML page (not conforming to the strict HTML 4.01 DTD) to XHTML using the strict XHTML DTD. We would have fared much better with the transitional XHTML DTD because the page incorporated the presentational and layout aspects within the HTML tags themselves rather than using stylesheets. If this page were written to conform to the strict HTML DTD, only minimal corrections would be necessary.

This leaves us with the question, "Which strategy should we use for dealing with existing HTML pages?" Unfortunately, no global strategy offers a best-case solution because we must consider conflicting factors. However, generally speaking, pages noncompliant with the strict HTML 4.01 DTD will always retain a certain amount of longevity if we bring them into compliance with the frameset XHTML DTD, therefore requiring only slight, general alteration. Pages being developed to interact with an existing site can still enjoy the relaxed restrictions that the frameset DTD offers and yet comply with the strict DTD. This decreases the necessity of converting the entire site if the need arises. When possible, comply with the strict DTD, thereby ensuring the site's viability for the future.

```
<?xml version="1.0" encoding="UTF-8"?>
<!DOCTYPE html PUBLIC "-//W3C//DTD XHTML 1.0 Strict//EN"
"http://www.w3.org/TR/xhtml1/DTD/xhtml1-strict.dtd">
<html xmlns="http://www.w3.org/1999/xhtml">
<head><title> DP Software Inc.</title></head>
<body>
<table border="0" cellpadding="0" cellspacing="2" >
<tr>
<td>
<table border="0" cellpadding="0" cellspacing="2"  width="500">
<tr>
<td align="right" > 
</td>
<td> 
</td>
<td><br />
<br />
<!--DP Software address-->
<h3>DP Software</h3>
<address>
PO Box 202 <br />
EAST NORWICH, N.Y. 11732<br/>
</address>
</td>
```

```
<td   rowspan="3" > </td>
<td rowspan="3"  valign="top"><br />
<br /><br /><br /><br /><br /><br /><br />
<!--DP Contact--><b>Tel: </b>(516) 922-2822<br />
<b>Fax: </b>(516) 922-2835
<br />
<br />
<b>Email:</b>
<br />
<a
href="mailto:dpeltzer@dpsoftware.com">dpeltzer@dpsoftware.com</
a>
<br />
</td>
</tr>
<tr>
<td colspan="3" >
<hr   />
</td>
</tr>
<tr>
<td align="right" ></td>
<td > </td>
<td align="right" valign="top"><!--Web Alliance Members-->
<h3>Web Alliance</h3>
<a href="http://www.st-eve.com" >St. Eve</a>
</td>
</tr>
</table></td>
</tr>
</table>
</body>
</html>
```

Figure 7.5   The correct DPS version

Summary

- XHTML is a remake of HTML version 4.01.
- XHTML conforms to XML.
- Your HTML document must be well formed because XHTML is an XML application.
- XHTML documents must conform to one of three DTDs:
  - Strict
  - Transitional
  - Framesets
- The XHTML transitional DTD allows most HTML and XHTML elements and attributes defined in HTML 4.0 with the exception of frames.
- The XHTML frameset DTD is similar to the transitional DTD, with the exception that frameset replaces the document body with appropriate frames.
- XHTML allows you to use general entities in your source documents.
- XHTML lets you define entity references in your pages.
- XML parsers use the encoding declaration to determine the character set.
- The XML prologue is not required in the XHTML document top.
- Your document must use either UTF-8 or UTF-16 encoding if the XML prologue is not declared.
- Use `xml:lang` and `html:lang` to identify the language of an element.
- Include CDATA in your XHTML document; however, browser support is missing for the most part.
- The XHTML family is designed with general user agent interoperability in mind.
- Through a new user agent and document profiling mechanism, servers, proxies, and user agents will be able to perform best-effort content transformation.
- Information is difficult to find because data resides in many different formats.

- Delineating chapter headings and subtitles and subdividing document segments into meaningful blocks of information facilitate searching.
- Well-structured documents and properly presented content bring consumers back to your web site, not glitzy pages.
- The XHTML standard adds Form Feed () and zero-width space (&#x200b) to the list of whitespace characters defined in the XML standard.

  The XHTML standard handles whitespace according to the following rules:

  - Remove all whitespace surrounding block elements.
  - Comments are removed entirely and do not affect whitespace handling. One whitespace character on either side of a comment is handled as two whitespace characters.
  - Convert line-feed characters within a block element into a space. If the attribute `preserve` is specified, the conversion will not occur.

- The document root element in XHTML is <html>, as defined in the DTD.
- The URL following the public identifier instructs the browser where to locate the DTD file.
- Both XHTML and XML well-formed documents require correct nesting.

Self-Review Exercises

The following statements are either true or false. If false, explain why.

1. Your source document must use either UTF-8 or UTF-16 encoding if the XML prologue is not declared.

2. A well-formed HTML source document is recognized by XML documents.

3. XHTML is a reformulation of HTML DTD version 4.0.

4. HTML is a standard generalized markup application (SGMA) and is widely recognized as the standard publishing language of the World Wide Web.

5. All major browsers, including Netscape and Internet Explorer, recognize the XHTML strict version.

6. XHTML's transitional DTD replaces HTML version 4.0.

7. XHTML's frameset DTD does not recognize HTML frames. (If false, write an XHTML document using frames.)

8. Functionality includes elements but not attributes in the new XHTML strict DTD.

9. A user agent retrieves and processes XHTML documents but does not render XHTML documents in HTML.

10. A strictly conforming XHTML document must be validated by the transitional DTD.

11. A DOCTYPE declaration must be declared in the document immediately following the root element.

12. The system identifier included in the DOCTYPE declaration must reference only the strict DTD, not the transitional DTD.

13. Explain why the root element in an XHTML source document must be defined as <html>.

Projects

1. What is the XHTML namespace? Provide an example.

2. Provide a basic XHTML declaration for the strict DTD.

3. Provide an XHTML declaration for the transitional DTD.

4. Write an XHTML document using the frameset DTD.

5. Write an XHTML program conforming to the strict DTD.

6. Write an XHTML program demonstrating how markup CDATA is used in a document conforming to the strict version.

7. Write a program containing an interactive JavaScript component. Use radio buttons to provide users with options to choose a specific hardware component, such as a choice of Ethernet cards.

8. Write an XHTML source document using other namespaces.

9. Write an XHTML source document demonstrating differences with HTML. Document these differences using both comments and examples.

8 Modularizing XHTML

PART 3
PRESENTATION

> **Note to Reader:** This chapter is advanced XHTML and focuses on
> *Modularization*. Unless you are going to design modules for digital
> devices, i.e. PDAs, or wish to learn more about XHTML in depth, you
> may skip to chapter 9 and learn how to map your data to a relational
> database.

8.1 XHTML Modularization

XHTML modules are Document Type Definition fragments. We can
merge them into the existing XHTML framework and build a new
markup language. Modularization provides the structure for creating
new markup languages with the XHTML framework module and
XHTML core modules. The W3C Working Draft Committee
for XHTML provides a template DTD with which we can build our
own modules. Before we create a new markup language, we will take
a close look at the XHTML strict DTD to understand how modularization works. Following that discussion, we will examine the DTD
template and import the Table module into the template, thereby creating a new markup language. Finally, we will build a DTD for
invoices and inventory.

XHTML is HTML
reformulated to
conform to the XML 1.0
Recommendation.

321

8.2   Parameter Entity Resolution

Let's begin with analysis of parameter entities as they function within
the XHTML strict DTD. When referenced, they expand in the DTD
itself. In essence, they serve as shorthand. For example, look at the
attributes for the h1 element. When defined, it is a replacement for
the complete ATTLIST declaration. We suggest that you navigate to
the strict XHTML DTD at http://www.w3.org/TR/xhtml11/ and follow
along as we traverse the parameter entity path:

```
<!ELEMENT h1    %Inline;>
<!ATTLIST h1
    %attrs;
    >
```

Element h1 contains entity %Inline and %attrs; %Inline is the
content model for h1. Here is its definition:

```
<!-- %Inline; covers inline or "text-level" elements -->
<!ENTITY % Inline "(#PCDATA | %inline; | %misc;)*">
```

This provides the content model with a choice between zero or
more #PCDATA, or content models listed by %Inline or %misc entities. Let's follow the path for parameter entities, beginning with
%inline:

```
<!ENTITY % inline "a | %special; | %fontstyle; | %phrase; |
%inline.forms;">
```

When expanded, it becomes the following:

```
<!ELEMENT h1 (#PCDATA |    a | %special; | %fontstyle; | %phrase;
| %inline.forms;")>
<!ENTITY %misc "ins | del | script | noscript">
```

Next, let's see what %special contains:

```
<!ENTITY % special    "br | span | bdo | object | img | map">
```

Now `h1` looks like the following:

```
<!ELEMENT h1 (#PCDATA |a | br | span | bdo | object | img |
 map | %fontstyle; | %phrase | %inline.forms;)>
```

Now `%fontstyle` needs resolution:

```
<!ENTITY % fontstyle "tt | i | b | big | small">
```

Next, `%phrase` contains the following:

```
<!ENTITY % phrase "em | strong | dfn | code | q | sub | sup |
samp | kbd | var | cite | abbr | acronym">
```

None of these requires resolution, so the only parameter entity to be resolved is `%inline.forms`:

```
<!ENTITY % inline.forms "input | select | textarea | label |
button">
```

We need to follow the `h1` `%attrs` path and resolve the attributes in the same manner in which we resolved the preceding parameter entities:

```
<!ENTITY % attrs "%coreattrs; %i18n; %events;">
```

`%coreattrs` is the next entity we need to pursue:

```
<!ENTITY % coreattrs
 "id          ID            #IMPLIED
  class       CDATA         #IMPLIED
  style       %StyleSheet;  #IMPLIED
  title       %Text;        #IMPLIED"
  >
```

Within %coreattrs, %StyleSheet and %Text are the next entities we must resolve:

```
<!ENTITY % StyleSheet "CDATA">
<!ENTITY % Text  "CDATA">
```

%StyleSheet indicates that it accepts all character data. The same is true for %Text. Now ATTLIST h1 looks like the following:

```
<!ATTLIST h1

    id          ID              #IMPLIED
    class       CDATA           #IMPLIED
    style       %StyleSheet;    #IMPLIED
    title       %Text;          #IMPLIED"
%il8n;
%events;
>
```

Expanding %il8n produces the following:

```
<!ENTITY % il8n
 "lang          %LanguageCode;  #IMPLIED
  xml:lang      %LanguageCode;  #IMPLIED
  dir           (ltr|rtl)       #IMPLIED"
  >
```

> **Note:** %il8n contains the definitions for internationalization.

lang is included for backward compatibility, and it identifies the language for specified content. dir (ltr|rtl) determines the direction in which a string is displayed in the browser. For example, this is a string is displayed as is if ltr is selected. Conversely, rtl displays the string as gnirts a si siht.

The %LanguageCode needs resolution:

```
<!ENTITY %LanguageCode  "NMTOKEN">
```

The %events entity contains the following entities:

```
<!ENTITY % events
 "onclick      %Script;      #IMPLIED
  ondblclick   %Script;      #IMPLIED
  onmousedown  %Script;      #IMPLIED
  onmouseup    %Script;      #IMPLIED
  onmouseover  %Script;      #IMPLIED
  onmousemove  %Script;      #IMPLIED
  onmouseout   %Script;      #IMPLIED
  onkeypress   %Script;      #IMPLIED
  onkeydown    %Script;      #IMPLIED
  onkeyup      %Script;      #IMPLIED"
  >
```

%Script is the only entity needing resolution:

```
<!ENTITY %Script    "CDATA">
```

Finally, we have completed our examination of parameter entities. Pursue the same path for any other element or attribute list included in the XHTML list.

8.3 Examining the XHTML DTD

The W3C Working Committee divided the XHTML DTD into separate abstract modules. Each module contains semantically grouped elements. Modules do not contain processing instructions; rather, they describe how modularization works. We can understand this better by examining two modules from the strict DTD for XHTML:

- Lists module
- Block module

We'll examine the Lists module first.

```
<!-- Lists Module (required)  ...... -->
<!ENTITY % xhtml-list.module "INCLUDE" >
<![%xhtml-list.module;[
<!ENTITY % xhtml-list.mod
```

```
PUBLIC "-//W3C//ELEMENTS XHTML 1.1 Lists 1.0//EN"
"xhtml 11-list-1.mod" >
%xhtml-list.mod;]]>
```

The INCLUDE attribute indicates the inclusion of this module in the DTD. The only option provided is either INCLUDE or IGNORE. The .module parameter entities use the suffix module when controlling the inclusion or exclusion of a DTD module.

The module begins with the usual header. Note that the <!ENTITY %xhtml-list.mod extension in this context informs us that .mod parameter entities use the suffix .mod to represent a DTD module, including a collection of elements, attributes, and parameter entities. Each module must be atomic and represented as an individual file entity. The block-level module contains a collection of parameter entities:

```
<!--=================== Block level elements
========================-->

<!ENTITY % heading "h1|h2|h3|h4|h5|h6">
<!ENTITY % lists "ul | ol | dl">
<!ENTITY % blocktext "pre | hr | blockquote | address">

<!ENTITY % block
"p | %heading; | div | %lists; | %blocktext; | fieldset |
table">

<!ENTITY % Block "(%block; | form | %misc;)*">

<!-- %Flow; mixes Block and Inline and is used for list items
etc. -->
<!ENTITY % Flow "(#PCDATA | %block; | form | %inline; |
%misc;)*">
```

The entity %heading contains the headings we are all familiar with. h1 displays an 1-point font size, whereas h2, h3, h4, and so on display smaller font sizes. No entity within this list requires resolution. The entity %lists offers a choice of the following three: ul | ol | dl.

The lists module offers list-oriented elements:

```
<!--===================== Lists ==================================-->

<!-- Unordered list -->

<!ELEMENT ul (li)+>
<!ATTLIST ul
  %attrs;
  >
<!-- Ordered (numbered) list -->
<!ELEMENT ol (li)+>
<!ATTLIST ol
  %attrs;
  >
<!-- list item -->

<!ELEMENT li %Flow;>
<!ATTLIST li
  %attrs;
  >
<!-- definition lists - dt for term, dd for its definition -->
<!ELEMENT dl (dt|dd)+>
<!ATTLIST dl
  %attrs;
  >
```

The `lists` module supports the elements and attributes in Table 8.1.

Table 8.1   List Elements and Attributes

Elements	Attributes	Minimal Content Model
dl	Common	(dt|dd)+
dt	Common	(PCDATA|Inline)*
dd	Common	(PCDATA|Inline)*
ol	Common	li+
ul	Common	li+
li	Common	(PCDATA|Inline)*

PART 3

PRESENTATION

The minimal content model represents a definition for indicating the elements or data allowed to be present within another element. The minimal content model for this module is (dl | dt | dd)+. This says the dl element is required to contain one or more instances of a dt element or dd element.

All W3C modules begin with commented information detailing the title of the module, the filename, a copyright statement, and revision data.

Figure 8.1 shows the abstract list module implementation.

```
<!-- XHTML Lists Module -->
<!-- file: xhtml-list-1.mod


    This is XHTML, a reformulation of HTML as a modular XML
application.
    Copyright 1998-2001 W3C (MIT, INRIA, Keio), All Rights
Reserved.
    Revision: $Id: xhtml-list-1.mod,v 4.0 2001/04/02 22:42:49
altheim Exp $ SMI
```

Figure 8.1 Abstract list modules

The next items are the PUBLIC and SYSTEM identifiers. PUBLIC and SYSTEM identify this DTD module:

```
PUBLIC "-//W3C//ELEMENTS XHTML Lists 1.0//EN"
SYSTEM "http://www.w3.org/TR/xhtml-modularization/DTD/xhtml-
list-1.mod"
Revisions:
  (none)
```

In this context, no revisions exist.

```
    .....................................................
    ............... -->
```

PART 3   PRESENTATION

This section provides a list of elements and their data types:

```
<!-- Lists
        dl, dt, dd, ol, ul, li
      This module declares the list-oriented element types
      and their attributes.-->
```

The following section presents definitions of qualified element names for the parameter entities:

```
<!ENTITY % dl.qname    "dl" >
<!ENTITY % dt.qname    "dt" >
<!ENTITY % dd.qname    "dd" >
<!ENTITY % ol.qname    "ol" >
<!ENTITY % ul.qname    "ul" >
<!ENTITY % li.qname    "li" >
```

The next section represents the single parameter entity for `dl:`, `<!ENTITY %dl.element`. Let's examine this section closely. The content model includes both the `%dt.qname` and `%dd.qname` parameter entities. The element declaration immediately following `dt.content` defines the element: `<!ELEMENT dl (dt | dd)+>`.

```
<!-- dl: Definition List ........................... -->
<!ENTITY % dl.element  "INCLUDE" >
<![%dl.element;[
<!ENTITY % dl.content  "( %dt.qname; | %dd.qname; )+" >
<!ELEMENT %dl.qname;  %dl.content; >
<!-- end of dl.element -->]]>
```

The attribute list works in the same way. A parameter entity declaration defines the entire `att list` using the INCLUDE keyword. The `Common attrib;` collection is referenced elsewhere in the DTD (refer to Table 8.1) using the `.attrib` suffixed parameter entity.

The same process continues throughout this module. The order is always `<!ENTITY content model` and then `<!ELEMENT declaration`.

PART 3 PRESENTATION

```
<!ENTITY % dl.attlist  "INCLUDE" >
<![%dl.attlist;[
<!ATTLIST %dl.qname;
     %Common.attrib;
>
<!-- end of dl.attlist -->]]>


<!-- dt: Definition Term ............................. -->


<!ENTITY % dt.element  "INCLUDE" >
<![%dt.element;[
<!ENTITY % dt.content
    "( #PCDATA | %Inline.mix; )*"
>
<!ELEMENT %dt.qname;  %dt.content; >
<!-- end of dt.element -->]]>
<!ENTITY % dt.attlist  "INCLUDE" >
<![%dt.attlist;[
<!ATTLIST %dt.qname;
     %Common.attrib;
>
<!-- end of dt.attlist -->]]>
<!-- dd: Definition Description ....................... -->
<!ENTITY % dd.element  "INCLUDE" >
<![%dd.element;[
<!ENTITY % dd.content
    "( #PCDATA | %Flow.mix; )*"
>
<!ELEMENT %dd.qname;  %dd.content; >
<!-- end of dd.element -->]]>


<!ENTITY % dd.attlist  "INCLUDE" >
<![%dd.attlist;[
<!ATTLIST %dd.qname;
     %Common.attrib;
>
<!-- end of dd.attlist -->]]>
```

```
<!-- ol: Ordered List (numbered styles) ................ -->

<!ENTITY % ol.element   "INCLUDE" >
<![%ol.element;[
<!ENTITY % ol.content   "( %li.qname; )+" >
<!ELEMENT %ol.qname;   %ol.content; >
<!-- end of ol.element -->]]>


<!ENTITY % ol.attlist   "INCLUDE" >
<![%ol.attlist;[
<!ATTLIST %ol.qname;
      %Common.attrib;
>
<!-- end of ol.attlist -->]]>
<!-- ul: Unordered List (bullet styles) ................ -->
<!ENTITY % ul.element   "INCLUDE" >
<![%ul.element;[
<!ENTITY % ul.content   "( %li.qname; )+" >
<!ELEMENT %ul.qname;   %ul.content; >
<!-- end of ul.element -->]]>


<!ENTITY % ul.attlist   "INCLUDE" >
<![%ul.attlist;[
<!ATTLIST %ul.qname;
      %Common.attrib;
>
<!-- end of ul.attlist -->]]>
<!-- li: List Item .................................... -->

<!ENTITY % li.element   "INCLUDE" >
<![%li.element;[
<!ENTITY % li.content
    "( #PCDATA | %Flow.mix; )*"
>
<!ELEMENT %li.qname;   %li.content; >
<!-- end of li.element -->]]>
```

```
<!ENTITY % li.attlist  "INCLUDE" >
<![%li.attlist;[
<!ATTLIST %li.qname;
     %Common.attrib;
>
<!-- end of li.attlist -->]]>
<!-- end of xhtml-list-1.mod -->
```

A minimal content model may also reference collections of elements known as the content set. For example:

```
<!ELEMENT dt %Inline;>
<!ATTLIST dt
%attrs;
>
```

This says the dt element can contain (#PCDATA) and any elements contained within the Inline content set. You will recall that we examined %Inline earlier in this chapter. Here is the information for your review:

```
<!-- %Inline; covers inline or "text-level" elements -->
<!ENTITY % Inline "(#PCDATA | %inline; | %misc;)*">
```

This provides the content model with a choice between zero or more #PCDATA, or content models listed by %Inline or %misc entities.

```
<!ENTITY % inline "a | %special; | %fontstyle; | %phrase; |
%inline.forms;">
```

8.4 Attribute List

XHTML uses attribute collections. The Table 8.2 provides a list of eight data types defined in the XHTML Recommendation version 1.0. These represent the allowable attribute data types in XHTML.

Table 8.2 Allowable Attributes

Attribute Type	Definition
CDATA	Character data
ID	A global unique ID
IDREF	Reference to an ID
IDREFS	A space-separated list of references to unique IDs
NAME	A name with the same character constraints as ID above
NMTOKEN	A name composed of only name tokens as defined in XML 1.0
NMTOKENS	One or more space-separated NMTOKENS values
PCDATA	Parsed character data

In addition to the eight predefined data types, the XHTML modularization DTD has defined a number of new data types, 19 to be precise (see Table 8.3).

Table 8.3 New Data Types Defined in XML

Data Type	Description of Data Type
Character	A character from any alphabet.
Charset	A character encoding as per [RFC2045], such as ISO-8859-1.
Charsets	A space-delimited list of character encodings defined by Charset.
Color	Any valid hexadecimal color, such as #C0C0C0, or one of 16 other named colors.
ContentType	A media type as defined in RFC2045.
ContentTypes	A comma-separated list of media types defined in ContentType.
Datetime	Date and time information.
FrameTarget	An XHTML frame name used as destination for results of specified actions.
LanguageCode	EN for English or FR for French, as defined in RFC1766.

Table 8.3   New Data Types Defined in XML, continued

Data Type	Description of Data Type
Length	A length specified in pixels or a percentage of available space.
LinkTypes	One or a list of names from a defined list of links.
MediaDesc	A comma-delimited list of media descriptors.
MultiLength	The value as a length or a relative length. A relative length has the format "i*" where "i" is an integer. Thus, the value "*" is equivalent to "1". For example, if 60 pixels of space is allocated, 1*, 2*, and 3* will be allocated 1 = 10 pixels, 2 = 20 pixels, and 3 = 30 pixels.
Number	One or more digits.
Pixels	A numeric value representing a number of pixels.
Script	Data passed to a script engine and not parsed by XHTML.
Text	Text-based data.
URI	A specified universal resource identifier as defined in RFC 1738.
URIs	A space-delimited list of URIs previously defined.

8.5 Defining the Type Modules

The following list describes the different type modules.

- The content model defines the structure of all elements declared in your markup language.

- The QName module contains the suffix `.mod`. This correlates with the parameter entity suffix utilized to identify it later when assembling all module components together.

- QNames parameter entities use the suffix `.QNames` when representing a qualified element name. The XML term "QNames" corresponds to qualified names. Namespaces define a globally unique domain in which one element is differentiated from another by defining its functionality. QNames modules contain parameter entities where QNames containing defined elements are stored.

- The declaration module contains a list of elements. When a referenced element requires a qualified name, retrieve it from the declaration module in fully qualified format. An example of qualified name `div` looks like the following: `dps:div`. Namespace delineates the difference in functionality and meaning.

- The `.content` parameter entities use the suffix `.content` when representing elements of the same class.

- The `.mix` parameter entities use the suffix `.mix` when representing a collection of element types from different classes.

- The `.attrib` parameter entities use `.attrib` when representing a group of tokens that represent one or more complete attribute specification within an `ATTLIST` declaration.

8.6 Examining the Skeletal DTD

In this section, we learn to utilize the template and include a predefined table module from the W3C strict DTD for creating newtable-markup.dtd. Here is Template.dtd in its entirety. Second, we insert the basic table module into the template. See Figure 8.2.

```
<!-- SKELETAL DTD
.................................................... -->
<!-- file: Template.dtd-->

<!-- SKELETAL DTD-->
<!-- This is a skeletal driver file. Modify it however you
want, paying careful attention to the embedded comments about
order.
```

```
       Please use this formal public identifier to identify it:

           "-//W3C//DTD XHTML-MYDTD//EN"-->
<!ENTITY % XHTML.version  "-//W3C//DTD XHTML-MYDTD//EN" >


<!-- Reserved for use with the XLink namespace:-->
<!ENTITY % XLINK.ns "" >
<!ENTITY % XLinkns.attrib "" >



<!-- reserved for future use with document profiles -->
<!ENTITY % XHTML.profile  "" >


<!-- Internationalization features
     Use this feature-test entity to declare elements
     and attributes used for internationalization support. Set
     it to INCLUDE or IGNORE as appropriate for your markup
     language.-->
<!ENTITY % XHTML.I18n  "IGNORE" >


<!-- Define the Content Model
     Remember that you can modify this content model or replace
     it simply by changing the following ENTITY declaration.-->
<!ENTITY % xhtml-model.mod
     PUBLIC "-//W3C//ENTITIES XHTML 1.1 Document Model 1.0//EN"
     SYSTEM "http://www.w3.org/TR/xhtml 11/DTD/xhtml 11-model-
     1.mod" >


<!-- Pre-Framework Redeclaration placeholder
.................... -->
```

```
<!-- this serves as a location to insert markup declarations
     into the DTD prior to the framework declarations.-->
<!ENTITY % xhtml-prefw-redecl.module "IGNORE" >
<![%xhtml-prefw-redecl.module;[
%xhtml-prefw-redecl.mod;
<!-- end of xhtml-prefw-redecl.module -->]]>


<!-- The events module should be included here if you need it.
     In this skeleton it is IGNOREd.-->
<!ENTITY % xhtml-events.module "IGNORE" >


<!-- Modular Framework Module
................................ -->
<!ENTITY % xhtml-framework.module "INCLUDE" >
<![%xhtml-framework.module;[
<!ENTITY % xhtml-framework.mod
PUBLIC "-//W3C//ENTITIES XHTML 1.1 Modular Framework 1.0//EN"
"xhtml 11-framework-1.mod" >
%xhtml-framework.mod;]]>


<!-- Post-Framework Redeclaration placeholder
................... -->
<!-- this serves as a location to insert markup declarations
     into the DTD following the framework declarations.-->
<!ENTITY % xhtml-postfw-redecl.module "IGNORE" >
<![%xhtml-postfw-redecl.module;[
%xhtml-postfw-redecl.mod;
<!-- end of xhtml-postfw-redecl.module -->]]>


<!-- Basic Text Module (Required)
............................ -->
<!ENTITY % xhtml-text.module "INCLUDE" >
<![%xhtml-text.module;[
<!ENTITY % xhtml-text.mod
PUBLIC "-//W3C//ELEMENTS XHTML 1.1 Basic Text 1.0//EN"
```

```
"xhtml 11-text-1.mod" >
%xhtml-text.mod;]]>


<!-- Hypertext Module (required)
.............................. -->
<!ENTITY % xhtml-hypertext.module "INCLUDE" >
<![%xhtml-hypertext.module;[
<!ENTITY % xhtml-hypertext.mod
PUBLIC "-//W3C//ELEMENTS XHTML 1.1 Hypertext 1.0//EN"
"xhtml 11-hypertext-1.mod" >
%xhtml-hypertext.mod;]]>


<!-- Lists Module (required)
.................................. -->
<!ENTITY % xhtml-list.module "INCLUDE" >
<![%xhtml-list.module;[
<!ENTITY % xhtml-list.mod
PUBLIC "-//W3C//ELEMENTS XHTML 1.1 Lists 1.0//EN"
"xhtml 11-list-1.mod" >
%xhtml-list.mod;]]>


<!-- Your modules can be included here.  Use the basic form
     defined above and be sure to include the public FPI
     definition in your catalog file for  each module that you
     define. You may also include W3C-defined modules at
     this point.-->


<!-- Document Structure Module (required)
..................... -->
<!ENTITY % xhtml-struct.module "INCLUDE" >
<![%xhtml-struct.module;[
<!ENTITY % xhtml-struct.mod
PUBLIC "-//W3C//ELEMENTS XHTML 1.1 Document Structure 1.0//EN"
"xhtml 11-struct-1.mod" >
%xhtml-struct.mod;]]>
```

```
<!-- end of SKELETAL DTD
.............................................. -->
<!--
.................................................................
........ -->
```

Figure 8.2 Skeletal DTD

This skeletal DTD allows you to assemble various module implementations to create a new XHTML markup language.

8.7 Including the Basic Table Module

Create the NewTable Markup.dtd file by including the basic core modules previously discussed. Additionally, add the W3C-defined basic *tables* module for completion of the new DTD.

```
<!--
.................................................................
........ -->
<!-- SKELETAL DTD
.................................................... -->
<!-- file: NewTableMarkup.dtd -->
```

Once the filename is declared, use the formal public identifier to identify the new filename:

```
<!-- This is a skeletal driver file. Modify it however you
want, paying careful attention to the embedded comments about
order.
    Use this formal public identifier to identify it:
```

```
"-//DPSoftware//DTD XHTML-NewTableMarkup.dtd//EN"-->
<!ENTITY % XHTML.version  "-//DPSoftware//DTD XHTML-
NewTableMarkup//EN" >
```

PART 3

PRESENTATION

```
<!-- Next, add the basic tables module using the same format as
for other modules:
Add the module here following the preceding commented section
in the template:-->

<!--Include your modules here.  Use the basic form defined
above and be sure to incorporate the public FPI definition in
your catalog file for each module that you define. -->
<!-- Basic Tables Module . . . . . . . . . . . . . . . . . .
. . . . . . . . . . . . .   -->
<!ENTITY % xhtml-basic-table-1.module "Include" >
<![ %xhtml-basic-table-1.module;[
<!ENTITY % xhtml-basic-table-1.mod
PUBLIC "-//W3C/ELEMENTS XHTML Basic tables 1.0//EN"
"xhtml-basic-table-1.mod"
%xhtml-basic-table-1.mod;]]>

<!--Modified Skeletal DTD -->
<!-- file: NewTableMarkup.dtd-->

<!--NEW SKELETAL DTD-->
<!-- This is a skeletal driver file. Modify it however
     you want, paying careful attention to the embedded
     comments about order. Please use this formal public
     identifier to identify it:-->
<! - The next line identifies the new dtd -->

"-//DPSoftware//DTD XHTML-NewTableMarkup.dtd//EN"-->
<!ENTITY % XHTML.version  "-//DPPSoftware//DTD XHTML-
NewTableMarkup//EN" >
```

```
<!-- Reserved for use with the XLink namespace:-->
<!ENTITY % XLINK.ns "" >
<!ENTITY % XLinkns.attrib "" >


<!-- reserved for future use with document profiles -->
<!ENTITY % XHTML.profile  "" >


<!-- Internationalization features
     This feature-test entity declares elements
     and attributes used for internationalization support. Set
     it to INCLUDE or IGNORE as appropriate for your markup
     language.-->
<!ENTITY % XHTML.I18n "IGNORE" >


<!-- Define the Content Model
     Remember, you can modify this content model or replace it
     simply by changing the following ENTITY declaration.-->
<!ENTITY % xhtml-model.mod
PUBLIC "-//W3C//ENTITIES XHTML 1.1 Document Model 1.0//EN"
SYSTEM "http://www.w3.org/TR/xhtml 11/DTD/xhtml 11-model-1.mod"
>


<!-- Pre-Framework Redeclaration placeholder
.................... -->
<!-- this serves as a location to insert markup declarations
     into the DTD prior to the framework declarations.-->
<!ENTITY % xhtml-prefw-redecl.module "IGNORE" >
<![%xhtml-prefw-redecl.module;[
%xhtml-prefw-redecl.mod;
<!-- end of xhtml-prefw-redecl.module -->]]>


<!--Insert the events module here if you need it. In this
```

```
        skeleton it is IGNOREd.-->
<!ENTITY % xhtml-events.module "IGNORE" >


<!-- Modular Framework Module
................................. -->
<!ENTITY % xhtml-framework.module "INCLUDE" >
<![%xhtml-framework.module;[
<!ENTITY % xhtml-framework.mod
PUBLIC "-//W3C//ENTITIES XHTML 1.1 Modular Framework 1.0//EN"
"xhtml 11-framework-1.mod" >
%xhtml-framework.mod;]]>


<!-- Post-Framework Redeclaration placeholder
................... -->
<!-- This serves as a location to insert markup declarations
     into the DTD following the framework declarations.-->
<!ENTITY % xhtml-postfw-redecl.module "IGNORE" >
<![%xhtml-postfw-redecl.module;[
%xhtml-postfw-redecl.mod;
<!-- end of xhtml-postfw-redecl.module -->]]>


<!-- Basic Text Module (Required)
................................ -->
<!ENTITY % xhtml-text.module "INCLUDE" >
<![%xhtml-text.module;[
<!ENTITY % xhtml-text.mod
PUBLIC "-//W3C//ELEMENTS XHTML 1.1 Basic Text 1.0//EN"
"xhtml 11-text-1.mod" >
%xhtml-text.mod;]]>


<!-- Hypertext Module (required)
................................. -->
<!ENTITY % xhtml-hypertext.module "INCLUDE" >
<![%xhtml-hypertext.module;[
<!ENTITY % xhtml-hypertext.mod
PUBLIC "-//W3C//ELEMENTS XHTML 1.1 Hypertext 1.0//EN"
```

```
"xhtml 11-hypertext-1.mod" >
%xhtml-hypertext.mod;]]>

<!-- Lists Module (required)
.................................. -->
<!ENTITY % xhtml-list.module "INCLUDE" >
<![%xhtml-list.module;[
<!ENTITY % xhtml-list.mod
PUBLIC "-//W3C//ELEMENTS XHTML 1.1 Lists 1.0//EN"
"xhtml 11-list-1.mod" >
%xhtml-list.mod;]]>

<!--Insert your modules here.  Use the basic form defined above
and be sure to incorporate the public FPI definition in your
catalog file for each module that you define. Add W3C-defined
modules at this point.-->

<!-- Include the basic tables module here -->
<!-- Basic Tables Module . .  . -->
<!ENTITY % xhtml-basic-table-1.module "Include" >
<![ %xhtml-basic-table-1.module;[
<!ENTITY % xhtml-basic-table-1.mod
PUBLIC "-//W3C/ELEMENTS XHTML Basic tables 1.0//EN"
"xhtml-basic-table-1.mod"
%xhtml-basic-table-1.mod;]]>

<!-- end of new basic-tables inclusion -->

<!-- Document Structure Module (required)
...................... -->
<!ENTITY % xhtml-struct.module "INCLUDE" >
<![%xhtml-struct.module;[
<!ENTITY % xhtml-struct.mod
PUBLIC "-//W3C//ELEMENTS XHTML 1.1 Document Structure 1.0//EN"
"xhtml 11-struct-1.mod" >
%xhtml-struct.mod;]]>
```

```
<!-- end of Modified Skeletal DTD
................................................ -->
```

Figure 8.3   NewTableMarkup.dtd

After completing the modified skeletal DTD, incorporate it into your XML source documents. Simply reference the modified DTD in your DOCTYPE declaration. The following example demonstrates how this is accomplished:

```
<!DOCTYPE html PUBLIC "-//DPSoftware/DTDS XHTML-NewTableMarkup
//EN" "http://www.DPSoftware.com/DTDs/NewTableMarkup.dtd">
<html
xmlns:ntm="http://www.DPSoftware.com/DTDs/NewTableMarkup.dtd">
```

This modified template processes correctly all submitted documents. However, if you create new elements and attributes, use a browser with a built-in parser such as the current version of the Internet Explorer browser. You must also include a stylesheet, such as XSLT or cascading style sheets, to render them in HTML.

8.8   Constructing the Invoice Module

Let's construct a new invoice module for incorporation into the template DTD provided by the W3C Working Draft Committee. The XHTML DTD serves as guide for our project as we build the QName, declaration, and driver XHTML modules.

TheXML document in Figure 8.4 serves as the document instance for our invoice module.

```xml
<?xml version="1.0" encoding="UTF-8"?>
<invoice>
<!-- invoice data should be placed here -->
    <invoiceData>
      <invoiceNum>L0105318</invoiceNum>
      <invoiceDate>05/30/03</invoiceDate>
      <orderNumber>16698</orderNumber>
      <purchaseOrder>3058</purchaseOrder>
    </invoiceData>
    <salesData>
        <cash>66.99</cash>
        <credit>NA</credit>
        <check>NA</check>
    </salesData>
<!-- place customer data here -->
    <soldTo>
      <custNumber>PD11</custNumber>
      <custName>Dwight Peltzer</custName>
      <address>PO Box 355</address>
      <city>East Meadow</city>
      <state>NY</state>
      <homePhone>516-666-3466</homePhone>
      <businessPhone>212-456-2359</businessPhone>
    </soldTo>
<!-- shipping information goes here -->
    <shipTo>
      <custName>Dwight Peltzer</custName>
      <address>PO Box 355</address>
      <city>East Meadow</city>
      <state>NY</state>
      <zipcode>11532</zipcode>
      <dateShipped>May 10, 20002</dateShipped>
    </shipTo>
<!-- inventory information goes here -->
    <inventory>
      <shelf>Available</shelf>
      <shelfItems>location</shelfItems>
      <itemNo>DL-DSH5</itemNo>
      <description>-D-Link -Port 10/100 Hub/Switch</description>
```

```
      <sku>DL-DSH510</sku>
      <quantity>1</quantity>
      <price>61.00</price>
      <tax>5.19</tax>
      <backOrder>NA</backOrder>
   </inventory>
</invoice>
```

Figure 8.4   Invoice.xml

Invoice.xml contains five categories: `invoiceData`, `salesData`, `soldTo`, `shipTo`, and `inventory`. The parser processes the data as #PCDATA. `invoiceData` contains the following elements:

- `invoiceNum`
- `invoiceDate`
- `orderNumber`
- `purchaseOrder`

Figure 8.5 shows the graphic representation of the document instance.

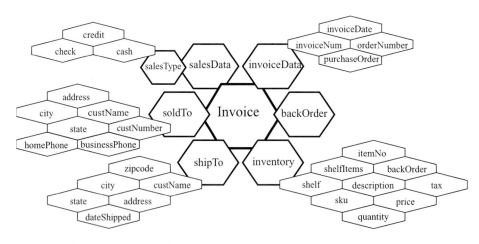

Figure 8.5   Invoice graphic representation

8.9   Defining a QName Module

The following process describes what a QName module is and
demonstrates how to build one. A QName module is an XML term
for qualified names. XML namespaces differentiate elements that
share the same name but contain different definitions. Usually the
namespaces come from more than one markup language. (Note:
Refer to Section 4.6 of Chapter 4, "Introducing Schemas," for a discussion of namespaces.) A perfect example of the namespace conflict
is the <title> element. In one context it means the following:

```
<title>XML Language Mechanics</title>
```

In another context, it would mean the title of an English gen-
tleman, as follows:

```
<title>Sir Winston Churchill</title>
```

Finally, here it is in a schema context:

```
<xsd:schema>
    . . . . . . . .
<xsd:element name="title">
   <xsd:complexType>
      <xsd:choice>
      <xsd:element name="Sir" type="xsd:string"/>
      <xsd:element name="Dr." type="xsd:string"/>
      <xsd:element name="Professor." type="xsd:string"/>
      <xsd:element name="XML Language Mechanics"
      type="xsd:string"/>
      </xsd:choice>
   </xsd:complexType>
 </xsd:schema>
```

XML namespaces identify which language a specified element
belongs to by means of appending a prefix, such as xhtml:title.
The QName module contains parameter entities used to store the
QNames of elements to be defined in a declaration module. The
given elements will be presented in fully qualified format. The
QName module begins with a commented section listing the module
name; the filename, public, and system identifiers used to reference

the module; and the namespace declaration. Construct the QName module as follows. The steps required to construct the invoice QName module are defined below.

1. Define a parameter entity `MODULE.prefixed`, announcing whether elements embedded within the module are using the XML namespace prefixed names. Note that this entity's default value is `"NS.prefixed;"`. The XHTML framework defines this parameter entity to be `IGNORE` by default, thereby serving as a switch for turning on or off prefixing for all specified namespaces. The example in Figure 8.6 indicates that we will use namespace prefixing, and it builds step by step the invoice module.

```
<!--(1). . . . . . . . . . . . . . . . . . . . . . .
. . . . . -->
<!-- Invoice QNames Module . . . . . . . . . . . . . .
. . . . . . . . . . . . . . . . . . .-->
<!--file: invoice-QNames-1.mod

PUBLIC  "-//DPSOFTWARE//ELEMENTS XHTML invoice QNames
1.0//EN SYSTEM "http://www.dpsoftware.com/DTDS/invoice-QNames-
1.mod"-->
```

Figure 8.6 Invoice QNames module

2. Define a parameter entity `MODULE.xmlns` containing the namespace identifier for our module. In our case, `invoice` is the identifier. This code is a fragment.

```
xmlns:invoice="http://www.dpsoftware.com/xmlns/invoice"
```

3. Declare the default value for prefixing this module's elements. Note that `NS.prefixed` will be overridden by the XHTML framework or by a document instance.

```
<!ENTITY %NS.prefixed  "IGNORE" >
<!ENTITY %  invoice.prefixed "%NS.prefixed;" >
```

4. Declare the actual namespace for this module.

```
<!ENTITY %  invoice.xmlns
"http://www.dpsoftware.com/xmlns/invoice" >
```

Note that `invoice` is the actual namespace for this module.

5. Define a parameter entity `MODULE.prefix` containing the default prefix string used when using prefixing.

```
<!ENTITY %  invoice.prefix "inventory" >
```

6. Declare the prefix for this module and any prefixed namespaces required by this module.

```
<![% invoice.prefixed;[
<!ENTITY % invoice.pfx "%invoice.prefix;:" >
<!ENTITY % invoice.xmlns.extra.attrib
"xmlns:% invoice.prefix;  %URI.datatype; #FIXED  '%
invoice.xmlns;'" >
]]>
<!ENTITY % invoice.pfx "" > <!-- not enabled -->
<!ENTITY % invoice.xmlns.extra.attrib " " > <!--not enabled-->
```

7. Declare the extra namespace that should be included in the XHTML elements.

```
<ENTITY % XHTML.xmlns.extra.attrib;
"%invoice.xmlns.extra.attrib;" >
```

PART 3
PRESENTATION

Now declare the qualified names for all of the elements in the module.

```
<!ENTITY % invoice.invoiceData.QNames
"%invoice.pfx;invoiceData" >
<!ENTITY % invoice.shelf.QNames "%invoice.pfx;shelf" >
<!ENTITY % invoice.shelfItems.QNames "%invoice.pfx;shelfItems"
>
<!ENTITY % invoice.invoiceNum.QNames "%invoice.pfx;invoiceNum"
>
<!ENTITY %invoice.invoiceDate.QNames "%invoice.pfx;invoiceDate"
>
<!ENTITY % invoice.orderNumber.QNames
"%invoice.pfx;orderNumber" >
<!ENTITY % invoice.purchaseOrder.QNames
"%invoice.pfx;purchaseOrder" >
<!ENTITY % invoice.salesType.QNames "%invoice.pfx;salesType" >
<!ENTITY % invoice.cash.QNames "%invoice.pfx;cash" >
<!ENTITY % invoice.credit.QNames "%invoice.pfx;credit" >
<!ENTITY % invoice.check.QNames "%invoice.pfx;check" >
<!ENTITY % invoice.soldTo.QNames "%invoice.pfx;soldTo" >
<!ENTITY % invoice.custNumber.QNames "%invoice.pfx;custNumber"
>
<!ENTITY % invoice.custName.QNames "%invoice.pfx;custName" >
<!ENTITY % invoice.address.QNames "%invoice.pfx;address" >
<!ENTITY % invoice.city.QNames "%invoice.pfx;city" >
<!ENTITY % invoice.state.QNames "%invoice.pfx;state" >
<!ENTITY % invoice.zip.QNames "%invoice.pfx;zip" >
<!ENTITY % invoice.homePhone.QNames "%invoice.pfx;homePhone" >
<!ENTITY % invoice.businessPhone.QNames
"%invoice.pfx;businessPhone" >
<!ENTITY % invoice.dateShipped.QNames
"%invoice.pfx;dateShipped" >
```

```
<!ENTITY % invoice.shipTo.QNames "%invoice.pfx;shipTo" >
<!ENTITY %invoice.salesData.QNames "%invoice.pfx;salesData" >
<!ENTITY %invoice.sku.QNames "%invoice.pfx;sku" >
<!ENTITY %invoice.quantity.QNames "%invoice.pfx;quantity" >
<!ENTITY %invoice.price.QNames "%invoice.pfx;price" >
<!ENTITY %invoice.tax.QNames "%invoice.pfx;tax" >
<!ENTITY %invoice.backOrder.QNames "%invoice.pfx;backOrder" >
<!ENTITY % invoice.description.QNames "%invoice.pfx;
description" >
```

This finishes the QName module declarations. Next, declare the declaration module.

8.10 Building the Invoice Declaration Module

The declaration module declares XML DTD elements and attribute lists. Constructing a XHTML declaration module uses the following rules defined in the XHTML modularization specification:

1. Define a parameter entity to use within the `ATTLIST` for each declared element. This parameter should include `%NS.decl.attrib` when `%MODULE.prefixed` is set to `INCLUDE`. Use `%NS.decl.attrib` plus `xmlns` `%URI.datatype;` `#FIXED 'MODULE.xmlns` when `%MODULE.prefixed` is set to `IGNORE`.

2. Declare all elements and attributes for the module. Within each `ATTLIST` for an element, include the parameter entity defined in the first rule so that all required `xmlns` attributes are available for each element in the module.

3. If the module adds attributes to specified elements defined in modules sharing the namespace of that module, declare those attributes so that they use the `%MODULE.pfx` prefix. An example of this follows:

   ```
   <!ENTITY % MODULE.img.dps.QNames "%MODULE.pfx;dps" >
   ```

```
<!ATTLIST %img.QNames;
    %MODULE.img.dps.QNames;   CDATA #IMPLIED>
```

This example adds the attribute `dps` to the `img` element of the image module. The attribute's name is the qualified name, including a prefix when prefixes are chosen for a source document. Add the `xmlns:MODULE_PREFIX` attribute to the `img` element's attribute list so that an XML namespace-aware parser knows how to resolve the namespace based on its prefix.

The declaration submodule contains all elements and attributes that make up this module. As usual, the submodule begins with the same type-commented sections we observed in the QNames submodule (see Figure 8.7).

```
<!--DPSoftware Invoice Module . . . . . . . . . . . . . .
. . . . .-->
<!--file: invoice-elements-1.mod
PUBLIC "-//DPSOFTWARE//ELEMENTS XHTML-DPSoftware invoice
1.0//EN" SYSTEM "http://www.dpsoftware.com/DTDs/invoice-
1.mod"dpsoftware
xmlns:invoice="http://www./DPSoftware.com/xmlns/invoice"
. . . . . . . . . . . . . . . . . .-->
```

Figure 8.7   Invoice declaration submodule

Following this section is another commented section naming the module, listing all elements to be declared and a description of the module's purpose:

```
<!-- DPSoftware invoice module-->
    invoice:invoiceData
    invoice:invoiceNum
    invoice:orderNumber
    invoice:invoiceData
    invoice:purchaseOrder
    invoice:salesData
    invoice:salesType
    invoice:cash
```

```
       invoice:credit
       invoice:check
       invoice:soldTo
       invoice:custNumber
       invoice:custName
       invoice:address
       invoice:city
       invoice:state
       invoice:zip
       invoice:homePhone
       invoice:businessPhone
       invoice:shipTo
       invoice:dateShipped
       invoice:shelf
       invoice:shelfItems

       invoice:itemNo
       invoice:description
       invoice:sku
       invoice:quantity
       invoice:price
       invoice:tax
       invoice:backOrder
<!--This module defines structural components for invoice -->
<!-- Define the global namespace attributes -->
<![%invoice.prefixed;[
<!ENTITY % invoice.xmlns.attrib
"%NS.decl.attrib;"
>
]]>
<!ENTITY % invoice.xmlns.attrib
"xmlns %URI.datatype;  #FIXED '%invoice.xmlns;'""
>
<!--Define a common set of attributes for all module elements
-->
<!ENTITY % invoice.Common.attrib "%invoice.xmlns.attrib;"
id          ID                #IMPLIED
>
```

```
<!-- Define the elements and attributes of the modules -->
<!ELEMENT %invoice.shelf.qname;
( %invoice.shelfItem.qname; )*>
<!ATTLIST %invoice.shelf.qname;
location    CDATA   #IMPLIED
%invoice.Common.Attrib;
>
<!ELEMENT %invoice.shelfItem.qname;
( %invoice.invoiceData.qname;,   %invoice.invoiceNum.qname;,
%invoice.invoiceDate.qname;,
%invoice.orderNumber.qname;, %invoice.purchaseOrder.qname;,
%invoice.salesData.qname;, %invoice.salesType.qname;,
%invoice.cash.qname;,%invoice.credit.qname;,
%invoice.check.qname;,   %invoice.soldTo.qname;,
%invoice.custNumber.qname;,
%invoice.custName.qname;, %invoice.address.qname;,
%invoice.city.qname;, %invoice.state.qname;,
%invoice.state.qname;, %invoice.zipCode.qname;,
%invoice.shipTo.qname;,
%invoice.dateShipped.qname;, %invoice.inventory.qname;,
%invoice.itemNo.qname;, %invoice.description.qname;,
%invoice.sku.qname;, %invoice.quantity.qname;,
%invoice.price.qname;,   %invoice.tax.qname;,
%invoice.backOrder.qname;) >
 location    CDATA   #IMPLIED
%invoice.Common.attrib;
>
<!ELEMENT %invoice.invoiceData.qname; ( #PCDATA ) >
<!ATTLIST %invoice.invoiceData.qname;
%invoice.Common.attrib;
>

<!ELEMENT %invoice.invoiceNum.qname; ( #PCDATA ) >
<!ATTLIST %invoice.invoiceNum.qname;
%invoice.Common.attrib;
>
<!ELEMENT %invoice.invoiceDate.qname; ( #PCDATA ) >
<!ATTLIST %invoice.invoiceDate.qname;
%invoice.Common.attrib;
>
```

```
<!ELEMENT  %invoice.orderNumber.qname; ( #PCDATA ) >
<!ATTLIST     %invoice.orderNumber.qname;
                    %invoice.Common.attrib;
>
<!ELEMENT  %invoice.purchaseOrder.qname; ( #PCDATA ) >
<!ATTLIST     %invoice.purchaseOrder.qname;
                    %invoice.Common.attrib;
>
<!ELEMENT  %invoice.salesData.qname; ( #PCDATA ) >
<!ATTLIST     %invoice.salesData.qname;
                    %invoice.Common.attrib;
>
<!ELEMENT  %invoice.salesType.qname; ( #PCDATA ) >
<!ATTLIST     %invoice.salesType.qname;
                    %invoice.Common.attrib;
>
<!ELEMENT  %invoice.cash.qname; ( #PCDATA ) >
<!ATTLIST     %invoice.cash.qname;
                    %invoice.Common.attrib;
>
<!ELEMENT  %invoice.credit.qname; ( #PCDATA ) >
<!ATTLIST     %invoice.credit.qname;
                    %invoice.Common.attrib;
>
<!ELEMENT  %invoice.check.qname; ( #PCDATA ) >
<!ATTLIST     %invoice.check.qname;
                    %invoice.Common.attrib;
>
<!ELEMENT  %invoice.soldTo.qname; ( #PCDATA ) >
<!ATTLIST     %invoice.soldTo.qname;
                    %invoice.Common.attrib;
>
<!ELEMENT  %invoice.custNumber.qname; ( #PCDATA ) >
<!ATTLIST     %invoice.custNumber.qname;
                    %invoice.Common.attrib;
>
<!ELEMENT  %invoice.custName.qname; ( #PCDATA ) >
<!ATTLIST     %invoice.custName.qname;
                    %invoice.Common.attrib;
>
<!ELEMENT  %invoice.address.qname; ( #PCDATA ) >
<!ATTLIS     %invoice.address.qname;
```

```
                          %invoice.Common.attrib;
      >
      <!ELEMENT %invoice.city.qname; ( #PCDATA ) >
      <!ATTLIST    %invoice.city.qname;
                          %invoice.Common.attrib;
      >
      <!ELEMENT %invoice.state.qname; ( #PCDATA ) >
      <!ATTLIST    %invoice.state.qname;
                          %invoice.Common.attrib;
      >
      <!ELEMENT %invoice.zipCode.qname; ( #PCDATA ) >
      <!ATTLIST    %invoice.zipCode.qname;
                          %invoice.Common.attrib;
      >
      <!ELEMENT %invoice.shipTo.qname; ( #PCDATA ) >
      <!ATTLIST    %invoice.shipTo.qname;
                          %invoice.Common.attrib;
      >
      <!ELEMENT %invoice.dateShipped.qname; ( #PCDATA ) >
      <!ATTLIST    %invoice.dateShipped.qname;
                          %invoice.Common.attrib;
      >
      <!ELEMENT %invoice.inventory.qname; ( #PCDATA ) >
      <!ATTLIST    %invoice.inventory.qname;
                          %invoice.Common.attrib;
      >
      <!ELEMENT %invoice.itemNum.qname; ( #PCDATA ) >
      <!ATTLIST    %invoice.itemNo.qname;
                          %invoice.Common.attrib;
      >
      <!ELEMENT %invoice.description.qname; ( #PCDATA ) >
      <!ATTLIST    %invoice.description.qname;
            %invoice.Common.attrib;
      >
      <!ELEMENT %invoice.sku.qname; ( #PCDATA ) >
      <!ATTLIST    %invoice.sku.qname;
                          %invoice.Common.attrib;
      >
      <!ELEMENT %invoice.quantity.qname; ( #PCDATA ) >
      <!ATTLIST    %invoice.quantity.qname;
                          %invoice.Common.attrib;
      >
```

```
<!ELEMENT %invoice.price.qname; ( #PCDATA ) >
<!ATTLIST    %invoice.price.qname;
                    %invoice.Common.attrib;
>
<!ELEMENT %invoice.tax.qname; ( #PCDATA ) >
<!ATTLIST    %invoice.tax.qname;
                    %invoice.Common.attrib;
>
<!ELEMENT %invoice.backOrder.qname; ( #PCDATA ) >
<!ATTLIST    %invoice.backOrder.qname;
                    %invoice.Common.attrib;
>
<!-- end of invoice-1.mod -->
```

8.11 Building a Driver

The driver is the file referenced by documents written in your new markup language. For the driver to work, each XHTML driver must contain the following elements:

- A definition of the parameter entity XHTML version. It should be set to the formal public identifier for your new markup language.
- A definition of the parameter entity xhtml-qname-extra.mod. This must be set to the qualified names collection module. A qualified names collection represents a module in which all of the QName modules are instantiated and the set of prefixed attributes are defined. A qualified name collection module contains the following:
  - A reference to the QName module of each non-XHTML module included. (We will discuss this further in another section.)

- A definition of the parameter entity
  `XHTML.xmlns.extra.mod` to be the collection of the
  `MODULE.xmlns.extra.attrib` parameter entities, one
  from each included module.

- A definition of the parameter entity `xhtml-model.mod`. This
  should be set to the model module. (The model module is an
  XHTML module that defines the content model for your new
  markup language. It can be simply a declaration of a parameter
  entity and inclusion of some other model module. It is, in
  essence, definitions of the structure of all elements in your
  markup language. We will see such a model shortly.)

- References to the modules that make up your DTD. This is an
  explicit list of XHTML modules, including modules you are
  modifying. The first module to be instantiated is the XHTML
  modularization framework module. This module manages incorporation of the XHTML infrastructure, merging it with your
  specified QNames, including your content model, and your
  newly declared modules.

Here is the DTD for `Invoice`:

```
<!-- Invoice DTD
...................................................... -->
<!-- file: Invoice.dtd-->

<!-- Invoice DTD-->
<!-- This is the DTD driver for Invoice.

    Please use this formal public identifier to identify it:

    "-//DPSoftware//DTD XHTML-invoice 1.0//EN"

    And this namespace for invoice-unique elements:
```

```
xmlns:invoice="http://www.DPSoftware.com/DTDs/invoice "-->
<!ENTITY % XHTML.version  "-//DPSoftware//DTD XHTML-INVOICE
1.0//EN" >
<!ENTITY %invoice-qname.mod SYSTEM "invoice-qname-1.mod">
%invoice-qname.mod;

<!ENTITY NS.prefixed.extras.attrib " ">

<!-- Reserved for use with the XLink namespace:-->
<!ENTITY % XLINK.ns "" >
<!ENTITY % XLinkns.attrib "" >

<!ENTITY %xhtml-model-1.mod "inventory-model-1.mod">

<!-- reserved for future use with document profiles -->
<!ENTITY % XHTML.profile  "" >

<!-- Internationalization features
     This feature-test entity is used to declare elements
     and attributes used for internationalization support. Set
     it to INCLUDE or IGNORE as appropriate for your markup
     language.-->
<!ENTITY % XHTML.I18n "IGNORE" >


<!-- Redeclare the Misc.extra to include INVOICE to hook it
     into the content model.-->

<!ENTITY % Misc.extra
     "| script | noscript | myml:myelement" >

<!-- Define the Content Model
```

PART 3 PRESENTATION

```
          Remember that you can modify this content model or replace
          it simply by changing the following ENTITY declaration.-->
<!ENTITY % xhtml-model.mod
PUBLIC "-//W3C//ENTITIES XHTML 1.1 Document Model 1.0//EN"
SYSTEM "http://www.w3.org/TR/xhtml 11/DTD/xhtml 11-model-1.mod"
>


<!-- Pre-Framework Redeclaration placeholder
.................... -->
<!-- this serves as a location to insert markup declarations
     into the DTD prior to the framework declarations.-->
<!ENTITY % xhtml-prefw-redecl.module "IGNORE" >
<![%xhtml-prefw-redecl.module;[
%xhtml-prefw-redecl.mod;
<!-- end of xhtml-prefw-redecl.module -->]]>


<!-- The events module should be included here if you need it.
     In this skeleton it is IGNOREd.-->
<!ENTITY % xhtml-events.module "IGNORE" >


<!-- Modular Framework Module
................................. -->
<!ENTITY % xhtml-framework.module "INCLUDE" >
<![%xhtml-framework.module;[
<!ENTITY % xhtml-framework.mod
PUBLIC "-//W3C//ENTITIES XHTML 1.1 Modular Framework 1.0//EN"
"xhtml 11-framework-1.mod" >
%xhtml-framework.mod;]]>


<!-- Post-Framework Redeclaration placeholder
.................... -->
<!-- this serves as a location to insert markup declarations
     into the DTD following the framework declarations.-->
```

```
<!ENTITY % xhtml-postfw-redecl.module "IGNORE" >
<![%xhtml-postfw-redecl.module;[
%xhtml-postfw-redecl.mod;
<!-- end of xhtml-postfw-redecl.module -->]]>

<!-- Basic Text Module (Required)
............................. -->
<!ENTITY % xhtml-text.module "INCLUDE" >
<![%xhtml-text.module;[
<!ENTITY % xhtml-text.mod
PUBLIC "-//W3C//ELEMENTS XHTML 1.1 Basic Text 1.0//EN"
"xhtml 11-text-1.mod" >
%xhtml-text.mod;]]>

<!-- Hypertext Module (required)
............................... -->
<!ENTITY % xhtml-hypertext.module "INCLUDE" >
<![%xhtml-hypertext.module;[
<!ENTITY % xhtml-hypertext.mod
PUBLIC "-//W3C//ELEMENTS XHTML 1.1 Hypertext 1.0//EN"
"xhtml 11-hypertext-1.mod" >
%xhtml-hypertext.mod;]]>

<!-- Lists Module (required)
.................................. -->
<!ENTITY % xhtml-list.module "INCLUDE" >
<![%xhtml-list.module;[
<!ENTITY % xhtml-list.mod
PUBLIC "-//W3C//ELEMENTS XHTML 1.1 Lists 1.0//EN"
"xhtml 11-list-1.mod" >
%xhtml-list.mod;]]>

<!-- Your modules can be included here.  Use the basic form
     defined above and be sure to include the public FPI
     definition in your catalog file for each module that you
     define. You may also include W3C-defined modules at
     this point.-->
```

```
<!-- My Invoice Module
..................................... -->
<!ENTITY % invoice-elements.mod
PUBLIC "-//DPSoftware//ELEMENTS XHTML-invoice 1.0//EN"
"http://www.DPSoftware/DTDs/invoice-elements-1.mod" >
%invoice.mod;>
<!-- Document Structure Module (required)
..................... -->
<!ENTITY % xhtml-struct.module "INCLUDE" >
<![%xhtml-struct.module;[
<!ENTITY % xhtml-struct.mod
PUBLIC "-//W3C//ELEMENTS XHTML 1.1 Document Structure 1.0//EN"
"xhtml 11-struct-1.mod" >
%xhtml-struct.mod;]]>


<!-- end of SKELETAL DTD -->
```

8.12 XHTML Driver 1.1

The following section is taken from the W3C XHTML modularization specification. It provides documentation on building drivers and serves as a nice conclusion to our discussion on modularization.

This section contains the driver for the XHTML 1.1 document type implementation as an XML DTD. It relies on XHTML module implementations defined in [XHTMLMOD] and in [RUBY].

```
<!-- XHTML 1.1 DTD -->
<!-- file: xhtml 11.dtd-->
```

```
<!-- XHTML 1.1 DTD

    This is XHTML, a reformulation of HTML as a modular XML
    application.

    The Extensible HyperText Markup Language (XHTML)
    Copyright 1998-2001 World Wide Web Consortium
    (Massachusetts Institute of Technology, Institut National de
    Recherche en Informatique et en Automatique, Keio
    University).
    All Rights Reserved.

    Permission to use, copy, modify, and distribute the XHTML
    DTD and its accompanying documentation for any purpose and
    without fee is hereby granted in perpetuity, provided that
    the above copyright notice and this paragraph appear in all
    copies.  The copyright holders make no representation about
    the suitability of the DTD for any purpose.

    It is provided "as is" without expressed or implied
    warranty.

    Author:    Murray M. Altheim <altheim@eng.sun.com>
    Revision:  $Id: xhtml 11.dtd,v 1.21 2001/05/29 16:37:01
    ahby Exp $-->
<!-- This is the driver file for version 1.1 of the XHTML DTD.

    Please use this formal public identifier to identify it:
```

```
                    "-//W3C//DTD XHTML 1.1//EN"-->
<!ENTITY % XHTML.version  "-//W3C//DTD XHTML 1.1//EN" >


<!-- Use this URI to identify the default namespace:

        "http://www.w3.org/1999/xhtml"

    See the Qualified Names module for information
    on the use of namespace prefixes in the DTD.
-->
<!ENTITY % NS.prefixed "IGNORE" >
<!ENTITY % XHTML.prefix "" >


<!-- Reserved for use with the XLink namespace:-->
<!ENTITY % XLINK.xmlns "" >
<!ENTITY % XLINK.xmlns.attrib "" >


<!-- For example, if you are using XHTML 1.1 directly, use the
FPI in the DOCTYPE declaration, with the xmlns attribute on the
document element to identify the default namespace:

        <?xml version="1.0"?>
        <!DOCTYPE html PUBLIC "-//W3C//DTD XHTML 1.1//EN" "xhtml
        11.dtd">
        <html xmlns="http://www.w3.org/1999/xhtml"
              xml:lang="en">
        ...
        </html>

    Revisions:
    (none)-->


<!-- reserved for future use with document profiles -->
<!ENTITY % XHTML.profile  "" >


<!-- Bidirectional Text features
     This feature-test entity is used to declare elements
```

```
    and attributes used for bidirectional text support.-->
<!ENTITY % XHTML.bidi  "INCLUDE" >


<?doc type="doctype" role="title" { XHTML 1.1 } ?>


<!-- Pre-Framework Redeclaration placeholder
.................. -->
<!-- this serves as a location to insert markup declarations
     into the DTD prior to the framework declarations.-->
<!ENTITY % xhtml-prefw-redecl.module "IGNORE" >
<![%xhtml-prefw-redecl.module;[
%xhtml-prefw-redecl.mod;
<!-- end of xhtml-prefw-redecl.module -->]]>


<!ENTITY % xhtml-events.module "INCLUDE" >


<!-- Inline Style Module
.................................... -->
<!ENTITY % xhtml-inlstyle.module "INCLUDE" >
<![%xhtml-inlstyle.module;[
<!ENTITY % xhtml-inlstyle.mod
PUBLIC "-//W3C//ELEMENTS XHTML Inline Style 1.0//EN"
"http://www.w3.org/TR/xhtml-modularization/DTD/
xhtml-inlstyle-1.mod" >
%xhtml-inlstyle.mod;]]>


<!-- declare Document Model module instantiated in framework
-->
<!ENTITY % xhtml-model.mod
PUBLIC "-//W3C//ENTITIES XHTML 1.1 Document Model 1.0//EN"
"xhtml 11-model-1.mod" >
```

PART 3

PRESENTATION

```
<!-- Modular Framework Module (required)
......................... -->
<!ENTITY % xhtml-framework.module "INCLUDE" >
<![%xhtml-framework.module;[
<!ENTITY % xhtml-framework.mod
PUBLIC "-//W3C//ENTITIES XHTML Modular Framework 1.0//EN"
"http://www.w3.org/TR/xhtml-modularization/DTD/
xhtml-framework-1.mod" >
%xhtml-framework.mod;]]>


<!-- Post-Framework Redeclaration placeholder
.................. -->
<!-- this serves as a location to insert markup declarations
     into the DTD following the framework declarations.-->
<!ENTITY % xhtml-postfw-redecl.module "IGNORE" >
<![%xhtml-postfw-redecl.module;[
%xhtml-postfw-redecl.mod;
<!-- end of xhtml-postfw-redecl.module -->]]>


<!-- Text Module (Required)
.................................... -->
<!ENTITY % xhtml-text.module "INCLUDE" >
<![%xhtml-text.module;[
<!ENTITY % xhtml-text.mod
PUBLIC "-//W3C//ELEMENTS XHTML Text 1.0//EN"
"http://www.w3.org/TR/xhtml-modularization/DTD/
xhtml-text-1.mod" >
%xhtml-text.mod;]]>


<!-- Hypertext Module (required)
.............................. -->
<!ENTITY % xhtml-hypertext.module "INCLUDE" >
<![%xhtml-hypertext.module;[
<!ENTITY % xhtml-hypertext.mod
PUBLIC "-//W3C//ELEMENTS XHTML Hypertext 1.0//EN"
"http://www.w3.org/TR/xhtml-modularization/DTD/
xhtml-hypertext-1.mod" >
%xhtml-hypertext.mod;]]>
```

PART 3
PRESENTATION

```
<!-- Lists Module (required)
..................................... -->
<!ENTITY % xhtml-list.module "INCLUDE" >
<![%xhtml-list.module;[
<!ENTITY % xhtml-list.mod
PUBLIC "-//W3C//ELEMENTS XHTML Lists 1.0//EN"
"http://www.w3.org/TR/xhtml-modularization/DTD/
xhtml-list-1.mod" >
%xhtml-list.mod;]]>

<!-- Edit Module
.............................................. -->
<!ENTITY % xhtml-edit.module "INCLUDE" >
<![%xhtml-edit.module;[
<!ENTITY % xhtml-edit.mod
PUBLIC "-//W3C//ELEMENTS XHTML Editing Elements 1.0//EN"
"http://www.w3.org/TR/xhtml-modularization/DTD/
xhtml-edit-1.mod" >
%xhtml-edit.mod;]]>

<!-- BIDI Override Module
....................................... -->
<!ENTITY % xhtml-bdo.module "%XHTML.bidi;" >
<![%xhtml-bdo.module;[
<!ENTITY % xhtml-bdo.mod
PUBLIC "-//W3C//ELEMENTS XHTML BIDI Override Element 1.0//EN"
"http://www.w3.org/TR/xhtml-modularization/DTD/xhtml-bdo-1.mod"
>
%xhtml-bdo.mod;]]>

<!-- Ruby Module
.............................................. -->
<!ENTITY % Ruby.common.attlists "INCLUDE" >
<!ENTITY % Ruby.common.attrib "%Common.attrib;" >
<!ENTITY % xhtml-ruby.module "INCLUDE" >
<![%xhtml-ruby.module;[
```

PART 3

PRESENTATION

367

```
<!ENTITY % xhtml-ruby.mod
PUBLIC "-//W3C//ELEMENTS XHTML Ruby 1.0//EN"
"http://www.w3.org/TR/ruby/xhtml-ruby-1.mod" >
%xhtml-ruby.mod;]]>


<!-- Presentation Module
....................................... -->
<!ENTITY % xhtml-pres.module "INCLUDE" >
<![%xhtml-pres.module;[
<!ENTITY % xhtml-pres.mod
PUBLIC "-//W3C//ELEMENTS XHTML Presentation 1.0//EN"
"http://www.w3.org/TR/xhtml-modularization/DTD/xhtml-pres-
1.mod" >
%xhtml-pres.mod;]]>


<!-- Link Element Module
....................................... -->
<!ENTITY % xhtml-link.module "INCLUDE" >
<![%xhtml-link.module;[
<!ENTITY % xhtml-link.mod
PUBLIC "-//W3C//ELEMENTS XHTML Link Element 1.0//EN"
"http://www.w3.org/TR/xhtml-modularization/DTD/
xhtml-link-1.mod" >
%xhtml-link.mod;]]>


<!-- Document MetaInformation Module
............................ -->
<!ENTITY % xhtml-meta.module "INCLUDE" >
<![%xhtml-meta.module;[
<!ENTITY % xhtml-meta.mod
PUBLIC "-//W3C//ELEMENTS XHTML Metainformation 1.0//EN"
"http://www.w3.org/TR/xhtml-modularization/DTD/
xhtml-meta-1.mod" >
%xhtml-meta.mod;]]>


<!-- Base Element Module
....................................... -->
<!ENTITY % xhtml-base.module "INCLUDE" >
<![%xhtml-base.module;[
<!ENTITY % xhtml-base.mod
```

```
PUBLIC "-//W3C//ELEMENTS XHTML Base Element 1.0//EN"
"http://www.w3.org/TR/xhtml-modularization/DTD/xhtml-base-
1.mod" >
%xhtml-base.mod;]]>

<!-- Scripting Module
........................................ -->
<!ENTITY % xhtml-script.module "INCLUDE" >
<![%xhtml-script.module;[
<!ENTITY % xhtml-script.mod
PUBLIC "-//W3C//ELEMENTS XHTML Scripting 1.0//EN"
"http://www.w3.org/TR/xhtml-modularization/DTD/xhtml-script-
1.mod" >
%xhtml-script.mod;]]>

<!-- Style Sheets Module
....................................... -->
<!ENTITY % xhtml-style.module "INCLUDE" >
<![%xhtml-style.module;[
<!ENTITY % xhtml-style.mod
PUBLIC "-//W3C//ELEMENTS XHTML Style Sheets 1.0//EN"
"http://www.w3.org/TR/xhtml-modularization/DTD/xhtml-style-
1.mod" >
%xhtml-style.mod;]]>

<!-- Image Module
............................................. -->
<!ENTITY % xhtml-image.module "INCLUDE" >
<![%xhtml-image.module;[
<!ENTITY % xhtml-image.mod
PUBLIC "-//W3C//ELEMENTS XHTML Images 1.0//EN"
"http://www.w3.org/TR/xhtml-modularization/DTD/xhtml-image-
1.mod" >
%xhtml-image.mod;]]>

<!-- Client-side Image Map Module
.............................. -->
<!ENTITY % xhtml-csismap.module "INCLUDE" >
<![%xhtml-csismap.module;[
<!ENTITY % xhtml-csismap.mod
PUBLIC "-//W3C//ELEMENTS XHTML Client-side Image Maps 1.0//EN"
```

```
"http://www.w3.org/TR/xhtml-modularization/DTD/
xhtml-csismap-1.mod" >
%xhtml-csismap.mod;]]>


<!-- Server-side Image Map Module
.............................. -->
<!ENTITY % xhtml-ssismap.module "INCLUDE" >
<![%xhtml-ssismap.module;[
<!ENTITY % xhtml-ssismap.mod
PUBLIC "-//W3C//ELEMENTS XHTML Server-side Image Maps 1.0//EN"
"http://www.w3.org/TR/xhtml-modularization/DTD/
xhtml-ssismap-1.mod" >
%xhtml-ssismap.mod;]]>


<!-- Param Element Module
..................................... -->
<!ENTITY % xhtml-param.module "INCLUDE" >
<![%xhtml-param.module;[
<!ENTITY % xhtml-param.mod
PUBLIC "-//W3C//ELEMENTS XHTML Param Element 1.0//EN"
"http://www.w3.org/TR/xhtml-modularization/DTD/
xhtml-param-1.mod" >
%xhtml-param.mod;]]>


<!-- Embedded Object Module
.................................. -->
<!ENTITY % xhtml-object.module "INCLUDE" >
<![%xhtml-object.module;[
<!ENTITY % xhtml-object.mod
PUBLIC "-//W3C//ELEMENTS XHTML Embedded Object 1.0//EN"
"http://www.w3.org/TR/xhtml-modularization/DTD/
xhtml-object-1.mod" >
%xhtml-object.mod;]]>


<!-- Tables Module
......................................... -->
<!ENTITY % xhtml-table.module "INCLUDE" >
<![%xhtml-table.module;[
<!ENTITY % xhtml-table.mod
```

```
PUBLIC "-//W3C//ELEMENTS XHTML Tables 1.0//EN"
"http://www.w3.org/TR/xhtml-modularization/DTD/
xhtml-table-1.mod" >
%xhtml-table.mod;]]>

<!-- Forms Module
............................................ -->
<!ENTITY % xhtml-form.module "INCLUDE" >
<![%xhtml-form.module;[
<!ENTITY % xhtml-form.mod
PUBLIC "-//W3C//ELEMENTS XHTML Forms 1.0//EN"
"http://www.w3.org/TR/xhtml-modularization/DTD/
xhtml-form-1.mod" >
%xhtml-form.mod;]]>

<!-- Legacy Markup
............................................ -->
<!ENTITY % xhtml-legacy.module "IGNORE" >
<![%xhtml-legacy.module;[
<!ENTITY % xhtml-legacy.mod
PUBLIC "-//W3C//ELEMENTS XHTML Legacy Markup 1.0//EN"
"http://www.w3.org/TR/xhtml-modularization/DTD/
xhtml-legacy-1.mod" >
%xhtml-legacy.mod;]]>

<!-- Document Structure Module (required)
...................... -->
<!ENTITY % xhtml-struct.module "INCLUDE" >
<![%xhtml-struct.module;[
<!ENTITY % xhtml-struct.mod
PUBLIC "-//W3C//ELEMENTS XHTML Document Structure 1.0//EN"
"http://www.w3.org/TR/xhtml-modularization/DTD/
xhtml-struct-1.mod" >
%xhtml-struct.mod;]]>

<!-- end of XHTML 1.1 DTD
............................................... -->
```

XHTML 1.1 Customizations

An XHTML family document type (such as XHTML 1.1) must define the content model that it uses. This is done through a separate content model module that is instantiated by the XHTML modular framework. The content model module and the XHTML 1.1 driver (shown in the preceding section) work together to customize the module implementations to the document type's specific requirements. The content model module for XHTML 1.1 is defined as follows:

```
<!-- XHTML 1.1 Document Model Module
..................................... -->
<!-- file: xhtml 11-model-1.mod

    This is XHTML 1.1, a reformulation of HTML as a modular
XML application.
    Copyright 1998-2001 W3C (MIT, INRIA, Keio), All Rights
Reserved.
    Revision: $Id: xhtml 11-model-1.mod,v 1.13 2001/05/29
16:37:01 ahby Exp $ SMI

    This DTD module is identified by the PUBLIC and SYSTEM
identifiers:

PUBLIC "-//W3C//ENTITIES XHTML 1.1 Document Model 1.0//EN"
SYSTEM "http://www.w3.org/TR/xhtml 11/DTD/xhtml 11-model-1.mod"

Revisions:
(none)

<!-- XHTML 1.1 Document Model
    This module describes the groupings of elements that make
```

```
up common content models for XHTML elements.
XHTML has three basic content models:
%Inline.mix;  character-level elements
%Block.mix;   block-like elements, e.g., paragraphs and lists
%Flow.mix;    any block or inline elements

Any parameter entities declared in this module may be used
to create element content models, but the above three are
considered 'global' (insofar as that term applies here).

The reserved word '#PCDATA' (indicating a text string) is now
included explicitly with each element declaration that is
declared as mixed content, as XML requires that this token
ccur first in a content model specification.
-->

<!-- Extending the Model

While in some cases this module may need to be rewritten to
accommodate changes to the document model, minor extensions
may be accomplished by redeclaring any of the three *.extra;
parameter entities to contain extension element types as
follows:

%Misc.extra;    whose parent may be any block or
                inline element.
%Inline.extra;  whose parent may be any inline element.
%Block.extra;   whose parent may be any block element.
If used, these parameter entities must be an OR-separated
```

list beginning with an OR separator ("|"), eg., "| a | b | c"

All block and inline *.class parameter entities not part
of the *struct.class classes begin with "| " to allow for
exclusion from mixes.-->

```
<!-- .............. Optional Elements in head
................. -->
<!ENTITY % HeadOpts.mix
    "( %script.qname; | %style.qname; | %meta.qname;
    | %link.qname; | %object.qname; )*"
>
<!-- ................ Miscellaneous Elements
................... -->
<!-- ins and del are used to denote editing changes
-->
<!ENTITY % Edit.class "| %ins.qname; | %del.qname;" >

<!-- script and noscript are used to contain scripts
    and alternative content-->
<!ENTITY % Script.class "| %script.qname; | %noscript.qname;" >

<!ENTITY % Misc.extra "" >
<!-- These elements are neither block nor inline and can
    essentially be used anywhere in the document body.-->
<!ENTITY % Misc.class
    "%Edit.class;
    %Script.class;
    %Misc.extra;"
>
<!-- .................... Inline Elements
...................... -->
<!ENTITY % InlStruct.class "%br.qname; | %span.qname;" >

<!ENTITY % InlPhras.class
```

```
        "| %em.qname; | %strong.qname; | %dfn.qname; |
        %code.qname;
            | %samp.qname; | %kbd.qname; | %var.qname; | %cite.qname;
            | %abbr.qname; | %acronym.qname; | %q.qname;" >

<!ENTITY % InlPres.class
        "| %tt.qname; | %i.qname; | %b.qname; | %big.qname;
            | %small.qname; | %sub.qname; | %sup.qname;" >
<!ENTITY % I18n.class "| %bdo.qname;" >
<!ENTITY % Anchor.class "| %a.qname;" >

<!ENTITY % InlSpecial.class
        "| %img.qname; | %map.qname;
            | %object.qname;" >

<!ENTITY % InlForm.class
        "| %input.qname; | %select.qname; | %textarea.qname;
            | %label.qname; | %button.qname;" >
<!ENTITY % Inline.extra "" >

<!ENTITY % Ruby.class "| %ruby.qname;" >
<!-- %Inline.class; includes all inline elements,
        used as a component in mixes-->
<!ENTITY % Inline.class
        "%InlStruct.class;
         %InlPhras.class;
         %InlPres.class;
         %I18n.class;
         %Anchor.class;
         %InlSpecial.class;
         %InlForm.class;
         %Ruby.class;
         %Inline.extra;"
>

<!-- %InlNoRuby.class; includes all inline elements
        except ruby, used as a component in mixes-->
<!ENTITY % InlNoRuby.class
        "%InlStruct.class;
```

```
        %InlPhras.class;
        %InlPres.class;
        %I18n.class;
        %Anchor.class;
        %InlSpecial.class;
        %InlForm.class;
        %Inline.extra;"
>


<!-- %NoRuby.content; includes all inlines except ruby-->
<!ENTITY % NoRuby.content
    "( #PCDATA
    | %InlNoRuby.class;
    %Misc.class; )*"
>


<!-- %InlNoAnchor.class; includes all nonanchor inlines,
    used as a component in mixes-->
<!ENTITY % InlNoAnchor.class
    "%InlStruct.class;
    %InlPhras.class;
    %InlPres.class;
    %I18n.class;
    %InlSpecial.class;
    %InlForm.class;
    %Ruby.class;
    %Inline.extra;"
>


<!-- %InlNoAnchor.mix; includes all nonanchor inlines-->
<!ENTITY % InlNoAnchor.mix
    "%InlNoAnchor.class;
    %Misc.class;"
>
<!-- %Inline.mix; includes all inline elements, including
%Misc.class;-->
<!ENTITY % Inline.mix
    "%Inline.class;
```

```
        %Misc.class;"
>


<!-- .................... Block Elements
..................... -->


<!-- In the HTML 4.0 DTD, heading and list elements were
included
     in the %block; parameter entity. The %Heading.class; and
     %List.class; parameter entities must now be included
     explicitly on element declarations where desired.-->
<!ENTITY % Heading.class
     "%h1.qname; | %h2.qname; | %h3.qname;
      | %h4.qname; | %h5.qname; | %h6.qname;" >
<!ENTITY % List.class "%ul.qname; | %ol.qname; | %dl.qname;" >
<!ENTITY % Table.class "| %table.qname;" >
<!ENTITY % Form.class  "| %form.qname;" >
<!ENTITY % Fieldset.class  "| %fieldset.qname;" >
<!ENTITY % BlkStruct.class "%p.qname; | %div.qname;" >
<!ENTITY % BlkPhras.class
     "| %pre.qname; | %blockquote.qname; | %address.qname;" >
<!ENTITY % BlkPres.class "| %hr.qname;" >
<!ENTITY % BlkSpecial.class
     "%Table.class;
      %Form.class;
      %Fieldset.class;"
>


<!ENTITY % Block.extra "" >
<!-- %Block.class; includes all block elements,
     used as an component in mixes-->
<!ENTITY % Block.class
     "%BlkStruct.class;
      %BlkPhras.class;
      %BlkPres.class;
      %BlkSpecial.class;
```

```
        %Block.extra;"
>

<!-- %Block.mix; includes all block elements plus %Misc.class;
-->
<!ENTITY % Block.mix
    "%Heading.class;
     | %List.class;
     | %Block.class;
     %Misc.class;"
>
<!-- ............... All Content Elements  ................
-->

<!-- %Flow.mix; includes all text content, block and inline-->
<!ENTITY % Flow.mix
    "%Heading.class;
     | %List.class;
     | %Block.class;
     | %Inline.class;
     %Misc.class;"
>
<!-- end of xhtml 11-model-1.mod -->
```

Summary

We consider this chapter's topic to be one of the most important technologies included in the XML family. We have learned how to
include modules from the XHTML specification and create a new
markup language using the DTD template provided for us to build
a DTD.

Implement XHTML modules as Document Type Definition fragments. You can assemble fragments in a specified order and create a
resulting DTD. Your XHTML document can then be validated against
this DTD.

The W3C Committee divides the XHTML DTD modules into separate categories called abstract modules. Each module contains semantically grouped elements.

The XHTML modularization is based on attribute collections defined in the XML 1.0 specification. The following eight data types are acceptable in XHTML:

- CDATA
- ID
- IDREF
- IDREFS
- NMTOKEN
- NMTOKENS
- PCDATA

Additionally, XHTML modularization has added several new data types. Table 8.2 provides information concerning them.

We learned that four collections make up the common collection, as follows:

- Core
- 118N
- Events
- Style

The XHTML strict DTD contains information about these.

Minimal content models define elements or data allowed within other elements. Examining the `dl` element defines a content model.

We learned how to utilize the template DTD to extract a predefined table in the W3C strict DTD for the purpose of creating a new DTD (see Section 8.6). Additionally, we built a custom DTD module (Section 8.8).

The DTD implementation contains two submodules: QNames and Declaration. In this section we learned how to build a submodule and then decompose it to provide a better understanding of how this works.

Finally, we demonstrated how to create a new markup module.

PART 3

PRESENTATION

Self-Review Exercises

1. Provide a detailed explanation of how to implement XHTML modules as DTDs.

2. What is a QName?

3. The W3C Working Committee divided the XHTML DTD into separate modules. What are they?

4. Provide a list of acceptable XML data types.

5. Describe the differences between the XHTML strict DTD, the transitional DTD, and the frameset DTD.

6. Attribute collections comprise the common collection. Four collections exist. Provide a detailed account of each and what it comprises.

7. What is a minimal content model? Provide an example.

8. Minimal content models frequently reference collections of elements commonly called content sets. Provide an explanation for them.

9. Write a program including a module from the strict DTD. Do not use the example listed in this chapter.

10. Write a purchase order XML source document and create a DTD for it.

11. Describe the importance of the XHTML framework module.

IMPLEMENTATION

PART 4

9 Mapping Your Data to a Database

9.1 Design Strategies for Mapping XML to Relational Databases

Mapping data from one format to another is the focus of this chapter. Part 1 of this book introduced numerous technologies for manipulating, searching, and transforming data. Part 2 of this book presents practical applications using XML technologies reviewed earlier. We will demonstrate how to parse raw data, use the DOM to generate an XML file, and in turn, save that document to various type repositories.

We begin by mapping a comma-delimited flat file, parsing it, and generating an XML document. Typically, flat files exist as comma-delimited, fixed-width, or tagged records.

Flat files contain data fields separated by commas or some other means of delineating separate fields, such as tab characters, colons, or pipe characters. Carriage return-line, line-feed combinations delimit individual records.

The second flat file type contains fixed-length fields in which a specified number of bytes is allocated for each field. The third file type uses tags for indicating the beginning of a new record.

The example in Figure 9.1 is comma delimited.

```
Dwight Peltzer,PO Box 335,
EastNorwich,NY,11773,11/01/2003,11/04/2002,
1,Silver TLZ6 phone,1,69.9,blue TLZ80
PDA,2,99.20,,0,0.00,,0,0.00,,0,0.00
Steven Heim,36-8 188th Street,Queens,NY,78462,
11/03/2003,11/05/2003,2,red Palm Pilot, 3,99.30,blue TLZ88
phone,11,89.9,,0,0.00,,0,0.00,,0,0.00
```

Figure 9.1   A comma-delimited file

This file contains the following invoice information: customer name, address, city, state, zip, purchase date, ship date, shipping code (UPS, FEDEX, USPS), and a three-item field indicating the type of wireless device, quantity, and price.

The same invoice presented in fixed-length form looks like Figure 9.2.

```
Dwight Peltzer        PO Box 355        Hicksville
NY11773
06/05/200206/9/2002
Steve George          PO Box 234        Flushing Meadows
NY16435
06/12/2002 06/13/2003
```

Figure 9.2   Fixed-length delimited file

The third type of flat file is the tagged record. The first field in the record indicates the type of record, such as (I) for invoice, (L) for line item, and (C) for a customer.

```
I,06/05/2002, 06/9/2003
C,Dwight Peltzer, PO Box 355, Hicksville, NY, 11772
L, 2, Silver T61Z phone, 1, 69.95
L,1, Gold T68 phone, 2, 79.95
```

Figure 9.3   Tagged-record flat file

9.2 Transforming a Flat File to Name/Value Pairs

The first thing we need to do is transform the comma-delimited flat file to name/value pairs. This will help us set up the information we need to parse the file and transform it to XML.

Examining the comma-delimited file, here is how our mapping looks. The [N] represents an indeterminate invoice. We use this notation when a flat file represents more than one invoice.

Table 9.1   Mapping Data to Name/Value Pairs

Value	Details	
record[N].field1	Data Type:	String
	Format:	varchar (20)
	Description	Customer name
record[N].field2	Data Type:	String
	Format:	varchar (30)
	Description	Customer address
record[N].field3	Data Type:	String
	Format:	varchar (20)
	Description	Customer city
record[N].field4	Data Type:	String
	Format:	char (2)
	Description	Customer state
record[N].field5	Data Type:	String
	Format:	#####-####
	Description	Customer zip code
record[N].field6	Data Type:	Datetime
	Format:	MM/DD/YYYY
	Description	Order date

Table 9.1 Mapping Data to Name/Value Pairs, continued

Value	Details	
record[N].field7	Data Type:	Datetime
	Format:	MM/DD/YYYY
	Description	Ship date
record[N].field8	Data Type:	Enumerated Values
	Format:	1:USPS
		2:UPS
		3:FEDEX
	Description	Shipping method
record[N].field9	Data Type:	String
	Format:	varchar (25)
	Description	Type of wireless device
		[color] [type] [device name]
record[N].field9	Data Type:	Quantity
	Format:	#####
	Description	Quantity of devices ordered
record[N].field11	Data Type:	Price
	Format:	####.##
	Description	Part price
record[N].field12	Data Type:	String
	Format:	varchar (25)
	Description	Type of wireless device
		[color] [type] [device name]
record[N].field13	Data Type:	Quantity
	Format:	#####
	Description	Quantity of devices ordered

Table 9.1   Mapping Data to Name/Value Pairs, continued

Value	Details	
record[N].field14	Data Type:	Price
	Format:	####.##
	Description	Part price
record[N].field15	Data Type:	String
	Format:	varchar (25)
	Description	Type of wireless device [color] [type] [device name]
record[N].field16	Data Type:	Quantity
	Format:	#####
	Description	Quantity of devices ordered
record[N].field17	Data Type:	Price
	Format:	####.##
	Description	Part price
record[N].field18	Data Type:	String
	Format:	varchar (25)
	Description	Type of wireless device [color] [type] [device name]
record[N].field19	Data Type:	Quantity
	Format:	#####
	Description	Quantity of devices ordered
record[N].field20	Data Type:	Price
	Format:	####.##
	Description	Part price

PART 4
IMPLEMENTATION

Table 9.1   Mapping Data to Name/Value Pairs, continued

Value	Details	
record[N].field21	Data Type:	String
	Format:	varchar (25)
	Description	Type of wireless device
		[color] [type] [device name]
record[N].field22	Data Type:	Quantity
	Format:	#####
	Description	Quantity of devices ordered
record[N].field23	Data Type:	Price
	Format:	####.##
	Description	Part price

Table 9.2 demonstrates how we link each field to a specific record component. `InvoiceInfo.Invoice[N]` points to `->Customer.Name`, and so on.

Table 9.2   Mapping Data Fields to XML

Origin	Target	Comments
record[N].field1	InvoiceInfo.Invoice[N]->Customer.Name	Create a new customer
record[N].field2	InvoiceInfo.Invoice[N]->Customer.address	Reference address
record[N].field3	InvoiceInfo.Invoice[N]->Customer.city	Reference the city

Table 9.2 Mapping Data Fields to XML, continued

Origin	Target	Comments
record[N].field4	InvoiceInfo.Invoice[N]->Customer.state	Reference the state
record[N].field5	InvoiceInfo.Invoice[N]->Customer.Zip	Reference the zip code
record[N].field6	InvoiceInfo.Invoice[N].order date	Reference order date
record[N].field7	InvoiceInfo.Invoice[N].ship date	Reference the ship date
record[N].field8	InvoiceInfo.Invoice[N].shipping method	Enumerated ship values: 1: USPS 2: UPS 3: FEDEX
record[N].field9	InvoiceInfo.Invoice.LineItem[1].Part.Name	
record[N].field9	InvoiceInfo.Invoice.LineItem[1].Part.Type	
record[N].field11	InvoiceInfo.Invoice.LineItem[1].Part.Color	
record[N].field12	InvoiceInfo.Invoice.LineItem[1].Part.Quantity	
record[N].field13	InvoiceInfo.Invoice.LineItem[1].Part.Price	

Table 9.2   Mapping Data Fields to XML, continued

Origin	Target	Comments
record[N].field14	InvoiceInfo.Invoice.LineItem[2].Part.Name	Blank if line 2 doesn't appear on invoice
record[N].field15	InvoiceInfo.Invoice.LineItem[2].Part.Type	
record[N].field16	InvoiceInfo.Invoice.LineItem[2].Part.Color	

9.3   Transforming Flat Files to XML

Several approaches for flat-file transformation to XML are as follows:

- Manual serialization
- SAX
- The DOM

One advantage of manually serializing a file is the small memory footprint. You create the file by appending strings and creating start and ending tags for them. Unfortunately, this method is error prone because you might overlook a start or ending tag. Additionally, this method is not a well-organized approach. The governing document, such as a DTD or schema, dictates the element order. We will leave this method for you to explore as an exercise.

The SAX method requires creating an event handler for processing strings passed to it. (Refer to Chapter 3, "Parsing Your XML Document," where we discussed the various parsing methods and presented an example of parsing with SAX.) You must create start and end tags for each individual component. The file must be created in the order dictated by a DTD or schema. We recommend this method for generating very large XML documents because the document is not stored in memory, as it is the case with the DOM.

The third method uses the DOM for creating a hierarchical tree. It loads the entire document in memory, providing random access to the source document, a major advantage. This method allows flexibility in determining document order because the target document provides no constraints. The drawback is caching the document in memory if the source file is large. For demonstration purposes, we will use VBScript for processing data and transforming it to XML. Figure 9.4 contains the script for creating InvoiceInfo.xml. We will walk you through the code so that you can learn how to process a flat file. The `sField` array contains 23 fields. This conforms to the mapping we did previously. Refer to Tables 9.1 and 9.2 for a detailed description of each field. As we parse the file, we collect data from three categories: invoice, part, and customer. When we ultimately generate the XML document, we organize the file to generate customer information first, followed by invoice data, and finally part information, as demonstrated here:

```
root.appendChild(customerContainer)
root.appendChild(invoiceContainer)
root.appendChild(partContainer)
```

Figure 9.4 shows the VBScript file.

```
Module Invoice

    Sub Main()
        Dim fstrObj, txtstr, sLine, s, sItem
        Dim elem, dom, root
        Dim iField, iNode
        Dim sField(23)
        Dim stName, sSType, sTColor
        Dim sType, sColor, sName, sAddress
        Dim iLineItem
```

Figure 9.4   Invoice.vbs

We track customer and part information by initializing `iCust` and `iPart`. By doing so, we are able to generate a unique ID for each element created. The delimiter is a comma, as indicated by `Delim=Chr(44)`. `Dim invContainer, partContainer, customerContainer`

We suggest that you refer to the source code on the accompanying CD and copy it into your favorite compiler's IDE and follow along as we step through the code.

```
Dim litem, newlin, iCust, iPart, cust, part, Delim

iCust = 1
iPart = 1
Delim = Chr(44)
```

Next we create two objects, `Scripting.FileSystemObject` and a DOM object. The `FileSystemObject` reads the flat file, and the DOM object creates the tree.

```
fstrObj = CreateObject("Scripting.FileSystemObject")
dom = CreateObject("Microsoft.XMLDOM")
root = dom.createElement("InvoiceData")
dom.appendChild(root)
```

`InvoiceContainer, partContainer,` and `customerContainer` serve as repositories holding information from each category. When we generate the XML file, they contain the data we need to output the information where necessary.

> **Note:** Document fragments usually do not have a root element; therefore they are not well-formed documents but exist instead as fragments.

```
invContainer = dom.createDocumentFragment()
partContainer = dom.createDocumentFragment()
customerContainer = dom.createDocumentFragment()
```

Open the flat file and read it. The VBScript function `Left` contains the following arguments: `Left(string, length)`. The `string` argument is the string being processed, whereas `length` returns the number of characters from the left of the string. Function `Instr` finds the starting position of one string within another. `Mid` returns a substring of a specified length from within a given string.

```
txtstr =
fstrObj.OpenTextFile("C:\VisualStudioExamples\Parse\invoicede-
lim.txt")Do While txtstr.AtEndOfStream <> True
s = txtstr.ReadLine
For iField = 1 To 22
sField(iField) = Left(s, InStr(s, Delim) - 1)
s = Mid(s, InStr(s, Delim) + 1)
Next
sField(23) = s

        elem = dom.createElement("Invoice")
```

' If the customer is located, set the customer IDREF attribute to point to it.

```
elem.setAttribute("customerIDREF", "NotFound")
newlin = customerContainer.childNodes
            For iNode = 0 To newlin.length - 1
            sName = newlin.item(iNode).getAttribute("name")
sAddress = newlin.item(iNode).getAttribute("address")
If sName = sField(1) And sAddress = sField(2) Then
 'If sName = sField(1) and sAddress = sField(2), we assume we
'have located this customer
elem.setAttribute("customerIDREF", _
newlin.item(iNode).getAttribute("customerID"))
                End If
            Next

If elem.getAttribute("customerIDREF") = "NotFound" Then
' create a new customer
cust = dom.createElement("Customer")
cust.setAttribute("customerID", "CUST" & iCust)
```

```
                cust.setAttribute("name", sField(1))
                cust.setAttribute("address", sField(2))
                cust.setAttribute("city", sField(3))
                cust.setAttribute("state", sField(4))
                cust.setAttribute("postalCode", sField(5))
                customerContainer.appendChild(cust)
                elem.setAttribute("customerIDREF", "CUST" &
                iCust)
                iCust = iCust + 1
            End If
    'Iterate through three-field set and set ship method
            elem.setAttribute("orderDate", sField(6))
            elem.setAttribute("shipDate", sField(7))
             If sField(8) = 1 Then
            elem.setAttribute("shipMethod", "USPS")
             If sField(8) = 2 Then
            elem.setAttribute("shipMethod", "UPS")
             If sField(8) = 3 Then
            elem.setAttribute("shipMethod", "FedEx")
             invContainer.appendChild(elem)

            For iLineItem = 1 To 5
                If sField(6 + iLineItem * 3) > " " Then
    ' lineItem exists
                    litem = dom.createElement("LineItem")
                    litem.setAttribute("quantity", sField(6 +
                    iLineItem * 3 + 1))
                    litem.setAttribute("price", sField(6 +
                    iLineItem * 3 + 2))

    ' parse the description field
    sItem = sField(6 + iLineItem * 3)
                stColor = Left(sItem, InStr(sItem, " ") - 1)
                sItem = Mid(sItem, InStr(sItem, " ") + 1)
                sSType = ""
                While InStr(sItem, " ") > 0
```

```
          sSType = sSType + Left(sItem, InStr(sItem, " "))
              sItem = Mid(sItem, InStr(sItem, " ") + 1)
              End While
              sSType = Left(sSType, Len(sSType) - 1)
              stName = sItem


              newlin = partContainer.childNodes
              litem.setAttribute("partIDREF", "NotFound")
              For iNode = 0 To newlin.length - 1
          sName = newlin.item(iNode).getAttribute("name")
          sType = newlin.item(iNode).getAttribute("type")
          sColor = newlin.item(iNode).getAttribute("color")
    If stName = sName And sSType = sType And sTColor = sColor _
                  Then
                      litem.setAttribute("partIDREF", _
          newlin.item(iNode).getAttribute("partID"))
                  End If
              Next
              If litem.getAttribute("partIDREF") =
"NotFound" Then

' Create a new part

                  part = dom.createElement("Part")
                  part.setAttribute("partID", "PART" &
                  iPart)
                  part.setAttribute("name", stName)
                  part.setAttribute("type", sSType)
                  part.setAttribute("color", sTColor)
                  partContainer.appendChild(part)
litem.setAttribute("partIDREF", "PART" & iPart)
                  iPart = iPart + 1
```

```
                              End If
                              elem.appendChild(litem)

                       End If
                 Next
           Loop
           txtstr.Close()
```
'parsing is finished. Append the data stored in the repositories.
```
           root.appendChild(customerContainer)
           root.appendChild(invContainer)
           root.appendChild(partContainer)
```

'Now, output the XML file.
```
           txtstr = fstrObj.CreateTextFile("C:\Parse.xml", True)
           txtstr.Write(dom.xml)
           txtstr.close()
           txtstr = Nothing

     End Sub

End Module
```

The XML file we generated is Parse.xml (see Figure 9.5).

```
<InvoiceData>
<Customer customerID="CUST1" name="Dwight Peltzer" address="PO
Box 335" city="EastNorwich" state="NY" postalCode="11773"/>
<Customer customerID="CUST2" name="Steven Heim" address="36-8
188th Street" city="Queens" state="NY" postalCode="78462"/>
<Invoice customerIDREF="CUST1" orderDate="11/01/2003"
shipDate="11/04/2002" shipMethod="USPS">
<LineItem quantity="1" price="69.9" partIDREF="PART1"/>
<LineItem quantity="2" price="99.20" partIDREF="PART2"/>
</Invoice>
<Invoice customerIDREF="CUST2" orderDate="11/03/2003"
shipDate="11/05/2002" shipMethod="UPS">
<LineItem quantity=" 3" price="99.30" partIDREF="PART3"/>
<LineItem quantity="11" price="89.9" partIDREF="PART4"/>
```

```
</Invoice>
<Part partID="PART1" name="phone" type="TLZ6" color="Silver"/>
<Part partID="PART2" name="PDA" type="TLZ80" color="blue"/>
<Part partID="PART3" name="Pilot" type="Palm" color="red"/>
<Part partID="PART4" name="phone" type="TLZ88" color="blue"/>
</InvoiceData>
```

Figure 9.5   Parse.XML

We can do various things with the generated XML file. Persisting the data to a file or to a database would be a logical thing to do. Before we make that decision, let's discuss data modeling before we proceed any further.

9.4 Modeling Your Data

Address the following key issues before beginning the initial design phase:

- Do we map data from XML to a relational database or vice versa?
- For what purpose do we design the data model?

Modeling data necessitates designing a mapping strategy. Two distinct concepts exist for modeling data: modeling for data and modeling for text. Modeling for data requires an entirely different approach than modeling for text. For example, let's examine the American League baseball standings example in which we model for structure.

Division	Team	won	lost	percentage	gamesBehind	home	away	div	streak
East	NY Yankees	29	22	.589	--	14-9	15-13	14-10	Lost 1
East	Boston	28	22	.560	1/2	17-10	11-12	16-10	Won 1
East	Toronto	26	26	.500	3 1/2	13-12	13-14	9-6	Lost 1
East	Baltimore	24	27	.471	5	14-14	10-13	12-14	Lost 3
East	Tampa Bay	15	37	.288	14/1/2	8-20	7-17	7-18	Lost 1

Figure 9.6   Baseball league standings

Wins and losses determine the overall structure of the team standings. Business model requirements dictate document structure.
Percentages based on the won/lost column provide information concerning a team's performance. Heaven forbid we should alter the
structure of the standings by moving Boston or Toronto into first
place. This destroys the meaning of the standings and produces undesirable results. Each column heading describes specific statistical
content. Moving data vertically or horizontally (meaning in columns
or rows, respectively) strips content of its meaning and relevance to
the entire document. Summing it up, structure is of the essence in this
example.

Two additional issues arise when we consider how to model data:
document size and performance. Are we modeling for readability or
computer processing? If we model for computer processing, simply
abbreviate descriptive element tag names and remove whitespace, as
demonstrated in the following example:

```
<b><W>29</W><L>22</L><PCT>589</PCT><GB>--</GB>,<H>14-
8</H>,<A>15-13</A>,<D>15-13</D>14-9<S>Lost 1</S></b>
```

This format is perfect for computer consumption. We retain structure and reduce document size.

9.5 Mapping Child Elements as Attributes

Elements map as attributes and require less bandwidth, as demonstrated here:

```
<L l= "22" pct=".589"  gb="--" h="14-8" />
```

A hierarchal tree consists of elements, attributes, processing instructions, comments, and so on and represents an XML source document. The DOM extracts content from attributes more efficiently than from elements because attributes consist of name/value pairs, whereas the element-only content model contains three separate pieces of information: opening tag, content, and closing tag. For example:

```
Tag         Content    Closing Element
_____

<Customer>DPSoftware</Customer>
<Address> PO Box 355</Address>
```

The parser must locate the element, process the opening tag and then its content, and finally process the closing tag. Now compare this format with the same data presented as attributes:

```
<Invoice
      CustomerName ="DPSoftware" CustomerAddress="PO Box 355"/>
```

Less processing is required in this context.

Referring back to the league standings, the columns map easily to a relational database. The elements `<AmericanLeague>`, `<Division>`, and `<Team>` map directly to table names. `Won`, `lost`, and so on map as attributes, reducing document size and facilitating efficient data processing and retrieval. Let's format the team statistics as attributes (see Figure 9.7).

```
<AmericanLeague
    Division="East">
      <Team
          Name="NY Yankees"
          won="29"
          lost="22"
          Percentage="589"
          GB=" "
          Home="14-9"
          Away="15-13"
          Div="14-9"/>
          Division="East"
```

PART 4

IMPLEMENTATION

```
                    Name="Boston"
                    won="28"
                    lost="22"
                    Pct.="560"
                    GB="1/2 "
                    Home="17-9"
                    Away="11-12"
                    Div="16-9"/>
                    Division="East"
                    Name="Toronto"
                    won="26"
                    lost="26"
                    Pct.="500"
                    GB="3 1/2 "
                    Home="13-12"
                    Away="13-14"
                    Div="9-6"/>
      </AmericanLeague>
```

Figure 9.7   Team standings mapped as attributes

Modeling data for text represents another type of mapping. It requires maintaining structure. The following excerpt from Shakespeare's *Hamlet* is marked up especially for print media. We divide scenes into substructures, meaning <SceneOne>, <SceneTwo>, and so on. (The latter scene is not included in this document fragment.) Paragraph headings delineate document structure, including both line and quote element tags within the paragraph block. Additionally, Hamlet.xml emulates the original document structure presented in Figure 9.8 without markup tags.

```
-  <Hamlet>

    -

-  <SceneOne>

    -

-  <paragraph>
   <line officer="Bernardo" />
   <quote>'Who's there?'</quote>
   <quote>'Answer me: stand, and unfold yourself.'</quote>
   <line officer="Bernardo" />
   <quote>"Long live the king!"</quote>

    -
```

```
<line officer="Francisco" />
<quote>"Bernardo"'</quote>
<line officer="Bernardo" />
<quote>"He"</quote>
<line officer="Francisco" />
<quote>"You come most carefully upon your hour"</quote>
<line officer="Bernardo" />
<quote>"Tis now struck twelve; get thee to bed, Francisco.
"</quote>
<line officer="Francisco" />
<quote>'For this relief much thanks; 'tis bitter cold, And I
am sick at heart'</quote>
<line officer="Bernardo" />
<quote>'Have you had quiet guard?'</quote>
<line officer="Francisco" />
<quote>'Not a mouse stirring.'</quote>
<line officer="Bernardo" />
<quote>'Well, good-night. If you do meet Horatio and Marcellus,
the rivals of my watch, bid them make haste'</quote>
<line officer="Francisco" />
<quote>'I think I hear them. Stand, ho! Who's there?'</quote>
</paragraph>
</SceneOne>
</Hamlet
```

Figure 9.8   Hamlet.xml displayed in Internet Explorer

What happens if we alter the document structure? Figure 9.9 answers this question.

```
<SceneOne>
<paragraph>
<line officer = "Francisco"/>
<quote>'For this relief much thanks; 'tis bitter cold, And I am
sick at heart'</quote>
<line officer= "Bernardo"/>
<quote>'Have you had quiet guard?'</quote>
<line officer = "Francisco"/>
<quote>'Not a mouse stirring.'</quote>
<line officer= "Bernardo"/>
```

```
<quote> 'Well, good-night. If you do meet Horatio and
Marcellus, the rivals of my watch, bid them make haste'
</quote>
<line officer="Francisco"/>
<quote> 'I think I hear them. Stand, ho! Who's there?'</quote>
<line officer="Bernardo"/>
<quote> 'Who's there?'</quote>
<line officer= "Francisco"/>
<quote> 'Answer me: stand, and unfold yourself.'
</quote>
</paragraph>
</SceneOne>
```

Figure 9.9   Altering *Hamlet*'s structure

Restructuring the data in this context eliminates both structure and meaning. It is always a good policy to bind source documents to a DTD or schema to assure proper document structure. Let's design a DTD for Hamlet. Defining a root element is the first task in DTD design. Document root element **<Hamlet>** contains child element **<SceneOne>**.

```
<?xml version="1.0" encoding="UTF-8"?>
<!ELEMENT Hamlet (SceneOne)>
Element <SceneOne> contains exactly one child element:
<paragraph>
<!ELEMENT SceneOne (paragraph)>
```

Figure 9.10   Hamlet.dtd

Define the content model for an attribute list as follows:

```
<!ELEMENT line EMPTY>
<!ATTLIST line
officer (Bernardo | Francisco) #REQUIRED
>
<!ELEMENT paragraph (line | quote)+>
<!ELEMENT quote (#PCDATA)>
```

Here are some tips for designing a DTD and mapping to a relational database, applicable to any DTD design:

1. Decide on your content model, meaning element-only, mixed, text-only, ANY, or EMPTY. Examine your document and list only elements initially.

```
<!Element Hamlet EMPTY>
<!Element SceneOne EMPTY>
<!Element line EMPTY>
<!Element Paragraph EMPTY>
```

2. Then add your child elements in the order you want them to appear in the source document.

   Element `Hamlet` can contain only one child element, `SceneOne`. Naturally, the play contains more than one scene, so you must add the various scenes to element `Hamlet` if you want to process the entire play. In this example, we are only presenting the first scene.

3. When we map elements to a relational database, represent them as a set of tables. Begin by doing the following steps:

   1. Create a primary key.

   2. Add a column that holds an automatically incremented integer key.

   3. Name the column corresponding to the element with an appended key.

   4. Set the column to be the primary key on the created table.

   5. For every structural element located in the DTD, create a table in the database.

   6. Add a column to the table that references the parent element (if the structural element has one allowable parent element or is the root element for the DTD).

   7. Create the foreign key.

   8. If an element contains text-only content, create a column in the database.

   9. Add a foreign key that represents the parent element that points to the corresponding record in a child table.

PART 4

IMPLEMENTATION

10. Make this column nullable.

11. If an element is text-only and may appear in a parent element more than once, create a table to hold the text values of the element.

12. Add a foreign key that relates back to the parent table.

13. Create an intermediate table to portray the relationship between each parent element and the element (if the element may appear in more than one parent element).

Unfortunately, we find it difficult to create a DTD for *Hamlet* that accurately portrays the play. For example, the occurrence compositor limits us when defining precisely the number of recurrences for an element. Additionally, we are limited to defining data types as only PCDATA or CDATA. Therefore, an XSD schema will allow us to portray *Hamlet* more accurately.

9.6 Designing a Schema for *Hamlet*

Defining data types and providing constraints for source documents is very limited using DTD methodology. DTDs focus on an XML instance from a document point of view, whereas schemas view document instances from a data type perspective. Let's create an XSD schema for Hamlet (see Figure 9.11) and review some of the advantages that schemas offer us.

```
<?xml version="1.0" encoding="UTF-8"?>
<xsd:schema xmlns:xsd="http://www.w3.org/2000/9/XMLSchema"
elementFormDefault="qualified">
   <xsd:element name="Hamlet">
     <xsd:complexType>
       <xsd:sequence>
          <xsd:element name="SceneOne" type="SceneOneType"/>
       </xsd:sequence>
     </xsd:complexType>
```

```
        </xsd:element>
        <xsd:complexType name="SceneOneType">
          <xsd:sequence>
            <xsd:element name="paragraph" type="paragraphType"/>
          </xsd:sequence>
        </xsd:complexType>
        <xsd:complexType name="lineType">
          <xsd:attribute name="officer" use="required">
            <xsd:simpleType>
              <xsd:restriction base="xsd:NMTOKEN">
                <xsd:enumeration value="Bernardo"/>
                <xsd:enumeration value="Francisco"/>
              </xsd:restriction>
            </xsd:simpleType>
          </xsd:attribute>
        </xsd:complexType>
        <xsd:complexType name="paragraphType">
          <xsd:choice maxOccurs="unbounded">
            <xsd:element name="line" type="lineType"/>
            <xsd:element ref="quote"/>
          </xsd:choice>
        </xsd:complexType>
        <xsd:element name="quote" type="xsd:string"/>
    </xsd:schema>
```

Figure 9.11   Hamlet.xsd

Compare Hamlet's DTD with the schema and note the compositors for child elements `line` and `quote`. The DTD plus (+) symbol only indicates that `line` and `quote` reappear repeatedly, limiting our capability to specify the precise number of times each character appears throughout the first scene (although, in this scene, it is not necessary to do so). In contrast, the schema provides the capability to specify child element recurrences using keywords `minOccurs="0"` and `maxOccurs="unbounded"`. Observe how to use `restriction` to define a new data type (see Figure 9.12).

```
        <xsd:complexType name="lineType">
                <xsd:attribute name="officer" use="required">
                    <!--this is the block we are discussing-->
```

PART 4
IMPLEMENTATION

405

```
<xsd:simpleType>
<xsd:restriction base="xsd:NMTOKEN">
<xsd:enumeration value="Bernardo"/>
<xsd:enumeration value="Francisco"/>
</xsd:restriction>
</xsd:simpleType>
</xsd:attribute>
</xsd:complexType>
```

Figure 9.12   Restriction base

Schemas allow us to define simple data types used specifically for attributes. You accomplish this by providing a label to the `simpleType` attribute containing the name of the new data type. Then use `restriction` to indicate that the newly declared data type is derived from the simple string data type. Subsequently, because of this derivation, the number of possible values restricts enumerated attributes `Bernardo` and `Francisco`, defined as `NMTOKEN`. Using named data types is analogous to defining a class and then using it to create an object. Extensibility enhances our ability to more accurately define Hamlet's data model. Considering the advantages that XML and schemas give us, we encourage our readers to migrate from DTDs to schema design as the chosen methodology for providing document structure and constraints, defining new data types, as well as a multitude of other major benefits.

9.7 Mapping Raw Data to XML

`<Invoice>` existed originally as an unformatted document. We converted the data to XML using the same parsing technique employed in Figure 9.4.

XML allows us to be very flexible in the manner in which we mark up data. Five content models exist for designing our documents. Standalone documents, though well formed, are not very useful. Unforeseen problems arise when mapping a poorly designed document to a relational database if not validated. We eliminate these problems by carefully selecting the proper content model before attempting any mapping. Let's examine the five content models, discuss the pros and cons of each, and learn how to apply them. First, however, we present the XML document in Figure 9.13 to serve as model for this discussion.

```
<?xml version="1.0" encoding="UTF-8"?>
<!DOCTYPE Invoice SYSTEM "C:\Documents and
Settings\Administrator\My
Documents\chapter9Examples\Invoice1.dtd">
<Invoice>
    <SoldTo>
        <soldToID>PD11</soldToID>
        <invoiceDate>05/29/2003</invoiceDate>
        <custPO>00</custPO>
        <CustID>90</CustID>
    </SoldTo>

    <!-- shipping elements go here -->
    <ShipTo>
      <Name>Joseph Fingers</Name>
      <Address>PO Box 355</Address>
      <City>East Meadow</City>
      <State>NY</State>
      <Zip>11542</Zip>
      <shipDate>05/30/2001</shipDate>
      <ShipMethod>UPS</ShipMethod>
    </ShipTo>
    <!-- product info goes here -->
    <Product>
      <ProdNum>DL-DSH5</ProdNum>
      <ProductDescription>D-Link Hub</ProductDescription>
    </Product>
    <!-- line items go here -->
    <LineItem>
        <invoiceNo>095318</invoiceNo>
        <ProductID>DSH</ProductID>
      <Quantity>1</Quantity>
      <PartNum>DSH5</PartNum>
      <unitPrice>61.00</unitPrice>
    </LineItem>
</Invoice>
```

Figure 9.13   Invoice.xml

9.8   Content Models

<Invoice> is the root element for this document. Sibling elements are <SoldTo>, <ShipTo>, <Product>, and <LineItem>. Designing the file with this structure makes it easy to search and map the data to a relational database. The following list contains the five content models discussed in the next chapter sections. Each content model presents unique approaches to mapping data:

- Element-only content
- Mixed
- ANY
- Text-only content
- EMPTY

Element-Only Content Model

The element-only content model allows only nested elements to appear within it. Consider the following document source:

```
<Invoice>
    <soldTo></soldTo>
    <shipTo></shipTo>
    <Product></Product>
    <LineItem></LineItem>
</Invoice>
```

Sibling elements SoldTo, ShipTo, Product, and LineItem are containers with subelements nested within them. Invoice represents a nice way of nesting more than one substructure within it. This structure becomes very significant when we apply the SQL query FOR XML EXPLICIT in the next chapter. These elements map directly as tables.

Examining the source document again, we need a method for displaying the relationship between tables. Add an automatic generated key, independent of the data bearing the name of the table. For example, the following four IDs map as table names and bear their respective names:

- `soldToKey` or `soldToID`
- `shipToKey` or `shipToID`
- `ProductKey` or `ProductID`
- `lineItemKey` or `lineItemID`

The script in Figure 9.14 uses these IDs.

```
Use Invoice
go
Create Table soldTo(
soldToID int PRIMARY KEY NOT NULL,
CustID int not null,
invoiceDate datetime not null,
shipDate datetime not null,
CustPO int not null)

Create Table lineItem(
lineItemID int PRIMARY KEY NOT NULL,
soldToID int not null,
invoiceNo int not null,
Quantity int not null,
unitPrice decimal not null,
ProductDescription varchar (255) not null
CONSTRAINT fk_lineItemSoldTo
FOREIGN KEY (soldToID)
REFERENCES soldTo (soldToID))
```

Figure 9.14   Create table `soldToLineItem` script

This mapping carries some overhead. Some controversy exists regarding the use of elements versus attributes. One point of view considers elements as containers of data, whereas an opposing view considers attributes as annotations to elements and provides additional information about the content of an element as well as the element itself. As previously stated, elements require both opening and closing tags, whereas attributes contain only a name and value

PART 4

IMPLEMENTATION

enclosed within quotes. Additionally, child elements are more flexible. Elements can contain child elements, whereas attributes include content only. The decision to use elements depends on whether it is necessary to break down element components to gain more information. If so, use them; otherwise, use attributes. Of course, this changes the content model. Attributes offer other advantages over elements because they provide more powerful constraints than elements. For example, they limit values of an attribute to a class of values, such as notation or entity names, or a list of enumerated acceptable values:

```
<!ELEMENT shipTo EMPTY>
<!ATTLIST shipTo shipMethod (FedEx | UPS |USPS) #REQUIRED
```

Figure 9.15 demonstrates `soldTo` and `lineItem` using attributes rather than elements.

```
<?xml version="1.0" encoding="UTF-8"?>

<!ELEMENT  soldTo EMPTY>
<!ATTLIST soldTo
   CustID            CDATA    #REQUIRED
   InvoiceDate       CDATA    #REQUIRED
   shipDate          CDATA    #REQUIRED
   custPO            CDATA    #REQUIRED>

  <!ELEMENT lineItem EMPTY>
  <!ATTLIST lineItem
  soldToID            CDATA    #REQUIRED
  invoiceNo           CDATA    #REQUIRED
  Quantity            CDATA    #REQUIRED
  unitPrice           CDATA    #REQUIRED
  ProductDescription CDATA    #REQUIRED>
```

Figure 9.15   Replacing elements with attributes

Describing Table Relationships in XML

Defining primary/foreign key relationships is one of the most important tasks in establishing table relationships. Displaying 1:1, 1:M, and

M:M relationships is important when relating groups of columns to other groups of semantically related columns. Figure 9.16 displays the 1:1 relationship with `lineItem (soldToID)` pointing back to `SoldTo (soldToID)`.

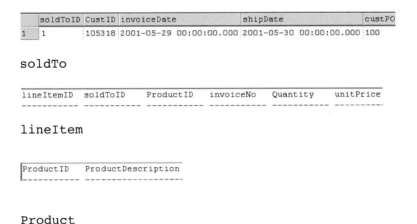

soldTo

lineItem

Product

Figure 9.16   `lineItem` References

Mapping very complex relationships is possible. Adding table `Product` demonstrates how to achieve this. A many-to-many relationship exists between `soldTo` and `Product` where `lineItem (ProductID)` points to `Product (ProductID)`.

Mixed Content Model

This content model allows a mixture of text and elements in any order. Furthermore, it does not specify the number of text or element occurrences; zero or more instances can appear. An example might be:

```
<! ELEMENT    Invoice(#PCDATA | LineItem |   CustName )*>
```

The mixed content model is not satisfactory for data modeling because subelements specified within the declaration can appear anywhere in any order. We do not recommend using this content model because elements do not map easily to relational tables.

ANY Content Model

This model, just like the mixed content model, is not satisfactory for mapping to a relational database. It is by far too permissive. Code for this model resembles the mixed content model; therefore, let's move on to the next category, text-only.

Text-Only Content Model

The text-only model allows text strings only within this type element. An example looks like this:

```
<CustName>Joseph Fingers</CustName>
```

Mapping `CustName`, `Address`, `City`, `State`, and `ZipCode` to a database using text-only is an excellent choice. These elements become column names in a table or fields in a flat file.

EMPTY Content Model

In this context, an element contains no information or data. See the following Customer example where the element is closed with a forward slash. First, the empty element tag, then the source document fragment.

```
<!ELEMENT  Customer EMPTY>
```

The source document fragment looks like this:

```
<Customer/>
```

Figure 9.17 presents salesData as elements. Figure 9.18 presents the elements as attributes.

```
<salesData>
    <storeNumber>01</storeNumber>
    <address>380 West Old Country Road</address>
    <city>East Meadow</city>
    <state>NY</state>
    <zipCode>11542</zipCode>
    <salesID>31</salesID>
    <salesName>Mike Alteman</salesName>
    <salesTerms>cash</salesTerms>
</salesData>
```

Figure 9.17   `salesData` elements

Figure 9.18 presents these elements as DTD attributes: in this context attributes map as column names in a SQL table.

```
<!ELEMENT  salesData EMPTY>
<!ATTLIST salesData
        storeNumber    CDATA       #REQUIRED
        address        CDATA       #REQUIRED
        city           CDATA       #REQUIRED
        state          CDATA       #REQUIRED
        zipCode        CDATA       #REQUIRED
        salesID        CDATA       #REQUIRED
        salesName      CDATA       #REQUIRED
        salesTerms     CDATA       #REQUIRED>
```

Figure 9.18   `salesData` DTD elements as attributes

Consider the following rules of thumb when modeling data:

- Never contain formatting information within an XML document or in a database.
- Calculate summaries and totals on-the-fly when needed.

This rule conforms to the concept of separating data from formatting instructions, as mandated in XHTML strict version 1.0. Use SQL Analyzer to query the data source if you want to reconstruct the original invoice document containing formatting and summary information. Remember, summary data is volatile. Summary-type

PART 4

IMPLEMENTATION

413

information should not be saved in a relational database. This is a disputed topic because many developers whose job is working with financial data insist on storing summary information in a repository. It really depends on the situation. No one correct answer exists. We recommend not saving summary information.

Finally, consider the performance aspect when modeling data. Extrapolating attribute-related values from a table is much more efficient than getting information from elements. This goes for both document-specific information searched via subheadings or titles, and transforming source documents for mapping purposes to a desired rendering or format using XSLT. The other point to be made here— smaller document size!

9.9 Parsing Documents—Revisiting Invoice.xml

`Invoice` contains a single document root. (Refer to Chapter 3 for a discussion on how XPath and the DOM view the root element.) All elements, attributes, text, processing instructions, entities, and comments are stored conceptually within this root element. Distinguishing between the document root and the source document root is based on how the document is parsed.

Various methods exist for parsing source documents. Employing the DOM represents one approach. For example, Microsoft's MSXML version 4.0 retains the entire source document in memory. (This topic is revisited in Chapter 11, "A Brief Introduction to .NET," where OPENXML and datasets are discussed.) The parser traverses the tree, instantiating an object for each node and copying the node name and content to an intermediate instruction tree. Subsequently, the result tree data is handed to XSLT, resulting in presentation in HTML or some other format.

An alternate parsing approach treats the source document as a series of events passed to an event handler for processing. Such parsers include SAX, XT, and XERCES. These are Java-based parsers. Parent elements semantically grouped into distinct categories enhance structure.

Figure 9.19 displays the four substructures in Internet Explorer 6.2 without exposing child elements contained within each group.

Mapping these categories to SQL Server is easy. Elements `soldTo`, `shipTo`, `lineItem`, and `Product` are mapped as tables in our `Invoice` database; subcategory child elements/attributes are mapped as intersecting columns containing content.

```
- <Invoice>
+ <soldTo>
+ <shipTo>
+ <lineItem>
+ <Product>
<Comments></comments>
</Invoice>
```

Figure 9.19   `Invoice` semantically grouped

Grouping these elements in substructures emulates the source document's structure. Element order is unimportant when modeling for data. Additionally, elements portray document meaning and structure, are simple to search and easy to read, and most important, facilitate efficient parsing. Figure 9.20 represents `<Invoice>` as a set of elements.

```
<!DOCTYPE Invoice SYSTEM "C:\Documents and
Settings\Administrator\My
Documents\chapter9Examples\Invoice1.dtd">
<Invoice>
   <SoldTo>
     <invoiceNo>095318</invoiceNo>
     <invoiceDate>05/29/2003</invoiceDate>
     <CustPO>16698</CustPO>
     <CustID>PD11</CustID>
   </SoldTo>
   <!-- shipping elements go here -->
   <ShipTo>
     <Name>Joseph Fingers</Name>
     <Address>PO Box 355</Address>
     <City>East Meadow</City>
     <State>NY</State>
     <Zip>11542</Zip>
     <shipDate>05/30/2003</shipDate>
     <ShipMethod>UPS</ShipMethod>
   </ShipTo>
```

```
        <!-- product info goes here-->
        <Product>
          <ProdNum>DL-DSH5</ProdNum>
          <ProductDescription>D-Link Hub</ProductDescription>
        </Product>
        <!-- line items go here -->
        <LineItem>
          <invoiceNo>095318</InvoiceNo>
          <Quantity>1</Quantity>
          <PartNum>DSH5</PartNum>
          <unitPrice>61.00</unitPrice>
        </LineItem>
</Invoice>
```

Figure 9.20   Expanded `Invoice` parent and child elements

Bind `<Invoice>` to Schema.xsd to ensure proper instance document structure. As previously mentioned, child elements map as attributes, thereby separating content from structure. Employ elements for structure and attributes for content.

Figure 9.21 demonstrates how to bind to the default namespace.

```
<?xml version = "1.0" encoding = "UTF-8"?>
<Invoice xmlns:xsi = "http//www.w3.org/2001/XMLSchema-instance"
xsi:noNameSpaceSchemaLocation = "Invoice.xsd">
```

Figure 9.21   Invoice.xml schema binding

A user-defined namespace (a significant schema benefit) has not been targeted in this example. In this context, use the keyword `noNameSpaceSchemaLocation` to define the namespace binding.

Text-Only Elements Relate to Columns

We have already seen how elements map to a relational database. When representing data in XML format, elements containing text-only data and defined as #PCDATA correspond to a database column. Elements represent structure, and attributes represent columns. This clearly delineates structure from content. Text-only mapping obfuscates differences between structure and content and should not be used.

Making Provisions for Null Values

An important feature that schemas offer makes provisions for null values. For example, within the source document, modify the `<shipDate>` column to indicate the status of a shipment by using `nillable`. For example:

```
<xsd:element name="shipDate" type="xsd:date" nillable="true"/>
```

We then indicate that `shipDate` has a `nil` value in the instance document:

```
<shipDate xsi:nil="true"></shipDate>
```

Declaring Unique ID Attributes

Define primary key and foreign key pointers between tables using ID and IDREF. The syntax for creating an ID as an attribute on an element is demonstrated here:

```
ELEMENT_NAME ID #REQUIRED
```

Declare globally unique IDs as attributes to an element. An example is shown in Figure 9.22.

```
<!ELEMENT soldTo EMPTY>
<!ATTLIST soldTo
     InvoiceID       ID       #REQUIRED
     InvoiceDate     CDATA    #REQUIRED
     OrderNumber     CDATA    #REQUIRED
     CustPO          CDATA    #REQUIRED
     CustIDREF       CDATA    #REQUIRED>
```

Figure 9.22   ELEMENT ID declaration

InvoiceID	InvoiceDate	OrderNumber	CustPO	CustIDREF

9.10 ID/IDREF and Foreign Keys

Add an ID to show a many-to-one relationship. If the child has more than one parent, add an IDREFS attribute to an element on the parent side. This way, the IDREFS points to the ID of the child element.

We have both a `Customer` and `Order` table relationship in this example. We display the Customer table first. Figure 9.23 is the Order table.

```
<!ELEMENT Customer Empty>
<!ATTLIST Customer
      CustomerID ID #REQUIRED
```

The corresponding instance document is as follows:

```
<Customer CustomerID="Customer2" />
```

Let's build on this example in Figure 9.23.

```
<!ELEMENT  Order (Customer, Invoice)>
<!ELEMENT Customer Empty>
<!ATTLIST Customer
      CustomerID    ID      #REQUIRED>

<!ELEMENT Invoice EMPTY>
<!ATTLIST Invoice
      InvoiceID     ID      #REQUIRED
      CustomerIDREF IDREF   #REQUIRED>
```

Figure 9.23   Defining ID/IDREF pointers

The ID corresponds to the IDREF attribute in the source document:

```
<Order>
    <Customer CustomerID="Customer 1234" />
    <Invoice InvoiceID ="15634" CustomerIDREF = "
    Customer1234" />
<Order>
```

Next, we shift our focus to attribute list declarations.

9.11 Attribute List Declarations

Attribute types include the following:

- Enumerated lists
- IDREF/IDREFS
- CDATA
- NMTOKEN/NMTOKENS
- ENTITY/ENTITIES

Let's examine enumerated lists first.

9.12 Enumerated Lists

Enumerated lists provide a mechanism for listing choices. For example, observe the following DTD:

```
<!ELEMENT Automobile EMPTY>
<!ATTLIST Automobile
        AutomobileType (Maxima | Altima | Sentra) #REQUIRED>
```

This model maps easily by creating a lookup table. The `AutomobileType` attribute must consist of the three listed values. The create SQL table script in Figure 9.24 maps our DTD to a relational database.

```
Create Table AutomobileTypeLookup (
AutomobileType integer,
Description varchar (255) not null
PRIMARY KEY (AutomobileType))

Create Table Automobile (
AutomobileKey integer not null,
AutomobileType integer
CONSTRAINT fk_AutomobileAutomobileTypeLookup FOREIGN KEY
(AutomobileType)
REFERENCES  AutomobileTypeLookup (AutomobileType))
INSERT AutomobileTypeLookup (AutomobileType,Description)
```

```
values ( 1, 'Maxima')
INSERT AutomobileTypeLookup (AutomobileType,Description)
values (2, 'Altima')
INSERT AutomobileTypeLookup (AutomobileType,Description)
values (3, 'Sentra')
```

Figure 9.24   SQL script

Map all records to `AutomobileType` values residing in the `AutomobileTypeLookup` table. The following screen capture demonstrates this table:

	AutomobileType	Description
1	1	Maxima
2	2	Altima
3	3	Sentra

9.13 Attribute IDREF/IDREFS

This category was discussed earlier in this chapter. Refer to the section on ID/IDREF for a review. Let's move on to a discussion about CDATA.

Attribute CDATA

Declare CDATA attributes in the following manner:

```
<!ELEMENT  Invoice EMPTY>
<!ATTLIST Invoice
     CustomerName     CDATA    #REQUIRED
     Address          CDATA    #REQUIRED
     City             CDATA    #REQUIRED
     State            CDATA    #REQUIRED
     CustomerType (Commercial | Consumer | Educational)
#REQUIRED>
```

DTDs specify three data type attributes:

- #FIXED
- #REQUIRED
- #IMPLIED

Mapping these attributes to a database requires special treatment.
`#FIXED` indicates that the system supplies the value. In this case, don't use `#FIXED`, whereas `#REQUIRED` is analogous to `NOT NULL` in a database. If `#IMPLIED` is specified, define the corresponding column as `NULL`.

NMTOKEN/NMTOKENS

NMTOKEN attributes consist of digits, letters, underscores, periods, and colons. A NMTOKEN is similar to CDATA with some restrictions. The following DTD shows how NMTOKENs are treated in the DTD:

```
<!ELEMENT Invoice EMPTY>
<!ATTLIST Invoice
InvoiceRef  NMTOKEN #REQUIRED>
```

A corresponding instance document would be as follows:

```
<Customer ReferenceNumber = "CR1254" />
```

A SQL table script for NMTOKENs is as follows:

```
Create Table Customer(
CustomerKey integer not null)
Create Table Reference(
ReferenceKey integer not null,
CustomerKey integer not null,
ReferenceNO varchar (12) not null)
```

ReferenceKey	CustomerKey	ReferenceNO

Table Reference

CustomerKey

Table Customer

In the event that two NMTOKENs are required, simply create one `Customer` row and two `RefNo` rows. An instance document fragment looks like this:

```
<Customer ReferenceNo = "CR1254  CR57683" />
```

9.14 ENTITY/ENTITIES Attributes

Entities associated with an element are not parsed. Let's see how DTDs represent unparsed entities:

```
<!NOTATION gif PUBLIC "GIF">
<!ENTITY DPS SYSTEM "dpsLogo.gif" NDATA gif>
<!ELEMENT logo EMPTY>
<!ATTLIST logo img ENTITY #REQUIRED>
```

The corresponding instance document is as follows:

```
<logo  img="dpsLogo" />
```

Store the value of this attribute just as you did with NMTOKENs and declare it as NMTOKEN.

Summary

You have learned how to map raw data to relational databases from raw XML and vice versa. Elements map directly as table names; attributes map as column names. Items covered include mapping data using the content models element-only, mixed content, ANY, text-only, and EMPTY.

Additionally, we compared DTDs with schemas and found the latter technology preferable when abstracting data separately from the document structure.

Armed with this newly acquired knowledge, you are prepared to work comfortably with the new functionality provided in SQL Server 2000. Let's dive right in and see how the new features enhance our ability to work with both XML and relational databases.

Self-Review Exercises

1. Modeling data necessitates designing a mapping strategy. Two distinct concepts exist for modeling data. What are they?

2. Extracting data from attribute/value pairs is more efficient than extrapolating information from elements. Why?

3. Write a small program demonstrating how to specify values as NULL in an XML document.

4. DTDs specify three data type attributes:

   a. #REQUIRED

   b. #FIXED

   c. #IMPLIED

   Describe how to use them in a DTD.

5. Section 9.5 described tips for designing a DTD and mapping a DTD to a database. Describe several of them.

6. Describe content models empty, element-only, mixed, and ANY.

Projects

1. Map the following source document by creating the database DesignPatterns.

```
<DesignPatterns>
    <Creational>
    <abstractFactory value="Interface"/>
    <Builder interface="nondependent"/>
    </Creational>

    <Structural>
    <Bridge interface="decouple"/>
    <Decorator benefit="dynamicCreation"/>
    </Structural>

    <Behavioral>
```

```
<Interpreter functionality="defineGrammarRepresentation"/>
<Template interface="skeletalStructure"/>
</Behavioral>
</DesignPatterns>
```

2. Map the tables to the database `DesignPatterns` by writing a SQL script to create the tables `Creational`, `Structural`, and `Behavioral`.

3. Create SQL scripts to populate the three tables.

4. Create a DTD for `DesignPatterns`.

5. Create an XSD schema for `DesignPatterns`.

6. Mark up a poem using attributes. Select a poem of your choice.

7. Design a DTD for the poem.

8. Based on the poem you have marked up in XML, provide a schema for it.

10 New SQL Server 2000 Features

10.1 SQL Server 2000 Provides New Functionality

In Chapter 9, we focused on mapping raw data from XML to a relational database. The five content models—element-only, ANY, mixed, text, and EMPTY—were examined the purpose of mapping data to a relational database context.

SQL Server 2000 provides several new features that facilitate saving and retrieving data in XML. They include the following:

- `FOR XML AUTO`
- `FOR XML RAW`
- `FOR XML EXPLICIT`
- Universal tables
- `OPENXML`
- Edge tables
- XPath query support
- Comparison between XDR and XSD schemas
- XML views
- Annotations and mapping schemas
- SQL Server 2000 `sql:field`, `sql:relation`, and `sql:relationship` specifiers
- Updategrams

We recommend that you download the Microsoft SQL Server 2000 Web Services Toolkit to obtain SQLXML 3.0.

PART 4

IMPLEMENTATION

In this chapter, we will put our mapping techniques to work and will learn how to utilize these innovative techniques. The preceding bulleted topics represent the features we examine in this chapter. Once we have thoroughly mastered these techniques, we will shift our attention to the .NET framework in Chapter 11 and web services (in Chapter 12). The focus is always on XML and persistence. Let's begin by discussing FOR XML AUTO.

10.2 FOR XML Clauses

The FOR XML clause comes in three different formats: FOR XML RAW, FOR XML AUTO, and FOR XML EXPLICIT. These formats allow us to write queries against a relational database and return a rowset in hierarchical XML tree format. Whereas Active Data Objects (ADO) recordsets return data in the traditional row/column manner, a format not suited for presenting documents in XML, SQL Server 2000 provides us with the tools to query a relational database and retrieve data formatted as XML (Note: ADO.NET is Microsoft's most recent data access technology). Before we examine the new functionality that SQL Server offers us, let's query the Invoice table and view the recordset as it is returned in ADO 2.6 (see Figure 10.1).

	InvoiceID	InvoiceDate	OrderNumber	CustPO	CustIDREF
1	1015318	2001-05-29 00:00:00.000	16698	PD11	1
2	1015319	2001-05-29 00:00:00.000	16699	PD13	2
3	1015320	2001-05-30 00:00:00.000	16700	PD127	3

Figure 10.1   A traditional recordset

Web applications need to access data quickly, regardless of how many users are logged on to the database. Unfortunately, ADO never provided us with the lightweight data access objects we needed to create scalable web applications. The Internet demands data access designed to provide speedy data retrieval to large numbers of clients. ADO 2.6 is built around a tightly coupled client/server architecture. It contains well-designed business services, data services, and user services. The middle-tier business layer manages database access and returns data as recordsets. Additionally, it requires a persistent connection to the back-end database. In contrast, web applications use the same N-tiered architecture but are loosely coupled, whereas the user services and business services communicate over HTTP, and the state is not persisted between calls.

ADO was integrated with OLEDB providers, thereby offering a flexible, easy-to-use interface. The negative side to this methodology is that ADO cannot manage XML and disconnected recordsets easily.

If our task is to have raw data returned as XML, we need a mechanism for retrieving data in a format suitable for our business requirements. Let's begin by examining the FOR XML clauses and see how we can apply them to our needs. In a mission-critical environment, time is of the essence, and these new features facilitate retrieving raw data presented in XML.

First let's query the Northwind sample database that comes bundled with SQL Server 2000 and append the FOR XML AUTO clause to the query (see Figure 10.2).

```
Select CustomerID, CompanyName, ContactName FROM Customers FOR
XML AUTO
```

```
XML_F52E2B61-18A1-11d1-B105-00805F49916B
2000<Customers CustomerID="ALFKI"
     CompanyName="Alfred Futterkiste"
     ContactName="Maria Anders"/>

<Customers CustomerID="ANATR"
     CompanyName="Ana Trujillo Emparedados y helados"
     ContactName="Ana Trujillo"/>
```

Figure 10.2 Northwind Customers query

Notice how the FOR XML AUTO query returns the recordset beginning with the root element in the format `<Element|attribute|values>`, followed by its child elements *and* attributes, just as specified in the query.

Let's look at the rowset from another point of view. It returns the same results:

```
<Customers>
     CustomerID="ALFKI" CompanyName="Alfreds Futterkiste"
     ContactName="Maria Anders"/>
     CustomerID="ANATR"  CompanyName="Ana Trujillo Emparedados
     y helados"  ContactName="Ana Trujillo"/>
</Customers>
```

This view clearly indicates how `<Customers>` maps to the database as the table name, whereas `CustomerID`, `CompanyName`, and `ContactName` map as columns. The query root element `<Customers>` returns an element containing attributes. The content model is empty, containing attribute values consisting of strings that are simple types in an XSD schema.

The BINARY Base64 argument specifies that binary data should be returned in the BINARY Base64-encoded format, and this is the default argument for the `AUTO` mode. BINARY Base64 is an encoding method utilized for encoding data transmitted to a browser. Subsequently, the browser decodes the data and displays the data in a format we can read.

Additionally, note when using the `FOR XML AUTO` clause you cannot use nested SELECT queries such as the following:

```
SELECT    *
FROM TABLE A
WHERE … SELECT * FROM TABLE A FOR XML AUTO
```

Next, by appending `XMLDATA` to the same query, SQL prepends a schema to the recordset, followed by the specified elements and attributes.

```
Select CustomerID, ContactName
FROM Customers
FOR XML AUTO, XMLDATA
```

The results are shown in Figure 10.3.

```
XML_F52E2B61-18A1-11d1-B105-00805F49916B
<Schema name="Schema1" xmlns="urn:schemas-microsoft-com:xml-
data"
xmlns:dt="urn:schemas-microsoft-com:datatypes">
<ElementType name="Customers" content="empty" model="closed">
<AttributeType name="CustomerID" dt:type="string"/>
<AttributeType name="ContactName" dt:type="string"/>
<attribute type="CustomerID"/>
<attribute type="ContactName"/>
</ElementType>
</Schema>
<Customers xmlns="x-schema:#Schema1" CustomerID="ALFKI"
ContactName="Maria Anders"/>
<Customers xmlns="x-schema:#Schema1" CustomerID="ANATR"
ContactName="Ana Trujillo"/>
```

Figure 10.3   FOR XML AUTO, XMLDATA

When defining schema for a particular class of documents, you specify what elements and attributes are allowed in the document and how these elements and attributes are related to each other. In the XML-Data Reduced (XDR) schema, specifying an `<ElementType ...>` and an `<AttributeType ...>` defines the elements and attributes, respectively, as well as their type. Then an instance of an element or an attribute is declared using `<element ...>` or `<attribute ...>` tags.

XMLDATA generates an XDR schema that maps to the default namespace `xmlns="urn:schemas-microsoft-com:xml-data`. What we previously stated concerning the content model is now confirmed once we add XMLDATA to the query. Additionally, the schema identifies the attribute type as string for both `CustomerID` and `ContactName`; the content model is `empty` and `closed`. This means elements and attributes must appear in the source document in the sequence specified in the schema. No additional elements are allowed to appear that would break the content model. Recall from Chapter 4, "Introducing Schemas," that when the content model is `empty`, elements cannot contain other nested elements. In that context, you will see the format listed here: `element name/attribute/value`. Thus, note the order of element/attributes residing in a universal table, as shown in Table 10.1.

PART 4 IMPLEMENTATION

Table 10.1 For XML AUTO, XMLDATA

Root Element	Attribute/Value	Attribute/Value
Customers	CustomerID="ALFKI"	ContactName="Maria Anders"

What is a universal table? One of the challenges is defining an industry-wide standard for XML message formats, one that can be shared by participating members of a profession-centric group. Referring specifically to SQL data structures, the challenge is extracting data and creating XML data structures that meet these industry-wide standards. One method of doing this is utilizing SQL SELECT statements to retrieve results in XML format, in particular the FOR XML EXPLICIT query. This allows you to map the internal structure to an external standard. The universal table represents this standard by allowing you to specify the shape of an XML query. The universal table contains all information concerning the XML tree. It contains metadata columns, a tag column that stores the tag number of the current element, and a parent column that stores the tag number of the parent element. See Table 10.2 and 3 for a detailed discussion on this topic.

10.3 FOR XML RAW

The recordset returned from a FOR XML RAW query varies slightly from the previous query. The RAW mode returns the result set with each result row wrapped with the generic identifier row. This format is permissible for further computer processing, but it is not acceptable for exchanges with external organizations. It requires adherence to industry standards and tags that are more descriptive.

Let's issue a query using the FOR XML RAW specifier and observe the changes (see Figure 10.4).

```
Use Northwind
Go
Select Customers.CustomerID, ContactName, OrderID
FROM Customers, Orders
```

```
WHERE Customers.CustomerID = Orders.CustomerID
ORDER BY Customers.CustomerID, OrderID
FOR XML RAW
```

Figure 10.4   FOR XML RAW query

Figure 10.5 represents the returned recordset in RAW format.

```
Select Customers.CustomerID, ContactName, OrderID
-----------------------------*/
XML_F52E2B61-18A1-11d1-B105-00805F49916B
-------------------------------------------------------------------
<row CustomerID="ALFKI" ContactName="Maria Anders" OrderID="10643"/>
```

Figure 10.5   Northwind FOR XML RAW recordset

The root element <Customers> is replaced with a generic <row> header followed by attribute/value pairs. Whereas a traditional recordset presents data in tabular column format, the default XML query is attribute centric. Remember that attributes map as columns in XML. Attribute-centric rowsets are particularly convenient for persisting data to a flat file format.

10.4 FOR XML EXPLICIT

FOR XML EXPLICIT is more complex but provides us with full control over the shape of our rowset. The clauses we have examined are useful. Unfortunately, we have little control over them other than specifying child element order in the query. What if we need a specific XML-formatted recordset? FOR XML EXPLICIT is the tool we need to accomplish this task.

The EXPLICIT clause requires some preliminary discussion before we can apply it against a database object. By providing metadata, we can control the format of the XML recordset returned by execution of the FOR XML EXPLICIT query. Invoice.xs and its source document Invoice2.xml will serve as basis for this discussion (see Figure 10.6).

```
<xs:schema xmlns:xs="http://www.w3.org/2001/XMLSchema"
elementFormDefault="qualified">
   <xs:complexType name="InvIDType">
     <xs:attribute name="id" type="xs:int" use="required"/>
     <xs:attribute name="date" type="xs:string"
     use="required"/>
   </xs:complexType>
   <xs:complexType name="InvInfoType">
     <xs:attribute name="id" use="required">
       <xs:simpleType>
          <xs:restriction base="xs:NMTOKEN">
            <xs:enumeration value="Ord1"/>
            <xs:enumeration value="Ord2"/>
            <xs:enumeration value="Ord3"/>
          </xs:restriction>
       </xs:simpleType>
     </xs:attribute>
     <xs:attribute name="SKU" use="required">
       <xs:simpleType>
          <xs:restriction base="xs:NMTOKEN">
            <xs:enumeration value="D100"/>
            <xs:enumeration value="Dlink"/>
            <xs:enumeration value="Intel20k"/>
            <xs:enumeration value="hp75"/>
          </xs:restriction>
       </xs:simpleType>
     </xs:attribute>
   </xs:complexType>
   <xs:element name="Invoice">
     <xs:complexType>
       <xs:choice maxOccurs="unbounded">
          <xs:element name="InvID" type="InvIDType"/>
          <xs:element name="InvInfo" type="InvInfoType"/>
       </xs:choice>
       <xs:attribute name="InvoiceID" type="xs:string"
       use="required"/>
       <xs:attribute name="name" type="xs:string"
       use="required"/>
     </xs:complexType>
   </xs:element>
</xs:schema>
```

Figure 10.6   Invoice.xs schema

The source document, Invoice.xml, adheres to the XSD schema just presented. Let's examine both documents, beginning with the XML XSD document.

The root element <Invoice> contains two complexType subelements, InvID and InvInfo, both containing simple type attributes. The root element identifies customer id as dps and customer name as Peltzer. InvID provides an ID for the invoice, the date attribute indicates the date of purchase, and InvInfo contains information concerning the products purchased.

Notice how we enumerate both order numbers and their product descriptions. We use base type NMTOKEN to restrict both order number and SKU descriptions. A restricted base type is always preceded with keyword <xs:simpleType> and is followed by using the restriction mechanism. This schema is an excellent example of how it clearly defines the source document structure. Discussing document structure will help us when we examine the structure of the universal table and how elements and attributes relate to this table. Figure 10.7 shows the source document as displayed in Internet Explorer 6.2.

```
<?xml version="1.0" encoding="UTF-8" ?>
- <Invoice InvoiceID="dps" name="Peltzer">
    <InvID id="105318" date="10/18/002" />
    <InvInfo id="Ord1" SKU="Dlink" />
    <InvInfo id="Ord2" SKU="hp75" />
    <InvID id="105318" date="10/20/002" />
    <InvInfo id="Ord3" SKU="Intel20k" />
    <InvInfo id="Ord2" SKU="D100" />
  </Invoice>
```

Figure 10.7 Invoice2.xml

The EXPLICIT mode transforms a rowset generated by the query into XML in a very specific layout. The SELECT query must be written so that it binds specified elements/attributes to an associated tag number in the first column, as shown in Table 10.2.

Table 10.2   Universal Table Format

Tag	Parent	Element|Attribute	Element|Attribute
1	NULL	ElementName!1!attribute	Name!1!name

The tag is an integer data type. The second column must be identified as the Parent tag number (in this case, it contains a NULL) of the parent element. This tag is also an integer data type. Note that, when using an id or idref (third column), they can only be applied to simple data types as defined in the scheme for schemas. By using these columns for defining table column structure, we construct the hierarchical parent-child relationship. Conceptually, we understand that the document root element cannot have a parent but stores all child elements, attributes, comments, and processing instructions within it. Therefore, the Tag column should be assigned integer 1, thereby identifying the root element. The Parent column must contain a NULL identifier for the root element and be placed at the top of the universal table. The columns are vertically aligned to contain child elements/attributes and a row identifier.

Table 10.3   Universal Table Example

Tag	Parent	Invoice!1!InvoiceID	Invoice!1!name
1	NULL	dps	Peltzer

The first column, Tag 1, identifies root element Invoice; the second column contains a NULL because the root may not have a parent. The third and fourth columns contain the ID and name attributes, respectively. Examining the source document, we note that the query assigns attribute values dps and Peltzer to their respective columns.

The universal table format is as follows:

```
elementName!TagNumber!PropertyName!Directive
```

The elementName specifier identifies the Invoice element, followed by the exclamation point delimiter and its attribute. The

`TagNumber` always bears the hierarchical order number of the nested elements. Each tag number corresponds directly to one element name. The `PropertyName` represents the attribute's name. `ID`'s value is `dps`, attribute `name`'s value is `Peltzer`, and so on.

Applying the Directive Mechanism

The `Directive` (fourth column) is always optional. This column is used to provide further control over how the data is represented. However, the `attributeName` must be included if `Directive` isn't specified. For example, the following element directive is implied: (`Invoice!1`). This is the shorthand version for (`Invoice!1!element`) because `Invoice` is an element. The `Directive` attributes are as follows:

- `element`   This is used to indicate that the data in this column should be encoded and represented as a subelement in the XML fragment.

- `xml`   This is used to indicate that the column should be represented as a subelement in the XML fragment. No encoding occurs in this instance.

- `hide`   This is used to indicate that a column should be present in the universal table but not in the document fragment returned.

- `xmltext`   This retrieves XML data from an overflow column and appends it to the current element.

- `cdata`   This is used to represent data in this column as CDATA.

- `ID, IDREF, IDREFS`   These are used with the `XMLDATA` option to return an inline schema with attributes of type `ID`, `IDREF`, or `IDREFS`. These are typically used to define relationships among several documents.

You should use `Directives` to provide instructions on how to map string data to XML by employing keywords `hide`, `cdata`, `element`, `xmldata`, and `xml`. Note that unless `xmldata` is specified, keywords `ID`, `IDREF`, and `IDREFS` have no effect. Let's examine each directive, beginning with element encoding.

PART 4 IMPLEMENTATION

435

Element Encoding

One consequence of specifying the `element` directive is how it encodes elements with characters such as <. Characters appear as `&lt;` or `&gt;` respectively in the source document. Consider code fragment in Figure 10.8, where we want to insert < into Peltzer.

```
<!-- encode the following character in name Pel<tzer -->
UPDATE Invoice
SET name='Pel<tzer'
WHERE name='Peltzer'
Go
```

Figure 10.8   Encoding element entity character data

The generated rowset displays the update as follows:

```
<Invoice CustID="dps">
<name>Pel&lt;tzer</name>
```

We restore the value `Peltzer` back to its original state with the query in Figure 10.9.

```
Select 1 as Tag, NULL as Parent,
      Invoice.InvoiceID as [Invoice!1! CustID],
      Invoice.name    as [Invoice!1!name!element]
FROM Invoice
ORDER BY [Invoice!1!Cust ID]
FOR XML EXPLICIT
UPDATE Invoice
SET name='Peltzer'
WHERE name='Pel<tzer'
```

Figure 10.9   Restoring nonentity encoding character data

The rowset generated by this query demonstrates two points:

1. The attribute `name` is contained as a child element `<name>` of `Invoice` rather than being generated as an attribute, as in `Invoice name= "Peltzer"`. In XML parlance, this is known as *element containment* because the root element con-

tains other nested elements. By virtue of the fact that `name` is generated as an element rather than as an attribute, the content model changes to elements-only (`content elt only`) in an XDR schema.

2. The name `Peltzer` is returned to its original state rather than being encoded, as was the case in the previous example.

Other concepts apply to the `element` directive. For example, let's assume we have an attribute we want to be formatted as an element. Examine the following code:

```
<InvoiceID="dps" name="Peltzer">
```

By specifying the `element` directive immediately following the attribute's name, the query will generate an element as demonstrated in Figure 10.10.

```
Select 1       as Tag,
       NULL as Parent,
       Invoice.InvoiceID as [Invoice!1!CustID],
       NULL as [Invoice!1!name!element],
<!-- place the element directive here -->
```

Figure 10.10   XML element containment

The following rowset demonstrates how `<name>` is generated as a contained element:

```
<Invoice CustID="dps">
    <name>Peltzer</name>
</Invoice>
```

In queries containing multiple `SELECT` statements, only column names specified in the initial query (universal table) are output, whereas column names specified in subsequent `SELECT` statements are ignored. This is indicated by examining the Tag column where integer 1 resides. The first `SELECT` query will select only `<Invoice>` attributes.

The second `SELECT` query selects table `InvID` elements and attributes, thereby bypassing the parent elements and their attributes. Note that a `UNION ALL` statement requires both tables to have an identical structure; otherwise, the statement will fall. Figure 10.11 shows the generated XML output.

```
<!--1ˢᵀ select QUERY -->
Select 1       as Tag,
       NULL as Parent,
       Invoice.InvoiceID as [Invoice!1!CustID],
       NULL as [Invoice!1!name!element],
UNION ALL
<!-- 2ᴺᴰ SELECT Query-->
 SELECT 2 as Tag,
1 as Parent
  InvID.id as [InvID!2!id],
  InvID.date as [InvID!2!.date]
```

Figure 10.11   Multiple SELECT statements

Applying the xml Directive

Specifying directive xml is essentially the same as the element directive (see the preceding section 10.), except that no character encoding takes place. That is, < or > remains as presented in the code: <Pel<tzer>.

Storing Overflow (Unconsumed) Data with xmltext

The xmltext directive is useful in storing overflow (unconsumed) XML data stored in a column contained within an OPENXML query. (We discuss both overflow and OpenXML later in this chapter.) Note that a column specifying xmltext must be a text type, such as varchar, char, text, ntext, or nvarchar.

Why would we need to store ancillary data in an overflow column? An example would be a database maintained by Broadcast Music Incorporated (BMI) called BMI Composers, which contains data concerning composers in the twentieth and twenty-first centuries. However, it contains no columns for adding new rock composers. Therefore, it requires altering the database and adding a new field labeled UnconsumedData to the NewComposers table. To do so, execute the following SQL command against the existing table: `ALTER TABLE NewComposers ADD Unconsumed Data NVARCHAR (1000)`. The table structure now looks like the example in Figure 10.12. First here's the `Create Table` SQL script.

```
Create Table ComposersTable(
ComposerID varchar (5) NOT NULL,
ComposerName varchar(25),
UnconsumedData nvarchar (1000) not null
)
```

Figure 10.12   The `NewComposers` table

The following is a screen shot displaying the columnar structure:

ComposerID	ComposerName	UnconsumedData

Let's assume BMI adds some new composers. The XML data would look like this:

```
<ComposersTable ID="C1" Name="JBird" bandLeader="Jon"
instrument="bassGuitar"/>

<ComposersTable Id="C2" Name="Robie" leadSinger="Rob"
instrument="drums"/>
```

Certain attributes can be added to our table, but we had no place to insert bandleader or instrument until we added the `UnconsumedData` field. We can now use SQL's `OPENXML` to add these two new composers to the `ComposersTable` with additional data. The `OPENXML` query looks like the following:

```
SELECT 1 AS Tag, 0 As Parent,
    ComposerID AS [ComposersTable!1!ComposerID!element],
    UnconsumedData AS [ComposersTable!1!xmlText]
FROM ComposersTable
FOR XML EXPLICIT
```

Now we can update `ComposersTable` by first using attributes and then specifying elements.

```
UPDATE ComposersTable SET UnconsumedData=
'ComposerElement="bandLeader= Jon"
WHERE ComposerID ='C1';

UPDATE ComposersTable SET UnconsumedData ='<ComposerElement>
leadSinger=Rob</ComposerElement>'
WHERE ComposerID='C2';
```

Here is the rowset:

	ComposerID	ComposerName	UnconsumedData
1	C1	Jon	ComposerElement attr="bandLeader" />
2	C2	Rob	<ComposerElement> leadSinger=Rob</ComposerElement>

This table contains the `UnconsumedData` column that stores the unconsumed data. However, an attribute name is not listed in the query; rather, the `xmltext` directive is specified, as in `overflow as [Parent!1!!xmltext]`. The consequence of the query appends attributes to the `<overflow>` element attribute list. Here's one other noteworthy item: The `ComposerID` attribute `[Parent!1!!xmltext]` conflicts directly with the `<Parent>` element at the same level (`!1!`), so attributes are ignored in this context. Attributes override attributes sharing the same name in the overflow column. Therefore, row two contains no attribute.

Figure 10.13 demonstrates how to construct an `OPENXML` SQL query that allows attributes to be appended to the query.

```
SELECT 1 as Tag, NULL as Parent,
    ComposerID as [Parent!1!BandID],
    ComposerName as [Parent!1!ComposerName],
    Overflow as [Parent!1!!xmltext]
<!-- No attributes are specified here-->
FROM NuMetalComposers
FOR XML EXPLICIT
```

Figure 10.13 Appending attributes to the `Overflow` column

We could also change the data in the table so that the `Overflow` column now contains the data in Figure 10.14.

```
UPDATE ComposersTable SET UnconsumedData='<ComposerElement>
attr="Joe" sideman </ComposerElement>'
WHERE ComposerID='C3';
```

Figure 10.14   The `Overflow` column

The query in Figure 01.15 contains more than one subelement.

```
UPDATE ComposersTable SET UnconsumedData ='<ComposerElement>
<ComposerElement2> additional Chris content</ComposerElement2>
more ComposerElement Chris content </ComposerElement>'
WHERE ComposerID='C4';
```

Figure 10.15   Subelements

Figure 10.16 shows the resultant rowset.

	C..	Co...	UnconsumedData
1	C1	Jon	ComposerElement attr="bandLeader" />
2	C2	Rob	<ComposerElement> leadSinger=Rob</ComposerElement>
3	C3	Joe	<ComposerElement> attr="Joe" sideman </ComposerElement>
4	C4	Chris	<ComposerElement> <ComposerElement2> additional Chris content</ComposerElement2> more ComposerElement Chris ...

Figure 10.16   Overflow-generated rowset

We can also retrieve data from the `Overflow` column. Before we proceed through the process of retrieving data from this column, we need to create a virtual directory in the IIS directory named Invoice. Begin by selecting Configure IIS Support-SQLXML-2.0 or 3.0; select the default web site. On the Action menu, select New and then select Virtual Directory. From the General tab, enter the name of your virtual directory. (In this case, enter **Invoice** or whatever name you want your directory to be named.) A typical path would be C:\Intetpub\wwwroot\Invoice. We assume you previously created this subdirectory before beginning this process. On the Security tab, select SQL Server and set up your password and valid login. From the Data Source tab, enter the name of your server (local). In the

Database dialog box, select the name of the database you want to use. The Settings tab will allow you to select the following items:

- Allow URL queries
- Allow template queries
- Allow XPath
- Allow post options

From the Virtual Names tab, click New. From the Type list, select Template and enter the path, such as C:\Inetpub\wwwroot\Composers\Template. Subdirectories for Schema and Template must exist. You will be asked to create virtual names for Schema, Template, and dbobject. Once these tasks are finished, save your settings. Finally, test your settings by typing the following URL in IE Explorer: http://localhost/Composers?sql=SELECT * FROM ComposersTable FOR XML AUTO&root=root. Then press Enter. You should see results similar to those we retrieved using Internet Explorer browser 6.0:

```
<?xml version="1.0" encoding="utf-8" ?>
- <root>
<ComposersTable ComposerID="C1" ComposerName="Jon"
UnconsumedData="ComposerElement attr="bandLeader" />"
<ComposersTable ComposerID="C2" ComposerName="Rob"
UnconsumedData="<ComposerElement>
leadSinger=Rob</ComposerElement>" />
<ComposersTable ComposerID="C3" ComposerName="Joe"
UnconsumedData="<ComposerElement> attr="Joe" sideman
</ComposerElement>" />
<ComposersTable ComposerID="C4" ComposerName="Chris"
UnconsumedData="<ComposerElement> <ComposerElement2> additional
Chris content</ComposerElement2> more ComposerElement Chris
content </ComposerElement>" />
</root>
```

Let's examine the URL:

```
http://localhost/Composers?sql=SELECT*%20from%20ComposersTable%
20for%20xml%20auto%20&root=root
```

The `root=root` following the query indicates that the root element should be named `root`. This is especially important when returning more than one element. However, you can otherwise name the root anything you'd like.

Table 10.4 provides information on the symbols embedded within the URL.

Table 10.4   URL Symbols

Name	Character	HexValue	URL
Ampersand	&	%26	Denotes entity encoding
Forward Slash	/	%2F	Directory separator
Percent	%	%25	Hex representation
Plus	+	%20	Denotes a space
Pound	#	%23	Denotes a bookmark
QuestionMark	?	%3F	Separates URL from its parameters

Now we will present a multiple SELECT-correlated query as it applies to the Invoice table (see Figures 10.17 and 10.18).

```
SELECT 1 as Tag, NULL as Parent,
I.InvoiceID            as [Invoice!1!InvoiceID],
I.name                 as [Invoice!1!name],
NULL                   as [InvID!2!id],
NULL                   as [InvID!2!date],
NULL                   as [InvInfo!3!id!id],
NULL                   AS [InvInfo!3!PID!idref]
from Invoice I

UNION ALL
SELECT 2 as Tag,
       1 as Parent,
       I.InvoiceID,
       NULL,
       O.id,
       O.date,
       NULL,
       NULL
```

```
FROM Invoice I, InvID O
WHERE I.InvoiceID = O.InvoicetID
UNION ALL

SELECT 3 as Tag,
       2 as Parent,
       I.InvoiceID,
       NULL,
       O.id,
       NULL,
       IOD.id,
       IOD.PID
FROM Invoice I, InvID O, [InvInfo] IOD
WHERE I.InvoiceID = O.InvoiceID
AND Oid = IOD.id
ORDER BY [Invoice!1!CustID],[InvID!2!id]
FOR XML EXPLICIT
```

Figure 10.17   Eight-column query

```
<Invoice custID="dps" name="Peltzer">
    <InvID id="105318" date="2003-10-18T00:00:00">
        <InvInfo id="105318" PID="105"/>
        <InvInfo id="105318" PID="200"/>
    </InvID>
</Invoice>

<Invoice InvoiceID="MWP" name="Waterman">
    <InvID id="105400" date="2003-11-10T00:00:00">
        <InvInfo id="105400" PID="3"/>
    </InvID>
</Invoice>
```

Figure 10.18   The generated rowset

Applying the CDATA Directive

CDATA contains content that is not encoded. AttributeName must not be specified when using this directive. Let's write a query using the above-mentioned information and observe the consequences of using this directive. If CDATA is specified, the character data is not encoded. See, for example, the query in Figure 10.19.

```
SELECT 1            as Tag,
NULL                as Parent,
Invoice.InvoiceID   as [Invoice!1!InvoiceID],
Invoice.name        as [Invoice!1!cdata]
FROM Invoice
ORDER BY [Invoice!1!CustID]
FOR XML EXPLICIT
```

Figure 10.19   A CDATA query

The returned rowset looks like this:

```
<Invoice InvoiceID="dps">
  <![CDATA[Peltzer]]>
</Invoice>
```

Applying the Hide Directive

Apply the Hide directive when an attribute should not appear in the
returned result. Such a query looks like Figure 10.20. Also, see
Figure 10.21 for the results from the query executed in Figure 10.20.

```
Select 1 as Tag,
        NULL              as Parent,
        Invoice.InvoiceID as [Invoice!1!CustID],
        NULL              as [InvID!2!id!hide]
FROM Invoice
UNION ALL
SELECT 2,
        1,
        Invoice.InvoiceID,
        InvID.id
FROM Invoice, InvID
WHERE Invoice.InvoiceID = InvID.InvoiceID
Order by [Invoice!1!InvoiceID],
        [InvID!2!id!hide]
FOR XML EXPLICIT
```

Figure 10.20   The hide directive

```
<Invoice InvoiceID="dps">
<InvID/>
</Invoice>
<Invoice InvoiceID="MWP">
<InvID/>
</Invoice>
```

Figure 10.21   Hide results

The result does not show the `InvID` id because the `hide` directive is specified. This is not a useful result, but it demonstrates how to use the `hide` directive. It also displays two queries: a beginning query and second query. The first `Select` query defines the rowset format so that the second query doesn't have to regenerate the column names. In addition, the second rowset must be identical to the first rowset for the `Union All` declaration to succeed. It then performs a table join. This time, the property tags specified in the first query are ignored.

Applying the ID/IDREF Directive

The following figure,10.22, provides an example of how we apply the `ID/IDREF` Directive.

```
select 1              as Tag,
NULL                  as Parent,
Customers.CustomerID  as [Customer!1!CustomerID!id],
NULL                  as [Order!2!OrderID!element],
NULL                  as [Order!2!CustomerID!idref],
NULL                  as [Order!2!OrderDate]
FROM Customers
UNION ALL
SELECT  2,
1,
Customers.CustomerID,
Orders.OrderID, Orders.CustomerID,
Orders.OrderDate
```

```
FROM Customers,Orders
WHERE Customers.CustomerID = Orders.CustomerID
ORDER BY [Customer!1!CustomerID!id],[Order!2!OrderID!element]
FOR XML EXPLICIT, xmldata
```

Figure 10.22   ID/IDREF query

The generated rowset is shown in Figure 10.23.

```
XML_F52E2B61-18A1-11d1-B105-00805F49916B
<Schema name="Schema1" xmlns="urn:schemas-microsoft-com:xml-
data"
xmlns:dt="urn:schemas-microsoft-com:datatypes">
<ElementType name="Customer" content="mixed" model="open">
    <AttributeType name="CustomerID" dt:type="id"/>
    <attribute type="CustomerID"/>
</ElementType>
<ElementType name="Order" content="mixed" model="open">
    <AttributeType name="CustomerID" dt:type="idref"/>
    <AttributeType name="OrderDate" dt:type="dateTime"/>
    <element type="OrderID"/>
    <attribute type="CustomerID"/>
    <attribute type="OrderDate"/></ElementType>
<ElementType name="OrderID" content="textOnly" model="closed"
dt:type="i4"/>
</Schema>
<Customer xmlns="x-schema:#Schema1" CustomerID="ALFKI">
    <Order CustomerID="ALFKI" OrderDate="2003-08-25T00:00:00">
    <OrderID>10643</OrderID>
    </Order>
    <Order CustomerID="ALFKI" OrderDate="2003-10-03T00:00:00">
    <OrderID>10692</OrderID>
    </Order>
    <Order CustomerID="ALFKI" OrderDate="2003-10-13T00:00:00">
    <OrderID>10702
```

```
</OrderID>
</Order>
<Order CustomerID="ALFKI" OrderDate="2003-01-15T00:00:00">
 <OrderID>10835</OrderID></Order>
 <Order CustomerID="ALFKI" OrderDate="2003-03-16T00:00:00">
```

Figure 10.23 ID/IDRFEF directive applied with `xmldata`

Notice the `ID` directive in the `CustomerID` column. Construct the query so that an `IDREF` in the `Orders` row points back to the `ID` in the `CustomerID` row.

```
SELECT 1            as   Tag,
NULL                as   Parent,
Customers.CustomerID as  [Invoice!1!InvoiceID!id],
NULL                as   [Order!2!OrderID]
NULL                as   [Order!2!CustomerID!idref]
FROM Customers
```

Figure 10.24 IDREF example

We have covered the `FOR XML EXPLICIT` basics. The next section discusses `OPENXML` and provides information concerning overflow columns.

10.5 OPENXML

When inserting, updating, or deleting data in a relational database, we need to provide data to the query. Traditionally, our data resides in flat-file format; however, if the data is in XML format, a method for creating a rowset and passing it to a SQL query is needed. `OPENXML` is precisely the tool we need. The rowset provider generates a view of an XML document, a replacement for a normal SQL

view in SQL queries. Let's examine the following aspects of
OPENXML. Use the following procedures to:

- Create an in-memory DOM representation of the XML source
  document.
- Use OPENXML to create a rowset view and then apply an XPath
  query to retrieve the desired data.
- Hand the rowset to an insert, update, or delete query to
  update the database.
- Remove the DOM representation from memory. OPENXML
  syntax looks like this:

```
OPENXML(idoc int [in],rowpattern nvarchar[in],[flags byte[in]])
[WITH (SchemaDeclaration | TableName)]
```

Let's clarify this syntax:

- The idoc type integer represents the document handle returned
  by the stored procedure sp_xml_preparedocument.
- The rowpattern represents an XPath expression in the following format:

```
/root/childnode/childnode/ element
```

For example, the following XML source document hierarchy
demonstrates this:

```
<root>
<Author>
        <Au_lastName>Peltzer</Au_lastName>
        <Publisher>Addison Wesley</Publisher>
</Author>
</root>
```

/root/Author/Au_lastName/Publisher identifies the
<Publisher> element's child element of the <root>.

- The Flags parameter determines how attributes/subelements
  map to the generated rowset in the XML source document. Set

value=1 for attribute-centric mapping, 2 for element-centric mapping, and 3 for mixed mapping. Use logical or, 1, and 2 to obtain value 3. Flag parameter 8 has a special application; combine it with the @mp:xmltext metaproperty to map this attribute to a column. Then the specified column will receive all unconsumed data.

- Use the With clause to provide a description of the rowset. Three options exist:
  - Specify an existing table name.
  - Specify the rowset schema (column names and data types and required mapping).
  - Use an edge table (a predefined rowset schema is used).

10.6 Defining Metaproperties

A query format begins with two declarations: stored procedure @idoc and type integer, providing the handle needed to pass the query to a SQL update, insert, or delete query.

idoc is an internal representation of the XML document called by sp_preparedocument. You must wrap the query with a <root> element to make the document XML compliant.

The second declaration, @doc, sets the memory allocation for the document to varchar (1000), which is determined by the size of the XML document @doc. Then we store the entire source document in @idoc. Make the document XML compliant by including an opening and closing <ROOT> element. Finally, call stored procedure sp_preparedocument and create an internal representation of it, such as EXEC sp_preparedocument @idoc OUTPUT @doc, followed by the SELECT statement using the OPENXML rowset provider. The format for the rowset provider is as follows:

```
/ROOT/Author/Publisher/PublisherDetails
```

It identifies the nodes in an XML document for processing by XPath.

The XPath pattern language represents the rowpattern as implemented in the MSXML XPath specification. For example, if a row ends with an element, the XPath expression creates a row specified by the `rowpattern` and ends with an element. As previously mentioned, the `flags` value specifies whether the row returns formatted as elements or attributes. If no `ColPattern` exists in the `SchemaDeclaration` (the `WITH` clause), the mapping specified in `flags` is implemented. Otherwise, the flag is ignored. The `SchemaDeclaration` has the following syntax format:

```
ColName, ColType [ColPattern |,[ Metaproperty] [, ColName
ColType [ColPattern | MetaProperty]…]
```

- `ColName` specifies the column name in the rowset.
- `ColType` defines the SQL data type of the column in the rowset. If column types differ from the corresponding XML data type of the attribute, type coercion occurs. If the column is defined as timestamp, the present value in the source document is ignored, and autofill values are returned.
- `ColPattern` specifies an XPath pattern describing how nodes are mapped to the columns. If `ColPattern` is not present, the default mapping occurs. XPath patterns support `MetaProperties`.
- `MetaProperty` is one of several metaproperties provided by `OPENXML`. They are listed below:
  - `@mp:id` provides a system-generated, document-wide identifier of the DOM node (element, attribute, and so on). An XML ID of 0 indicates that the element is the root node. The parent's ID is `NULL`.
  - `@mp:localname` stores the local part of the name of the node. It prefixes a namespace URI and names element or attribute nodes.
  - `@mp:namespaceuri` provides the namespace URI of the current element. If the value is `NULL`, no namespace is present.
  - `@mp:prefix` stores the namespace prefix of the current element name.
  - `@mp:prev` stores the previous sibling relative to a specified node. It provides information concerning the element order. It also contains the XML ID of the previous sibling having the same name. If the element is at the beginning of the list, the attribute is `NULL`.

PART 4
IMPLEMENTATION

451

- `@mp:text` is used for processing overflow information.
- `@mp:parentid` corresponds to `../@mp:id`.
- `@mp:parentlocalname` corresponds to `../@mp:localname`.
- `@mp:parentnamespaceuri` corresponds to `../@mp:namespaceuri`.
- `@mp:parentprefix` corresponds to `../@mp:prefix`.

Now that we have listed the metaproperties and described OPENXML basics, let's examine a query and see how to implement these metaproperties.

Defining an OPENXML Query

The following query contains the elements `<Author>`, `<Publisher>`, and `<PublisherDetails>`. The OPENXML statement retrieves `<Author>` information in a rowset consisting of two rows. The procedure for executing this query is as follows:

Call the `sp_preparedocument`-stored procedure to obtain the document handle and pass it to OPENXML. The following example defines the `rowpattern`:

```
SELECT * FROM OPENXML (@idoc, '/ROOT/Author',1)
WITH (AuthorID  varchar(10),
      Name      varchar(25))
EXEC sp_removedocument @idoc
```

The path descends through top-level `root` to the next level node, which is element `<Author>`. The specified `ColName` values match the corresponding XML document attributes, so do not specify the `ColPattern` parameter in the `Schema Declaration`. This query maps directly as attributes because the `flag` value is set to 1. The document in Figure 10.25 demonstrates how to insert values into a table. Assuming we have a Customer table with structure `[ID] int` and `[Name] varchar (50)`, here is the query.

```
Use RegistrationProcess
go
DECLARE @idoc int
exec sp_xml_preparedocument @idoc OUTPUT,'
<Root>
  <Customer>
    <Name>James</Name>
  </Customer>
</Root>'
insert Customer(ID, Name)
select *
from openxml (@idoc, 'Root/Customer')
with (ID int '@mp:id',
[Name] Varchar(50) 'Name')
```

Figure 10.25   Insert values

Using ColPattern for Mapping Attributes and Elements

The next example demonstrates how the `ColPattern` determines the rowpattern; therefore, the `flags` specifier is not present in the query. The `rowpattern` identifies the nodes to process: `/root/Author/Publisher/PublisherDetails', 2)`. Although the `flags` property has been set to element centric, the mapping specified in the `ColPattern` maps the columns to attributes. In addition, within the `SchemaDeclaration`, `ColPattern` defines both `ColName` and `ColType` parameters, as follows:

ColName	ColType	Path
auid	varchar(25)	'../@auid',
ISBN	varchar(25)	'@ISBN',
Category	varchar(10)	'@Category',
name	varchar(25)	'@name'

    `auid` identifies the parent `<Author>` node. `ISBN` and `Category` map directly to the `<PublisherDetails>` tag. Figure 10.26 demonstrates how to apply `ColPattern` when mapping your data.

```
DECLARE @idoc int
DECLARE @doc varchar (1000)
SET @doc ='
<root>
   <Author auid="DPS">
     <Publisher pubID="awl" auid="DPS">
        <PublisherDetails ISBN="01 200 30456 01" Category="CS"
        name="Peltzer"/>
        <PublisherDetails ISBN="01 200 30586 01" Category="IT"
        name="Heim"/>
     </Publisher>
   </Author>
</root>'

EXEC sp_xml_preparedocument @idoc OUTPUT, @doc
   SELECT *
FROM OPENXML (@doc, '/root/Author/Publisher/PublisherDetails',
1)
WITH (auid        varchar(25)          '../@auid',
      ISBN        varchar(25)          '@ISBN',
      Category    varchar(10)          '@Category',
      name        varchar(25)          '@name')
EXEC sp_xml_removedocument @idoc'
```

Figure 10.26 Specifying `ColPattern` for mapping

The results are shown in Figure 10.27.

auid	ISBN	Category	name
DPS	01 200 30456 01	CS	Peltzer
DPS	01 200 30586 01	IT	Heim

Figure 10.27 Attribute-centric results

Forming Element-Centric Queries

The next example builds on the element specifier found at the end of the OPENXML expression. This query specifies <AuthorID> and <Publisher> as elements. Flags parameter 2 defines the query as element centric (see Figure 10.28).

```
DECLARE @idoc int
DECLARE @doc varchar (1000)
SET @doc ='
<root>
  <Author>
    <AuthorID>DPS</AuthorID>
      <Publisher>Addison Wesley</Publisher>
      <PublisherDetails ISBN="01 200 30456 01" Category="CS"
      name="Peltzer"/>
      <PublisherDetails ISBN="01 200 30586 01" Category="IT"
      name="Heim"/>
    </Author>
</root>'
EXEC sp_xml_preparedocument @idoc OUTPUT, @doc
  SELECT *
FROM OPENXML (@idoc, '/root/Author',2)
WITH   (AuthorID       varchar(25),
        Publisher      varchar(25))
EXEC sp_xml_removedocument @idoc
```

Figure 10.28 An element-centric query

We have set the flag to 2 to generate the output as elements. See Figure 10.29.

```
AuthorID       Publisher
────────────── ──────────────

DPS            Addison Wesley
(1 row(s) affected)
```

Figure 10.29 Element Results

Defining Combination Attribute/Elementric Mapping

Figure 10.30 sets the `flags` parameter to 3, thereby indicating that both attribute and element mapping will occur. In this scenario, attributes map first and then elements map to columns not yet handled.

```
DECLARE @idoc int
DECLARE @doc varchar (1000)
SET @doc ='
<root>
<Author AuthorID = "DPS">
<PublisherName>Addison Wesley</PublisherName>
<PublisherDetails ISBN="01 200 30456 01" Category="CS"
name="Peltzer"/>
<PublisherDetails ISBN="01 200 30586 01" Category="IT"
name="Heim"/>
</Author>
</root>'
EXEC sp_xml_preparedocument @idoc OUTPUT, @doc
SELECT *
FROM OPENXML (@idoc, '/root/Author',3)
WITH    (AuthorID          varchar(25),
         PublisherName     varchar(25))
EXEC sp_xml_removedocument @idoc
```

Figure 10.30   Combining attribute-centric and element-centric mapping

The results are as follows:

```
AuthorID        PublisherName
_____    _____

DPS             Addison Wesley
```

Specifying the Text() Function

An XPath query specifies `Text()` in the `ColPattern` (see Figure 10.31). This overwrites the attribute-centric mapping indicated in `flags`. The column contains a leaf-value string of the `<Order>` element content.

```
AuthorID        PublisherName
_____    _____

DPS             Addison Wesley


DECLARE @idoc int
DECLARE @doc varchar (1000)
SET @doc ='
<root>
<Author AuthorID = "DPS" name="Peltzer"  locality="New York">
<Order OrderID = "PO1" date="10/20/2003" amt = "200.5"/>
<Order OrderID = "PO2" date="12/22/2003" amt = "535.45">Next
Day Delivery
</Order>
</Author>
<Author AuthorID = "SHH" name="Heim"   locality="Flushing
Meadows">
<Order OrderID = "PO3" date="11/20/2003" amt = "4.55"/>
<Order OrderID = "PO4" date="12/22/2003" amt = "10.05">Rush
order
</Order>
</Author>
</root>'
EXEC sp_xml_preparedocument @idoc OUTPUT, @doc
   SELECT *
FROM OPENXML (@idoc, '/root/Author/Order',3)
     with (OrderID varchar(10),
     amt                             float,
     comment                  ntext 'text()')
EXEC sp_xml_removedocument @idoc
```

Figure 10.31   XPath `Text()` query

Here are the query results:

OrderID	amt	comment
PO1	200.5	NULL
PO2	535.45000000000005	Next Day Delivery
PO3	4.5499999999999998	NULL
PO4	10.050000000000001	Rush order

Specifying a Table in the WITH Clause

The script in Figure 10.32 creates a table in which the query names the table in the WITH clause rather than naming the schema declaration. In this scenario, no column patterns are required. The flags parameter specifies the query as attribute centric.

```
Create Table Table1(OrderID char(6), date datetime, amount int)
DECLARE @idoc int
DECLARE @doc varchar (1000)
SET @doc ='
<root>
<Author AuthorID = "DPS" name="Peltzer"  locality="New York">
<Order OrderID = "PO1" date="10/20/2003" amount = "200"/>
<Order OrderID = "PO2" date="12/22/2003" amount = "535">Next
Day Delivery
</Order>
</Author>
<Author AuthorID = "SHH" name="Heim"  locality="Flushing
Meadows">
<Order OrderID = "PO3" date="11/20/2003" amount = "455"/>
```

```
<Order OrderID = "PO4" date="12/22/2003" amount = "1005">Keep
this order quiet
</Order>
</Author>
</root>'

EXEC sp_xml_preparedocument @idoc OUTPUT, @doc
SELECT *
FROM OPENXML (@idoc, '/root/Author/Order',1)
with Table1

EXEC sp_xml_removedocument @idoc
```

Figure 10.32   Named table query

Here are the results:

```
OrderID date                           amount
____    _____       _____

PO1     2003-10-20 00:00:00.000        200
PO2     2003-12-22 00:00:00.000        535
PO3     2003-11-20 00:00:00.000        455
PO4     2003-12-22 00:00:00.000        1005
```

@Attribute Ending Queries

Query attributes demonstrate how to end a `rowpattern` with an attribute. Create a row for each attribute node specified in the XML query. Notice that the `flags` parameter is not specified. Alternatively, identify the mappings in the `ColPattern` parameter. The `<Category>` attribute identifies parent node (`PublisherDetails`). The same is true for the `ISBN` attribute.

```
DECLARE @idoc int
DECLARE @doc varchar (1000)
SET @doc ='
<root>
<Author auid="DPS"  Au_name="Dwight Peltzer">
<Publisher pubId="aw1" auid="DPS">
<PublisherDetails ISBN="01 200 30456 01" Category="CS"
name="Peltzer"/>
<PublisherDetails ISBN="01 200 30586 01" Category="IT"
name="Heim"/>
</Publisher>
</Author>
</root>'
EXEC sp_xml_preparedocument @idoc OUTPUT, @doc
SELECT *
FROM OPENXML (@idoc,
'/root/Author/Publisher/PublisherDetails/@Category')
with (
      Category  varchar(10)       '../@Category',
      ISBN      varchar(25)       '../@ISBN',
      name      varchar(25)       '../@name',
      auid      varchar (10)      '../../@auid')
EXEC sp_xml_removedocument @idoc
```

Figure 10.33   Query attributes

The results are:

Category	ISBN	name	auid
CS	01 200 30456 01	Peltzer	DPS
IT	01 200 30586 01	Heim	DPS

Handing Queries to Update Tables

You can pass `OPENXML` queries to `select`, `update`, and `delete` queries. To achieve this, do the following steps:

1. Declare an `@idoc` handle.
2. Declare stored procedure `@doc` to store the source document.
3. Create the source file.
4. Call stored procedure `sp_preparedocument` to generate an in-memory document and return a document handle.
5. Pass the handle to `OPENXML`.
6. Define your `SELECT` query.
7. Pass the document handle to a SQL query for `UPDATE`, `DELETE`, or `SELECT` statements.
8. Call stored procedure `sp_removedocument` when finished to free memory and destroy the handle.

Let's examine the syntax for this sequence of steps. Assume you have created the Authors table. After executing the `OPENXML` statement, pass the handle to the SQL statement as demonstrated in Figure 10.34.

```
DECLARE @idoc int
DECLARE @doc varchar (1000)
SET @doc ='
<root>
  <Author AuthorID = "DPS">
      <PublisherName>Addison Wesley</PublisherName>
      <PublisherDetails ISBN="01 200 30456 01" Category="CS"
      name="Peltzer"/>
      <PublisherDetails ISBN="01 200 30586 01" Category="IT"
      name="Heim"/>
  </Author>
</root>'
EXEC sp_xml_preparedocument @idoc OUTPUT, @doc
  SELECT *
```

PART 4
IMPLEMENTATION

```
FROM OPENXML (@idoc, '/root/Author',3)
WITH    (AuthorID          varchar(25),
         PublisherName     varchar(25))

INSERT INTO  Author
SELECT * FROM OPENXML(@idoc,'/root/Author')
WITH Author
EXEC sp_xml_removedocument @idoc
```

Figure 10.34   Passing the handle to a SQL query

The results are as follows:

```
AuthorID          PublisherName
_____    _____

DPS               Addison Wesley
```

10.7 Edge Tables

An *edge table* is aptly named because each edge in the source XML maps to a row in the result. This means that each element is described by a row containing metadata.

MetaProperty attributes describe the properties of an XML element, attribute, or DOM node. They do not actually appear in the document; however, OPENXML supplies these properties for all XML elements/attributes. (The metaproperties were listed in section 10.6.)

You can access them by using the namespace urn:schemas-microsoft-com:xml-metaprop. (Note: These properties do not allow XPath expressions.) The edge table contains one column for each MetaProperty attribute with one exception: xmltext.

The example in Figure 10.35 returns the rowset as an edge table.

```
DECLARE @idoc int
DECLARE @doc varchar(1000)
SET @doc ='
<root>
 <Customer cid= "Cust1" name="Dwight" city="East Norwich">
```

```
<Order oid="Ord1" empid="1" >
<orderdate>10/12/2001</orderdate>
<requireddate>10/20/2001</requireddate>
note="ship 2nd day UPS" />
</Order>
<Order oid="Ord2" empid="1" >
<orderdate>11/2/2001</orderdate>
<requireddate>11/10/2001</requireddate>
</Order>
</Customer>
<Customer cid="C2" name="James" city="New York" >
<Order oid="Ord3" empid="2" >
<orderdate>11/13/2001</orderdate>
<requireddate>11/15/2001</requireddate>
</Order>
<Order oid="Ord4" empid="3" >
<orderdate>12/23/2001</orderdate>
<requireddate>12/24/2001</requireddate>
</Order>
</Customer>
</root>
'
EXEC sp_xml_preparedocument @idoc OUTPUT, @doc

SELECT   *
FROM   OPENXML (@idoc, '/root/Customer/Order', 3)
       WITH ( oid           varchar(20),
             CustName      varchar(10)  '../@name',
             UniqueIDVal   int          '@mp:id',
             ParentNameID  varchar(10)  '@mp:parentlocalname',
             NodeName      varchar(10)  '@mp:localname',
             NodeSibling   varchar(10)  '@mp:prev')

EXEC sp_xml_removedocument @idoc
```

Figure 10.35   An edge table query

The results are shown in Figure 10.36.

oid	CustName	UniqueIDVal	ParentNameID	NodeName	NodeSibling
Ord1	Dwight	6	Customer	Order	NULL
Ord2	Dwight	12	Customer	Order	6
Ord3	James	21	Customer	Order	NULL
Ord4	James	26	Customer	Order	21

Figure 10.36   Edge table results

The `@mp:id` provides a system-generated identifier of the DOM node. The `@mp:localname` names the element or attribute nodes. The `@mp:parentlocalname` is `Customer`.

If you want to find out how many `<Customer>` elements exist in the document, add the following code to the document just before the `EXEC sp_removedocument` expression:

```
SELECT count(*)
FROM OPENXML (@idoc , '/')
WHERE localname = 'Customer'
```

Many other `MetaProperty` features offer useful information. We leave these to the reader as an exercise. Before shifting our focus to XML views, one other feature needs mentioning: the `xmltext` over-flow feature.

Figure 10.37 demonstrates how `OPENXML` creates a one-column rowset view of the following document. The column `Col1` maps to the `xmlText` metaproperty, thereby creating an overflow column. Figure 10.38 follows this example with the query results.

```
DECLARE @idoc int
DECLARE @doc varchar(1000)
SET @doc ='
<root>
 <Customer cid= "Cust1" name="Dwight" city="East Norwich">
   <Order oid="Ord1" empid="1" >
     <orderdate>10/12/2003</orderdate>
     <requireddate>10/20/2003</requireddate>
     note="ship 2nd day UPS" />
   </Order>
   </Customer>
</root>
'
EXEC sp_xml_preparedocument @idoc OUTPUT, @doc
SELECT   *
FROM    OPENXML (@idoc, '/root')
WITH (Col1 ntext '@mp:xmltext')
EXEC sp_xml_removedocument @idoc
```

Figure 10.37   xmlText query


```
<root>
    <Customer cid="Cust1" name="Dwight" city="East Norwich">
    <Order oid="Ord1" empid="1">
      <orderdate>10/12/2003</orderdate>
      <requireddate>10/20/2003</requireddate>
      note="ship 2nd day UPS" /&gt;
    </Order>
    </Customer>
</root>
```

Figure 10.38   xmlText query results

xmlText overflow creates a rowset view of the XML document using OPENXML. It demonstrates how to retrieve unconsumed data by mapping the xmlText metaproperty attribute to a rowset column.

Figure 10.39 identifies the comment column that is mapped to `@mp:xmlText`. The `flags` parameter 9 indicates attribute-centric mapping. Only unconsumed data is copied to `comment`. Figure 10.40 is the retured result for Figure 10.39.

```
DECLARE @idoc int
DECLARE @doc varchar(1000)
SET @doc ='
<root>
 <Customer cid= "Cust1" name="Dwight" city="East Norwich">
   <Order oid="Ord1" empid="1" >
     <orderdate>10/12/2003</orderdate>
     <requireddate>10/20/2003</requireddate> ship on time.
     note="ship 2nd day UPS" />
   </Order>
   </Customer>
</root>
'

EXEC sp_xml_preparedocument @idoc OUTPUT, @doc

SELECT   *
FROM    OPENXML (@idoc, '/root/Customer/Order', 9)
WITH (oid char(5),
      date datetime,
      comment ntext '@mp:xmltext')
EXEC sp_xml_removedocument @idoc
```

Figure 10.39 `xmlText` overflow

```
oid           date                      comment
───────       ──                        ──────-
Ord1                                    NULL
<orderdate>10/12/2003</orderdate>
<requireddate>10/20/2003</requireddate>  ship on time.
note="ship 2nd day UPS" /&gt;
</Order>
```

Figure 10.40 `xmltext` query results

Now let's shift our focus to an examination of XML views in which we can query a relational table as if it were XML formatted.

10.8 Annotated Mapping Schemas– A Comparison Between XDR and XSD Schemas

Because annotations play a major role in mapping schemas, we will briefly compare the differences between XDR schemas and their updated successor, XSD schemas, with a view toward understanding how they both employ annotations for defining an XML view.

A typical schema validates document structure and data types, whereas mapping schemas assist in forming the data. To recognize the variance in roles that schemas play, let's begin by first examining the XDR schema, its syntax, and functionality. After a brief overview, we will discuss mapping schemas and the role they play in defining an XML view. You will see both XDR and XSD schemas used in creating views.

Annotations allow us to define mapping of elements and attributes to database tables and columns. Specifically, annotations provide a view of relational data. The default namespace for annotations is as follows:

```
xmlns=úrn:schemas-microsoft-com:xml-data"
xmlns:sql="urn:schemas-microsoft-com:xml-sql">
```

The namespace for data types is as follows:

```
<Schema xmlns="urn:schemas-microsoft-com:xml-data"
xmlns:sql="urn:schemas-microsoft-com:xml-sql"
xmlns:dt="urn:schemas-microsoft-com:datatypes">
```

Before we can annotate our XDR schemas, we must specify these namespaces. You preface the namespace declaration with `<Schema>`. Specifically, prefix `sql` differentiates annotations in this namespace from other namespaces.

Table 10.6 provides a list of annotations.

Table 10.6   Annotations Table

Annotation	Description
`sql:relationship`	Denotes the relationship between XML elements. The following attributes define the relationship: `key`, `key-relation`, `foreign-key`, `foreign-relation`.
`sql:field`	Denotes a mapping between element/attribute and database field.
`sql:id-prefix`	Prepends a prefix to a database field. It creates `valid id`, `idref`, and `idrefs`.
`sql:is-constant`	This allows you to include an item in a source document that is not linked to a column or table. Set it to true (1), which generates a constant in the output.
`sql:key-fields`	Specifies a field(s) that uniquely identifies table rows. Proper nesting is a consequence of using this specifier.
`sql:limit-field`	This filters the result.
`sql:limit-value`	When combined with `field`, it provides a filtered value.
`sql:map-field`	This annotation allows specified items to be excluded from the result.
`sql:overflow-field`	This specifies an overflow column where unconsumed data is stored.
`sql:relation`	This maps between element/attributes and database table/columns. This allows you to name elements/attributes that contain names different from columns in the database.
`sql:target-namespace`	Puts query results in a targeted namespace that is not the default.
`sql:use-cdata`	Allows you to specify CDATA for certain elements.

Providing annotations to the XML schema generates the view. Divide the schema into two separate parts:

- An XDR or XSD schema
- Specified annotations

The schema describes the structure of an XML document; annotations describe the relationships between the database and XML.

In Microsoft SQL Server 2000, use can use either type to create a schema. By using annotations, you can map the schema to tables and columns. Then XPath queries are applied against the view, and the results are returned in XML format. This procedure is much easier than writing OPENXML queries. Figure 10.41 is an example of a XDR schema.

```
<?xml version="1.0" encoding="UTF-8"?>
<Schema xmlns="urn:schemas-microsoft-com:xml-data"
xmlns:dt="urn:schemas-microsoft-com:datatypes"
xmlns:sql="urn:schemas-microsoft-com:xml-sql">
    <ElementType name="Employee" sql:relation="Salesreps">
      <AttributeType name="EmpID"/>
      <AttributeType name="Name"/>
      <AttributeType name="Title"/>

      <attribute type="EmpID" sql:field="Empl_Num"/>
      <attribute type="FName" sql:field="Name"/>
      <attribute type="Title" sql:field= "Title"/>

    </ElementType>
</Schema>
```

Figure 10.41 An XDR schema

Let's examine this schema, beginning with the namespace declaration:

```
<Schema xmlns="urn:schemas-microsoft-com:xml-data"
xmlns:dt="urn:schemas-microsoft-com:datatypes"
xmlns:sql="urn:schemas-microsoft-com:xml-sql">
```

This, followed by the `ElementType` declaration, distinguishes the XDR schema from its XSD counterpart. In contrast, the default XSD namespace declaration is as follows:

```
<xsd:schema xmlns:xsd="http://www.w3.org/2001/XMLSchema"
```

Next, `<ElementType name="Employee"` is usually followed by the content model, meaning `<ElementType name="ID" content ="textOnly"/>`, or other content models such as `elt only`, `mixed`, or `empty`. Also, note the difference between the element declaration in uppercase versus the lowercase element listed later in the schema. The uppercase `<Element>` represents the element declaration, whereas the lowercase `<element>` is considered an instance of the declared element. Once you have declared an element, you can reference it within scope of the `<ElementType>`.

Notice that `sql:relation` maps the `<Salesreps>` table to the `<Employees>` table (not shown). Furthermore, use attributes `EmpID`, `Name`, and `Title` to map directly to `Empl_Num` and `Title`. Once this view is created, query it as if it were XML.

The relationships between `<Attributes>` and `<attributes>` are similar to elements, with the exception that attributes appear either once or not at all in a given element. In addition, attribute order is not constrained. Refer again to the schema section where `<Attributes>` are declared and instances of them (`attribute`) are created to reference the attribute declaration.

Declaring data types in XDR schemas must be preceded by the data type namespace listed here: `xmlns:dt="urn:schemas-microsoft-com:datatypes"`. The syntax would look something like this:

```
<?xml version='1.0' ?>
<Schema xmlns="urn:schemas-microsoft-com:xml-data"
xmlns:dt="urn:schemas-microsoft-com:xml:datatypes"
xmlns:sql="urn:schemas-microsoft-com:xml-sql">
<ElementType name="CustomerID" dt:type="int" />
<ElementType name="CustomerName" dt:type="string" />
<ElementType name="Address" dt:type="string" />
```

```
<ElementType name="root" sql:is-constant='1' />
<element type="Customers" />
</ElementType>
<ElementType name="Customers    " sql:relation="Cust" />
<element type="CustomerID"        sql:field="CustomerID" />
<element type="CustomerName"      sql:field="CustomerName" />
<element type="Address"           sql:field="Address" />
</ElementType>
</Schema>
```

Notice how we use annotations to map the Customers element to the Cust table followed by mapping the attributes to the database columns.

An XSD schema, the recent update to schemas, provides more flexibility than the XDR schema. Here is the same data mapped to an XSD schema:

```
<xsd:Schema xmlns:xsd="http://www.w3.org/2002/XMLSchema"
xmlns:sql="urn:schemas-microsoft-com:mapping-schema">
<xsd:Element name="Customers" sql:relation="Cust" >
<xsd:complexType>
<xsd:sequence>
<xsd:element name="CustomerID"        type="xsd:int" />
<xsd:element name="CustomerName"      type="xsd:string" />
<xsd:element name="address"           type="xsd:string" />
</xsd:sequence>
</xsd:complexType>
</xsd:Schema>
```

Although they perform many of the same functions, the differences are enormous. One of the most significant features that XSD schemas offer us is the ability to declare our own user-defined data types. Inheritance is another unique feature that XDR schemas do not offer. Additionally, XSD schemas allow us to define keys on data elements for uniqueness. You will recall that ID, IREF, and IDREFS can only be applied to integers. In addition, they are unique throughout the entire document, whereas key and keyref can be applied on an individual basis to individual elements bearing data types other than integers. Many other differences exist. SQL Server 2000 beta versions 2.0 and 3.0 still support XDR schemas. BizTalk Server 2000 uses XDR schemas exclusively, although eventually it will support both type schemas.

The main emphasis of this discussion is placed on the role that schemas and mapping schemas play in defining the shape of XML rowsets, so let's return to our examination of XML views. Refer to Chapter 3, "Parsing Your XML Document," for a comprehensive discussion of XSD schemas.

The next example, xs:CustomerInfo (see Figure 10.42), is based on the Business database we created in SQL Server 2000. Note: xs and xsd are interchangeable.

```
<xs:schema xmlns:xs="http://www.w3.org/2001/XMLSchema"
elementFormDefault="qualified" attributeFormDefault="unquali-
fied">
    <xs:element name="CustomerInfo">
      <xs:complexType>
        <xs:sequence>
        <xs:element name="Cust_Num" type="xs:string"/>
        <xs:element name="Company" type="xs:string"/>
        <xs:element name="Cust_Rep" type="xs:string"/>
        <xs:element ref="Orders"/>
        </xs:sequence>
      </xs:complexType>
    </xs:element>

    <xs:element name="Orders">
    <xs:complexType>
      <xs:sequence>
        <xs:element ref="OrderInfo"/>
      </xs:sequence>
          <xs:attribute name="Order_Num" type="xs:integer"/>
          <xs:attribute name="OrderDate" type="xs:date"/>
    </xs:complexType>
```

```
        </xs:element>

        <xs:element name="OrderInfo">
            <xs:complexType>
                <xs:sequence>
                    <xs:element ref="Purchased_Items"/>
                </xs:sequence>
                    <xs:attribute name="Amount"
                    type="xs:integer"/>
                    <xs:attribute name="Quantity"
                    type="xs:integer"/>
        </xs:complexType>
        </xs:element>

        <xs:element name="Purchased_Items" type="Products"/>
            <xs:complexType name="Products">
                <xs:sequence>
                    <xs:element name="Product_Id" type="xs:string"/>
                    <xs:element name="Price" type="xs:integer"/>
                    <xs:element name="Qty_On_Hand"
                    type="xs:integer"/>
                </xs:sequence>
            </xs:complexType>
</xs:schema>
```

Figure 10.42   xs:CustomerInfo

This schema mirrors the content and format of our
`<CustomerInfo.xml>` source document. Root element
`<CustomerInfo>` contains subelement levels `<Orders>`,
`<OrderInfo>`, and `<PurchasedItems>`.

CustomerInfo contains three children elements: Cust_Num,
Company, and Cust_Rep.

Orders contain the child elements Product_Id, Order_Num,
Order_Date, Rep, and CustNum.

OrderInfo provides order detail information, such as the product
ID, price, and quantity on hand. If you scrutinize the annotated
schema in Figure 10.43, the final part of the schema defines the

PART 4
IMPLEMENTATION

primary key/foreign key relationship, and all other field mapping details map to the tables.

```
<xsd:annotation>
   <xsd:appinfo>
    <sql:relationship name="customers"
                parent="Customers"
                parent-key="Cust_Num"
                child="Orders"
                child-key="CustNum" />
    <sql:relationship name="OrderOrders"
                parent="Orders"
                parent-key="Product_Id"
                child="[OrderInfo]"
                child-key="OrderID" />
     <sql:relationship name="OrderInfoProducts"
                parent="[OrderInfo]"
                parent-key="Product_ID"
                child="Products"
                child-key="Product_ID
   </xsd:appinfo>
</xsd:annotation>
```

Figure 10.43   Annotated schema segment

The following example displays the source document for our annotated schema:

```
<CustomerInfo xmlns:xsi="http://www.w3.org/2001/XMLSchema-
instance"
xsi:noNamespaceSchemaLocation="C:\XML\CustomerInfo.xsd">
   <Cust_Num>2102</Cust_Num>
   <Company>Jones MFG</Company>
   <Cust_Rep>101</Cust_Rep>
   <Orders>
     <OrderInfo>
       <Purchased_Items>
           <Product_Id>2A45C</Product_Id>
           <Price>70</Price>
```

```
        <Qty_On_Hand>210</Qty_On_Hand>
      </Purchased_Items>
    </OrderInfo>
  </Orders>
</CustomerInfo>
```

A traditional rowset doesn't exactly match an XML document. We should form our SQL queries so that the data is written to an output stream rather than to a traditional recordset. This brings us closer to the format we desire. Writing to a stream allows us to shape the data in an XML format we need. Additionally, once the data is returned in this format, several options exist for doing something with the data, including passing it to the DOM for parsing, applying an XSLT stylesheet for rendering in HTML, or exposing the data to the web via http.

We have previously examined the three forms of FOR XML. For example, FOR XML RAW returns the data in XML format. If the query in Figure 10.44 were written using this clause, it would bring us closer to emulating the XSD schema we introduced earlier.

```
Use Business
go
SELECT Customers.Cust_Num,Customers.Company,
Orders.Product_Id, Orders.Order_Date,
Orders.Qty, Orders.Amount,
Products.Price, Products.Qty_On_Hand
FROM
Customers, Orders, Products
WHERE Customers.Cust_Num = Orders.Cust_Num
and
Orders.Product_Id = Orders.Product_Id and
Orders.MFR_Id=Products.Mfr_Id
and Customers.Cust_Num='2101'
FOR XML RAW
```

Figure 10.44   FOR XML RAW

The query results are as follows:

```
<row Cust_Num="2101" Company="JONES MFG." Product_Id="114   "
Order_Date="2003-01-03T00:00:00" Qty="6" Amount="1458"
Price="148" Qty_On_Hand="115"
```

PART 4
IMPLEMENTATION

The rowset still doesn't match our schema. Let's use the FOR XML AUTO clause to bring us closer to the results we desire (see Figure 10.45).

```
Public Function FOR XML AUTOQuery()
Dim adoConn         As New ADODB.Connection
Dim adoCmd          As New ADODB.Command
Dim adoStream       As New ADODB.Stream
AdoConn.Open        "provider=sqlxmloledb;DATA " & _
"provider=sqloledb;Server=(local);Database=Business;UID=sa;PWD=
;"
Set adoCmd.ActiveConnection = adoConn
AdoCmd.CommandType =adCmdText
AdoCmd.CommandText="Select  Customers.Cust_Num,  " & _
     "Customers.Company, " & _
     "Orders.Product_Id, Orders.Order_Date, Orders.Qty, " & _
     "Orders.Amount " & _
     "Products.Price, Products.Qty_On_Hand& _
     "From Customers, Orders, Products " & _
     "Where Customers.Cust_Num = Orders.Cust_Num " & _
     "and Orders.Product_Id =Orders.Product_Id " & _
     "and Orders.MFR_Id = Products.MFR_Id " & _
     "and Customers.Cust_Num='2101' FOR XML AUTO" _

adoStream.Open
adoCmd.Properties ("Output Stream").Value =adoStream
adoCmdText ,  adExecuteStream
Debug.Print adoStream.ReadText
End Function
```

Figure 10.45   FOR XML AUTO stream query

This query returns the stream shown in Figure 10.46.

```
<Customers Cust_Num="2101" Company="JONES MFG.">
<Orders Product_Id="114"  " Order_Date="2003-01-03T00:00:00"
Qty="6" Amount="1458">
<Products Price="148" Qty_On_Hand="115"/>
<Products Price="243" Qty_On_Hand="15"/>
</Orders>
</Customers>
```

Figure 10.46   FOR XML AUTO stream format

This is much better. However, the AUTO mode provides very limited control over the shape of the XML document, as we previously experienced. Therefore, we need to seek another alternative. Fortunately, FOR XML EXPLICIT allows us to have complete control over the rowset, as we saw earlier in this chapter. However, there is yet another method we should pursue: XML views that contain an annotated schema.

10.9 XML Views Containing Annotated Schemas

Annotations provide default element mapping to table names in XML views, and attribute names map to column names. A major feature that annotations provide allows us to represent hierarchical relationships. Consider the following code fragment:

```
<ElementType name="Employee" sql:relation="Employees">.
sql:relation
```

This defines the relationship between tables, whereas sql:field specifies a column mapping. Additionally, we use sql:relationship to define primary key/foreign key relationships. Let's redo our schema, add some annotations, and see if it works for us (see Figure 10.47).

```
<xsd:schema xmlns:xs="http://www.w3.org/2001/XMLSchema"
xmls:sql="urn:schemas-microsoft-com:mapping-schema">
elementFormDefault="qualified" attributeFormDefault=
"qualified">
<xs:element name="CustomerInfo"  sql:relation="customers">
<xs:complexType>
<xs:sequence>
<xs:element name="CustNum"  sql:field="Cust_Num"
type="xsd:string" />
 <xs:element name="CompanyName"  sql:field="Company"
type="xsd:string" />
 <xs:element name="Rep" sql:field= "Cust_Rep" type
="xsd:string" />
```

```
<xs:element ref="Order"        sql:relationship= "CustOrders" />
</xs:sequence>
<xs:attribute name="ID"   sql:field="Cust_Num" type="xsd:string"
/>
</xsd:complexType>
</xsd:element>


<xsd:element name="Order" sql:relation= "Orders">
<xsd:complexType>
<xsd:sequence>
<xsd:element ref="Items"   sql:relationship= "OrderOrders"/>
</xsd:sequence>
<xsd:attribute name="Order_Num" type="xsd:int"/>
<xsd:attribute name="DateOrdered" sql:field="Order_Date"
type="xsd:datetime"/>
</xsd:complexType>
</xsd:element>


<xsd:element name="OrderItems" sql:relation="[Order Info]">
<xsd:complexType>
<xsd:sequence>
<xsd:element ref="PurchasedItems"
sql:relationship="OrderInfoProducts"/>
</xsd:sequence>
<xsd:attribute name="UnitPrice" sql:field="Price"
type="xsd:int"/>
<xsd:attribute name="Quantity"   sql:field="Qty"
type="xsd:int"/>
</xsd:complexType>
</xsd:element>
<xs:element name="PurchasedItems" type="Product" sql:rela-
tion="Products" />
<xsd:complexType name="Products">
<xsd:sequence>
```

```
<xsd:element name="ProductName"    sql:field="Product_Id"
type="xsd:string" />
<xsd:element name="AvailableStock" sql:field="Qty_On_Hand"
type="xsd:int" />
        </xsd:sequence>
        </xsd:complexType>"
<xsd:annotation>
   <xsd:appinfo>
        <sql:relationship name="customers"
                    parent="Customers"
                    parent-key="Cust_Num"
                    child="Orders"
                    child-key="CustNum" />
        <sql:relationship name="OrderOrders"
                    parent="Orders"
                    parent-key="Product_Id"
                    child="[OrderInfo]"
                    child-key="OrderID" />

    <sql:relationship name="OrderInfoProducts"
                    parent="[OrderInfo]"
                    parent-key="Product_ID"
                    child="Products"
                    child-key="ProductID
   </xsd:appinfo>
  </xsd:annotation>

</xsd:schema>
```

Figure 10.47   Defining schema annotations

This schema represents an abstract layer over the database. We used `sql:prefix` to specify an XML for SQL server namespace. Then we used `sql:field` to map elements and attributes to columns in the database. Next we used the `sql:relation` annotation to map elements to tables. Finally, we used the `sql:relationship` annotation to specify three join relationships.

PART 4
IMPLEMENTATION

10.10 Creating XPath Queries

XPath is the querying language employed for XML views. (Refer to Chapter 6, "Applying XPath," for a review of XPath technology.) XPath selects nodes based on node sets selected by a previous XPath operator.

Let's write an ADO query and observe how XPath functions in this context (see Figure 10.48).

```
Public Function XPathQuery()

    Dim adoConn      As New ADODB.Connection
    Dim adoCmd       As New ADODB.Command
    Dim adoStream    As New ADODB.Stream

    adoConn.Open "provider=sqlxmloledb;data " & _
    provider=sqloledb;Server=(localhost);Database=northwind;
    UID=sa;PWD=;"
    Set adoCmd.ActiveConnection = adoConn
    adoCmd.CommandType = adCmdText
    adoCmd.Dialect = "{EC2A4293-E898-11D2-B1B7-00C04F680C56}"
    adoCmd.Properties("Mapping Schema") = "customers.xsd"
    adoCmd.CommandText = "/CustomerRecord[@ID='GROSR']"

    adoStream.Open
    adoCmd.Properties("Output Stream").Value = adoStream
    adoCmd.Execute , , adExecuteStream

    Debug.Print adoStream.ReadText

End Function
```

Figure 10.48   ADO query

The XPath query is the new item added here. Also, notice the `Dialect` for XPath:

```
adoCmd.Dialect = "{EC2A4293-E898-11D2-B1B7-00C04F680C56}"
```

The mapping schema property for the command has been set, thereby providing the file path to the schema. The returned rowset is the desired result. One problem remains: An XML document must have a <Root> element.

Write the query in the following manner to get the results we want:

```
/CustomerRecord[@ID='GROSR']/order/Items/ItemPurchased
```

Accessing XML data can be accomplished using several different methods. One method retrieves data with an XPath query in an Active Server Page (ASP) client. For example, the following partial script written in VBScript uses the SQLOLEDB provider to access the XML data (see Figure 10.49). Always prefix the query with <Root> when querying a database with XPath expressions, as demonstrated in the following query.

```
<%@ Language=VbSCRIPT %>

<%
'Const DBGUID_DEFAULT as String"{C8B521FB-5CF3-11CE-ADE5-
00AA0044773D}"
'Const DBGUID_SQL as String="{C8B522D7-5CF3-11CE-ADE5-
00AA0044773D}"
'Const DBGUID_MSSQLXML as String="{5D531CB2-E6Ed-11D2-B252-
00C04F681B71}"
'Const DBGUID_XPATH as String="{ec2a4293-e898-11d2-b1b7-
00c04f680c56}"

dim cn
dim cmd
dim textQryString
'get query string from user's request
textQryString =trim(cstr(Request.QueryString("XPathRequest") ))
'create a connection object
set cn=Server.CreateObject("adodb.connection")
'set the connection for the command object
cn.Open "PROVIDER=SQLOLEDB;Data Source=(localhost);
database=Invoice;uid=sa; PWD="
Set cmd.ActiveConnection = cn
```

'set command type for an XPath query. This is where you specify the particular dialect to be used for the 'CommandString or CommandText properties. It is a Globally Unique Identifier which permits the data provider to support multiple dialects. Its primary use is for XML generated recordsets. It identifies which form of XML the recordset is persisted in. The default SQL XML format is:

```
'"{5D531CB2-E6Ed-11D2-B252-00C04F681B71}"
'The standard SQL dialect is: ={C8B522D7-5CF3-11CE-ADE5-
00AA0044773D}
'The dialect we use for this query is the dialect display in
the next row of text in this query
cmd.Dialect ="{ec2a4293-e898-11d2-b1b7-00c04f680c56}"
cmd.Properties("Base Path") = "C:\VirtualRoot\Schema"
cmd.Properties("Mapping Schema") = "Invoice.xsd"
cmd.Properties("Output Stream") = Response
if len(trim(textQryString)) > 0 then
cmd.CommandText = trim(textQryString)
else
   cmd.CommandText = "Invoice"
end if

Response.Write("<root>)
cmd.Execute 1024
Rresponse.Write("</root>)
cn.Close
Set cn=nothing
Set cmd= Nothing

%>
```

Figure 10.49 Setting the `Dialect` property

Following this script, you need to create the Invoice schema and then create an HTML page to display the query. Load the document using `ActiveXObject` and refer to the MSXML 4.0 Parser. The final step is creating an xpath.xsi file and applying an XSLT template to transform the document. Use the Invoice.xml file presented earlier in this chapter as the source document.

10.11 Template Queries

The next type query we present demonstrates the basics for creating a template query. Template queries are essentially XML files with queries placed in query elements, which are defined in namespace `urn:schemas-microsoft-com:xml-sql">`. Within these templates, we can insert results of stored procedures and put complete SQL queries within these elements. The query in Figure 10.50 demonstrates syntax for a template query.

```
<ROOT xmlns:sql="urn:schemas-microsoft-com:xml-sql">
    <sql:query>
    SELECT * FROM Invoice FOR XML AUTO
    </sql:query>
</ROOT>
```

Figure 10.50 Constructing template queries

Here are the results:

```
<ROOT xmlns:sql="urn:schemas-microsoft-com:xml-sql">
    <Invoice CustID="dps" name="Peltzer" />
    <Invoice CustID="MWP" name="Waterman" />
</ROOT>
```

We could also place the entire query in the URL as demonstrated here:

```
http://localhost/Invoice?template=<ROOT+xmlns:sql="urn:schemas-
microsoft-com:xml-sql"><sql:query>
SELECT%20+*+FROM+iNVOICE+FOR+XML+AUTO</sql:query></ROOT>
```

Unfortunately, this task is undesirable for two reasons:

• It is cumbersome to enter the URL.
• Security becomes an issue.

It is preferable to store queries on the web server and then call them when necessary. We can also run multiple queries in templates, providing structure for them as shown in Figure 10.51.

```
<ROOT xmlns:sql="urn:schemas-microsoft-com:xml-sql">
    <SQLList>
    <sql:query>
    SELECT * FROM Authors FOR XML AUTO
    </sql:query>
    </SQLList>

    <ComposerList>
    <sql:query>
    SELECT * FROM NuMetalComposers FOR XML AUTO
    </sql:query>
    </ComposerList>

    <InvoiceList>
    <sql:query>
    SELECT * FROM Invoice FOR XML AUTO
    </sql:query>
    </InvoiceList>
</ROOT>
```

Figure 10.51   A multiple-template query

The results from this query are shown in Figure 10.52.

```
- <ROOT xmlns:sql="urn:schemas-microsoft-com:xml-sql">
- <SQLList>
 <Authors PublisherName="Addison Wesley" PublisherDetails="" />
 <Authors />
 <Authors />
 <Authors PublisherName="Addison Wesley" PublisherDetails="" />
 <Authors PublisherName="Addison Wesley" PublisherDetails="" />
</SQLList>
<ComposerList>
<NuMetalComposers BandID="Blood Fusion Theory"
ComposerName="JonathanP"        Overflow="JP<dps><address> 172
Radcliff Dr</address></dps>" />
```

```
</ComposerList>
<InvoiceList>
<Invoice CustID="dps" name="Peltzer" />
<Invoice CustID="MWP" name="Waterman" />
</InvoiceList>
</ROOT>
```

Figure 10.52   Multiple-template query result

10.12 Providing Parameters for Template Queries

Providing parameters for templates is accomplished by writing the query in Figure 10.53.

```
<ROOT xmlns:sql="urn:schemas-microsoft-com:xml-sql">
    <sql:header>
    <sql:param name="ID">1</sql:param>
    </sql:header>
    <SQLList>
    <sql:query>
    SELECT * FROM Authors WHERE CategoryID=@ID FOR XML AUTO
    </sql:query>
    </SQLList>
    <ComposerList>
    <sql:query>
    SELECT * FROM NuMetalComposers WHERE CategoryID=@ID FOR XML
    AUTO
    </sql:query>
    </ComposerList>

    <InvoiceList>
    <sql:query>
    SELECT * FROM Invoice WHERE CategoryID=@ID FOR XML AUTO
    </sql:query>
    </InvoiceList>
</ROOT>
```

Figure 10.53   Passing parameters to a query

The final task we need to do is provide the parameter in the URL, just as we do in Figure 10.54.

```
http://localhost/Invoice/template/MyParamTemplate.xml?ID=2
```

Figure 10.54   A parameter URL

The consequence of this query would return the rows in `Authors`, `NuMetalComposers`, and `Invoice`, where the `Category` column would be `2`.

You can see how XML views save us a lot of work. This discussion has demonstrated how we can query a relational database as if the data were formatted in XML.

10.13 New SQL XML Features

Other features provided in SQL Server 2000 and SQL XML 3.0 include BulkLoad and Updategrams. They allow you to persist changes to XML views by using the annotated mapping schema mechanism for converting XML to relational tables. If you have large amounts of data to insert into a relational database, use BulkLoadforXML for your tasks. We focus on Updategrams in this section.

Use XML templates to execute updategrams. The user specifies both the before and after XML document instances. You map updategrams to the namespace `urn:schemas-micosoft-com:xml-updategram`.

Modifying Data Utilizing Updategrams

The definitions for `<sync>`, `<before>`, and `<after>` reside in the namespace `urn:schemas-micosoft-com:xml-updategram`. The prefix you use for it is your choice. The syntax for an updategram is shown in Figure 10.55.

```
<ROOT xmlns;updg="urn:schemas-micosoft-com:xml-updategram">
    <updg:header [nullvalue="is NULL"]
    <updg:param name="paramName"/>
                    .  .  .  .
    </updg:header>

    <updg:sync [mapping-schema="schemaDocument.xml"]
    [updg:nullvalue="isNull"]

    <updg:before>
    <elementName attribute="value"    />
                    .  .  .
    </updg:before>
    <updg:after  [updg:returned="iVar1   iVar2     "]>
    <ElementName [updg:id="value"]  [updg:at-identity="iVar"]
    [updg:guid="gVar"]
    attribute="value" attribute="value"     />
    </updg:after>
                    .  .  .
    </updg:sync>
</ROOT>
```

Figure 10.55   Updategram syntax

Updategram keywords require some explanation:

• `<before>` identifies the present state of the record instance.
  Two scenarios exist: Either a SQL statement will appear in the
  `<before>` block, or nothing will exist (see Figure 10.56).

```
<ROOT xmlns:updg="urn:schemas-microsoft-com:xml-updategram">
    <updg:sync>
    <updg:before>
    ' The before state indicates a delete operation will occur
    <Orders_x0020_OrderInfo Order_Num="112961    "
    Product_Id="2A44L"/>
    </updg:before>
```

```
    <updg:after>
    </updg:after>
    </updg:sync>
</ROOT>
```

Figure 10.56   Delete `OrderInfo`

The next example demonstrates an updategram in which nothing appears in the `before` block. Therefore, values `Order_Num` "112961" and `Product_Id="2A44L"` will be inserted into the `OrderInfo` table in the Business database (see Figure 10.57).

```
<ROOT xmlns:updg="urn:schemas-microsoft-com:xml-updategram">
    <updg:sync>
    <updg:before>
    </updg:before>

    <updg:after>
    <Orders_x0020_OrderInfo Order_Num="112961 "
    Product_Id="2A44L"/>
    </updg:after>
    </updg:sync>
</ROOT>
```

Figure 10.57   Insert `OrderInfo`

One more scenario exists, an update. Consider the code in Figure 10.58.

```
<ROOT xmlns:updg="urn:schemas-microsoft-com:xml-updategram">
    <updg:sync>
    <updg:before>
    <Orders_x0020_OrderInfo Order_Num="112961 "
    Product_Id="2A44L"/>
    </updg:before>

    <updg:after>
```

```
<Orders_x0020_OrderInfo Order_Num="112961"
Product_Id="41003"/>
</updg:after>
</updg:sync>
</ROOT>
```

Figure 10.58   An update operation

In this case, we have updated the `Product_Id` because the order has been changed.

- `<sync>` contains the `<before>` and `<after>` blocks. Note that a `<sync>` block may contain more than one set of `<before>` and `<after>` blocks. If more than one block is specified, they must be specified as pairs. Consider each `<sync>` block as a single transaction, meaning everything within that block must be executed or not at all. A final note: When more than one `<sync>` blocks exist, a failure in one block will not preclude the execution of other blocks.

Modifying a database (`insert`, `update`, or `delete`) from an existing XML document can occur by using either OPENXML Transact-SQL or an updategram. The OPENXML function slices the existing XML document and makes available a rowset that can be handed to an INSERT, UPDATE, or DELETE statement to execute the operation against the repository tables. In contrast, the updategram works against XML views provided by the mapping schema. The mapping schema maps XML elements and attributes to matching tables and columns.

Two methods exist for mapping XML data: implicit and explicit. The default mapping is implicit, meaning that each element in the `<before>` or `<after>` block maps to a table, and each subelement's child element or attribute maps to a column in the repository.

Let's view such a scenario. The updategram in Figure 10.59 performs an implicit operation. Because nothing is specified in the `<before>` block, the updategram inserts a new customer in the `Invoice` table. The `Invoice` element maps directly to the `Invoice` table and `InvoiceID` and `name` map directly as attributes to the corresponding columns in the `Invoice` table.

PART 4

IMPLEMENTATION

```
<ROOT xmlns:upgr="urn:schemas-microsoft-com:xml-updategram">
   <upgr:sync >
   <upgr:before>
   </upgr:before>

   <upgr:after>
   <Invoice InvoiceID "jwp" name="Waterman"/>
   </upgr:after>
   </upgr:sync >
</ROOT>
```

Figure 10.59   Implicit mapping—an insert operation

Mapping explicitly causes the updategram to use the corresponding schema for determining which tables and columns are updated.
We previously created a mapping schema for the
NuMetalComposers example. The syntax for explicit schema
mapping is shown in Figure 10.60.

```
<ROOT xmlns:sql="urn:schemas-microsoft-com:xml-sql">
   <sql:xpath-query mapping-schema="MyMappingSchema.xml">
   /Orders
   </sql:xpath-query>
</ROOT>
```

Figure 10.60   Explicit schema mapping

Two forms exist for mapping:

- Element-centric mapping
- Attribute-centric mapping

The first category uses elements containing other elements to
denote the properties of the specified element. For example, the
Invoice element may contain ID and name subelements, as shown
in Figure 10.61.

```
<ROOT xmlns:upgr="urn:schemas-microsoft-com:xml-updategram">
    <upgr:sync>
    <upgr:before>
    </upgr>

    <upgr:after>
    <Invoice>
    <InvoiceID>dps</InvoiceID>
    <Name>Chris Peltzer</Name>
    </Invoice>
    </upgr:after>
    </upgr:sync>
</ROOT>
```

Figure 10.61   Element-specific mapping containing subelements

Figure 10.62 demonstrates how we write an updategram attribute-centric query.

```
<ROOT xmlns:upgr="urn:schemas-microsoft-com:xml-updategram">
<upgr:sync>
    <upgr:before>
    </upgr>

    <upgr:after>
    <Invoice CustID ="dps" name="Chris Peltzer" />
    <InvID id="105318" date'"2003-10-18" />
    </upgr:after>
    </upgr:sync>
</ROOT>
```

Figure 10.62   An attribute-centric query

As we have stated throughout this text, whether you decide to utilize element-centric or attribute-centric queries is a matter of personal choice, but also you must consider performance issues and processing power. Processing elements requires three separate steps, whereas attributes require only two steps. For example, the following code using elements-only requires three steps to process: `<Employee>Chris Peltzer</Employee>`. Once the parser locates the element's opening tag (step one), it must then process the contained data (step two). Finally, it encounters the element closing tag (step three), acknowledging it and advancing to the next element. In contrast, once the parser encounters the opening element tag (step one), it recognizes the attribute keyword and processes its value (step two). This is followed by recognizing the closing forward slash and continuing to the next element.

Certain situations exist in which elements are necessary because multiple attributes bearing the same name on an element are not permissible. For example, the following code is illegal:

```
<Table columnName="id" columnName="FName", columnName="LName"
/>
```

10.14 Addressing Special Issues with Updategrams

Several issues exist in which writing Updategrams requires special attention:

- Generating GUIDs
- Returning an `identity` column value
- Handling `null` values
- Managing characters valid in SQL but not in XML
- Data type conversion issues

The first item we want to address is generating Globally Unique Identifiers (GUIDs). A GUID is a 16-byte binary value that ensures that the GUID will be universally unique.

For example, let's assume the Business database we created in SQL requires a separate table for storing information concerning demographics for a specified county in Virginia. We are doing research for Corporation X. The company has subcontracted the research to AC Nielsen, which specializes in gathering information and generating reports. Corporation X is trying to decide whether to open a new retail outlet in Fairfax County, Virginia. (Incidentally, it is one of the most affluent counties in America.) We first need to create a new table in our Business database called `Research`. The code for creating the new table is shown in Figure 10.63.

```
Create table Research
Use Business
Go
( ResearchId    uniqueidentifier(16)   not null,
  RData                 ntext                    (16) )
```

Figure 10.63 Create a table named `Research`

Next we need to create the updategram that inserts a new row into the `Research` table. The Updategram uses the `updg:guid` attribute to generate the GUID value that is placed in placeholder `gValue`. The `NEWID()` `T-SQL` function is called when the SQL ISAPI extension DLL recognizes the GUID. Figure 10.64 shows the Updategram code.

```
<ROOT xmlns:updg="urn:schemas-microsoft-com:xml-updategram">
   <updg:sync>

   <updg:after>
   <Research updg:guid="gValue">
   <ResearchId>gValue</ResearchId>
   <RData>Affluent- Average:MBA </RData>
   </Research>
   </updg:after>
   </updg:sync>
</ROOT>
```

Figure 10.64   Updategram GUID.xml

GUID.xml is saved to the C:\virtual directory\template\GUID.xml subdirectory. To test the template, we typed the following URL in IE Explorer 6.2:

`http://localhost/Invoice/template/GUID.xml.`

PART 4

IMPLEMENTATION

The result returned in the browser is as follows:

```
<ROOT xmlns:updg="urn:schemas-microsoft-com:xml-updategram" />
```

We then queried the database in the SQL query analyzer that returned confirmation that the insert was successful:

```
Use Business
Go
SELECT * FROM Research
ResearchId                                    RData
──────────────────────────────────────────   ─────-


3CA92548-68FA-4A78-8538-28FE0663F713 Affluent- Average:MBA
```

We can also return the unique identifier using the code in Figure 10.65.

```
<ROOT xmlns:updg="urn:schemas-microsoft-com:xml-updategram">
    <updg:sync>
    <updg:before>
    </updg:before>

    <updg:after updg:returnid="gValue">
    <Research updg:guid="gValue">
    <ResearchId>gValue</ResearchId>
    <RData>Affluent</RData>
    </Research>
    </updg:after>
    </updg:sync>
</ROOT>
```

Figure 10.65   ReturnID

The returned result in the browser is as follows:

```
-<ROOT xmlns:updg="urn:schemas-microsoft-com:xml-updategram">
  - <returnid>
    <gValue>1A95213C-0C4D-4745-8362-0E2738CC88FC</gValue>
  </returnid>
</ROOT>
```

Now that we have learned how to create a GUID and return that ID, we can also handle NULL values. Use the `xsi_nil` attribute and specify the corresponding element it should be applied to, as shown in Figure 10.66.

```
<xsd:element name="fname" sql:field="firstName"
type="xsd:string" nillable="true"/>
```

Figure 10.66   Inserting an `xsi:nill` attribute

The corresponding mapping schema must specify `xsi:nil="true"`, as demonstrated in Figure 10.67.

```
<ROOT xmlns="urn:schemas-microsoft-com:xml-sql"
   xmlns:updg="urn:schemas-microsoft-com:xml-updategram"
   xmlns:xsi="http://www.w3.org/2001/XMLSchema-instance">

   <updg:sync mapping-schema="MySchema.xml">
   <updg:before/>
   <updg:after>
   <Employee EID="e103457" lname="Montaine">
   <fname xsi:nil="true">
   </fname>
   </Employee>
   </updg:after>
   </updg:sync>

</ROOT>
```

Figure 10.67   The mapping schema for `xsi:nil`

The updategram specifies the `<fname>` element as `xsi:nil` in the `<after>` block. Therefore, when the updategram is executed, the NULL value will be inserted in the `fname` column.

SQL Server allows spaces to exist in names (such as Order Info), whereas in XML, this constitutes an invalid, ill-formed portion of a source document. All we need to do is use character encoding. Consider the code in Figure 10.68.

```
<ROOT xmlns:updg="urn:schemas-microsoft-com:xml-updategram">
   <updg:sync>
   </updg:before >
   <updg:after>
   <Invoice_x0020_Info OrderNum= "813531" date="2003-10-18"
   ProductID="PD11" UnitPrice="$25.0" Qty="1"/>
   </updg:after>
   </updg:sync>
</ROOT>
```

Figure 10.68   Handling spaces in Updategrams

By inserting the x0020 between Invoice and Info, we easily eliminate the problem. The syntax is always `'_XHHHH_'`, where HHHH represents the four-digit hexadecimal UCS-2 code for the character in the most significant bit-first order.

Data type conversions are easily handled in Updategrams.

We assume the UnitPrice in a mapping schema is type money. Therefore, it is important to convert from a string to a money type. The dollar sign must be included as part of the data value. The updategram examines the Unit Price. If the first character is a dollar sign, the necessary conversion is applied. If a mapping schema is specified and the column data type is specified as dt:type=fixed.14.4, the dollar sign is not required. The mapping schema is responsible for applying the appropriate conversions to the Unit Price.

Summary

You have learned to apply newly acquired mapping techniques to your arsenal of programming techniques in XML. Here are the FOR XML clauses covered in this chapter:

- `FOR XML AUTO`
- `FOR XML RAW`
- `FOR XML EXPLICIT`

Each clause returns rowsets in a distinct format. Depending on the particular scenario, each querying technique retrieves raw data in a particular way. Specify column order using `FOR XML AUTO`. Elements map as table names, and attributes map as column names. Additionally, the `auto` mode provides control over tags but little control over the structure. Query results return as nested elements in tree format.

`FOR XML RAW` returns a rowset in which each row maps to a generic element named `<row>` in the `SELECT` query. Columns appear as attributes, whereas elements are prefixed with element `row`. A significant difference between `FOR XML AUTO` and `FOR XML RAW` exist: The `raw` query returns a rowset lacking a hierarchal tree format. The results are flattened and map easily to a relational database of other flat file repository.

`FOR XML EXPLICIT` offers full control over how we want rowsets to be formatted. Several unique features we covered include the following:

- Metadata provides information concerning column formatting.
- Tags describe the element tag number, usually defined as value 1.
- Tags specify the parent of the element being processed.
- Universal tables describe the metadata columns, thereby providing control over the shape of the XML tree.
- `OPENXML` provides a rowset view of an XML document.
- A `rowpattern` identifies the nodes in an XML document and is written using XPath pattern language.

PART 4

IMPLEMENTATION

- OPENXML allows us to specify default mapping by offering three choices: element-centric, attribute-centric, or mixed-mode mapping.
- The flags parameter specifies the mapping. The SchemaDeclaration and ColPatterns determine the mapping.
- Two stored procedures are called to obtain a document handle to pass to OPENXML:
  - sp_xml_preparedocument procures the document handle.
  - sp_xml_removedocument removes the DOM internal representation of the XML document from memory.
- A rowpattern identifies the nodes to process. ColName values match the corresponding XML attribute names.
- Pass the @idoc handle to a SQL query, including select, update, insert, or delete values specified in the OPENXML query.
- Create a table and pass the table name to a query in the WITH clause to provide a description of the rowset. Other options include specifying the rowset schema (column names, data type, and required mapping) or using an edge table.

Several metaproperty attributes provide an author with the capability to query data and return information about the query. In addition, several directives allow you to define the element/column relationship using the ID/IDREFS(s). You can also use the hide directive to exclude specified column names from a returned rowset. Other directives support element-returned rowsets, xml, CDATA, and xmlText. The latter directive is used to create an overflow column to hold elements/element data not stored in a relational table.

Retrieve the unconsumed data via a SQL query. Finally, function Text() allows you to store text comments with a document.

You learned how relational database tables could be queried as though the data resides in XML format. XML views provide a flexibility that the other SQL Server features do not. Views define the shape of an XML source document. Annotations, an important feature of XML views, allow us to describe the table/column relationship just as can be done in traditional SQL queries. We can also define primary key/foreign key relations; describe 1:1, 1: M, and M:N relationships; and perform joins of all types. An XSD schema defines the structure of an XML document. XPath queries are executed against the raw flat-formatted data and return it in XML format. We can also apply template queries against the relational data. Views are powerful tools for mapping to and from XML. You also learned the basics of updategrams and the numerous features they offer.

In conclusion, the new features in SQL Server 2000 empower the author to extend the traditional techniques used in normal SQL technology and forever influence the way we design interactive database applications for the future.

Self-Review Exercises

The following statements are either true or false. If they are false, provide an explanation of why you think the statement is incorrect.

1. SQL Server 2000 provides new functionality, which in reality is just old methods wrapped in new terminology.

2. ADO database technology has been enhanced in SQL Server 2000.

3. Columns map to table names, and elements map to columns.

4. `FOR XML` clauses come in three different formats: `OPENXML`, `FOR XML AUTO`, and `FOR XML EXPLICIT`.

5. ADO allows us to read relational database-formatted data as XML.

6. ADO queries return rowsets using a data provider.

7. The `FOR XML RAW` clause returns recordsets as element-centric formatted data.

8. `FOR XML AUTO` queries return recordsets mapped to a generic `<raw>` element.

9. `FOR XML AUTO, XMLDATA` returns rowsets formatted as attribute-centric formatted data.

10. Reserved keyword `XMLData` returns a schema appended to an XML query.

11. `FOR XML EXPLICIT` returns query rowsets in mixed mode.

12. A universal table specifies the shape of an XML query.

13. A FOR XML EXPLICIT query allows us to specify three type results:

    a. Mixed mode

    b. Element centric

    c. Attribute centric

14. Specifying xmlText allows us to return rowsets as text.

15. A schema declaration allows us to query relational data as though it were XML.

16. You can specify a table name in the WITH clause in XML views.

The next set of questions requires an explanation of *why* and *how* a directive or query keyword functions, such as how an OPENXML universal table maps elements/attributes.

17. You can return a rowset as an edge table. Explain what this means.

18. Explain how an XML view uses annotations. Provide an example.

19. Provide a description of how the directive xmlText functions.

20. What does "unconsumed data" mean? Demonstrate how this directive is used.

Projects

1. Create a four-tiered XML document.

2. Generate a DTD for this document.

3. Create an XSD schema for this document.

4. Map the XML document to a database.

5. Create the tables for this database.

6. Populate the database tables.

7. Write a SQL query using the FOR XML clause and using the XML document created in the first project. Also specify xmldata.

8. Write a SQL query using the FOR XML RAW clause for the XML document created in the first project.

9. Create a set of tables for a typical registration process. The tables should include Student, Professors, Course, CourseSchedule, and Classroom. Add primary keys.

10. Create an OPENXML query and specify the query as element centric.

11 A Brief Introduction to .NET

11.1 Introduction to the .NET Framework

The .NET Framework represents a completely new model for building systems on the Windows platform. In this chapter, we provide a thumbnail sketch of .NET to introduce you to this model. We highlight the essential features and increase your basic understanding of VB.NET and the .NET Framework with examples. This introduction does not serve as a comprehensive review; rather, it exists solely to get you started thinking about .NET. It is not possible to do this vast new technology justice in one or even several chapters. Another book being written by this author will cover the full complement of services and features that the .NET Framework offers you. However, for the present, we intend to whet your appetite and hope you will migrate to VB.NET from VB 6.0.

We recommend that you install Visual Studio.Net and the .NET Framework before you can work with the source code in this chapter.

11.2 .NET Framework: A Brief Description

.NET contains three .NET Framework specifications that serve as host for the primary group of programming languages, including VB.NET, Visual C++.NET, and C#. Visual Studio.NET provides an

PART 4
IMPLEMENTATION

Integrated Development Environment (IDE). Underlying all of this is the .NET Framework. The three specifications are as follows:

- Common Language Runtime (CLR)
- Common Type Specification (CTS)
- Common Language Specification (CLS)

In addition, .NET provides base class libraries that the primary programming languages targeting the .NET Framework share. Many third-party vendors are also providing .NET implementations for Perl, Python, and COBOL.

11.3 The Common Language Runtime

The Common Language Runtime (CLR) contains two core entities: runtime engine mscoree.dll and base class library mscorlib.dll. The CLR's primary task is to locate an assembly and find the required type within the binary. It reads the assembly's metadata and then compiles the Intermediate Language (IL) code into a platform-specific set of application-specific instructions. As an added bonus, it provides cross-language exception handling and cross-language debugging, something we all need.

The CLR offers total code integration. For example, a .NET-aware compiler can compile preexisting COM binaries and interact with new .NET binaries without conflict.

Another important task that the CLR performs is generating a .NET Assembly. When a .NET-aware compiler creates an EXE or DLL, the resulting module is the `Assembly`. It contains Microsoft Intermediate Language code as well as metadata describing in detail every type existing within the binary. It also contains the Assembly version. (This is why COM binaries can intermingle with .NET binaries without creating a crash).

The .NET Assembly contains a .NET Manifest (see Figure 11.1). It provides a detailed description of the Assembly and specifies a list of externally referenced assemblies required for execution.

```
.assembly extern mscorlib
{
  .publickeytoken = (B7 7A 5C 56 19 34 E0 89 )        // .z\V.4..
  .ver 1:0:3300:0
}
.assembly extern Microsoft.VisualBasic
{
  .publickeytoken = (B0 3F 5F 7F 11 D5 0A 3A )    // .?_....:
  .ver 7:0:3300:0
}
.assembly extern System
{
  .publickeytoken = (B7 7A 5C 56 19 34 E0 89 )        // .z\V.4..
  .ver 1:0:3300:0
}
.assembly extern System.Data
{
  .publickeytoken = (B7 7A 5C 56 19 34 E0 89 )  // .z\V.4..
  .ver 1:0:3300:0
}
.assembly extern System.Xml
{
  .publickeytoken = (B7 7A 5C 56 19 34 E0 89 )  // .z\V.4..
  .ver 1:0:3300:0
}
.assembly ViewAssembly
{
  .custom instance void
[mscorlib]System.Reflection.AssemblyTrademarkAttribute::.ctor(s
tring) =
 ( 01 00 00 00 00 )
  // —— The following custom attribute is added automatically,
do not uncomment ——
  //  .custom instance void
[mscorlib]System.Diagnostics.DebuggableAttribute::.ctor(bool,
```

```
       //
bool) = ( 01 00 01 01 00 00 )
   .custom instance void
[mscorlib]System.Runtime.InteropServices.GuidAttribute::.ctor(s
tring) =
   ( 01 00 24 41 43 34 31 41 45 33 31 2D 43 37 44 43    //
..$AC41AE31-C7DC
        2D 34 45 35 34 2D 39 37 45 46 2D 30 32 43 41 36    // -
4E54-97EF-02CA6   43 45 30 32 39 34 45 00 00 )
// CE0294E..
   .custom instance void
[mscorlib]System.CLSCompliantAttribute::.ctor(bool) = ( 01 00
01 00 00 )
   .custom instance void
[mscorlib]System.Reflection.AssemblyProductAttribute::.ctor(str
ing) = ( 01 00 00 00 00 )
   .custom instance void
[mscorlib]System.Reflection.AssemblyCopyrightAttribute::.ctor(s
tring) = ( 01 00 00 00 00 )
   .custom instance void
[mscorlib]System.Reflection.AssemblyCompanyAttribute::.ctor(str
ing) = ( 01 00 00 00 00 )
   .custom instance void
[mscorlib]System.Reflection.AssemblyDescriptionAttribute::.ctor
(string) = ( 01 00 00 00 00 )
   .custom instance void
[mscorlib]System.Reflection.AssemblyTitleAttribute::.ctor(strin
g) = ( 01 00 00 00 00 )
   .hash algorithm 0x00008004
   .ver 1:0:907:22791
}
.module ViewAssembly.exe
// MVID: {6E7682F1-0E71-4169-A9D9-2CC80CBD0545}
.imagebase 0x11000000
.subsystem 0x00000003
.file alignment 511
.corflags 0x00000001
// Image base: 0x03190000
```

Figure 11.1 Displaying the Manifest

The CLR generates single-file assemblies and multifile assemblies. The first type represents a single binary. The latter type contains more than one binary, called a module. Modules allow you to partition a multifile assembly, thereby facilitating the creation of an easy deployment model.

> **Note:** "Managed code" is the term used to describe instances of objects you create that are managed by the runtime. The container holding the IL code is the Assembly.

The CLR offers memory management and tracks references to objects. When all references are no longer present, it removes them from memory through a process called garbage collection.

11.4 The Common Type Specification (Data Types and Namespaces)

A *type* refers to a collection of classes, interfaces, structures, delegates, and enumerations, supported by the runtime engine. You can build your own custom types and group them into unique namespaces. This eliminates name conflicts between assemblies.

Table 11.1 provides an overview of the .NET namespaces.

Table 11.1   .NET Namespaces

.NET Namespace	Practical Meaning
System	A set of classes pertaining to garbage collection, primitive types, math manipulations, and so on.
System.Collections	This defines container objects such as ArrayLists, Queues, and so on.
System.Data.Oledb	These namespaces are all commonly linked to database functionality.
System.Data	
System.Data.Common	
System.Data.SqlClient	

PART 4
IMPLEMENTATION

507

Table 11.1   .NET Namespaces, continued

.NET Namespace	Practical Meaning
`System.IO`	This namespace deals with File IO and so on.
`System.Reflection.Emit` `System.Reflection`	Reflection allows you to examine IL code and assemblies at runtime. It also supports dynamic creation.
`System.Net`	This contains types related to network programming.
`System.Diagnostics`	This allows language-neutral debugging.

`System.Drawing`
`System.Drawing2D`
`System.Drawing.Printing`
	This namespace deals with GDI, bitmaps, icons, fonts, and so on.

`System.Runtime.InteropServices` `System.Runtime.Remoting`	This allows you to interact with unmanaged code such as COM Servers, Win32 DLLs, and so on.
`System.Threading`	This enables multithreading, including types Mutex, Thread, and Timeout.
`System.Security`	This deals with .NET security such as classes that support permissions and so on.
`System.Windows.Forms`	This namespace allows the construction of dialog boxes, windows, and so on.
`System.Web`	This category includes a number of namespaces dealing with building web services, web applications, ASP.NET.
`System.Xml`	These are classes representing core XML primitives and types enabling interaction with XML data.

The Common Type Specification "structure" replaces VB 6.0 types. You may recall how VB 6.0 supported the `Type` keyword, allowing you to create a user-defined type (UDT). In the .NET world, structure defines numerical types such as rectangles, complex numbers, and so on. The CTS provides information on all data types supported by the runtime. It specifically describes how these data types can interact with each other by examining metadata describing these types. Note how the CTS defines a common set of types, thereby allowing .NET binaries to interact across all platforms with languages conforming to the .NET Framework. Structures can implement an infinite number of interfaces but are not allowed to derive from other base types. This means they are sealed.

The .NET module represents a class type.

Note: Public functions, subroutines, and member variables declared within a module scope are "shared" members, directly accessible throughout the entire application. In essence, a module is global in scope. One caveat exists: Modules are not creatable.

11.5 The Common Language Specification

The Common Language Specification contains guidelines describing in detail the set of rules that a .NET compiler must support for generated code to be eligible for hosting by the CLR. By doing so, all languages targeting the .NET platform share the IL code. Here is a brief summary of the rules:

- CLS rules apply to only CLS types.
- Public member definitions should be CLS types.
- Method parameters should be CLS types.
- Public members accessible to subclasses must be CLS types.

Table 11.2 provides information concerning CLS data types:

PART 4
IMPLEMENTATION

Table 11.2   CLS Data Types

VB.NET Type	.NET Base Type	CLS Compliant
Byte	System.Byte	Yes
System.SByte	System.SByte	Not supported
Short	System.Int16	Yes
Integer	System.Int32	Yes
Long	System.Int64	Yes
System.UInt16	System.UInt16	Not supported
System.Uint32	SystemUInt32	Not supported
System.Uint32	System.UInt32	Not supported
System.Uint64	System.Uint64	Not supported
Single	System.Single	Yes
Double	System.Double	Yes
Boolean	System.Boolean	Yes
Object	System.Object	Yes
Char	System.Char	Yes
String	System.String	Yes
Decimal	System.Decimal	Yes
IntPtr	System.IntPtr	Yes
UIntPtr	System.UIntPtr	Not supported

The CLS is still in a state of flux, but the basics are established. Always make sure you program with CLS-compliant data types to ensure interoperability with various other .NET languages. These rules apply only to externally exposed items. Private variables declared within a function or subroutine can use nonsupported data types and still maintain interoperability.

11.6 Examining Microsoft Intermediate Language (IL)

Let's examine the MSIL to get a feeling for an IL Assembly and view its contents. Figure 11.2 presents a simple class named `MaxValue`. (It is a code fragment.) Once the compiler compiles this code, it generates a single file Assembly containing a Manifest, IL instructions, and metadata. The latter category provides information concerning each module item. See Section 11.6 for a description of metadata.

```
int maximum (int x, int y, int z)
{
    int max = x;
    if (y > max)
    max = y;
    if z > max)
    max = z;
    return max;
}
```

Figure 11.2   Class `MaxValue`

A Description of Metadata

Metadata is information about data. Metadata is the key to understanding how .NET functions. The compiler generates metadata and stores it in an executable (EXE) or DLL. A major benefit that the .NET Framework offers is the set of application programming interfaces (APIs) it provides to export metadata to and from an XML schema or COM type library. Figure 11.3 represents the IL code for the class `MaxValue`.

```
C:\VisualStudioExamples\ViewAssembly\obj\Debug\ViewAssembly.exe
MANIFEST
ViewAssembly
    Module1
        .class private auto ansi sealed
        .custom instance void
        [Microsoft.VisualBasicMicrosoft.VisualBasic.CompilerServi
        ces.StandardModuleAttribute::..clon()=(01 00 00 00)
        MaxValue
        .class nested public auto ansi
        .ctor:void()
        SelectMax : int32(int32,int32)
        Main : void()
```

Figure 11.3   Class `MaxValue` IL Manifest

The following items exist within the deployment unit (Assembly):

- Name, version, and culture
- A public key providing verification
- All types exported by the assembly
- Existing dependencies, meaning other Assemblies that this assembly depends on
- Security
- Attributes created by the user (custom)
- Compiler-defined attributes
- Base classes and/or interfaces that the Assembly utilizes

The ILDasm.exe tool provided by Visual Studio.NET allows us to peek under the hood to view both the Manifest and the Assembly for class `MaxValue`. Notice the icon representing a module. The metadata describes the class as private. The sealed class designation means `MaxValue` cannot function as a base class for other classes. `MaxValue` contains a single function called `SelectMax`: `int32(int32,int32)`. `Sub Main()` is the class entry point.

Table 11.3 will help you understand the code we examine in the Manifest.

Table 11.3 Manifest Intermediate Language Tags

Manifest Tag	Interpretation
`.Assembly`	Denotes the Assembly declaration
`.file`	Denotes files existing in the Assembly
`.Assembly extern`	The assembly reference indicating that another Assembly contains items referenced by the current module
`.class extern`	Classes exported by the Assembly but declared in another module
`.exeloc`	Provides information concerning the location of the executable for the assembly

Table 11.3   Manifest Intermediate Language Tags, continued

Manifest Tag	Interpretation
`.module`	Denotes a *.netmodule
`.module extern`	Denotes that other modules contained within this module have items referenced within this module
`.publickey`	Represents bytes of the public key
`.publickeytoken`	Contains a token of the public key

Let's view the manifest by double-clicking MANIFEST to display the metadata. Note the Assembly version; also observe the references to namespaces. Every assembly contains an associated Manifest. It contains metadata specifying the name and version of the Assembly. For example, the mscorlib carries version 1:0:3300:0. The publickeytoken is present only because the assembly is configured as a shared assembly and references the public key of the binary. (You'll learn more about shared assemblies later in this chapter when we discuss the Global Assembly Cache.)

The first portion of the Assembly references all external assemblies required by the current Assembly to operate successfully. The Manifest makes use of mscorlib.dll, meaning .Assembly extern mscorlib.

The second segment of the Manifest enumerates each module contained within the Assembly. `.custom instance void [mscorlib]System.Reflection.AssemblyDescriptionAttribute::.ctor(string) = ( 01 00 00 00 00 )` demonstrates how `Reflection` gathers metadata at runtime about the Assembly. You can load the assembly at runtime and procure a list of all types contained within a module. This includes methods, events, fields, and properties. The next item of interest is the underlying IL code (see Figure 11.4).

PART 4

IMPLEMENTATION

```
 MaxValue::SelectMax : int32(int32,int32)

.method public instance int32  SelectMax(int32 x,
                   int32 y) cil managed
{
 // Code size      21 (0x15)
 .maxstack  2
 .locals init ([0] int32 SelectMax)
 IL_0000: nop
 IL_0001: Idarg.1
 IL_0002: Idarg.2
 IL_0003: ble.s    IL_0009
 IL_0005: Idarg.1
 IL_0006: stloc.0
 IL_0007: br.s     IL_0013
 IL_0009: nop
 IL_000a: Idarg.1
 IL_000b: Idarg.2
 IL_000c: bge.s    IL_0012
 IL_000e: Idarg.2
 IL_000f: stloc.0
 IL_0010: br.s     IL_0013
 IL_0012: nop
 IL_0013: Idloc.0
 IL_0014: ret
} // end of method MaxValue::SelectMax
```

Figure 11.4   Viewing IL code

If you double-click on `.class nested public auto ansi`, you will see the underlying code:

```
  MaxValue
    ▶ .class nested public auto ansi
```

```
.class auto ansi nested public MaxValue
       extends [mscorlib]System.Object
{
} // end of class MaxValue
```

The next item of interest is the actual metadata for each type contained within the Manifest (see Figure 11.5).

```
TypeDef #2
_____

   TypDefName: MaxValue   (02000003)
   Flags     : [NestedPublic] [AutoLayout] [Class] [AnsiClass]
(00000002)
```

```
Extends    : 01000001 [TypeRef] System.Object
EnclosingClass : ViewAssembly.Module1 (02000002)
Method #1
————————————————————————————

    MethodName: .ctor (06000002)
    Flags      : [Public] [ReuseSlot] [SpecialName]
    [RTSpecialName] [.ctor]   (00001806)
    RVA         : 0x00002088
    ImplFlags : [IL] [Managed]  (00000000)
    CallCnvntn: [DEFAULT]
    hasThis
    ReturnType: Void
    No arguments.


Method #2
————————————————————————————

    MethodName: SelectMax (06000003)
    Flags      : [Public] [ReuseSlot]  (00000006)
    RVA         : 0x00002094
    ImplFlags : [IL] [Managed]  (00000000)
    CallCnvntn: [DEFAULT]
    hasThis
    ReturnType: I4
    2 Arguments
      Argument #1:   I4
      Argument #2:   I4
    2 Parameters
        (1) ParamToken : (08000001) Name : x flags: [none]
        (00000000)
        (2) ParamToken : (08000002) Name : y flags: [none]
        (00000000)
```

Figure 11.5   Viewing the Manifest metadata

The .NET runtime uses this metadata to locate the assembly, invoke methods, and create object instances.

Examining Common Type Specification Types

The Common Type System specifies how all types—classes, interfaces, enums, and structures—must be defined to qualify as a member of the Common Type System.

> **Note:** All Common Type structures derive from the common base class System.ValueType. This base class enforces structure behavior, meaning it ensures that the structure functions as a stack-based entity rather than a heap-based entity.

- Structures can implement limitless numbers of interfaces. However, they are sealed, meaning they cannot function as a base class for other classes.
- CTS classes (like all classes) contain public and private properties, public member functions, and visibility characteristics. They include public, protected, friend, and private traits. These traits determine whether other assemblies can or cannot use this class. These traits are declared as follows:
  - MustInherit
  - Shadows
  - Shared

  MustInherit supports polymorphic behavior on derived types, whereas Shadows hides base class implementations. Shared means that class members must be bound at either the class level or the object level. The latter is the default.
- CTS interfaces represent an assemblage of methods, properties, and events.
- Interfaces can derive from other interfaces.

Single and Multifile Shared Assemblies

So far, we have examined a single Assembly and its Manifest. A single Assembly can also consist of multiple modules. A private Assembly is meant for use by an application residing on a single machine. It is time to build an Assembly containing a client. Let's build a type library in VB.NET called RegistratrionProcess. The scope of this project is simple and goes like this: RegistrationProcess represents a university student registration system. You can register new students, assign them to classes, check for registration payment, list professors, and so on. This simple application provides us with the opportunity to examine how to create and use a library, set properties, view collections of objects, create client classes to test the primary application, discuss events in Visual Basic.NET, and generate a strong name for an Assembly. Additionally, we will discuss the Global Assembly Cache and learn how to use it. Let's get started.

Building Your First Class Library

In Visual Studio.NET, create a new project and name it RegistrationProcess.

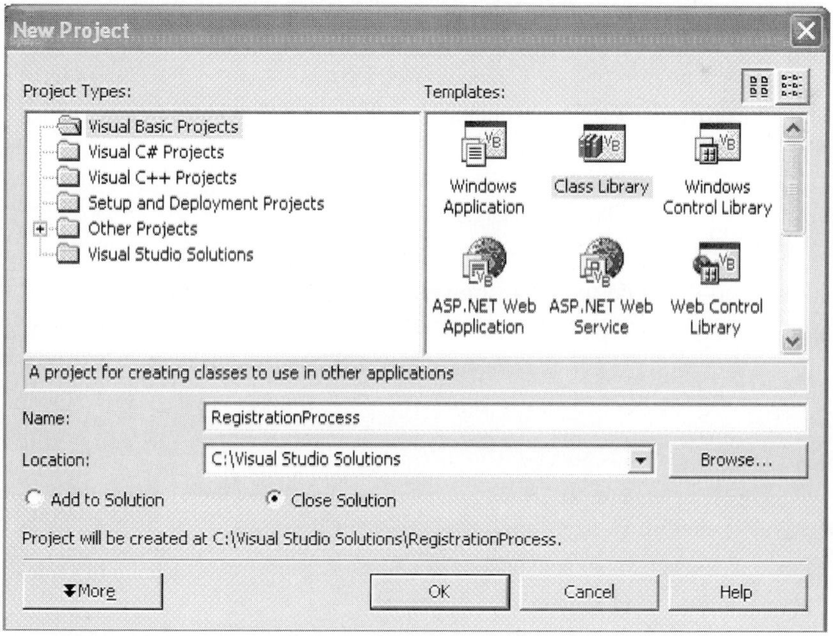

Figure 11.6   Creating your first Class library

From the View menu, select the Solution Explorer and note how Visual Studio.NET has created a single class called Public Class Class1. Rename it Public Class Student. Also, notice that Class1.vb should be renamed Student.vb. You accomplish this by right-clicking the Class1.vb icon and selecting Rename. Make sure your project name is RegistrationProcess.

In VB.NET, a module contains a .vb extension. Additionally, your source code can contain more than one class. We will demonstrate this shortly with some code examples.

Several other notable items may appear new to you if this is your first visit to the Visual Studio.NET IDE. A constructor is missing, as is the designer. However, you can change this by selecting the project name, RegistrationProcess, and clicking on Add Component. When the dialog window appears, select the Component class (see Figure 11.7).

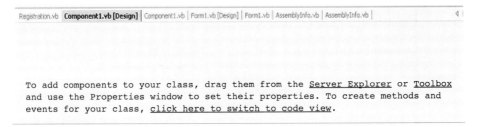

Figure 11.7   Adding a Component class

When you select 'click here to switch to code view', it brings you to the code window shown in Figure 11.8.

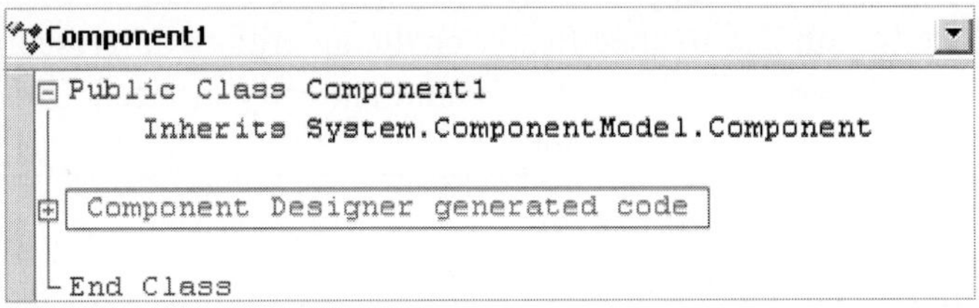

Figure 11.8   Component1.vb

This class allows you to drag controls onto it and create other data components. Public Class Component1.vb inherits from base class Component in System.ComponentModel.

Adding Properties to Your RegistrationProcess Class

Let's create a new student name and begin the registration process (see Figure 11.9).

```
Public Class Student
    Dim msStudentName As String

Public Property StudentName () As String
      Get
          Return msStudentName
      End Get
      Set(ByVal Value As String)
          msStudentName = Value
      End Set
End Property
End Class
```

Figure 11.9   Creating a new student name

First, we declare msStudentName As String. Following the declaration, when you typed Property StudentName() As String, some code was automatically added for you. All you need to do is fill in the following code in the Get/Set segment: Return msStudentName. In the Set section, add the following code: msStudentName=Value. That was easy.

PART 4
IMPLEMENTATION

> **Note:** In VB6.0, you had to specifically create an argument to receive a value. In VB.NET, an incoming value is automatically inserted. This represents a significant improvement.

Although our class has only one property so far, let's create a test client and make sure our code works.

11.7 Building a Test Client

Select 'New' from the File menu to generate a Windows application (see Figure 11.10).

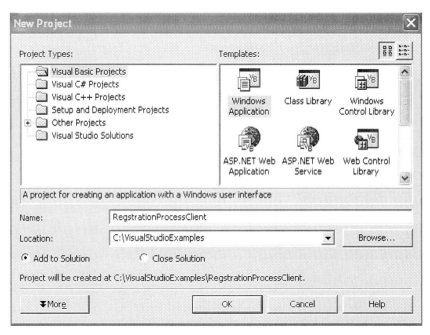

Figure 11.10   Creating a Windows project

Additionally, check to make sure you add this new Windows application to the solution. You could also create a client and close the existing project. Then you would have to add an `Imports` statement to access the class library code. In any case, add the following statement to your class: `'Imports RegistrationProcess'`. Make sure you add it before the `Public Class` declaration. Now right-click 'RegistrationProcessClient' in Solution Explorer to set it as the startup project (see Figure 11.11).

Figure 11.11   Setting the client as startup project

Setting RegistrationProcessClient as the startup project highlights it in bold. Next let's add some code to Form1.vb. From the View menu, select Toolbars.

Drag a button onto the form. Change the text property to Click Me. Then double-click the button to access the button1 subroutine:

```
Private Sub Button1_Click(ByVal sender As System.Object, ByVal
e As System.EventArgs) Handles msFirstName.Click
        Dim myStudent As New RegistrationProcess.Student()
        myStudent.StudentName = "Steve Heim"
        MsgBox(myStudent.StudentName)
```

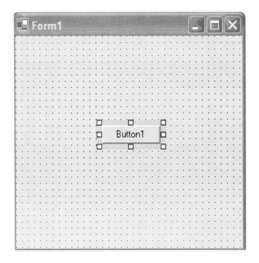

In Solution Explorer, right-click the References node for the RegistrationProcessClient project. Select the Projects tab. The dialog box displays the RegistrationProcessClient.dll in the upper window.

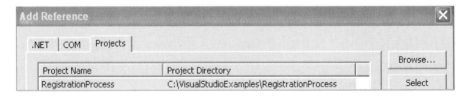

Select the project name so that it displays in the lower
Components window.

Component Name	Type	Source	Remove
RegistrationProcess	Project	C:\VisualStudioExamples\Regist...	

Selected Components:

OK   Cancel   Help

You have just imported the namespace containing the Student
class.

> **Note:** In VB.NET, all projects have a default namespace. Both project
> name and namespace share the same name.

From the Build menu, select Build RegistrationProcess to compile
the Assembly. You have two options for building it:

• Debug mode
• Release Mode

The first option compiles with debug information but does not
include any code optimizations. The second option compiles without
any symbolic debug information. Obviously, when you have completed your application and thoroughly debugged it, you should
choose the 'Release' mode. However, we are just beginning to build
the classes, so select the Debug option.

PART 4
IMPLEMENTATION

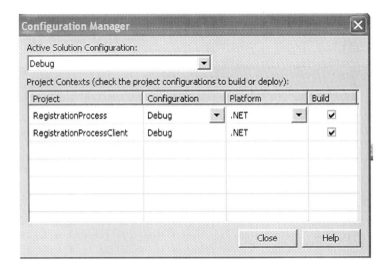

Let's investigate the compilation process and examine the project directory. Two files now reside in the bin directory:

- RegistrationProcess.dll
- RegistrationProcess.pdb

The .dll extension is the assembly. The .pdb extension is the debug file accompanying the RegistrationProcess.dll. PDB means program database.

Now let's run the application and view the generated output.

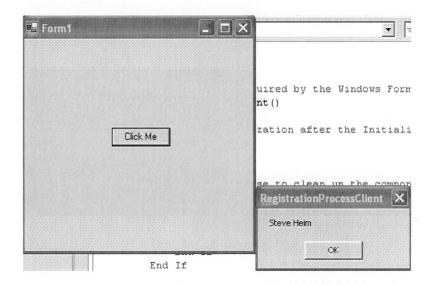

Voila! It works. Before examining the Assembly, let's continue exploring some other exciting new features that VB.NET offers. Here are some of the items we'll explore:

- Creating objects in memory using the New keyword
- WithEvents
- RaiseEvents
- AddHandler
- Adding methods to your class
- Default properties
- Parameterized properties

11.8 Creating Objects in Memory Using the New Keyword

Let's examine the code we previously entered:

```
Dim myStudent As New RegistrationProcess.Student ()
```

PART 4
IMPLEMENTATION

525

The New keyword creates the object in memory immediately. This is a significant improvement over VB 6.0, where you had to check to make sure the object was instantiated in memory.

11.9 Using the Event Keyword

You can apply the Event keyword to check whether a student has paid his registration bill before admitting him to classes. Two options are available:

- The WithEvents keyword
- The AddHandler keyword.

Let's examine the following code:

```
Event PayBill(ByVal PaymentType As String)
    Public Property StudentID() As String
        Get
            Return msStudID
        End Get
        Set(ByVal Value As String)
            msStudID = Value
            'check to see if bill is paid
            RaiseEvent PayBill ("BillPaid")
        End Set
    End Property
```

First we create a variable as follows for the preceding code:

```
Dim msStudID As String
```

Then you need to declare your object, along with the accompanying WithEvents keyword. Global scope is an issue here. Modules are global. Therefore, declare WithEvents at module level because you cannot declare the keyword inside a procedure.

You could also do the following:

```
Dim WithEvents Student as New Student
```

The second option, AddHandler, is preferable. Let's explain why. First, using AddHandler eliminates the need to define a new class to use the WithEvents keyword. Simply include an AddHandler statement; bind the specified event with the newly created procedure to handle your event. Second, you can create a single procedure to handle more than one event.

```
Protected Sub Button1_Click(ByVal sender as Object,_
  ByVal e As System.EventArgs) Handles Button1.Click
      Dim Student as New Student()
      AddHandler Student.PayBill, AddressOf
Me.CheckBillHandler

Private Sub CheckBillHandler(ByVal PayBill as String)
    ' other code goes here
End Sub
```

11.10 Creating Methods in Your Class

Once a student has settled his account, admissions can accept him as a matriculating student. Here is code for the Admit() function.

```
Public Function Accept() As Boolean
        'Add student to class roster
        Return True
End Function
End Class
```

Once you have created this function, you can call it like this:

```
If Student.Admit Then 'AssignClasses'
```

11.11 Using Parameterized Properties

A student attends many classes and has more than one professor. We can add a ProfessorList as follows:

First declare the `ProfessorList` as a collection of names:

```
Dim ProfessorList As New Collection()
```

Then add this code to your class:

```
Default Public ReadOnly Property Professors _
(ByVal iIndex As Integer) As Professor
    Get
        Return CType(ProfessorList (iIndex), Professor)
    End Get
End Property
```

A few items need clarification. Notice how you can declare a `Default` property. This is possible only if the property contains more than one parameter, as is the case here. Another important item concerns this line of code:

```
Return CType (ProfessorList(iIndex), Professor)
```

Because `OptionStrict` (the default) is on, it prevents a conversion from a `Collection` type to a `Professor` type. Therefore, use `CType` and the conversion succeeds. Simply pass in both object (`ProfessorList`) and the class type (`Professor`).

11.12 Examining the Delegate Keyword

Let's examine the Delegate keyword and observe the following list:

- .NET delegates represent a class deriving from MulticastDelegate. The delegate is object oriented and type safe.
- A delegate contains three important pieces of information:
  - The method name it calls
  - Arguments passed to the method, if any
  - The return value
- Delegate types represent pointers referencing methods it calls rather than pointing to a specified memory address.

> **Note:** VB 6.0 pointers reference a specific memory address, in direct contrast to .NET delegates.

Understanding .NET Events

In this section, we examine the .NET Events keyword. The following list provides information on this keyword.

- The .NET delegate serves as the backbone for the .NET `Event` keyword. For example, you use the .NET `Event` keyword to create a new delegate.
- Send an event using the `RaiseEvent` keyword. The consequence of this is that the underlying IL automatically calls `System.MultiDelegate.Invoke()`.
- Use the `VB.NET AddressOf` keyword to create a new instance of the `MultiCastDelegate` type. It points automatically to the designated method.
- Delegates are also useful for callback functions.
- The new `Handles` keyword syntactically binds a method name to a particular event. The name of a method event is irrelevant when applying this keyword.
- The `Handles` keyword allows you to configure multiple methods to listen to the same event.

The compiler automatically generates the following information each time you declare a new event:

- Add a new, nested, hidden delegate to your class. The delegate name is always <EventName>EventHandler.
- Add two hidden public functions: the first containing an `add_` prefix and the second having a `remove_` prefix.

PART 4
IMPLEMENTATION

11.13 Adding a New Class

It is possible to add a new class by doing the following:

```
Public Class Professor
    Dim miProfID As Integer
    Public Property ProfessorID() As Integer
        Get
            Return miProfID
        End Get
        Set (ByVal Value As Integer)
            miProfID = Value
        End Set
    End Property

    Public ReadOnly Property GradeStatus() As String
        Get
            'Check database for any failing grades
            'Grant Degree if all classes are completed
        End Get
    End Property
End Class
```

For classes to be covered, we need to create `Class Professor` and create a variable `miProfID` as an `Integer` type. We also create a `Read Only Property GradeStatus`, hereby allowing the registrar to make sure the student completes all academic obligations before he can graduate.

We need a driver to take advantage of our classes, therefore it is useful to compile the code and then discuss a multifile Assembly, the Global Assembly Cache, and learn how the runtime engine locates the Assembly. Examine the code in Figure 11.12 and observe the Registration Process in action.

```
Imports RegistrationProcess
Public Class Student
    Dim msStudentName As String
    Dim msStudID As String
    Dim Professor As String
    Dim ProfessorList As New Collection()
```

```
    Public Property StudentName() As String
        Get
            Return msStudentName
        End Get
        Set (ByVal Value As String)
            msStudentName = Value
        End Set
    End Property

    Default Public ReadOnly Property Professors _
    (ByVal iIndex As Integer) As Professor
        Get
            Return CType (ProfessorList (iIndex), Professor)
        End Get
    End Property

    Event PayBill (ByVal PaymentType As String)
    Public Property Student ID() As String
        Get
            Return msStudID
        End Get
        Set (ByVal Value As String)
            msStudID = Value
            'Check to see if bill is paid
            RaiseEvent PayBill ("BillPaid")
        End Set
    End Property

    Public Function Accept () As Boolean
        'Add student to class roster
        Return True
    End Function
End Class


Public Class Professor
    Dim miProfID As Integer
    Public Property ProfessorID() As Integer
        Get
            Return miProfID
        End Get
```

```
        Set (ByVal Value As Integer)
            miProfID = Value
        End Set
    End Property


    Public ReadOnly Property GradeStatus() As String
        Get
            'Check database for any failing grades
            'Grant Degree if all classes are completed
        End Get
    End Property
End Class
```

Figure 11.12   Public Class RegistrationProcess

Let's compile it to make sure it is correct. It does compile successfully.

One of the goals of object-oriented programming is reuse of code. We would like to use the Assembly in other applications. The following section discusses this topic beginning by creating a 'strong name', thereby making the assembly global in scope. You must create the *'strong name'* before you can drag it into the *Global Cache Assembly*. Then the assembly becomes visible and accessible to other applications. Let's see how this works in the next section.

11.14 Making RegistrationProcess.dll Reusable

It is possible to make an Assembly global in scope by creating a new Windows project and adding a reference to it, just as we did with the RegistrationProcessClient earlier in this chapter. Then we create a 'strong name'. It contains the following information:

```
' Version information for the Assembly consists of the follow-
  ing four values:
  '
  '       Major Version
```

```
'       Minor Version
'       Build Number
'       Revision
'
' You can specify all the values or you can default the Build
  and Revision Numbers
' by using the '*' as shown below:
```

```
<Assembly: AssemblyVersion("1.0.*")>
```

The assembly's 'identity', its 'simple text name', version number, and culture information, as well as a public key and digital signature ensure the assembly's global identity. The strong name is generated from the Assembly file containing the Manifest, which in turn contains names and hashes of all files that comprise the Assembly.

Strong names guarantee name uniqueness by relying on unique key pairs. Additionally, a strong name protects the version you have created. No one can produce another version of your assembly. Another important aspect of a strong name is that it provides a strong security check. However, do not think a strong name implies a level of trust. It does not.

Versioning is the mechanism for allowing conflicting name Assemblies sharing the same name to live side by side. This prevents DLL hell! Note that strong-named Assemblies can only reference other strong-named Assemblies.

As previously mentioned, an Assembly's version identifier contains two basic pieces of information:

- A friendly text string name
- A numeric identifier

The first and second digits identify the major and minor version of the assembly, 1.0 in this case. The third digit marks the build number, followed by a current revision number (if any). The .NET runtime utilizes the assembly version to ensure that the appropriate binary is loaded on behalf of the client.

PART 4
IMPLEMENTATION

533

11.15 Creating a Strong Name

Early beta versions of Visual Studio.NET listed Strong Name on the Tools menu. This is no longer the case. Don't despair, however, because creating a strong name for an assembly is essential. Microsoft has provided an alternative way for you to do so. Let's step through the process. To create a strong name, do the following:

From the Tools menu, select External Tools. The following dialog box will appear:

Then select 'Add' and, in the 'Title' field, type an appropriate name. (Create Strong Name is appropriate.) Make sure the title relates to this topic. In the 'Command' field, double-click the ellipsis and browse the path to "C:\ProgramFiles\Visual Studio.Net\FrameworkSDK\bin". Double-click on 'sn.exe' to place it in this field.

Bin				▼	⇦ ▾ 🔄	🔍 ✕ 📋	▦ ▾ Tools ▾

Name ▲	Size	Type	Date Modified ⌃
mscordmp	60 KB	Application	1/5/2002 1:32
nmake	80 KB	Application	1/5/2002 6:49
PermView	56 KB	Application	1/5/2002 1:32
PEVerify	56 KB	Application	1/5/2002 1:32
ResGen	36 KB	Application	1/5/2002 1:00
SecUtil	16 KB	Application	1/5/2002 1:01
setreg	55 KB	Application	9/12/2001 4:2
signcode	26 KB	Application	9/12/2001 4:2
sn	68 KB	Application	1/5/2002 1:32

This utility creates the SNK file. Several flags exist for creating the Strong Name. The only one we are currently concerned with is the '–k' flag. The template looks like this: `<filename>.snk`. It is wise to provide a name representing your class. Then select <initial directory> and specify where you want to store your strong name. We placed it in the project directory for easy access. Check the output window so that you can see your Strong Name being created. Finally, select 'OK'. From the Tools directory, you will find Strong Name listed. Select it to create a strong name for your Assembly. Look in your project directory to ensure that your strong name is actually there.

RegistrationProcess				▼	← ▾ 🔄	🔍 ✕ 📋	▦ ▾ Tools ▾

Name ▲	Size	Type	Date Modified
bin		File Folder	7/3/2002 4:22 PM
obj		File Folder	7/3/2002 4:08 PM
AssemblyInfo.vb	2 KB	Visual Basic Source	7/10/2002 11:58 /
Component1.resx	2 KB	.NET XML Resource ...	9/19/2001 6:24 PI
Component1.vb	2 KB	Visual Basic Source	7/3/2002 4:11 PM
Registration	1 KB	Strong name key	7/10/2002 11:55 /
Registration.vb	2 KB	Visual Basic Source	7/5/2002 12:03 PI
RegistrationProcess	2 KB	Visual Studio Solution	7/3/2002 4:22 PM
RegistrationProcess	1 KB	Strong name key	7/5/2002 12:04 PI
RegistrationProcess	4 KB	Visual Basic .NET Pr...	7/3/2002 4:22 PM
RegistrationProcess.vbproj	2 KB	Visual Studio Projec...	7/11/2002 12:04 F

It is indeed there. One final step is to use `gacutil.exe`, also located in the same directory as the `sn.exe` utility. Then copy the assembly to the Global Assembly Cache so that it is available for reuse by other applications. Then, from the Command window, type the following to place the Assembly in the GAC: **gacutil /i Registration.dll.** A much easier method is available, however; drag and drop the assembly to GAC located in C:\Windows\Assembly. Note: from the command line, use the gacutil.exe.

Global Assembly Name	Type	Version	Culture	Public Key Token
Microsoft.VisualStudioAnalyzer.EventSubscriber		7.0.3300.0		b03f5f7f11d50a3a
Microsoft.VisualStudioAnalyzer.PrimaryEventCollector		7.0.3300.0		b03f5f7f11d50a3a
Microsoft.Vsa		7.0.3300.0		b03f5f7f11d50a3a
Microsoft.Vsa.Vb.CodeDOMProcessor		7.0.3300.0		b03f5f7f11d50a3a
Microsoft.VSDesigner	Native Images	7.0.3300.0		b03f5f7f11d50a3a
Microsoft.VSDesigner	Native Images	7.0.3300.0		b03f5f7f11d50a3a
Microsoft.VSDesigner	Native Images	7.0.3300.0		b03f5f7f11d50a3a
Microsoft_VsaVb		7.0.3300.0		b03f5f7f11d50a3a
msatinterop		7.0.3300.0		b03f5f7f11d50a3a
mscorcfg		1.0.3300.0		b03f5f7f11d50a3a
mscorlib	Native Images	1.0.3300.0		b77a5c561934e089
MSDATASRC		7.0.3300.0		b03f5f7f11d50a3a
MSDDSLMP		7.0.3300.0		b03f5f7f11d50a3a
MSDDSP		7.0.3300.0		b03f5f7f11d50a3a
Office		7.0.3300.0		b03f5f7f11d50a3a
Regcode		1.0.3300.0		b03f5f7f11d50a3a
RegistrationProcess		1.0.921.19495		6cf7280fa2c28aa9

You can see RegistrationProcess residing within the GAC.

RegistrationProcess	1.0.921.19495	6cf7280fa2c28aa9

You can also verify that a Strong Name has been created by right-clicking 'RegistrationProcess' in the Solution Explorer.

- **RegistrationProcessClient**
  - References
    - RegistrationProcess

Select 'Properties' and the Strong Name field displays as True.

> **Note:** If your Srong name does not appear automatically in the Solutions Explorer window, check to make sure it has actually been created. In our case, although we created the Strong name from the Tools menu, the Strong Name property remained False. The solution to this is as follows: Select 'AssemblyInfo.vb' and open the dialog box to see if the following assembly key is present.

```
Imports System.Reflection
Imports System.Runtime.InteropServices

' General Information about an assembly is controlled throug
' set of attributes. Change these attribute values to modify
' associated with an assembly.

' Review the values of the assembly attributes

<Assembly: AssemblyTitle("")>
<Assembly: AssemblyDescription("")>
<Assembly: AssemblyCompany("")>
<Assembly: AssemblyProduct("")>
<Assembly: AssemblyCopyright("")>
<Assembly: AssemblyTrademark("")>
<Assembly: CLSCompliant(True)>

'The following GUID is for the ID of the typelib if this pro
<Assembly: Guid("53FD0A45-9139-46E2-AF79-A09EDCDBC65B")>

' Version information for an assembly consists of the follow
'
'        Major Version
'        Minor Version
'        Build Number
'        Revision
'
' You can specify all the values or you can default the Buil
' by using the '*' as shown below:

<Assembly: AssemblyVersion("1.0.*")>
```

You don't see the Assembly key, so take the following steps to ensure that the Strong Name will generate the key.

1. Copy `<Assembly: AssemblyVersion ("1.0.*")>` and paste it to the next line.

2. Add the following code:

```
<Assembly: AssemblyKeyFile
("..\\..\\Registration.snk")>
```

Repeat the same process for both Assembly.vb files. Then recompile your assembly and check your Registration property. It verifies that your Strong Name has been created.

PART 4

IMPLEMENTATION

```
<Assembly: AssemblyVersion ("1.0.*")>
<Assembly: AssemblyKeyFile ("..\\..\\Registration.snk")>
```

Now drag the Assembly to the GAC.

11.16 Discovering How .NET Locates Your Assembly

The application you created calls a referenced assembly containing information about the Assembly, such as name, version, culture, and public key. It first examines a configuration file. If you think it necessary to update your assembly, you can create a configuration file that looks something like this:

```
<configuration>
<runtime>
<assemblyBinding xmlns="urn:schemas-microsoft-com:asm.v1">
    <dependentAssembly>
      <AssemblyIdentity name="RegistrationProcess"
        <publicKeyToken="6cf7280fa2c28aa9" />
          <bindingRedirect oldVersion="1.0.0.0"
          newVersion="2.0.0.0" />
    </dependentAssembly>
    <publisherPolicy apply="yes" />
    <probing privatePath = "c:\Visual Studio
    Solutions\RegistrationProcess" />
  </assemblyBinding>
  <gcConcurrent enable="true">
  </runtime>
</configuration>
```

You can also use another tool called 'mscorcf.msc' to configure and manage the assembly. It is located in C:\Windows\Microsoft.Net\Framework\.

```
.NET Framework Configuration
.NET Framework Configuration allows you to configure assembiles,
remoting services, and code access security policy.

Tasks
Manage the Assembly Cache
   The assembly cache stores assemblies that are designed to be
   shared by several applications. Use the assembly cache to view,
   add, and remove the managed components that are installed on
   this computer.
Managed Configured Assemblies
   Configured assemblies are the set of assemblies from the assem-
   bly cache that have an associated set of rules. These rules can
   determine which version of the assembly gets loaded and the
   location used to load the assembly.
Configure Code Access Security Policy
   The common language runtime uses code access security to con-
   trol applications' access to protected resources. Each applica-
   tion's assemblies are evaluated and assigned permissions based
   on factors that include the assemblies' origin and author.
Adjust Remoting Services
   Use the Remoting Services Properties dialog box to adjust com-
   munication channels for all applications on this computer.
Manage Individual Applications
   Each application can have its own set of configured assemblies
   and remoting services.
```

You must have a client application before you can use this tool.

Probing

Probing means that the runtime looks for your Assembly following established criteria.

First, the runtime examines the GAC file to see if the Assembly contains a strong name. Naturally, if the assembly is private, the search is conducted within the application's root directory, commonly referred to as the 'AppBase' directory. If it sees a reference to an assembly, it searches for RegistrationProcess.dll.

If the Assembly is not in AppBase, the runtime searches the configuration file for any path specified therein. If assembly is still not present, it examines the 'bin' directory until, ultimately, it locates the Assembly.

Using a Codebase

A <codebase> element specifies where the Common Language Runtime can find an assembly. The runtime can use the <codebase> in a configuration file only if the file includes a Redirect Assembly

PART 4

IMPLEMENTATION

539

version. After determining the proper version to use, the runtime applies the codebase setting from the file determining the assembly version. If no codebase exists, probing continues in the normal manner. Here is an example:

```
<configuration>
    <runtime>
        <assemblyBinding xmlns="urn:schemas-microsoft-
        com:asm.v1">
            <dependentAssembly name="RegistrationProcess"
                publicKeyToken="6cf7280fa2c28aa9"
                culture="en-us" />
        <codeBase version="2.0.0.0"
        href="http://www.dps.com/RegistrationProcess.dll"/>
            </dependentAssembly>
        </assemblyBinding>
    </runtime>
</configuration>
```

> **Note:** This element is available for use in an application configuration file, machine configuration file (machine.config), and the publisher policy file.

Create a new project (codeBaseAsmClient) that makes use of the RegistrationProcess.dll version 2.0.0.0. Once you have created the test application, place a copy of the new version 2.0.0.0 in a folder on your C drive, perhaps in C:\myAssemblies. Next, open the mscorcf.msc file (refer to Section 11.15 for instructions on where to find this tool). Then add this client to a list of configured assemblies. Select 'Configure an Assembly' from the Assembly Cache, and select the 'RegistrationProcess.dll.' Finally, from the Codebase tab, map the new version 2.0.0.0 to the C:\myAssemblies subdirectory.

The URI should specify the protocol used during the probe; the XML file is generated for you:

```
<?xml version='1.0' ?>
<configuration>
  <runtime>
    <assemblyBinding xmlns="urn:schemas-microsoft-com:asm.v1">
      <dependentAssembly>
        <AssemblyIdentity name="RegistrationProcess"
              publicKeyToken="6cf7280fa2c28aa9"/>
          <codebase version="2.0.0.0"
          href="file:///c:\myAssemblies "/>
        </.dependentAssembly>
      </assemblyBinding>
    </runtime>
</configuration>
```

Finally, let's fire up ilasm.exe and view the public key for our DLL (see Figure 11.13).

```
.publickey=(00 24 00 00 04 80 00 00 94 00 00 00 06 02 00 00 //
          .$..............
 00 24 00 00 52 53 41 31 00 04 00 00 01 00 01 00 // .$..RSA1 ........
 2B 15 57 cc 38 07 11 79 70 5A 9B A9 6C 40 5E 69 // +.W.8..ypZ..|@^i
 B4 72 70 36 1C 95 9E 29 99 B3 CE 55 E3 31 D0 35 // .rp6...)...U.1.5
 57 79 35 53 66 49 24 07 2B FC 7E 39 20 B9 84 46 //Wy5Sfl$.+.~9 ..F
 26 E4 8C 87 0B E6 FC 11 0A 8A F5 AD 37 2C 57 // &....J.......7.W
 28 42 91 0C 5A 8D 83 73 9F D3 29 60 CA 0E 7C 0D // (B..Z..s..)'..|.
 C3 1A EA 5D 8C D1 FB A6 AC 8B A1 65 FA C0 45 // ...].......Me..E
 BC 91 2A 1A 80 40 85 3E 78 84 3D 60 0B 25 48 90 // ..*..@.>x.=.'.%H.
 A9 32 EF 4F 53 DD FD 29 DA 5F E5 01 62 DF 4C C5)// .2.OS..).._..b.L.
.hash algorithm 0x00008004
.ver 1:0:922:15208
.
mresource public RegistrationProcessComponent1.resources
[
.
module RegistrationProcess.dll
//MVID:{9D1D6BE3-86BA-4B8C-91C1-378740312B4F}
imagebase 0x11000000
subsystem 0x00000002
file alignment 512
corflags 0x00000009
//Image base:0x030b0000
```

Figure 11.13 A shared Assembly public key

Before closing this discussion, understand that many other important topics—including reflection, inheritance, and declaring properties under Visual Basic.NET—require extensive coverage. These will be covered in another text currently being written by this book's author. The .NET Framework, VB.NET, and C# represent a major step forward in building applications on the Windows platform. We look forward to Microsoft porting .NET to other platforms.

11.17 Some Closing Thoughts

Although we have provided you with a only brief introduction to the .NET Framework and VB.NET, our intent is to introduce you to some basics and fundamentals so that you can begin making the transition from VB 6.0 to the .NET environment and VB.NET. The learning curve is initially steep, but in the end the effort is worthwhile. Once you understand how the .NET Framework integrates with the three specifications and are able to read the Manifest and Assembly, everything falls into place.

Reflection and inheritance are essential topics that you should explore in more depth. Inheritance brings VB.NET in line with the object-oriented programming languages C# and C++. This is a valuable update for VB programmers. You should also make ADO.NET and ASP.NET an integral part of your arsenal of programming tools. They represent significant changes and can help you write integrated, language-agnostic, and platform-independent applications. Now that you have read this chapter, you can easily understand the integral role that XML and schemas play in each aspect of the .NET environment. Happy XML programming!

Summary

The .NET Framework represents a new model for building systems on the Windows platform. We have learned how three .NET specifications serve as host for Visual C++, C#, and Visual Basic.NET.

Visual Studio.NET offers a user-friendly IDE for developing applications of your choice sharing a Common Language Runtime library. The three primary languages share the same libraries; the compiler generates 'Intermediate Language' code. The three .NET specifications that provide unique integration between the three primary programming languages are:

- Common Language Runtime
- Common Type Specification
- Common Language Specification

The Common Language Runtime contains two core entities: runtime engine mscoree.dll and mscorlib.dll. The basic functionality that CLR supports is generating and locating an Assembly and discovering the required types within the binary to execute an application. It reads the Assembly's metadata and subsequently compiles the IL code to application-specific instructions. The CLR also supports cross-language error handling and debugging.

Perhaps one of the most important features that .NET offers is versioning. The runtime checks the version and compares it with the Assembly determining the version number. The CLR checks the Assembly for its name, version, and culture. It also ascertains whether the assembly is strongly named by checking for a publickey-token, and it checks all types exported by the assembly.

The CLR generates both single file assemblies and multifile assemblies. Additionally, the CLR offers memory management through a process called garbage collection.

The second .NET specification shared by the three primary programming languages is the Common Type Specification. This specification refers to a collection of classes, interfaces, structures, delegates, and enumerations supported by the CLR engine. You can also build your own custom types and group them into unique namespaces. This eliminates name conflicts between assemblies. Table 11.1 described the Specification namespaces in detail.

PART 4

IMPLEMENTATION

The third type specification that .NET adheres to is the Common Language Specification. It contains guidelines describing in detail the set of rules that a .NET compiler must support for generated code to be eligible for hosting by the CLR. Table 11.2 provided information concerning CLS data types. Although the CLS is still a work in progress, the basics are established. Refer to Table 11.3 for a description of Manifest Intermediate Language tags. This serves as a refresher for understanding the Manifest.

We learned how to build a class library and build an assembly that's shareable by client applications. Creating a Strong Name makes the Assembly global in scope and reusable by other applications such as a Console application, a Windows application, and so on.

A review of some of the essential features of Visual Basic.NET provided you with the opportunity to view several of VB.NET's changes. We discussed topics such as adding properties to your class, referencing your assembly from a client, using parameterized properties, and creating objects immediately in memory with the `New` keyword.

We discussed two options for utilizing `WithEvents`, `RaiseEvents`, and `AddHandler`. The latter option is preferable because it eliminates the need to define a new class to apply `WithEvents`. Additionally, `AddHandler` can handle more than one event. We learned how the keyword `Delegate` is type safe, object oriented, and a class derived from `MulticastDelegate`. `Delegate` contains three important pieces of information:

- The method name it calls
- Arguments passed to the method
- The return value

Most important, the .NET delegate serves as the backbone for the .NET `Event` keyword. You can use the VB.NET `AddressOf` keyword to create a new instance of the `MultiCastDelegate` type. It points automatically to the designated method. Delegates are also convenient for callback functions.

The new `Handles` keyword binds a method name to a particular event. While the name of the method is irrelevant, it allows you to configure multiple methods to listen to the same event.

Finally, you learned how the CLR locates an Assembly through a process called probing and how to use a `<codebase>` element to specify where the assembly is located. The configuration file is an essential ingredient for providing instructions to the runtime where your Assembly resides. You can redirect the search to force the runtime to employ an updated version of an assembly.

Self-Review Questions

(Note that no solutions are provided for Chapters 11 and 12.)

1. Describe three important tasks that the Common Language Runtime performs.

2. Describe the role that the Common Type Specification plays.

3. Provide a description of the role that the Common Language Specification plays.

4. Describe how you create a strong name for BookingManager and place the shared assembly in the Global Assembly Cache.

5. How do you construct a configuration file for BookingManager?

6. What is a `<codebase>`? When is it applied?

7. Write a short document explaining how the CLR locates an assembly.

8. Open the Manifest and Assembly for BookingManager, examine them, and explain the IL code generated by the CLR.

9. Describe the advantages that `AddHandler` provides.

10. Describe how to apply a delegate and address more than one event.

PART 4
IMPLEMENTATION

12 Creating Distributed Applications and Web Services

12.1 Leveraging .NET Distributed Applications and Web Services

A web service resides somewhere on the Internet and exposes its services to clients. For example, you can enter a URL such as http://www.someAddress.com in your Netscape or Internet Explorer browser, navigate to a specified web site, and then buy an antique or book travel arrangements, among a myriad of possibilities. To secure your purchase or reservations, you submit your credit card to the web service. Your software application employs a mechanism called discovery for locating the web service, querying the kinds of services it offers. If a match occurs, you submit your request and complete the transaction.

You can download the SOAP Toolkit 3.0 before you begin studying this chapter. It allows you to add XML Web Service functionality to your existing COM applications and components.

Leveraging components distributed on remote machines is essential to handle the large number of users consuming web services on the Internet. Hundreds of millions of consumers visit popular web sites daily. Utilizing load balancing and distributing components on the web is essential. An example of a component-based application is an e-commerce business in which foreign currency exchange requires submitting customer orders to a back-end enterprise resource planning (ERP) set of components. The application can reside on multiple platforms hosting different operating systems, such as Unix on one platform, Windows XP on another platform, and so on.

The client request can use one of the following methods for submitting the order to a web server residing somewhere on the Internet:

- HTTP GET
- HTTP POST
- Simple Object Access Protocol (SOAP)

The request may consume the services of a credit-card component for processing the transaction and returning a response providing credit approval or denial.

DCOM allows an application to invoke COM components installed on different servers. Another service, CORBA, is limited to applications and components installed within the corporate data center. Both DCOM and CORBA use proprietary, tightly coupled protocols. Unfortunately, clients face several barriers when communicating with the servers. They encounter firewalls restricting the use of open ports, making calls in an open environment difficult. Another problem both DCOM and CORBA face is that they are both connection oriented, thereby limiting their use as distributed services. They cannot easily manage interruptions such as external calls from other clients. If you are making calls via the Internet, you are not able to control your connection. Although the connection might succeed, the next call may fail if an interruption occurs. Designing load-balanced connections between client and server is difficult. You may not reroute a new request to another server. The connection must be preserved to maintain the integrity of the currently processed transaction.

12.2 Designing a New Approach (Web Services)

Realizing the difficulties encountered using DCOM or CORBA, you must consider developing several criteria for accommodating remote procedure calls (RPCs):

- **Interoperability.** Clients on other platforms must freely use a remote service.

- **Strongly typed interfaces.** Data types being transmitted to and from the client must map easily to data types defined by most procedural programming languages.

- **Support for any language.** The implementation of a remote service should use existing Internet standards, thereby eliminating the necessity to reinvent the wheel. Java, Perl, C#, Visual Basic, C++ must all have access to the web service.

- **Support for any distributed component infrastructure.** Avoid tightly coupled components.

- **Security for RPC calls.** Security is always of utmost important. Make sure security is an integral part in making RPC calls.

12.3 Defining a Web Service

Web services expose an interface to invoke an activity for a client. The following items represent the building blocks we use for building those services:

- **Encoding.** Data transmitted between client and server requires encoding the message body. XML is the host language for serializing data to a stream, a file, or in memory. Additionally, XML represents the standard solution for describing information exchanged between diverse systems. In plain English, XML is fundamental to web services.

- **Description.** A web service provides an endpoint. Once the point is located, the client requires information on how to interact with the service. The description of the web service provides structured metadata about the service it provides. Grouping similar, related services into interfaces and providing a means of describing those services is the task the Web Services Description Language (WSDL) performs.

- **Discovery.** A client needs to access web services by locating the services required to successfully submit a call and receive a return response. Universal Description, Discovery, and Integration (UDDI) fulfills this function. We call this process discovery. UDDI enables providers of web services to advertise their services in a standard format, allowing client service authors to gather information they need for building a client component.

- **Messaging format.** Both the client and server must agree on a common protocol for encoding and formatting messages. Today, SOAP is the preferred protocol.
- **Transport.** Once the message is formatted and data is serialized into the body of the message, the service executes transmission between client and server using a specified protocol.

In this chapter, we begin by building a simple distributed application using Visual Basic 6.0. This allows us to view some of the differences between Visual Basic 6.0 and Visual Basic.NET. Then we will provide a fictitious case study and business model called International Foreign Currency Exchange (IFCE) to serve as the basis for developing a web service using Visual Studio.NET and Visual Basic.NET. IFCE sells foreign currencies to both cash and credit-card clients.

Through discussion of web services, we'll explore UDDI, DISCO, WSDL, and SOAP, and we'll extol the benefits of migrating to VB.NET. Let's get started.

12.4 Building a Distributed Application

Microsoft provides a product called SOAP Toolkit 3.0 that's bundled with a number of samples to give you a jumpstart on using SOAP. Each implementation demonstrates various toolkit APIs with languages such as Visual Basic, C++, ASP/JScript, and so on. The samples work only with Visual Studio 6.0. We include samples from this toolkit to get you up and running. Then we shift our focus to Visual Basic.NET and learn to build web services and clients in that environment.

You can download the SOAP Toolkit beta version 3.0: Simply use a search engine to locate the Toolkit.

Then, begin by creating a virtual directory for your examples:

1. Create a folder on the server called **MySOAPExamples**, such as C:\MySOAPExamples.

2. Open the Control Panel in Windows 2000 or Windows XP, select Administrative Tools, and then choose Internet Information Services. Open IIS, right-click on the default web site, point to New, and click Virtual Directory. The dialog box in Figure 12.1 will appear on your screen.

Figure 12.1 The IIS Virtual Directory Wizard

3. Select Next. Enter **SOAPExamples** in the Alias box and then click Next.

4. Type **C:\MySOAPExamples** and then click Next. Once more, click Next. Finally, click Finish to complete the wizard.

5. Open a command prompt window and change your directory to C:\Program Files\MSSOAP\Binaries.

PART 4

IMPLEMENTATION

6. Type the following: **soapdir.cmd UPDATE MySOAPExamples**. You can see the script configuring the newly created MySOAPExamples virtual directory. Once this is accomplished, you can take advantage of the Internet Server API (ISAPI) handler bundled with this toolkit.

```
C:\Program Files\MSSOAP\Binaries>soapvdir.cmd UPDATE MySOAPExamples
Registered virtual DIR:
  IIS://localhost/w3svc/1/Root/MySOAPExamples
with addition scriptmap entry:
  .wsdl,C:\Program Files\Common Files\MSSoap\Binaries\SOAPIS30.dll,1,GET,POST
```

> **Note:** Add Client and Server folders to this directory. If you open the IIS directory, you can observe the following directory structure:
>
>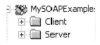

Creating an ActiveX File

We need to create various components on both server and client:

- Implement the server by creating a Visual Basic 6.0 ActiveX DLL called **SelectMaxSize**. You should also create a Web Services Description Language (WSDL) file listing both the service and its operations.
- Generate a Web Services Meta Language (WSML) file. This maps operations contained within the WSML file to methods in the COM object.
- Write a Visual Basic scripting application for calling operations from the server.

First, begin by creating an ActiveX DLL Project in VB 6.0. Name the project **Sample1Service** and name the class **Sample1**. Then select Sample1Service Properties. Select the Unattended Execution and Retained in Memory options on the General tab. Add the following code:

```
Public Function AddNumbers (ByVal NumberOne As Double, _
    ByVal NumberTwo As Double) _As Double
    AddNumbers = NumberOne + NumberTwo
End Function
Public Function SubtractNumbers (ByVal NumberOne As Double, _
    ByVal NumberTwo As Double) _As Double
    SubtractNumbers = NumberOne - NumberTwo
End Function
```

Save the file in C:\MySOAPExamples\Sample1\Server. From the File menu, select Make Sample1Service.dll and save it in the MySOAPExamples\Sample1\Server folder.

The WSDL Generator

The next step creates the Sample1.wsdl and Sample1.wsml files. These files describe the operations `AddNumbers` and `SubtractNumbers`. The WSDL file provides metadata about data input and output. It also defines the specified format that a client must observe when creating a SOAP message for requesting an operation defined in the web service. Additionally, it identifies the server as either an ASP listener or Internet server (ISAPI). Finally, it specifies a `location` `<soap:address>` for the child element and port specified by the service.

The following steps are required for creating the WSDL and WSML files:

1. Select the WSDL/WSML generator utility from the SOAP Toolkit group. The Toolkit Wizard will appear.

2. Select 'Next' twice.

3. Enter **Sample1** as the service name in the 'Select the COM .dll file to analyze' dialog box.

4. Specify the location of the COM object (Sample1Service.dll), as in C:\MySOAPExamples\Server\Service1.dll.

5. Select 'Next.'

6. Select services you want to expose. In this example, the two services are as follows:

- AddNumbers

- SubtractNumbers

7. In the SOAP Listener information dialog box:

a. Enter **http://*Server*/MySOAPExamples/Server/**. This is where you specify your IIS server name.

b. In the Listener URI, select ISAPI.

c. In the location for the new WSDL and WSML files dialog box, click Next.

d. Select Finish. The necessary WSDL and WSML files are created for the Sample1 service.

The client Sample1.vbs application is a Microsoft Visual Basic 6.0 VBScript application. It first creates the SOAPClient30 object:

```
Dim SoapClient3
set Soapclient3 = CreateObject("MSSOAP.SoapClient30")
```

It then calls the mssoapinit method:

```
Call SoapClient3.mssoapinit("Sample1.wsdl",
"Sample1","Sample1SoapPort")
Here is the VBScript code:
Option Explicit
Dim SoapClient3
set Soapclient3 = CreateObject("MSSOAP.SoapClient30")
on Error Resume Next
Call SoapClient3.mssoapinit("Sample1.wsdl",
"Sample1","Sample1SoapPort")
if err <> 0 then
wscript.echo "initialization failed " + err.description
end if
wscript.echo SoapClient3.AddNumbers (47, 56)
if err <> 0 then
wscript.echo err.description
wscript.echo "faultcode=" + SoapClient3.faultcode
```

```
   wscript.echo   "faultstring=" + SoapClient3.faultstring
   wscript.echo   "faultactor=" + SoapClient3.faultactor
   wscript.echo   "detail=" + SoapClient3.detail
end if
wscript.echo SoapClient3.SubtractNumbers (47, 56)
if err <> 0 then
   wscript.echo   err.description
   wscript.echo   "faultcode=" + SoapClient3.faultcode
   wscript.echo   "faultstring=" + SoapClient3.faultstring
   wscript.echo   "faultactor=" + SoapClient3.faultactor
   wscript.echo   "detail=" + SoapClient3.detail
end if
```

The initialization binds the methods in the specified port to the
`SOAPClient30` object. The calls to `AddNumbers` and
`SubtractNumbers` are sent to the server as a SOAP message and
are returned as a response to the client. One thing you must do before
running this sample is copy the Sample1.wsdl file from the server file
to your client folder. Save it and run the clientSample1.vbs application. Open a command prompt window and type the following:
cscript clientSample1.vbs. You will see the following return
response:

```
 Directory of C:\MySOAPExamples\Client

06/10/2002   05:45 PM    <DIR>          .
06/10/2002   05:45 PM    <DIR>          ..
06/10/2002   04:21 PM                957 clientSample1.vbs
06/10/2002   03:51 PM              3,872 Sample1.WSDL
               2 File(s)          4,834 bytes
               2 Dir(s)   6,624,489,984 bytes free

C:\MySOAPExamples\Client>cscript clientSample1.vbs
Microsoft (R) Windows Script Host Version 5.6
Copyright (C) Microsoft Corporation 1996-2001. All rights reserved.

103
-9
```

It is instructive to examine the Sample1 WSDL file. `<defini-
tions>` is the root for this file. The `definitions` element serves
much the same role as the root element does in an `xsd:schema`. The
child elements define a specific service.

PART 4

IMPLEMENTATION

```
<definitions
name='Sample1'
targetNamespace='http://tempuri.org/Sample1/wsdl/'
xmlns:wsdlns='http://tempuri.org/Sample1/wsdl/'
xmlns:typens='http://tempuri.org/Sample1/type/'
xmlns:soap='http://schemas.xmlsoap.org/wsdl/soap/'
xmlns:xsd='http://www.w3.org/2001/XMLSchema'
xmlns:stk='http://schemas.microsoft.com/soap-toolkit/wsdl-
extension'
xmlns:dime='http://schemas.xmlsoap.org/ws/2002/04/dime/wsdl/'
xmlns:ref='http://schemas.xmlsoap.org/ws/2002/04/reference/'
xmlns:content='http://schemas.xmlsoap.org/ws/2002/04/
content-type/'
xmlns:wsdl='http://schemas.xmlsoap.org/wsdl/'
xmlns='http://schemas.xmlsoap.org/wsdl/'>
```

Figure 12.2 The `definitions` root element

A WSDL file defines its own namespace. It adds a `targetNamespace` attribute to the `definitions` element. One important restriction: The value of the `targetNamespace` attribute cannot use a relative URI. The namespace allows you to qualify references to entities contained within the WSDL document. We set the `targetNamespace` in this document to http://tempuri.org/Sample1/wsdl. (Note: In a production environment, set the `targetNamespace` to your own.) Then the WSDL file assigns the prefix `wsdlns` to reference the namespace. This prefix fully qualifies all references to entities contained within the document. Additionally, it sets prefixes for the `Type` element as well as SOAP. The `XSD:Schema` is also referenced. A `definitions` element defines boundaries for a specified name. All elements declared within the WSDL document define entities for messages and ports. Assign entities a name using the `name` attribute.

The `<types>` element contains schema information listed in the WSDL document. The `XSD:Schema` is the default type system supported by WSDL. Note that, if the schema defines the types contained within the types element, the schema element appears as an immediate child of <types>, just as it does in this document. <types> also functions as a container for defining complex data types used in exchanging SOAP messages. (Note: No complex data types exist in this sample, just simple types. Refer to Chapter 4, "Introducing Schemas," for a discussion about complex data types.)

It is also possible to use other type systems using the extension attribute. The element name defines the type. In this discussion, we refer only to the default type, Schemas, used in web services created targeting the .NET platform. Let's examine the <types> element displayed in Figure 12.3.

```
<types>
<schema  targetNamespace='http://tempuri.org/Sample1/type/'
xmlns='http://www.w3.org/2001/XMLSchema'
xmlns:SOAP- NC='http://schemas.xmlsoap.org/soap/encoding/'
xmlns:wsdl='http://schemas.xmlsoap.org/wsdl/'
elementFormDefault='qualified'>

<import namespace='http://schemas.xmlsoap.org/soap/encoding/'/>
<import namespace='http://schemas.xmlsoap.org/wsdl/'/>
<import namespace='http://schemas.xmlsoap.org/ws/2002/04/
reference/'/>
<import namespace='http://schemas.xmlsoap.org/ws/2002/04/
content-type/'/>
</schema>
</types>
```

Figure 12.3   The <types> element

The <message> element

The <message> element contains descriptions for logical contents of the messages. A message is composed of parts described by the part child element transmitted between client and server. The part is a parameter passed to the method. The message name is

`Sample1.AddNumbers`. `NumberOne` is the `part` (parameter). The data type is `xsd:double`.

```
<message name='Sample1.AddNumbers'>
        <part name='NumberOne' type='xsd:double'/>
        <part name='NumberTwo' type='xsd:double'/>
</message>
```

For every message, a `Response` method exists, with `part` `Result` as type `double`. The same format exists for the second call to method `SubtractNumbers`.

```
<message name='Sample1.AddNumbersResponse'>
        <part name='Result' type='xsd:double'/>
</message>
```

```
<message name='Sample1.SubtractNumbers'>
        <part name='NumberOne' type='xsd:double'/>
        <part name='NumberTwo' type='xsd:double'/>
</message>
```

```
<message name='Sample1.SubtractNumbersResponse'>
        <part name='Result' type='xsd:double'/>
</message>
```

Defining the <portType>

The `<portType>` provides a list of operations, each individually assigned to a specified `<operation>` child element. The operations in our example are `AddNumbers` and `SubtractNumbers`. Additionally, each operation further contains two child elements, `<input>` and `<output>`. Their task describes the input and output for each operation. The `parameterOrder` determines the order in which parameters are defined.

```
<portType name='Sample1SoapPort'>

<operation name='AddNumbers' parameterOrder='NumberOne
NumberTwo'>
<input message='wsdlns:Sample1.AddNumbers'/>
<output message='wsdlns:Sample1.AddNumbersResponse'/>
</operation>
```

```
<operation name='SubtractNumbers' parameterOrder='NumberOne
NumberTwo'>
<input message='wsdlns:Sample1.SubtractNumbers'/>
<output message='wsdlns:Sample1.SubtractNumbersResponse'/>
</operation>

</portType>
```

Describing the <binding> Element

A `<binding>` element corresponds to a `<portType>` element. This element defines the protocol information for a specified operation. The `<binding>` element contains three child elements:

- `<stk:binding>`
- `<soap:binding>`
- `<operation>`

The `<type>` attribute provides the name of the `<portType>`.

```
<binding name='Sample1SoapBinding'
type='wsdlns:Sample1SoapPort' >
```

The `preferredEncoding` determines the character encoding used by the `SoapClient30` and `SoapServer30` objects.

```
<stk:binding preferredEncoding='UTF-8'/>
```

`<soap:binding>` uses these attributes to define protocol-specific information. For example, the `style` attribute indicates that the two operations are Remote Procedure Calls (RPC). The `transport` attribute value signifies HTTP transmission of SOAP messages.

The `<soap:operation>` element indicates that both client and server objects use the value of the `soapAction` attribute:

```
<soap:binding style='rpc'
transport='http://schemas.xmlsoap.org/soap/http'/>
<operation name='AddNumbers'>
```

```
<soap:operation
soapAction='http://tempuri.org/Sample1/action/Sample1.AddNumber
s'/>
```

Both `<input>` and `<output>` elements include a `<soap:body>` element, indicating that the SOAP request and response messages contain only the SOAP body but no header. If the request or response includes a SOAP header, a `<soap:header>` would be included in both `input` and `output` elements. When serializing a SOAP message, you can use either encoded or literal formats. The `use` attribute specifies the encoding type to execute on the various parts of the message.

```
<input>
<soap:body
use='encoded'
```

`rpc` is the `style` attribute, meaning that each message part is embedded within an RPC-wrapper element within the SOAP body element. The `namespace` attribute denotes the namespace for each RPC wrapper.

```
namespace='http://tempuri.org/Sample1/message/'
encodingStyle='http://schemas.xmlsoap.org/soap/encoding/'
parts='NumberOne NumberTwo'/>
</input>
<output>
<soap:body
use='encoded'
namespace='http://tempuri.org/Sample1/message/'
encodingStyle='http://schemas.xmlsoap.org/soap/encoding/'
parts='Result'/>
</output>
</operation>

<operation name='SubtractNumbers'>
<soap:operation
soapAction='http://tempuri.org/Sample1/action/Sample1.
SubtractNumbers'/>
<input>
<soap:body
use='encoded'
```

```
namespace='http://tempuri.org/Sample1/message/'
encodingStyle='http://schemas.xmlsoap.org/soap/encoding/'
parts='NumberOne NumberTwo'/>
</input>
<output>
<soap:body
use='encoded'
namespace='http://tempuri.org/Sample1/message/'
encodingStyle='http://schemas.xmlsoap.org/soap/encoding/'
parts='Result'/>
</output>
</operation>
</binding>
```

Describing the <service> Element

The SOAP client must identify a specified service, including the port and operation desired as well as input parameter values. The <service> element provides this information. The service element consists of the following items:

- The name attribute
- The binding attribute
- soap:address

The name attribute provides a unique name to distinguish it from other included ports in a WSDL document. The binding attribute refers to the binding defined previously in the binding element. The soap:address element offers the address of the server-side SOAP request handler.

```
<service name='Sample1' >
<port name='Sample1SoapPort'
binding='wsdlns:Sample1SoapBinding' >
<soap:address
location='http://ECOM3/MySOAPExamples/Server/Sample1.WSDL'/>
</port>
</service>
</definitions>
```

PART 4

IMPLEMENTATION

12.5 Examining the WSML File

The WSML file's responsibility is to map the operation in a service defined in a WSDL document to a specified method in a COM object residing on the server. The `<servicemapping>` element wraps the contents of the WSML file. The fragment in Figure 12.4 demonstrates the beginning of the `service` element. The `<using>` element identifies the COM object.

```
<?xml version='1.0' encoding='UTF-8' ?>
 <!-- Generated 06/10/02 by Microsoft SOAP Toolkit WSDL File
Generator, Version 3.00.1124.0 -->
```

Figure 12.4   Sample1 WSML file

The `<servicemapping>` element identifies the `<service>` as `Sample1`. The WSDL Extension for SOAP in DIME Specification defines XML elements and attributes in a WSDL document, describing the encapsulation of a SOAP message with Binary64 and/or hexBinary content in a Direct Internet Exchange (DIME) message. (The DIME documentation is located at the following URL: http://gotdotnet.com/team/xml__wsspecs/dime/WSDL-Extension-for-Dime.htm. A discussion of the DIME is beyond the purview of this chapter.) We leave it to you to pursue this subject further if interested.

```
<servicemapping name='Sample1' xmlns:dime='http://schemas.xml-
soap.org/ws/2002/04/dime/wsdl/'>
```

The `<service>` element employs the `<using>` element to identify the COM object. The `PROGID` attribute identifies the class implementing all methods. Boolean attribute `cacheable` determines whether the object stays in memory as long as the `SoapServer` object is in memory. Value `0` indicates that the object is not cached. Note that if the COM object is single threaded, the flag is ignored. The `ID` refers to the object.

```
  <service name='Sample1'>
  <using PROGID='Service1.Sample1' cacheable='0'
ID='Sample1Object' />
```

The `<port>` element specifies the `portType` element defined in the WSDL file.

```
<port name='Sample1SoapPort'>
  <operation name='AddNumbers'>
```

The `<execute>` element maps the operation to the COM object. Within this element, the `uses` attribute contains the identical ID as the ID of the COM object. The `method` attribute identifies the method in the COM object. The `dispID` attribute provides the dispatch ID for the method. The `parameter` element describes the method parameters. `parameter` contains three attributes:

- `callIndex` determines the parameter order, such as 1 is the first parameter, 2 is the second parameter, and so on.
- The `name` attribute identifies the unique name for the parameter.
- The `element` name identifies the element name, in this case `Result`.

```
<execute uses='Sample1Object' method='AddNumbers'
dispID='1610809344'>
<parameter callIndex='-1' name='retval' elementName='Result' />
<parameter callIndex='1' name='NumberOne'
elementName='NumberOne' />
<parameter callIndex='2' name='NumberTwo'
elementName='NumberTwo' />
</execute>
</operation>
<operation name='SubtractNumbers'>
<execute uses='Sample1Object' method='SubtractNumbers'
dispID='1610809345'>
<parameter callIndex='-1' name='retval' elementName='Result' />
<parameter callIndex='1' name='NumberOne'
elementName='NumberOne' />
<parameter callIndex='2' name='NumberTwo'
elementName='NumberTwo' />
```

```
</execute>
</operation>
</port>
</service>
</servicemapping>
```

We have now covered the details for both a WSDL document and a WSML file. For information purposes, it is important to understand the basics for a web service. However, you needn't concern yourself with how to write this information because the WSDL generator takes care of this procedure for you.

If you want, examine the other samples provided in the SOAP Toolkit 3.0. The example we used is simple and only provides you with a brief overview of how to develop a distributed application using SOAP.

You also now understand how Visual Basic 6.0 manages web services. However, let's move on to Visual Studio.NET and observe how it automatically takes care of many details for you (which we describe as they occur).

12.6 Creating a Web Service Using Visual Studio.NET

You may have already noticed that web services consist of several technologies: WSDL, HTTP GET, HTTP POST, and SOAP. Additionally, web services contain a discovery service (*.vsdisco). In this section, you'll learn how to construct a simple web service for selecting a maximum value.

You can think of a web service as a chunk of code that is activated using HTTP requests. As previously mentioned, access to remote binary code requires platform-specific protocols. DCOM and CORBA are classic examples of this type of distributed application. A problem with this approach is they are proprietary protocols, requiring a tight connection to the remote source.

One of the main advantages you experience with the .NET Framework is that it is language agnostic. You can use C#, C++, VB.NET, and so on to build types extending across programming language boundaries. HTTP represents a protocol that all platforms understand. Combining HTTP with SOAP allows you to manage web services easily. A .NET web service consists of a number of classes, structures, and interfaces that provide the functionality you need to access remote services.

Here are the required components for creating a web service:

- An invocation protocol (HTTP GET, HTTP POST, or SOAP)
- A description service (such as WSDL) providing information concerning the services it offers
- A discovery service such as *.vsdisco

The invocation protocol transmits information between a web service client and a web service using XML. SOAP transmits the message, containing XML metadescriptions of the various services and objects.

Table 12.1 provides an overview of the web service namespaces.

Table 12.1 Web Service Namespaces

Web Service Namespace	Description
System.Web.Services	These contain the set of types required to build a web service.
System.Web.Services.Description	These types allow you to interact programmatically with WSDL.
System.Web.Services.Discovery	These types, used along with *. vsdisco, allow a web client to programmatically discover the web services installed on a specified machine.
System.Web.Services.Protocols	The XML data transmitted between a web client and a web service can be transmitted using HTTP GET, HTTP POST, or SOAP.

PART 4
IMPLEMENTATION

565

12.7 Describing the System.Web.Services Namespace

Table 12.2 provides information about the System.Web.Services namespace.

Table 12.2   System.Web.Services Namespace Members

System.Web.Services Type	Description
WebMethodAttribute	Adding the <WebMethod> attribute to a method enables the method to be called from a remote client using HTTP.
WebService	This defines the base class for web services.
WebServiceAttribute	This attribute is available for providing additional information concerning the web service.
WebServiceBindingAttribute	This identifies the binding protocol that a specified web service method is using.

Here are the core files for a web service in a VS.NET web service project:

- ***.vsdisco**   This file extension represents the discovery of web services. It contains an XML description of the web services at a specified URL.
- ***.asmx**   These files define methods for your web service. Note that each ***.asmx** file has a corresponding *.vb file to contain the code behind.
- ***.asmx.vb**   This relates to the previous description of the file extension.

Let's add some functionality to the Service1 class. Note that we have not included error handling for the sake of brevity, nor have we made provisions for the case in which x is equal to y. Figure 12.5 resolves that issue. Add the code shown in Figure 12.5.

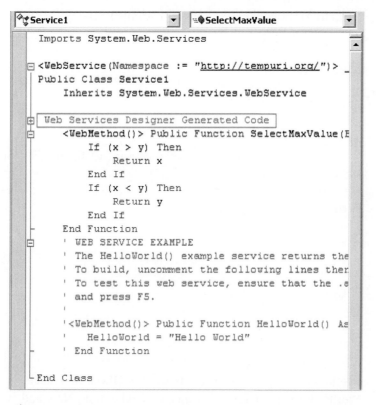

Figure 12.5 Adding the SelectMaxValue method code

```
<WebMethod()> Public Function SelectMaxValue(ByVal x As
Integer, ByVal y As Integer) As Integer
        If (x > y) Then
            Return x
        End If
        If (x < y) Then
            Return y
        End If
    End Function
```

The following example is an improvement over the preceding one. Can you see why?

```
int maximum( int, int, int); //function prototype
int main()
{ int a, b, c;
    cout << "Enter three integers: ";
    cin >> a >> b >> c;
    cout << "Maximum value is: " << maximum(a, b, c ) << endl;
    return 0;
}
int maximum( int x, int y, int z)
{
  int max = x;
  if( y > max)
  max = y;
  if (z > max )
  max = z;
  return max;
}
```

Note how simple it is to set up a web method. Just place <WebMethod()> before your method declaration. Now add any other methods in a similar fashion and compile your code (see Figure 12.6).

```
<WebMethod()> Public Function AddValues (ByVal x As Integer,
ByVal y As Integer) As Integer
        Return (x + y)
    End Function


<WebMethod()> Public Function SubtractValues(ByVal x As
Integer, ByVal y As Integer) As Integer
        Return (x - y)
    End Function


<WebMethod()> Public Function MultiplyValues(ByVal x As
Integer, ByVal y As Integer) As Integer
        Return (x * y)
    End Function
```

```
<WebMethod()> Public Function DivideValues(ByVal x As Integer,
ByVal y As Integer) As Integer
        If (y = 0) Then
            Throw New DivideByZeroException("You can't divide
            by zero!")
        End If
        Return x / y
    End Function
```

Figure 12.6   Adding additional methods

The results are shown in Figure 12.7.

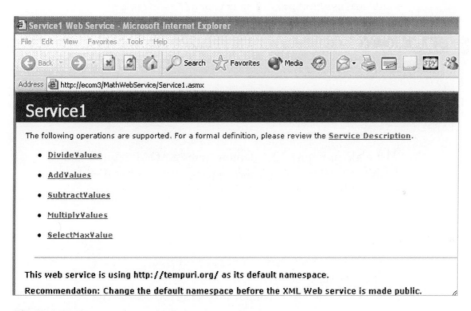

Figure 12.7   Viewing a web service response

Your machine functions as a temporary client and provides an HTML view of methods you entered and identified with the `<WebMethod>` attribute. Let's test the various methods and examine the web services in more depth. We'll test the `SelectMaxValue` first. A SOAP HTTP GET request submits the values entered.

SelectMaxValue

Test

To test the operation using the HTTP GET protocol, click the 'Invoke' button.

Parameter	Value
x:	32
y:	45

We display the result next:

```
<?xml version="1.0" encoding="utf-8" ?>
<int xmlns="http://tempuri.org/">45</int>
```

> **Note:** In a production environment, change the xmlns to your own, such as the following:
>
> ```
> <int xmlns=http://www.dpsoftware.com/results/>
> ```

The code in Figure 12.8 demonstrates a SOAP request and response. The placeholders shown need to be replaced with actual values.

```
POST /MathWebService/Service1.asmx HTTP/1.1
Host: ecom3
Content-Type: text/xml; charset=utf-8
Content-Length: length
SOAPAction: "http://tempuri.org/SelectMaxValue"
<?xml version="1.0" encoding="utf-8"?>
<soap:Envelope
xmlns:xsi="http://www.w3.org/2001/XMLSchema-instance"
xmlns:xsd="http://www.w3.org/2001/XMLSchema"
xmlns:soap="http://schemas.xmlsoap.org/soap/envelope/">
  <soap:Body>
    <SelectMaxValue xmlns="http://tempuri.org/">
      <x>int</x>
      <y>int</y>
    </SelectMaxValue>
  </soap:Body>
</soap:Envelope>
```

```
HTTP/1.1 200 OK
Content-Type: text/xml; charset=utf-8
Content-Length: length

<?xml version="1.0" encoding="utf-8"?>
<soap:Envelope
xmlns:xsi="http://www.w3.org/2001/XMLSchema-instance"
xmlns:xsd="http://www.w3.org/2001/XMLSchema"
xmlns:soap="http://schemas.xmlsoap.org/soap/envelope/">
  <soap:Body>
    <SelectMaxValueResponse xmlns="http://tempuri.org/">
      <SelectMaxValueResult>int</SelectMaxValueResult>
    </SelectMaxValueResponse>
  </soap:Body>
</soap:Envelope>
```

Figure 12.8   SOAP request and response

In the next section, we'll display the Web Service Description Language document for all web methods. We list the file without comment. If you want to refresh your memory about the WSDL file, refer to Figure 12.2 where we began with a discussion on the `<Types>` element.

12.8 A WSDL Document for SelectMaxValue Web Service

In Figure 12.9 we present a WSDL document for the SelectMaxValue Web Service.

```
<?xml version="1.0" encoding="utf-8" ?>
- <definitions
xmlns:http="http://schemas.xmlsoap.org/wsdl/http/"
xmlns:soap="http://schemas.xmlsoap.org/wsdl/soap/"
xmlns:s="http://www.w3.org/2001/XMLSchema"
xmlns:s0="http://tempuri.org/"
xmlns:soapenc="http://schemas.xmlsoap.org/soap/encoding/"
xmlns:tm="http://microsoft.com/wsdl/mime/textMatching/"
xmlns:mime="http://schemas.xmlsoap.org/wsdl/mime/"
targetNamespace="http://tempuri.org/"
xmlns="http://schemas.xmlsoap.org/wsdl/">
```

```
+ <types>
+ <message name="SelectMaxValueSoapIn">
+ <message name="SelectMaxValueSoapOut">
+ <message name="AddValuesSoapIn">
+ <message name="AddValuesSoapOut">
+ <message name="SubtractValuesSoapIn">
+ <message name="SubtractValuesSoapOut">
+ <message name="MultiplyValuesSoapIn">
+ <message name="MultiplyValuesSoapOut">
+ <message name="DivideValuesSoapIn">
+ <message name="DivideValuesSoapOut">
+ <message name="SelectMaxValueHttpGetIn">
+ <message name="SelectMaxValueHttpGetOut">
+ <message name="AddValuesHttpGetIn">
+ <message name="AddValuesHttpGetOut">
+ <message name="SubtractValuesHttpGetIn">
+ <message name="SubtractValuesHttpGetOut">
+ <message name="MultiplyValuesHttpGetIn">
+ <message name="MultiplyValuesHttpGetOut">
+ <message name="DivideValuesHttpGetIn">
+ <message name="DivideValuesHttpGetOut">
+ <message name="SelectMaxValueHttpPostIn">
+ <message name="SelectMaxValueHttpPostOut">
+ <message name="AddValuesHttpPostIn">
+ <message name="AddValuesHttpPostOut">
+ <message name="SubtractValuesHttpPostIn">
+ <message name="SubtractValuesHttpPostOut">
+ <message name="MultiplyValuesHttpPostIn">
+ <message name="MultiplyValuesHttpPostOut">
+ <message name="DivideValuesHttpPostIn">
+ <message name="DivideValuesHttpPostOut">
+ <portType name="Service1Soap">
+ <portType name="Service1HttpGet">
+ <portType name="Service1HttpPost">
+ <binding name="Service1Soap" type="s0:Service1Soap">
+ <binding name="Service1HttpGet"
type="s0:Service1HttpGet">
+ <binding name="Service1HttpPost"
type="s0:Service1HttpPost">
+ <service name="Service1">
  </definitions>
```

Figure 12.9   A WSDL document

12.9 Describing the WebMethod Attribute Types

Apply the `WebMethod` attribute to each method you want to expose via HTTP. The attributes are as follows:

- `<WebMethod(Description:=" ")>`
- `EnableSession`
- `MessageName`
- `TransactionOption`

The `Description` attribute provides additional documentation about your `WebMethod`. The `EnableSession` attribute by default is set to true. It configures this method to maintain session state. The `MessageName` attribute is available for avoiding namespace name clashes. You simply provide a unique message name to avoid the namespace clash. Finally, the `TransactionOption` functions as root of a COM+ transaction.

12.10 Building a Web Service for the International Foreign Currency Exchange

It is time to introduce the business model and case study named International Foreign Currency Exchange. The International Foreign Currency Exchange provides the following foreign currency exchange services for clients:

- Managing currency exchanges
- Ordering foreign currency
- Offering availability of foreign currency services at all bank branches
- Providing convenient locations throughout the United States, Canada, United Kingdom, France, Germany, and Italy
- Buying and selling foreign cash and travelers checks based on current exchange rates

PART 4
IMPLEMENTATION

International Finance Corporation services both customer accounts and nonaccount clients. The latter category offers cash-only services, whereas bank customers can use credit cards, personal checks, and other forms of payment.

All branch offices receive individual-country, current buy-and-sell-rate reports. These contain information concerning the country currency name and denominations of both cash and traveler checks. In addition, the report includes individual restrictions for each type of currency.

Account executives and cashiers provide customers with currency information, offer exchange rates, and place orders for currencies. Throughout the day, cashiers and account executives receive updates on currency availability at each branch.

Requests for currencies exceeding individual country restrictions are rejected. Three categories exist for fulfilling orders:

- Pending
- Current orders
- Order fulfillment

Pending orders occur only if currency stock is not available in cash drawers or in local branches. The standard procedure for such an occurrence is procuring requested currencies from regional branches. The bank notifies the customer when the currency is available to the local branch for order fulfillment.

The financial transaction is complete when an auditor checks a cashier's drawer and reconciles any discrepancy. If excess currencies exceed the normal limits that a drawer should hold, the central branch stock returns the excess currencies to the stock. A balance shortfall prompts a request for currency replenishment from a central bank supply.

The IFCE adheres to rules and regulations defined by the following tables and use cases. Each use case describes procedures that the IFCE must follow. The Security Exchange Commission dictates the business rules that each bank must follow before being allowed to buy and sell currencies. The bank utilizes these tables to define and detail their business practices.

A termination result must accompany each type of transactional event.

Table 12.3 Textual Use Case Model

Use Case #	Name describing the nature of the use case.
Topic	Group the use cases.
Transactional Event	Describe in a paragraph the type event. These events are object oriented, meaning a trigger fires when an event occurs such as a purchase. They must be atomic.
Participants	Identify the participant by its ID, such as a piece of hardware or software package, a consumer, and so on.
Use Case Description	Describe the overview of the role that the use case plays in the transaction or event. (Do not describe process or enforcement of business rules.)
Constraints or Preexisting Conditions	Provide a description of the system state. For example, the state must be altered to conform to the rules or else a trigger fires to flag an overdraft or nonexisting account.
Termination Results	Provide a description of termination results. Describe preexisting conditions before termination and results after termination.
Use Case Description	Offer a description of events leading to successful or unsuccessful termination.
Input and Output Data Types	Give a description of data types for input and output.

Table 12.4   A Two-Tiered Truth Table for Termination Conditions

Termination Conditions:				
Condition 1	T	F	F	F
Condition 2		T	F	F
Condition 3			T	F
Termination Results:				
Termination result #1	1			
Termination result #2		2		
Termination result #3			3	
Termination result #?				4

Table 12.5   Scenario Description of Events

Scenario #	Create a sequential number identifying the scenario.
Use case number	This unique number is linked with the scenario #.
Termination results	The termination result corresponds to a scenario.
Scenario description	This description should be detailed.

Table 12.6   Flow of Events Template

Event	Participant/OS	Use Case Event	Use Case Data Elements	Event Validation	Steps Required to Accomplish a Task	Comments

Table 12.7   Event Steps Decision Table

Termination Results#
Condition Affecting Termination Results:

Condition #1	T	F	F	F
Condition #2		T	F	F
Condition #n			T	F
System event #1	n			n
System event #2		n	n	
System event #n				n

Table 12.8   System Sequence Diagram

Participant	**Operating System**
1: Event 1 (participant)	⇨
2. Event 2 (system)	⇦
3. Event 3 (participant)	⇨
4. Event n (system)	⇦

Table 12.9   A Participant Role Template

Participant name	Name the role a participant plays in interacting with an event.
Role description	In a paragraph or two, describe the role a participant plays.
Role status	Define the primary or secondary participant's role.
Relationships	Define your relationships.
Inheritance1	Specify the superclass (identify the parent class).
Inheritance2	Detail the subclass for specification (define the purpose for subclassing).

12.11 Describing IFCE's Business Rules

The following list contains the business rules for this case study.

1. Nonaccount customers can only purchase currency with cash.

2. The IFCE must verify that the customer has a valid account. The teller must enter an account number or name to ensure that the account is currently active.

3. Procure today's date from the software's system date. When the transaction is registered, it must contain a timestamp.

4. The form's first name field cannot exceed 15 characters.

5. The middle name field cannot exceed 15 characters.

6. The last name cannot exceed 20 characters.

7. The address field is obligatory.

8. Store the form in the system's database.

9. The type of currency that a customer requests must originate from one the following countries: a) United States, b) Canada, c) Britain, d) France, e) Italy, or f) Germany.

   If the requested currency is not offered by the IFCE, terminate the transaction.

10. A customer cannot purchase more than the maximum amount of currency permitted by each country for exchange within a 24-hour period by an individual.

11. The amount of currency that a customer requests must reside within the IFCE or one of its branches before a transaction can be completed; otherwise, the transaction status reverts to a pending status.

12. The teller must be able to fulfill the customer's full request for currency for a transaction to obtain completion status. The procedures for completing a transaction are as follows:

    • Check for available cash in the teller's drawer.

    • Enter the transaction and pay the customer if sufficient currency is available.

    • Check the system for sufficient currency within the branch if it is not available locally.

- Issue a request to the system for the additional funds.
- Enter the transaction and update the database to show the increase in local cash-drawer currency so that the cash drawer remains in balance.
- If the total amount is not available in the branch, offer the following options to customers:

    1. Customers can adjust the requested amount to be equal to or less than the amount currently in the branch.

    2. Customers can accept the amount available and return for the remaining balance at a later time.

    3. Generate a pending transaction for this scenario:

        a. The additional currency will be available the next business day.

        b. The customer can decide to wait until the entire amount of currency requested is available.

        c. Generate a pending transaction for the following scenario:

            i. The full amount of currency will be available the next business day.

            ii. The customer can decide to cancel the currency-exchange request.

13. Record the country's currency being paid.

14. Enter the country's currency being purchased.

15. Record the number for each currency denomination being paid.

16. Call on the system method to multiply the number for each currency denomination being paid out. Then add and total each denomination.

17. The total amount of currency being paid to the customer must equal the total that the system shows on teller's screen.

18. Give each teller a unique ID number.

19. Assign each workstation a unique workstation ID.

20. Provide each branch with a unique ID.

21. Each transaction can have only one status, which is determined based on the events preceding the creation of the transaction.

Account Customer Business Rules

Credit Card:

22. Only an account customer can use a credit card for purchasing currency.

    • The teller must enter the account number into the system.

23. Only one credit card account per request can be used.

    • The customer can submit multiple forms for using multiple credit cards.

24. MasterCard, Visa, and American Express are the only valid credit cards accepted.

25. The customer must have a valid IFCE account for purchasing currency with a credit card. The name on the credit card and the customer's name on his or her account must match.

26. The teller must view the customer's expiration date on the credit card to ensure its validity.

    • If valid, the teller must check "yes" in the expiration date validate flag.

    • If not valid, the teller must check "no" in the expiration date validate flag.

    • Terminate the transaction.

27. The teller must view the customer's credit card and one other ID to ensure that the signatures match.

    • If the signature is present and matches the other ID, the teller must check "yes" in the signature validate flag.

    • If the signature doesn't match, the teller must check "no" in the signature validate flag.

    • Terminate the transaction.

28. If the expiration date validate flag and the signature validate flag are both "yes," process the credit card through the credit card authorization system.

29. Only one approval/disapproval code per credit card authorization request is allowed.

    * If credit card request is disapproved, terminate the transaction. The credit card issuer performing the validation handles approval reasons.

Personal Checks:

30. The teller must verify that the check is not drawn on a fraudulent account.

    * Utilize the checkmate system. This system scans the check to ensure that the checking account is valid.

        1. If the checking account is valid, check "yes" in the checking account validate flag.

        2. If the checking account is not valid, check "no" in the checking account validate flag.

            a. If the checking account validate flag is "no," terminate the transaction.

31. Only an account customer can use a personal check for purchasing currency. Enter the checking account number into the system.

Nonaccount Cash Customer:

32. A nonaccount cash customer must present a valid picture ID.

    * If a nonaccount cash customer does not have a valid picture ID, terminate the transaction.

33. The nonaccount cash customer's picture ID card must match other forms of identification.

    * If a nonaccount cash customer's picture does not match the person requesting the cash, terminate the transaction.

34. The nonaccount customer's picture ID must contain a number present on the card that can be recorded in the system. ID numbers can be a driver's license number, social security number, employee ID number, or student ID.

    * If one of these numbers is not available, terminate the transaction.

PART 4
IMPLEMENTATION

35. Valid picture ID cards are driver licenses, state ID cards, employee ID cards, bank-issued photo IDs and school-issued ID cards.

    • If none of these cards is available, terminate the transaction.

36. Nonaccount customers can only purchase currency with cash.

    • If a nonaccount cash customer does not have cash to purchase currency, cancel the transaction.

37. The teller can only accept cash or travelers checks as a method of payment for a nonaccount cash customer.

It is time to implement these business rules. Create a Visual Basic.NET project in Visual Studio.NET of type ASP.NET web service. Name the project **International Foreign Currency Exchange**. When the project loads, select Solution Explorer to view the files automatically generated for you (see Figure 12.11).

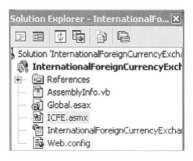

Figure 12.11   IFCE files in Solution Explorer

Next right-click on Service1.asmx and rename it as **ICFE.asmx**. Then double-click on the ASMX file to view the code-behind for this file. Ignore the commented out Hello World code. The significant item here is the function's name: `<WebMethod()>`. This designates the method as callable from a client via HTTP over the web.

Add the code in Figure 12.12 to facilitate IFCE's ability to convert a client's requested foreign currency to U.S. dollars. Our example demonstrates how to convert British sterling, French francs, German marks, and Italian lire to U.S. currency. Of course, in a real-world application, the IFCE would query a central bank database to determine the current exchange rate. This is necessary because the IFCE business rules inform us that the exchange rate is updated three times daily from agencies like Reuters or Bloomberg.

```
Imports System.Web.Services


<WebService(Namespace := "http://tempuri.org/")> _
Public Class Service1
    Inherits System.Web.Services.WebService


#Region " Web Services Designer Generated Code "


    Public Sub New()
        MyBase.New()
        'This call is required by the Web Services Designer.
        InitializeComponent()
        'Add your own initialization code after the
InitializeComponent() call
    End Sub
    'Required by the Web Services Designer
    Private components As System.ComponentModel.IContainer
    'NOTE: The following procedure is required by the Web
Services Designer
    'It can be modified using the Web Services Designer.
    'Do not modify it using the code editor.
    <System.Diagnostics.DebuggerStepThrough()> Private Sub
    InitializeComponent()
        components = New System.ComponentModel.Container()
    End Sub
    Protected Overloads Overrides Sub Dispose(ByVal disposing
    As Boolean)
        'CODEGEN: This procedure is required by the Web
        Services Designer
        'Do not modify it using the code editor.
        If disposing Then
        If Not (components Is Nothing) Then
        components.Dispose()
        End If
```

```
        End If
        MyBase.Dispose(disposing)
    End Sub
#End Region
    <WebMethod()> Public Function IFCECurrencyConvert(ByVal
    dAmt As Decimal, _
     ByVal sOrigCurr As String, ByVal sDestCurr As String) As
    Decimal
        Select Case sOrigCurr
            Case "Sterling"
                Return CDec(dAmt * 1.57)
            Case "Francs"
                Return CDec(dAmt * 1.27)
            Case "Marks"
                Return CDec(dAmt * 1.73)
            Case "Lire"
                Return CDec(dAmt * 100.76)
        End Select
    End Function


    ' WEB SERVICE EXAMPLE
    ' The HelloWorld() example service returns the string
      Hello World.
    ' To build, uncomment the following lines, then save, and
      build the project.
    ' To test this web service, ensure that the .asmx file is
      the start page
    ' and press F5.


    '<WebMethod()> Public Function HelloWorld() As String
    'HelloWorld = "Hello World"
    ' End Function

End Class
```

Figure 12.12   IFCE WebMethod code

The method takes two parameters: the amount of currency entered
for conversion and the type of currency the method will convert to.
We could use an `if` statement to determine the `conversion` method
or employ a `Select Case` statement as we demonstrate here.

Finally, build the web service. You can view the service either by selecting E5 or right-clicking IFCE.asmx and selecting View in Browser.

Note: You might have trouble viewing the following page and receive a message stating the following: "You are trying to download the file from HTTP://localhost and *name of file.asmx*, would you like to open it or save it to a file?" Additionally, you will receive an HTTP error stating that the page cannot be found. A solution exists. .vsdisco (dynamic discovery) is a feature on Visual Studio.NET computers only, and it is turned off by default. You can turn this feature on for each computer by using machine.config or for each application by using web.config. To enable dynamic discovery, change the following line in the machine.config file:

```
<!--add verb="*" path="*.vsdisco"
type="System.Web.Services.Discovery.DiscoveryRequestHandler,
System.Web.Services, Version=1.0.3300.0, Culture=neutral,
PublicKeyToken=b03f5f7f11d50a3a" validate="false"/-->
```

Change it to the following:

```
<add verb="*" path="*.vsdisco"
type="System.Web.Services.Discovery.DiscoveryRequestHandler,
System.Web.Services, Version=1.0.3300.0, Culture=neutral,
PublicKeyToken=b03f5f7f11d50a3a" validate="false"/>.
```

Just remove the comment <-- from the front of the line and end of the line, and you will have no trouble locating the page, viewing it, and browsing the .vsdisco file. You can find this file at the following location: http://support.microsoft.com/?scid=kb;en-us;Q307303. This advice is courtesy of Microsoft Support for Visual Studio.NET.

Select the IFCEcurrencyConverter button to bring up the dialog box in Figure 12.13.

Enter your data in the respective fields and click on the Invoke button to view the results.

PART 4 IMPLEMENTATION

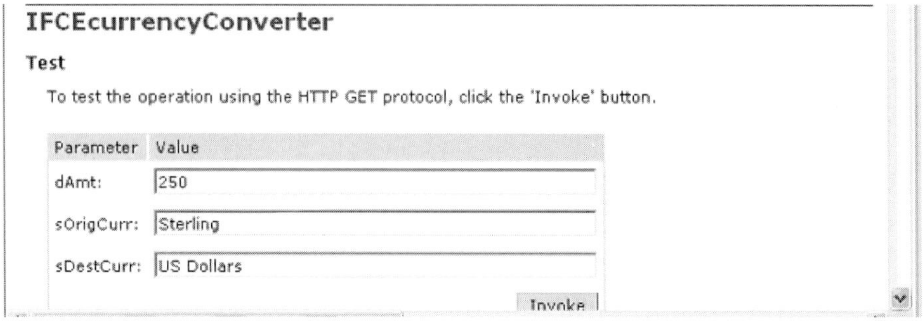

IFCEcurrencyConverter

Test

To test the operation using the HTTP GET protocol, click the 'Invoke' button.

Parameter	Value
dAmt:	250
sOrigCurr:	Sterling
sDestCurr:	US Dollars

Invoke

Figure 12.13   Default web service page

You can also build a data-driven web service with ADO.NET. SQL Server 2000 allows you to access data via HTTP. It is also possible to

```
<?xml version="1.0" encoding="utf-8" ?>
<decimal xmlns="http://tempuri.org/">360.825</decimal>
```

create a web service in ASP.NET.

Summary

A web service is a software component residing on the Internet and exposing its services to clients. You can access it via HTTP, make a request such as converting a foreign currency to U.S. dollars, and vice versa. Three options exist for submitting requests to a web service:

- HTTP GET
- HTTP POST
- Simple Object Access Protocol (SOAP)

Web services expose an interface for invoking an activity of behalf of a client. We use the following building blocks for building a web service:

- XML encoding
- WSDL (Description, XML Schema)
- Discovery (UDDI, Disco)
- Messaging (SOAP)
- Transport (HTTP, SOAP, FTP)

A WSDL file provides metadata about data input and output; it defines the specific format that a client must observe when creating SOAP messages. Additionally, a WSDL file defines its own namespace by adding a `targetNamespace` to the `Definitions` element. Finally, it identifies the server as either an ASP listener or intern (ISAPI).

The WSML file's responsibility is to match an operation in a service defined in a WSDL document to a specified method in a COM object residing on the server. The `<serviceMapping>` element wraps the contents of the WSML file.

You can build a data-driven web site using SQL Server 2000 in combination with ADO.NET or an ASP.Net application.

We hope the brief introduction provided in Chapters 11 and 12 will serve as stimulus to further explore the .NET Framework and .NET language of your choice. It is well worth the effort.

One final thought concerning the IFCE case study: We leave it to you as an exercise to implement them fully by considering applying a design pattern such as the decorator pattern, as well as other patterns derived from the Gang Of Four's (Gamma, Helm, Johnson, and Vlissides) seminal book "Design Patterns—Elements of Reusable Object-Oriented Software" published by Addison Wesley. One of the most beneficial features of the .NET Framework is the inclusion of numerous interfaces. Explore them and design patterns. You will benefit immeasurably from them.

PART 4
IMPLEMENTATION

A XHTML Strict DTD Version 1.0

We include the XHTML strict DTD version 1.0 as a reference for when you design your XHTML documents. We refer you to the W3C when comparing this DTD with HTML's DTD.

```
<!--
    Extensible HTML version 1.0 Strict DTD

    This is the same as HTML 4.0 Strict except for
    changes due to the differences between XML and SGML.

    Namespace = http://www.w3.org/1999/xhtml

    For further information, see: http://www.w3.org/TR/xhtml1

    Copyright (c) 1998-2000 W3C (MIT, INRIA, Keio),
    All Rights Reserved.

    This DTD module is identified by the PUBLIC and SYSTEM
    identifiers:

    PUBLIC "-//W3C//DTD XHTML 1.0 Strict//EN"
    SYSTEM "http://www.w3.org/TR/xhtml1/DTD/xhtml1-strict.dtd"

    $Revision: 1.14 $
```

```
    $Date: 2000/01/25 23:52:20 $

-->

<!--================= Character mnemonic entities
=========================-->

<!ENTITY % HTMLlat1 PUBLIC
    "-//W3C//ENTITIES Latin 1 for XHTML//EN"
    "xhtml-lat1.ent">
%HTMLlat1;

<!ENTITY % HTMLsymbol PUBLIC
    "-//W3C//ENTITIES Symbols for XHTML//EN"
    "xhtml-symbol.ent">
%HTMLsymbol;

<!ENTITY % HTMLspecial PUBLIC
    "-//W3C//ENTITIES Special for XHTML//EN"
    "xhtml-special.ent">
%HTMLspecial;

<!--=================== Imported Names
======================================-->

<!ENTITY % ContentType "CDATA">
    <!-- media type, as per [RFC2045] -->

<!ENTITY % ContentTypes "CDATA">
    <!-- comma-separated list of media types, as per [RFC2045]
    -->

<!ENTITY % Charset "CDATA">
    <!-- a character encoding, as per [RFC2045] -->

<!ENTITY % Charsets "CDATA">
    <!-- a space separated list of character encodings, as per
    [RFC2045] -->

<!ENTITY % LanguageCode "NMTOKEN">
```

```
            <!-- a language code, as per [RFC1766] -->

<!ENTITY % Character "CDATA">
    <!-- a single character from [ISO10646] -->

<!ENTITY % Number "CDATA">
    <!-- one or more digits -->

<!ENTITY % LinkTypes "CDATA">
    <!-- space-separated list of link types -->

<!ENTITY % MediaDesc "CDATA">
    <!-- single or comma-separated list of media descriptors
    -->

<!ENTITY % URI "CDATA">
    <!-- a Uniform Resource Identifier, see [RFC2396] -->

<!ENTITY % UriList "CDATA">
    <!-- a space separated list of Uniform Resource Identifiers
    -->

<!ENTITY % Datetime "CDATA">
    <!-- date and time information. ISO date format -->

<!ENTITY % Script "CDATA">
    <!-- script expression -->

<!ENTITY % StyleSheet "CDATA">
    <!-- style sheet data -->

<!ENTITY % Text "CDATA">
    <!-- used for titles etc. -->

<!ENTITY % FrameTarget "NMTOKEN">
    <!-- render in this frame -->

<!ENTITY % Length "CDATA">
    <!-- nn for pixels or nn% for percentage length -->

<!ENTITY % MultiLength "CDATA">
    <!-- pixel, percentage, or relative -->
```

```
<!ENTITY % MultiLengths "CDATA">
    <!-- comma-separated list of MultiLength -->

<!ENTITY % Pixels "CDATA">
    <!-- integer representing length in pixels -->

<!-- these are used for image maps -->

<!ENTITY % Shape "(rect|circle|poly|default)">

<!ENTITY % Coords "CDATA">
    <!-- comma separated list of lengths -->

<!--==================== Generic Attributes
===================================-->

<!-- core attributes common to most elements
  id        document-wide unique id
  class     space separated list of classes
  style     associated style info
  title     advisory title/amplification
-->
<!ENTITY % coreattrs
 "id          ID              #IMPLIED
  class       CDATA           #IMPLIED
  style       %StyleSheet;    #IMPLIED
  title       %Text;          #IMPLIED"
  >

<!-- internationalization attributes
  lang        language code (backwards compatible)
  xml:lang    language code (as per XML 1.0 spec)
  dir         direction for weak/neutral text
-->
<!ENTITY % i18n
 "lang        %LanguageCode; #IMPLIED
  xml:lang    %LanguageCode; #IMPLIED
  dir         (ltr|rtl)      #IMPLIED"
  >

 <!-- attributes for common UI events
```

```
      onclick     a pointer button was clicked
      ondblclick  a pointer button was double clicked
      onmousedown a pointer button was pressed down
      onmouseup   a pointer button was released
      onmousemove a pointer was moved onto the element
      onmouseout  a pointer was moved away from the element
      onkeypress  a key was pressed and released
      onkeydown   a key was pressed down
      onkeyup     a key was released
  -->
  <!ENTITY % events
   "onclick        %Script;        #IMPLIED
    ondblclick     %Script;        #IMPLIED
    onmousedown    %Script;        #IMPLIED
    onmouseup      %Script;        #IMPLIED
    onmouseover    %Script;        #IMPLIED
    onmousemove    %Script;        #IMPLIED
    onmouseout     %Script;        #IMPLIED
    onkeypress     %Script;        #IMPLIED
    onkeydown      %Script;        #IMPLIED
    onkeyup        %Script;        #IMPLIED"
    >


  <!-- attributes for elements that can get the focus
     accesskey    accessibility key character
     tabindex     position in tabbing order
     onfocus      the element got the focus
     onblur       the element lost the focus
  -->
  <!ENTITY % focus
   "accesskey      %Character;     #IMPLIED
    tabindex       %Number;        #IMPLIED
    onfocus        %Script;        #IMPLIED
    onblur         %Script;        #IMPLIED"
    >


  <!ENTITY % attrs "%coreattrs; %i18n; %events;">


  <!--===================== Text Elements
  ======================================-->


  <!ENTITY % special
```

```
          "br | span | bdo | object | img | map">

<!ENTITY % fontstyle "tt | i | b | big | small">

<!ENTITY % phrase "em | strong | dfn | code | q | sub | sup |
                   samp | kbd | var | cite | abbr | acronym">

<!ENTITY % inline.forms "input | select | textarea | label |
button">

<!-- these can occur at block or inline level -->
<!ENTITY % misc "ins | del | script | noscript">

<!ENTITY % inline "a | %special; | %fontstyle; | %phrase; |
%inline.forms;">

<!-- %Inline; covers inline or "text-level" elements -->
<!ENTITY % Inline "(#PCDATA | %inline; | %misc;)*">

<!--==================== Block level elements
===============================-->

<!ENTITY % heading "h1|h2|h3|h4|h5|h6">
<!ENTITY % lists "ul | ol | dl">
<!ENTITY % blocktext "pre | hr | blockquote | address">

<!ENTITY % block
     "p | %heading; | div | %lists; | %blocktext; | fieldset |
table">

<!ENTITY % Block "(%block; | form | %misc;)*">

<!-- %Flow; mixes Block and Inline and is used for list items
etc. -->
<!ENTITY % Flow "(#PCDATA | %block; | form | %inline; |
%misc;)*">

<!--==================== Content models for exclusions
======================-->

<!-- a elements use %Inline; excluding a -->
```

```
<!ENTITY % a.content
    "(#PCDATA | %special; | %fontstyle; | %phrase; |
%inline.forms; | %misc;)*">

<!-- pre uses %Inline excluding img, object, big, small, sup or
sup -->

<!ENTITY % pre.content
    "(#PCDATA | a | br | span | bdo | map | tt | i | b |
       %phrase; | %inline.forms;)*">

<!-- form uses %Block; excluding form -->

<!ENTITY % form.content "(%block; | %misc;)*">

<!-- button uses %Flow; but excludes a, form and form controls
-->

<!ENTITY % button.content
    "(#PCDATA | p | %heading; | div | %lists; | %blocktext; |
      table | %special; | %fontstyle; | %phrase; | %misc;)*">

<!--================= Document Structure
===================================-->

<!-- the namespace URI designates the document profile -->

<!ELEMENT html (head, body)>
<!ATTLIST html
  %i18n;
  xmlns       %URI;        #FIXED
'http://www.w3.org/1999/xhtml'
  >

<!--================= Document Head
===================================-->

<!ENTITY % head.misc "(script|style|meta|link|object)*">

<!-- content model is %head.misc; combined with a single
     title and an optional base element in any order -->
```

```
<!ELEMENT head (%head.misc;,
    ((title, %head.misc;, (base, %head.misc;)?) |
     (base, %head.misc;, (title, %head.misc;))))>

<!ATTLIST head
  %i18n;
  profile      %URI;          #IMPLIED
  >


<!-- The title element is not considered part of the flow of
     text. It should be displayed, for example as the page
     header or window title. Exactly one title is required per
     document.
     -->
<!ELEMENT title (#PCDATA)>
<!ATTLIST title %i18n;>


<!-- document base URI -->


<!ELEMENT base EMPTY>
<!ATTLIST base
  href         %URI;          #IMPLIED
  >


<!-- generic metainformation -->
<!ELEMENT meta EMPTY>
<!ATTLIST meta
  %i18n;
  http-equiv   CDATA          #IMPLIED
  name         CDATA          #IMPLIED
  content      CDATA          #REQUIRED
  scheme       CDATA          #IMPLIED
  >


<!--
  Relationship values can be used in principle:

    a) for document specific toolbars/menus when used
       with the link element in document head e.g.
       start, contents, previous, next, index, end, help
```

```
        b) to link to a separate style sheet (rel="stylesheet")
        c) to make a link to a script (rel="script")
        d) by stylesheets to control how collections of
            html nodes are rendered into printed documents
        e) to make a link to a printable version of this document
            e.g. a PostScript or PDF version (rel="alternate"
            media="print")
    -->


    <!ELEMENT link EMPTY>
    <!ATTLIST link
      %attrs;
      charset       %Charset;        #IMPLIED
      href          %URI;            #IMPLIED
      hreflang      %LanguageCode;   #IMPLIED
      type          %ContentType;    #IMPLIED
      rel           %LinkTypes;      #IMPLIED
      rev           %LinkTypes;      #IMPLIED
      media         %MediaDesc;      #IMPLIED
      >


    <!-- style info, which may include CDATA sections -->
    <!ELEMENT style (#PCDATA)>
    <!ATTLIST style
      %i18n;
      type          %ContentType;    #REQUIRED
      media         %MediaDesc;      #IMPLIED
      title         %Text;           #IMPLIED
      xml:space     (preserve)       #FIXED 'preserve'
      >


    <!-- script statements, which may include CDATA sections -->
    <!ELEMENT script (#PCDATA)>
    <!ATTLIST script
      charset       %Charset;        #IMPLIED
      type          %ContentType;    #REQUIRED
      src           %URI;            #IMPLIED
      defer         (defer)          #IMPLIED
      xml:space     (preserve)       #FIXED 'preserve'
      >
```

```
<!-- alternate content container for nonscript-based rendering
-->

<!ELEMENT noscript %Block;>
<!ATTLIST noscript
  %attrs;
  >


<!--===================== Document Body
========================================-->

<!ELEMENT body %Block;>
<!ATTLIST body
  %attrs;
  onload          %Script;    #IMPLIED
  onunload        %Script;    #IMPLIED
  >

<!ELEMENT div %Flow;>  <!-- generic language/style container-->
<!ATTLIST div
  %attrs;
  >


<!--==================== Paragraphs
========================================-->

<!ELEMENT p %Inline;>
<!ATTLIST p
  %attrs;
  >


<!--==================== Headings
=========================================-->

<!--
  There are six levels of headings from h1 (the most important)
  to h6 (the least important).
-->

<!ELEMENT h1   %Inline;>
<!ATTLIST h1
```

```
      %attrs;
      >


<!ELEMENT h2 %Inline;>
<!ATTLIST h2
      %attrs;
      >


<!ELEMENT h3 %Inline;>
<!ATTLIST h3
      %attrs;
      >


<!ELEMENT h4 %Inline;>
<!ATTLIST h4
      %attrs;
      >


<!ELEMENT h5 %Inline;>
<!ATTLIST h5
      %attrs;
      >


<!ELEMENT h6 %Inline;>
<!ATTLIST h6
      %attrs;
      >


<!--==================== Lists
========================================-->

<!-- Unordered list -->

<!ELEMENT ul (li)+>
<!ATTLIST ul
  %attrs;
  >

<!-- Ordered (numbered) list -->

<!ELEMENT ol (li)+>
<!ATTLIST ol
```

```
  %attrs;
  >


<!-- list item -->

<!ELEMENT li %Flow;>
<!ATTLIST li
  %attrs;
  >


<!-- definition lists - dt for term, dd for its definition -->

<!ELEMENT dl (dt|dd)+>
<!ATTLIST dl
  %attrs;
  >


<!ELEMENT dt %Inline;>
<!ATTLIST dt
  %attrs;
  >


<!ELEMENT dd %Flow;>
<!ATTLIST dd
  %attrs;
  >


<!--===================== Address
=============================================-->

<!-- information on author -->

<!ELEMENT address %Inline;>
<!ATTLIST address
  %attrs;
  >


<!--===================== Horizontal Rule
===================================-->

<!ELEMENT hr EMPTY>
<!ATTLIST hr
```

```
  %attrs;
  >


<!--==================== Preformatted Text
==================================-->

<!-- content is %Inline; excluding
"img|object|big|small|sub|sup" -->

<!ELEMENT pre %pre.content;>
<!ATTLIST pre
  %attrs;
  xml:space (preserve) #FIXED 'preserve'
  >


<!--==================== Block-like Quotes
==================================-->

<!ELEMENT blockquote %Block;>
<!ATTLIST blockquote
  %attrs;
  cite          %URI;           #IMPLIED
  >


<!--==================== Inserted/Deleted Text
============================-->

<!--
  ins/del are allowed in block and inline content, but it's
  inappropriate to include block content within an ins element
  occurring in inline content.
-->
<!ELEMENT ins %Flow;>
<!ATTLIST ins
  %attrs;
  cite          %URI;           #IMPLIED
  datetime      %Datetime;      #IMPLIED
  >


<!ELEMENT del %Flow;>
<!ATTLIST del
  %attrs;
```

```
   cite         %URI;               #IMPLIED
   datetime     %Datetime;          #IMPLIED
   >


<!--=================== The Anchor Element
===================================-->

<!-- content is %Inline; except that anchors shouldn't be
nested -->

<!ELEMENT a %a.content;>
<!ATTLIST a
  %attrs;
  charset      %Charset;       #IMPLIED
  type         %ContentType;   #IMPLIED
  name         NMTOKEN         #IMPLIED
  href         %URI;           #IMPLIED
  hreflang     %LanguageCode;  #IMPLIED
  rel          %LinkTypes;     #IMPLIED
  rev          %LinkTypes;     #IMPLIED
  accesskey    %Character;     #IMPLIED
  shape        %Shape;         "rect"
  coords       %Coords;        #IMPLIED
  tabindex     %Number;        #IMPLIED
  onfocus      %Script;        #IMPLIED
  onblur       %Script;        #IMPLIED
  >


<!--======================= Inline Elements
=================================-->

<!ELEMENT span %Inline;> <!-- generic language/style container
-->
<!ATTLIST span
  %attrs;
  >


<!ELEMENT bdo %Inline;>  <!-- I18N BiDi over-ride -->
<!ATTLIST bdo
  %coreattrs;
  %events;
  lang         %LanguageCode; #IMPLIED
```

```
    xml:lang     %LanguageCode; #IMPLIED
    dir          (ltr|rtl)      #REQUIRED
    >

<!ELEMENT br EMPTY>   <!-- forced line break -->
<!ATTLIST br
  %coreattrs;
   >

<!ELEMENT em %Inline;>   <!-- emphasis -->
<!ATTLIST em %attrs;>

<!ELEMENT strong %Inline;>   <!-- strong emphasis -->
<!ATTLIST strong %attrs;>

<!ELEMENT dfn %Inline;>   <!-- definitional -->
<!ATTLIST dfn %attrs;>

<!ELEMENT code %Inline;>   <!-- program code -->
<!ATTLIST code %attrs;>

<!ELEMENT samp %Inline;>   <!-- sample -->
<!ATTLIST samp %attrs;>

<!ELEMENT kbd %Inline;>  <!-- something user would type -->
<!ATTLIST kbd %attrs;>

<!ELEMENT var %Inline;>   <!-- variable -->
<!ATTLIST var %attrs;>

<!ELEMENT cite %Inline;>   <!-- citation -->
<!ATTLIST cite %attrs;>

<!ELEMENT abbr %Inline;>   <!-- abbreviation -->
<!ATTLIST abbr %attrs;>

<!ELEMENT acronym %Inline;>   <!-- acronym -->
<!ATTLIST acronym %attrs;>

<!ELEMENT q %Inline;>   <!-- inlined quote -->
<!ATTLIST q
  %attrs;
```

```
   cite          %URI;              #IMPLIED
   >


<!ELEMENT sub %Inline;>   <!-- subscript -->
<!ATTLIST sub %attrs;>


<!ELEMENT sup %Inline;>   <!-- superscript -->
<!ATTLIST sup %attrs;>


<!ELEMENT tt %Inline;>   <!-- fixed pitch font -->
<!ATTLIST tt %attrs;>


<!ELEMENT i %Inline;>    <!-- italic font -->
<!ATTLIST i %attrs;>


<!ELEMENT b %Inline;>    <!-- bold font -->
<!ATTLIST b %attrs;>


<!ELEMENT big %Inline;>   <!-- bigger font -->
<!ATTLIST big %attrs;>


<!ELEMENT small %Inline;>   <!-- smaller font -->
<!ATTLIST small %attrs;>


<!--====================== Object
=======================================-->
<!--
   object is used to embed objects as part of HTML pages.
   param elements should precede other content. Parameters
   can also be expressed as attribute/value pairs on the
   object element itself when brevity is desired.
-->


<!ELEMENT object (#PCDATA | param | %block; | form | %inline; |
%misc;)*>
<!ATTLIST object
   %attrs;
   declare       (declare)       #IMPLIED
   classid       %URI;           #IMPLIED
   codebase      %URI;           #IMPLIED
   data          %URI;           #IMPLIED
   type          %ContentType;   #IMPLIED
```

```
         codetype      %ContentType;   #IMPLIED
         archive       %UriList;       #IMPLIED
         standby       %Text;          #IMPLIED
         height        %Length;        #IMPLIED
         width         %Length;        #IMPLIED
         usemap        %URI;           #IMPLIED
         name          NMTOKEN         #IMPLIED
         tabindex      %Number;        #IMPLIED
         >


<!--
    param is used to supply a named property value.
    In XML it would seem natural to follow RDF and support an
    abbreviated syntax where the param elements are replaced
    by attribute value pairs on the object start tag.
-->
<!ELEMENT param EMPTY>
<!ATTLIST param
    id            ID              #IMPLIED
    name          CDATA           #IMPLIED
    value         CDATA           #IMPLIED
    valuetype     (data|ref|object) "data"
    type          %ContentType;   #IMPLIED
    >


<!--===================== Images
=================================================-->


<!--
    To avoid accessibility problems for people who aren't
    able to see the image, you should provide a text
    description using the alt and longdesc attributes.
    In addition, avoid the use of server-side image maps.
    Note that in this DTD there is no name attribute. That
    is only available in the transitional and frameset DTD.
-->

<!ELEMENT img EMPTY>
<!ATTLIST img
  %attrs;
  src           %URI;           #REQUIRED
  alt           %Text;          #REQUIRED
```

```
    longdesc     %URI;           #IMPLIED
    height       %Length;        #IMPLIED
    width        %Length;        #IMPLIED
    usemap       %URI;           #IMPLIED
    ismap        (ismap)         #IMPLIED
    >


<!-- usemap points to a map element which may be in this
     document or an external document, although the latter is not
     widely supported -->


<!--==================== Client-side image maps
==============================-->


<!-- These can be placed in the same document or grouped in a
       separate document although this isn't yet widely supported
-->


<!ELEMENT map ((%block; | form | %misc;)+ | area+)>
<!ATTLIST map
    %i18n;
    %events;
    id           ID              #REQUIRED
    class        CDATA           #IMPLIED
    style        %StyleSheet;    #IMPLIED
    title        %Text;          #IMPLIED
    name         NMTOKEN         #IMPLIED
    >


<!ELEMENT area EMPTY>
<!ATTLIST area
    %attrs;
    shape        %Shape;         "rect"
    coords       %Coords;        #IMPLIED
    href         %URI;           #IMPLIED
    nohref       (nohref)        #IMPLIED
    alt          %Text;          #REQUIRED
    tabindex     %Number;        #IMPLIED
    accesskey    %Character;     #IMPLIED
    onfocus      %Script;        #IMPLIED
    onblur       %Script;        #IMPLIED
    >
```

```
<!--================= Forms
===================================================-->
<!ELEMENT form %form.content;>   <!-- forms shouldn't be nested
-->

<!ATTLIST form
  %attrs;
  action        %URI;           #REQUIRED
  method        (get|post)      "get"
  enctype       %ContentType;   "application/x-www-form-urlen-
coded"
  onsubmit      %Script;        #IMPLIED
  onreset       %Script;        #IMPLIED
  accept        %ContentTypes;  #IMPLIED
  accept-charset %Charsets;     #IMPLIED
  >

<!--
  Each label must not contain more than ONE field
  Label elements shouldn't be nested.
-->
<!ELEMENT label %Inline;>
<!ATTLIST label
  %attrs;
  for           IDREF           #IMPLIED
  accesskey     %Character;     #IMPLIED
  onfocus       %Script;        #IMPLIED
  onblur        %Script;        #IMPLIED
  >

<!ENTITY % InputType
  "(text | password | checkbox |
    radio | submit | reset |
    file | hidden | image | button)"
  >

<!-- the name attribute is required for all but submit & reset
-->

<!ELEMENT input EMPTY>     <!-- form control -->
```

```
<!ATTLIST input
  %attrs;
  type         %InputType;      "text"
  name         CDATA            #IMPLIED
  value        CDATA            #IMPLIED
  checked      (checked)        #IMPLIED
  disabled     (disabled)       #IMPLIED
  readonly     (readonly)       #IMPLIED
  size         CDATA            #IMPLIED
  maxlength    %Number;         #IMPLIED
  src          %URI;            #IMPLIED
  alt          CDATA            #IMPLIED
  usemap       %URI;            #IMPLIED
  tabindex     %Number;         #IMPLIED
  accesskey    %Character;      #IMPLIED
  onfocus      %Script;         #IMPLIED
  onblur       %Script;         #IMPLIED
  onselect     %Script;         #IMPLIED
  onchange     %Script;         #IMPLIED
  accept       %ContentTypes;   #IMPLIED
  >

<!ELEMENT select (optgroup|option)+> <!-- option selector -->
<!ATTLIST select
  %attrs;
  name         CDATA            #IMPLIED
  size         %Number;         #IMPLIED
  multiple     (multiple)       #IMPLIED
  disabled     (disabled)       #IMPLIED
  tabindex     %Number;         #IMPLIED
  onfocus      %Script;         #IMPLIED
  onblur       %Script;         #IMPLIED
  onchange     %Script;         #IMPLIED
  >

<!ELEMENT optgroup (option)+>   <!-- option group -->
<!ATTLIST optgroup
  %attrs;
  disabled     (disabled)       #IMPLIED
  label        %Text;           #REQUIRED
  >
```

```
<!ELEMENT option (#PCDATA)>        <!-- selectable choice -->
<!ATTLIST option
  %attrs;
  selected    (selected)      #IMPLIED
  disabled    (disabled)      #IMPLIED
  label       %Text;          #IMPLIED
  value       CDATA           #IMPLIED
  >


<!ELEMENT textarea (#PCDATA)>    <!-- multi-line text field -->
<!ATTLIST textarea
  %attrs;
  name        CDATA           #IMPLIED
  rows        %Number;        #REQUIRED
  cols        %Number;        #REQUIRED
  disabled    (disabled)      #IMPLIED
  readonly    (readonly)      #IMPLIED
  tabindex    %Number;        #IMPLIED
  accesskey   %Character;     #IMPLIED
  onfocus     %Script;        #IMPLIED
  onblur      %Script;        #IMPLIED
  onselect    %Script;        #IMPLIED
  onchange    %Script;        #IMPLIED
  >


<!--
  The fieldset element is used to group form fields.
  Only one legend element should occur in the content
  and if present should only be preceded by whitespace.
-->
<!ELEMENT fieldset (#PCDATA | legend | %block; | form |
%inline; | %misc;)*>
<!ATTLIST fieldset
  %attrs;
  >


<!ELEMENT legend %Inline;>       <!-- fieldset label -->
<!ATTLIST legend
  %attrs;
  accesskey   %Character;     #IMPLIED
  >
```

```
<!--
 Content is %Flow; excluding a, form and form controls
-->
<!ELEMENT button %button.content;>  <!-- push button -->
<!ATTLIST button
   %attrs;
   name         CDATA          #IMPLIED
   value        CDATA          #IMPLIED
   type         (button|submit|reset) "submit"
   disabled     (disabled)     #IMPLIED
   tabindex     %Number;       #IMPLIED
   accesskey    %Character;    #IMPLIED
   onfocus      %Script;       #IMPLIED
   onblur       %Script;       #IMPLIED
   >


<!--========================= Tables
=========================================-->


<!-- Derived from IETF HTML table standard, see [RFC1942] -->

<!--
 The border attribute sets the thickness of the frame around
 the table. The default units are screen pixels.

 The frame attribute specifies which parts of the frame around
 the table should be rendered. The values are not the same as
 CALS to avoid a name clash with the valign attribute.
-->
<!ENTITY % TFrame
"(void|above|below|hsides|lhs|rhs|vsides|box|border)">

<!--
 The rules attribute defines which rules to draw between cells:

 If rules is absent then assume:
     "none" if border is absent or border="0" otherwise "all"
-->
```

```
<!ENTITY % TRules "(none | groups | rows | cols | all)">

<!-- horizontal placement of table relative to document -->
<!ENTITY % TAlign "(left|center|right)">

<!-- horizontal alignment attributes for cell contents

  char        alignment char, e.g. char=':'
  charoff     offset for alignment char
-->
<!ENTITY % cellhalign
  "align       (left|center|right|justify|char) #IMPLIED
   char        %Character;     #IMPLIED
   charoff     %Length;        #IMPLIED"
  >

<!-- vertical alignment attributes for cell contents -->
<!ENTITY % cellvalign
  "valign      (top|middle|bottom|baseline) #IMPLIED"
  >

<!ELEMENT table
     (caption?, (col*|colgroup*), thead?, tfoot?,
(tbody+|tr+))>
<!ELEMENT caption %Inline;>
<!ELEMENT thead    (tr)+>
<!ELEMENT tfoot    (tr)+>
<!ELEMENT tbody    (tr)+>
<!ELEMENT colgroup (col)*>
<!ELEMENT col      EMPTY>
<!ELEMENT tr       (th|td)+>
<!ELEMENT th       %Flow;>
<!ELEMENT td       %Flow;>

<!ATTLIST table
  %attrs;
  summary     %Text;          #IMPLIED
  width       %Length;        #IMPLIED
  border      %Pixels;        #IMPLIED
  frame       %TFrame;        #IMPLIED
  rules       %TRules;        #IMPLIED
  cellspacing %Length;        #IMPLIED
```

```
  cellpadding %Length;         #IMPLIED
  >


<!ENTITY % CAlign "(top|bottom|left|right)">


<!ATTLIST caption
  %attrs;
  >


<!--
colgroup groups a set of col elements. It allows you to group
several semantically related columns together.
-->
<!ATTLIST colgroup
  %attrs;
  span          %Number;      "1"
  width         %MultiLength; #IMPLIED
  %cellhalign;
  %cellvalign;
  >


<!--
 col elements define the alignment properties for cells in
 one or more columns.

 The width attribute specifies the width of the columns, e.g.

     width=64        width in screen pixels
     width=0.5*      relative width of 0.5

 The span attribute causes the attributes of one
 col element to apply to more than one column.
-->
<!ATTLIST col
  %attrs;
  span          %Number;      "1"
  width         %MultiLength; #IMPLIED
  %cellhalign;
  %cellvalign;
  >


 <!--
```

```
      Use thead to duplicate headers when breaking table
      across page boundaries, or for static headers when
      tbody sections are rendered in scrolling panel.

      Use tfoot to duplicate footers when breaking table
      across page boundaries, or for static footers when
      tbody sections are rendered in scrolling panel.

      Use multiple tbody sections when rules are needed
      between groups of table rows.
-->
<!ATTLIST thead
   %attrs;
   %cellhalign;
   %cellvalign;
   >

<!ATTLIST tfoot
   %attrs;
   %cellhalign;
   %cellvalign;
   >

<!ATTLIST tbody
   %attrs;
   %cellhalign;
   %cellvalign;
   >

<!ATTLIST tr
   %attrs;
   %cellhalign;
   %cellvalign;
   >


<!--Scope is simpler than headers attribute for common tables--
>
<!ENTITY % Scope "(row|col|rowgroup|colgroup)">

<!--this for headers, td for data and for cells acting as both
-->
```

```
<!ATTLIST th
  %attrs;
  abbr          %Text;        #IMPLIED
  axis          CDATA         #IMPLIED
  headers       IDREFS        #IMPLIED
  scope         %Scope;       #IMPLIED
  rowspan       %Number;      "1"
  colspan       %Number;      "1"
  %cellhalign;
  %cellvalign;
  >

<!ATTLIST td
  %attrs;
  abbr          %Text;        #IMPLIED
  axis          CDATA         #IMPLIED
  headers       IDREFS        #IMPLIED
  scope         %Scope;       #IMPLIED
  rowspan       %Number;      "1"
  colspan       %Number;      "1"
  %cellhalign;
  %cellvalign;
```

Bibliography

Amaya 5.3 Public Release (December18, 2001), W3C.org

BizTalk.org (www.biztalk.org)

DOM Level 1, W3C.org

DOM Level 2, HTML, W3C.org

DOM Level 3, Abstract Schemas and Load and Save, W3C.org

DOM Level 3, XPath Specification, W3C.org

HTML 4.01 Specification, W3C.org

IBM's DOM Implementation in C++

Modularization of XHTML, W3C.org

Schema.NET (www.schema.net)

Schema for XML, Norman Walsh, July 1999, W3C.org

SMIL 1.0 W3C Recommendation, W3C.org

SMIL 2.0 W3C Recommendation, W3C.org

SOAP Toolkit Version 2.0

SOAP Version 1.2 Part 1, Messaging Framework Working Draft,
    W3C.org

SOAP Version 1.2 Part 2, Adjuncts, W3C.org

W3C Vector Graphics, 1.0, W3C.org

W3C XML Pointer, XBase, and Xlink, W3C.org

XHTML 1.0 Specification, W3C.org

XHTML 1.1 Specification, W3C.org

XML 1.0 Recommendation, W3C.org

XML Base 1.0, W3C.org

XML Linking Language (Xlink), Recommendation 1.0

XML.org (www.xml.org)

XML Path Language Version 1.0, W3C.org

XML Query Requirements 2.0, W3C.org

XML Query Use Cases, W3C.org

XML Schema Part 0, Primer, W3C.org

XML Schema Part 1, Structures, W3C.org

XML Schema Part 2, DataTypesSchema for Object-Oriented XML, W3C.org

XML Schema Tutorial by Roger L. Costello, 2001, W3C.org

XQuery 2.0 and XPath 2.0 Functions and Operators 1.0, W3C.org

XSLT 1.0, 1.1, W3C.org

Appleman, Dan. *Moving to VB.NET*. NewYork: Springer Verlag, 2001.

Brady, Tim. *Annotated XML Specification*. http://www.xml.com/axml/testaxml.htm

Brownell, David. *SAX2*. North Sebastopol, CA: O'Reilly, 2002.

Burke, Paul. *Professional SQL Server 2000 XML*. Birmingham, UK: Wrox Press, 2001.

Carlson, David. *Modeling XML Applications with UML*. Upper Saddle River, NJ: Pearson Publishing, 2001.

Castro, Elizabeth. *XML for the World Wide Web*. Berkeley, CA: Peachpit Press, 2001.

Conrad, Aaron. *A Survey of Microsoft SQL Server 2000 XML Features*. MSDN Library (Microsoft Corporation), 2001.

Fung, Kyun Yee. *XSLT, Working with XML and HTML*. Reading, MA: Addison-Wesley, 2000.

Gardner, John Robert, and Zarella L. Rendon. *XSLT and XPath, A Guide to XML Transformations*. Upper Saddle River, NJ: Prentice Hall, 2001.

Goldfarb, *Charles. XML Handbook, 4th Edition*. Upper Saddle River, NJ: Prentice Hall, 2002.

Harold, Elliote Rusty. *XML Bible*. Indianapolis: Hungry Minds, 2001.

Kay, Michael. *XSLT, 2nd Edition*. Birmingham, UK: Wrox Press, 2001.

Ladd, O'Donnell. *Using XHTML and Java2*. New York: Que Books, 2001.

Musciano, Chuck, and Bill Kennedy. *HTML and XHTML*. Sebastapol, CA: O'Reilly, 2000.

Navarro, Ann. *XHTML by Example*. Indianapolis: Que Books, 2001.

Pardi, William J. *XML in Action*. Redmond, WA: Microsoft Press, 1999.

Sceppa, David. *Programming ADO*. Redmond, WA: Microsoft Press, 2000.

Schmidt, Eric. *Using Schema and Serialization to Leverage Business Logic*. MSDN Library (Microsoft Corporation), 2001.

Short, Scott. *Building Web Services for the Microsoft .NET Platform*. Redmond, WA: Microsoft Press, 2002.

Troelsen, Andrew. *Visual Basic.NET, and the .NET Platform*. New York: Springer Verlag, 2001.

Utley, Craig. *A Programmer's Introduction to Visual Basic.NET*. Indianapolis: Sams Publishing, 2002.

Valentine, Chelsea. *XML Schemas*. Alameda, CA: Sybex, 2002.

Williams, Kevin. *Professional XML Databases*. Birmingham, UK: Wrox Press, 2000.

Wille, Christoph. *Presenting C#*. Indianapolis: Sams Publishing, 2002.

Wyke, R. Allen. *XML Programming*. Redmond, WA: Microsoft Press, 2002.

Index

types, deriving, 165–166
updategrams, 489
VBScript, 391–397
XML source document,
parsing, 96
ISO-8859-1 (Latin-1) character
set, 27, 36
item property, 121
IXMLDOM... objects, 123
IXMNamespace... interfaces,
124
IXMWriter interface, 124

J

Java language
extension functions, 290–291
parsers written in, 414
variable bindings for, 195
JavaScript
DOM interface, 106
extension functions, 290–291
objects embedded in, 309
JumpStart, 85–87

K

Kay, Michael (Saxon XSLT
processor), 198
`Key` and `Keyref` elements,
175, 179–180
key element in XSLT,
202–203
`key()` function, 281–282
keys, foreign. *see* foreign keys
keys, public. *see* public keys

L

`lang` attribute, 283
language
identifying, 347
independence, 85, 98
support, 549
LanguageCode data type in
XML, 333
`last()` function, 287
Latin-1 (ISO-8859-1) character
set, 27, 36
`lax` validation keyword, 162
Length data type in XML, 334
length property, 121
less than (< or &lt) operator,
284, 288
less than or equal to (<=) operator, 284
`letter-value` attribute, 283

`level` attributes, 282
leveraging remote components,
547–548
lexical representation, 132
LinkTypes data type in XML,
334
list method for deriving types,
139–140
lists
enumerated, 419–420
formatting in XSLT, 235–242
`%lists` entity, 326
lists module of strict DTD,
325–332
literals in schemas, 134–135
`local-name()` function, 288
local scope, 144–145, 151–156
locating root element, 209,
211–213, 215
location path, 292
location steps, 263–265
logic, separating from data, 26
logical structure, 4
lowercase tags, 10, 311
lt predefined entity, 51
Lumeria, 72

M

managed code, 507
Manifest
description, 504
example, 505–506
IL tags, 512–513
type metadata for, 514–515
manual serialization of files,
390
many-to-many relationships,
70, 410–411
many-to-one relationships, 418
mapping
attribute-centric, 450,
490–492
attribute/element combined,
456
attributes from child elements, 398–404
CDATA to database, 420–421
data to XML, 406–407
element-centric, 450,
490–492
ENTITIES attribute type to
database, 421–422
explicit and implicit, 489–490

invoice example, 384–390,
399, 406–407
NMTOKENs to databases,
421–422
raw data to XML, 406–407
strategy, 397
XML to relational databases,
27–30, 383–384, 403–404
mapping schemas, annotated
XDR-XSD comparision,
467–477
in XML views, 477–479
matching any element, 201
MediaDesc data type in XML,
334
memory, creating objects in,
525–526
memory-constrained environment, 84
memory-intensive processing,
96
memory management, 507
`<message>` element,
557–558
messaging format, 550
metadata
Common Language Runtime
(CLR), 504
Common Type Specification
(CTS), 509
description, 511–516
edge tables, 462
.NET Framework, 511–516
universal tables, 430
`FOR XML EXPLICIT`
clauses, 431
metaproperties
attributes, purpose of, 462
`WITH` clause, 458–459
ColPattern, 453–454
description, 450–452
edge tables, 462–467
element-centric queries, 455
mapping attributes and elements, 453–454
mapping attributes/elements
combined, 456
OPENXML query, defining,
452–453
`Text()` function, 457–458
updating tables, 461–462
`MetaProperty` parameter,
451
methods

About the Source Code:

Create a folder on your hard drive named XMLSourceCode or name you decide to use. Open the CD and copy folders for Chapters 1–11 into the XMLSourceCode folder. Each individual folder contains source code for that particular chapter. Most source code for Chapters 1–9 is written and tested in XML Spy by Altova, the accompanying disk included with this book. You may access the source code in more than one way:

1. Open source code in XML Spy

2. Open code in Notepad.

3. Chapter 9 and 10 examples are written in Q&A, SQL Server 2000.

4. Open Chapter 11 code in Visual Studio.NET or other favorite editor of your choice.

5. Chapter 12 source code is not on the CD. You may download Chapter 12 from Addison Wesley's web site. Open code for Chapter 12 in Visual Studio.NET.